The Cambridge Guide to African American History

This book emphasizes blacks' agency and achievements in the nineteenth and twentieth centuries, notably outcomes of the Civil Rights Movement. To consider the means or strategies that African Americans utilized in pursuing their aspirations and struggles for freedom and equality, readers can consult subjects delineating ideological, institutional, and organizational aspects of black priorities, with tactics of resistance or dissent, over time and place. The entries include but are not limited to Afro-American Studies; Anti-Apartheid Movement; Antilynching Campaign; Antislavery Movement; Black Power Movement; Constitution, US (1789); Conventions, National Negro; Desegregation; Durham Manifesto (1942); Feminism; Four Freedoms; Haitian Revolution; Jobs Campaigns; the March on Washington (1963); March on Washington Movement (MOWM); New Negro Movement; Niagara Movement; Pan-African Movement; Religion; Slavery; Violence, Racial; and the Voter Education Project. While providing an important reference and learning tool, this volume offers a critical perspective on the actions and legacies of ordinary and elite blacks and their nonblack allies.

Raymond Gavins is professor of history at Duke University. He is the author of *The Perils and Prospects of Southern Black Leadership* (1993) and dozens of scholarly articles, essays, book chapters, and reviews. He co-edited *Remembering Jim Crow* (2001). The co-recipient of the Oral History Association Distinguished Project Award (1996) and the Lillian Smith Book Award (2002), he received the John W. Blassingame Award for "distinguished scholarship and mentorship in African American history" (2008).

The Cambridge Guide to African American History

RAYMOND GAVINS
Duke University

CAMBRIDGE
UNIVERSITY PRESS

CAMBRIDGE
UNIVERSITY PRESS

32 Avenue of the Americas, New York, NY 10013-2473, USA

Cambridge University Press is part of the University of Cambridge.

It furthers the University's mission by disseminating knowledge in the pursuit of education, learning, and research at the highest international levels of excellence.

www.cambridge.org
Information on this title: www.cambridge.org/9781107501966

© Raymond Gavins 2016

This publication is in copyright. Subject to statutory exception and to the provisions of relevant collective licensing agreements, no reproduction of any part may take place without the written permission of Cambridge University Press.

First published 2016

Printed in the United States of America

A catalog record for this publication is available from the British Library.

Library of Congress Cataloging in Publication Data
Gavins, Raymond, author.
The Cambridge guide to African American history /
Raymond Gavins, Duke University.
pages cm
Includes bibliographical references and index.
ISBN 978-1-107-10339-9 (hardback) – ISBN 978-1-107-50196-6 (pbk.)
1. African Americans–History.   I. Title.
E185.G33   2015
973'.0496073–dc23   2015029273

ISBN 978-1-107-10339-9 Hardback
ISBN 978-1-107-50196-6 Paperback

Cambridge University Press has no responsibility for the persistence or accuracy of URLs for external or third-party Internet Web sites referred to in this publication and does not guarantee that any content on such Web sites is, or will remain, accurate or appropriate.

Contents

Preface

Scholarly accounts of blacks date from the 1880s, owing especially to black Union veteran and legislator George Washington Williams's *History of the Negro Race in America from 1619 to 1880* (two volumes, 1882). Black scholars W. E. B. Du Bois and Carter G. Woodson made vital contributions. Du Bois formed the Atlanta Conference of Negro Problems, publisher of nineteen Atlanta University Studies (1896–1917), including *The Negro Church* (1903) and *The Common School and the Negro American* (1911). Edited mostly by Du Bois, those works enlarged blacks' scholarly foundations. The "Father of Black History," Woodson founded the Association for the Study of Negro Life and History (1915), *Journal of Negro History* (1916), Associated Publishers (1921), Negro History Week (1926), and *Negro History Bulletin* (1937). Publishing many books, Woodson and his associates firmly shaped Negro history long before the *Brown v. Board of Education* decision of 1954 disallowed segregation in education.

The Civil Rights, Black Power, women's, Hispanic, Indian, and other rights movements in the 1960s influenced colleges, universities, and schools' consent to create black, minority, and women's courses and programs. Intersecting the New Social History, which integrated non-elite and marginalized people, African American history increasingly gained recognition in historical scholarship and proceeded apace. It now stands at the cutting edge of studies of not only black experiences from slavery to contemporary times but also race, ethnic, gender, and class relations and the state, politics, and culture in the United States, African diaspora, Atlantic World, and across the globe. Blacks and women "are so essential to American history that it is perverse to think of it without them," Nathan I. Huggins stated in 1986, assessing their roles in the "new social history" and the "reconstruction of American history." Race, ethnicity, class, gender, and injustice were contexts "whereby previously mute and unsummoned witnesses could offer testimony" (Huggins, 1986, p. 157). With blacks and women paving the way, more and more natives and immigrants, working and underclass groups of color began gaining visibility in historiography. Historiographies of slavery, abolition, racism, colonialism, decolonization, and national independence in the African, Atlantic, and global world appropriate African American themes of agency, freedom, civil and human rights, too. Gerald D. Jaynes, ed., *Immigration and Race: New Challenges for American Democracy* (2000) and Mary L. Dudziak, *Cold War Civil Rights: Race and the Image of American Democracy* (2000) attest to such relationships.

My goal in this book, intended for secondary school and college students, teachers, adult educational groups, and general readers alike, is to inform the study, teaching, and understanding of African American history. Building on Earl E. Thorpe's seminal work, *The Central Theme of Black History* (1969), I posit that the central theme is the quest of African Americans for dignity, freedom, citizenship, and equality. To learn, teach, and understand blacks' means or strategies in pursuing and sustaining that quest, as an example, I would suggest that readers consult the essays depicting ideologies, institutions, and movements over time and place. These include but are not limited to the Antilynching Campaign, Antislavery Movement, Black Nationalism, Black Power Movement, Civil Rights Movement, Conventions, National Negro, Education, Emancipation, Interracial Relations, Reconstruction, Religion, Segregation, Societies, Mutual Aid, and Student Activism. They explore ideological, institutional, and organizational aspects of blacks' priorities in and tactics of dissent, of nonviolent direct action and self-defense approaches. Each suggests accessible sources for Further Reading, which could supplement critical discussion, thinking, and writing. The entries increase numerically after 1770 and particularly in the nineteenth and twentieth centuries, although those on Africa, Family, Music, Religion, Slavery, and others cover important pre-1770 developments. I emphasize the later periods to portray black life and thought before and after the Civil War and emancipation; institution-building and struggle during the Jim Crow era; the evolution and consequences of the modern civil rights movement; and stride toward equity in post–civil rights America.

Reference

Huggins, Nathan I., "Integrating Afro-American History into American History." In Hine, Darlene Clark, ed., *The State of Afro-American History: Past, Present, and Future*. Baton Rouge: Louisiana State University Press, 1986, p. 157.

Cross References

Reference	See
Aaron, Henry L. (Hank)	Sports
Abernathy, Ralph D.	Southern Christian Leadership Conference (SCLC)
African American Women in Defense of Ourselves (1991)	Feminism
African Heritage Studies Association	Afro-American Studies
African Liberation Support Committee	Black Nationalism
African National Congress (ANC)	Apartheid
Africanisms	Afro-American Studies
Afro-Christianity	Afro-American Studies
Afrocentrism	Afro-American Studies
Agricultural Adjustment Administration (AAA)	Great Depression
Albert, Lawrence A.	Music
Alexander, Clifford L.	Equal Employment Opportunity Commission (EEOC)
Alexander, Raymond P.	Law Enforcement
Allen, Richard	Music
Alridge, Ira F.	Theatre
American Anti-Slavery Society	Antislavery Movement
American Civil Liberties Union ACLU)	Interracial Relations
American Colonization Society	Antislavery Movement
American Council on Race Relations	Interracial Relations
American Federation of Labor (AFL)	Labor
American Friends Service Committee (AFSC)	Interracial Relations
American Indian Movement (AIM)	Civil Rights Movement
American Teachers' Association (ATA)	Education

Reference	See
Coachman, Alice	Sports
Cobb, Charles	Science
Cobb, W. Montague	Medicine
Cole, Nat (King)	Music
Colored Farmers' Alliance	Agriculture
Colored Officers' Training Camp	Military
Coltrane, John	Music
Commission on Civil Rights, US	Civil Rights Act of 1957
Commission on Interracial Cooperation (CIC)	Interracial Relations
Committee on Fair Employment Practice (FEPC)	March on Washington Movement (MOWM)
Communist Party (CP)	Politics
Comprehensive Employment and Training Act (1973)	Family
Congressional Black Caucus (CBC)	Politics
Conservatives	Politics
Cook, Sam	Music
Cornely, Paul B.	Medicine
Council on American-Islamic Relations	Civil Rights Movement
Crop-Lien System	Agriculture
Crummell, Alexander	Scholarship
Davis, Miles	Music
Derricotte, Juliette	Medicine
Dessalines, Jean-Jacques	Haitian Revolution
Doby, Lawrence E. (Larry)	Sports
Domestic Slave Trade	Slavery
Dorsey, Thomas	Music
Double-V Campaign	World War II
Douglas, Aaron	Art
Draft Riots (1863)	Violence, Racial
Eaton, Hubert	Gibson, Althea; Medicine
Eaton v. Board of Managers of the James Walker Memorial Hospital (1950)	Medicine
Ebonics	Afro-American Studies
Edmonds, Helen G.	Scholarship
Ellington, Edward (Duke)	Music
Emancipation Day	Emancipation
Emancipation Proclamation (1863)	Emancipation
Equal Employment Opportunity Commission (EEOC)	Civil Rights Act of 1964
Equal Rights Amendment (1972)	Feminism
Extended Family	Family
Fair Housing Act	Civil Rights Act of 1968
Farm Security Administration (FSA)	Great Depression

Reference	See
Fifteenth Amendment (1870)	Constitution, US (1789)
Fisk Jubilee Singers	Music
Ford, Johnny L.	Politics
Fraternal Council of Negro Churches	Religion
Free Speech Movement	Student Activism
Freedom Forum	Journalism
Freedom's Journal (1827)	Journalism
Fourteenth Amendment (1868)	Constitution, US (1789)
Fuller, Metta Vaux Warrick	Art
Gandhi, Mahatma	Thurman, Howard
Garrison, William Lloyd	Antislavery Movement
Gillespie, John	Music
Giovanni, Nikki	Theatre
Girl Scouts of America	Education
Goode, Malvin R.	Journalism
Greene, Lorenzo J.	Scholarship
Grand United Order of True Reformers	Business
Gutman, Herbert G.	Scholarship
Hampton Singers	Music
Hansberry, Lorraine	Theatre
Harding, Vincent	Institute of the Black World (IBW)
Hayes, Roland	Music
Haynes, George E.	National Urban League
Harris, Patricia Roberts	Sororities
Henderson, Stephen	Institute of the Black World (IBW)
Higginbotham, Evelyn Brooks	Scholarship
Highlander Folk School	Clark, Septima P.; Parks, Rosa L.
Hill, Herbert	Labor
Hill, Oliver W.	National Association for the Advancement of Colored People (NAACP)
Hill-Burton Act	Medicine
Hill-Thomas Hearings	Thomas, Clarence
Hine, Darlene Clark	Scholarship
Holiday, Billie	Music
Holmes, Hamilton E.	Journalism
House, Callie	Religion
Hunter-Gault, Charlayne	Journalism
Jackson, James E.	Student Activism
Jackson, Joseph H.	Religion
Jackson, Maynard H.	Politics
James, Sherman A.	John Henryism

Reference	See
Jim Crow	Segregation
Johnson, Charles S.	Harlem Renaissance
Johnson, Edward A.	Negro History Movement
Johnson, Joshua	Art
Johnson, James Weldon	"Lift Every Voice and Sing"; Music; NAACP
Johnson, J. Rosamond	"Lift Every Voice and Sing"; Music
Joint Center for Political and Economic Studies	Politics
Jones, Absalom	Free African Society
Joplin, Scott	Music
Jordan, Vernon E. Jr.	National Urban League
Julian, Percy L.	Science
Juneteenth	Emancipation
King, Horace	Architecture
King, B. B.	Music
Koontz, Elizabeth D.	Education
Latimer, Louis H.	Technology
Lawrence, Jacob A.	Art
Lawyers' Committee for Civil Rights Under Law	Affirmative Action
Leadership Conference on Civil Rights (LCCR)	Interracial Relations
League of United Latin American Citizens (LOLAC)	Civil Rights Movement
Lewis, David L.	Scholarship
Liberalism	Politics
Liberty Party	Antislavery Movement
Lincoln, C. Eric	Religion
Litwack, Leon F.	Scholarship
Locke, Alain	Harlem Renaissance
Logan, Rayford	Scholarship
L'Ouverture, Toussaint	Haitian Revolution
Los Angeles Riot (1992)	Violence, Racial
Lynching	Violence, Racial
Major League Baseball (MLB)	Sports
Marable, Manning	Scholarship
Marsalis, Wynton	Music
McCarthy, Senator Joseph	Anticommunism
McDaniel, Hattie	Film
Middle Passage	Africa, Slavery
Million Man March	Farrakhan, Louis A.
Million Woman March (1997)	Feminism
Monk, Thelonious	Music

Reference	See
Morgan, Garrett A.	Technology
Morgan, Irene	*Morgan v. Virginia* (1946)
Moses, Robert P.	Science
Moynihan, Daniel Patrick	Moynihan Report
Muslims	Religion
Nat Turner's Revolt	Slavery
NAACP Legal Defense and Educational Fund	National Association for the Advancement of Colored People (NAACP)
National Association for Equal Opportunity in Higher Education	Education
National Association of 'Black Journalists	Journalism
National Basketball Association (NBA)	Sports
National Black Farmers Association	Agriculture
National Black Feminist Organization (1973)	Feminism
National Black Police Association	Law Enforcement
National Black United Front (NBUF)	Black Nationalism
National Collegiate Athletic Association (NCAA)	Sports
National Conference of Black Lawyers	Law Enforcement
National Council for Black Studies	Afro-American Studies
National Education Association (N EA)	Education
National Football League (NFL)	Sports
National Medical Association (NMA)	Medicine
National Negro Business League	Business
National Negro Insurance Association	Business
National Negro League	Sports
National Newspaper Publishers Association	Journalism
National Women's Law Center	Affirmative Action
Negro History Movement	Afro-American Studies
Newkirk, Pamela	Journalism
Newton, Huey P.	Black Panther Party
Norman, Jessye	Music
Northern Student Movement	Student Activism
Office of Economic Opportunity (OEO)	Business
Oliver, Joseph	Music
Owen, Chandler	A. Philip Randolph
Parker, Charlie	Music
Payne, Daniel A.	Gospel of Freedom
Paterson, David A.	Politics
Patrick, Deval L.	Politics
Patterson, Frederick D.	United Negro College Fund (UNCF)
Patton, Charley	Music

Reference	See
Southern Negro Youth Congress (SNYC)	Student Activism
Southern Poverty Law Center (SPLC)	Interracial Relations
Southern Regional Council (SRC)	Interracial Relations
Southern Student Organizing Committee	Student Activism
Southern Tenant Farmers' Union (STFU)	Agriculture
Special Field Order 15 (1865)	"Forty Acres and a Mule"
Stampp, Kenneth M.	Scholarship
Stokes, Carl B.	Politics
Student Organization for Black Unity	Student Activism
Students for a Democratic Society (SDS)	Student Activism
Sullivan, Louis W.	Science
Sweatt, Heman	*Sweatt v. Painter* (1950)
Tandy, Jewel V. W.	Architecture
Tanner, Henry Ossawa	Art
Tate, Merze	Scholarship
Taylor, A. A.	Scholarship
Taylor, Gardner C.	Religion
Taylor, Robert R.	Architecture
Tharpe, Rosetta	Music
The Negro in Business (1899)	Business
Thirteenth Amendment (1865)	Constitution, US
Thorpe, Earl E.	Scholarship
Till, Emmett	Johnson, John H.
Turner, Nat	Slavery
Tuskegee Airmen	Military
United Auto Workers of America (UAW)	Labor
United Farm Workers (UFW)	Labor
United States Colored Golfers Association	Sports
United States Professional Tennis Association	Sports
Universal Negro Improvement Association (UNIA)	Business
Vesey, Denmark	Slavery
Virginia Negro League	Sports
Wagner, Robert F.	Wagner Act (1935)
Walker's Appeal (1829)	Slavery
Walker, LeRoy T.	Sports
Waller, Calvin A. H.	Persian Gulf War
Watt, Melvin	*Shaw v. Reno* (1993)
Weather Underground Organization (WHO)	Student Activism
Wesley, Charles H.	Scholarship
Williams, Daniel Hale	Medicine
Williams, Frances Barrier	DePriest, Oscar
Williams, George Washington	Negro History Movement; Scholarship

Reference	See
Williams, Hosea	Southern Christian Leadership Conference (SCLC)
Williams, Serena J.	Sports
Williams, Venus E.	Sports
Wilson, August	Theatre
Women	Family; Feminism; Slavery
Women Accepted for Volunteer Emergency Service (WAVES)	Military
Women's Auxiliary Army Corps (WACS)	Military
Woodard, C. Vann	Scholarship
Wright, Louis T.	Medicine
Young Men's Christian Association (YMCA)	Education
Young Women's Christian Association (YWCA)	Education

Entries

ABBOTT, ROBERT S.   JOURNALIST

Born: November 28, 1868, Frederica, GA
Education: Beach Institute, Claflin College, 1886–89; Hampton Institute, graduated 1893 (printing), 1896 (academics); Kent College of Law LL.B., 1899
Died: February 22, 1940, Chicago, IL

Establishing the *Chicago Defender* in 1905, Abbott made it the largest and most outspoken black weekly before the 1920s.

Initially, he printed, folded, and sold copies. By 1912 he had expanded to paperboy deliveries and newsstand sales for a circulation of 20,000. To sell ads and collect news, he solicited churches and organizations on the South Side, a destination of southern black migrants. Circulation began spiraling with his coverage of the Brownsville, Texas riot (1906). Accused of killing one white man and wounding another, three companies of the all-black 25th Infantry Regiment were discharged dishonorably without court martial. Abbott's editorials denounced army racism.

His reputation soared. He vitalized newspaper publishing with an eight-column, eight-page extra on Booker T. Washington's death (1915). Decrying segregation, disfranchisement, and lynching in the South, he initiated "The Great Northern Drive" editorial series (1917). Print runs peaked at 230,000 during World War I and averaged 180,000 after the "Red Summer" of 1919, which witnessed twenty-five major riots, including the one in Chicago. A member of the Chicago Commission on Race Relations, whose report deplored that conflict, he also founded *Abbott's*

Monthly (1933). In the meantime, unlike most of its competitors, the *Defender* raised revenue mainly from subscriptions.

Further Reading

Reed, Christopher Robert. *Knock at the Door of Opportunity: Black Migration to Chicago, 1900–1919.* Carbondale: Southern Illinois University Press, 2014.

Rice, Myiti Sengstacke. *Chicago Defender.* Charleston, SC: Arcadia Publishing, 2012.

ABELE, JULIAN F.   ARCHITECT

Born: April 29, 1881, Philadelphia, PA
Education: Cheyney University, 1896; Pennsylvania Museum and School of Industrial Art, 1898; University of Pennsylvania, B.S., 1902
Died: April 23, 1950, Philadelphia, PA

The first black graduate of Penn's Architecture Department, Abele was the first black architect to impact large building design. In spite of the "color line" at Penn, he won designing awards and was the Architectural Society president in his senior year. But after graduating, he was ignored by Philadelphia architects, except for nightwork. To survive, he exhibited designs, moved to Idaho with his sister and her husband, and became a postal clerk. Also, with help from Philadelphia architect Horace Trumbauer, he traveled in Europe, studied Revival architecture, and honed a distinctive style.

Trumbauer hired Abele in 1906. "I hire my brains," he stated. Abele soon became chief designer; Trumbauer approved and signed blueprints. After Trumbauer's death in 1938, Abele co-headed the firm but worked behind the scenes. In 1941 the all-white American Institute of Architects elected him to membership. His contributions include the Philadelphia Museum of Art; Widener Library, Harvard University; and fifty-three buildings, notably Duke Chapel, at Duke University. Reportedly, when he visited the campus during construction, "a Durham North Carolina hotel ... refused to give him a room ..., while accommodating his white associate" (King, p. 1). Abele's portrait is in the foyer of Duke's administrative Allen Building.

Further Reading

King, William E. "Abele, Julian Francis (1881–1950)." *North Carolina Builders & Architects: A Biographical Dictionary.* Retrieved from http://ncarchitects.lib.ncsu.edu/people/P000277.

Tifft, Susan E. "Out of the Shadows: After Decades of Obscurity, African American Architect Julian Abele is Finally Getting Recognition for His Contributions to Some of 20th-Century America's Most Prestigious Buildings." *Smithsonian Magazine* (February 2005). Retrieved from www.smithsonianmag.com/history/out-of-theshadows-85569503/.

AFFIRMATIVE ACTION

Executive Order 10925 (1961) created the Committee on Equal Employment Opportunity, which required federal contractors to "take affirmative action" against discrimination. The 1964 Civil Rights Act banned discrimination on the basis of race, ethnicity, and sex (later including sexual identity and physical condition). It also formed the Equal Employment Opportunity Commission (EEOC); affirmative action became shorthand for ensuring equal economic, educational, and political opportunities.

African Americans pursued equality in education, employment, housing, and more. The Lawyers' Committee for Civil Rights Under Law and National Women's Law Center, among other groups, provided crucial assistance. In the meantime, federal courts began a retreat from remedies for inequalities such as de facto segregated schools. In 1974 the Supreme Court disallowed a lower court's order requiring that suburban school districts bus students as part of an adjacent urban district's desegregation plan. Opponents called affirmative action "reverse discrimination" or "race preferences" as it saw growing opposition. However, the second Clinton administration "vowed to 'mend not end' affirmative action." It did so largely by reducing cash payments and job-training programs that crucially helped welfare recipients. In a 1997 Gallup Poll, 79 percent of whites believed black applicants had an equal opportunity to be hired, compared to 51 percent of blacks.

[*See also Bakke v. Board of Regents of California* (1978); Civil Rights Act of 1964.]

Further Reading

Anderson, Terry H. *The Pursuit of Fairness: A History of Affirmative Action.* New York: Oxford University Press, 2004.

Golland, David Hamilton. *Constructing Affirmative Action: The Struggle for Equal Employment Opportunity.* Lexington: University Press of Kentucky, 2011.

AFRICA

Motherland of African Americans, Africa is the second largest continent. Her 12 million square miles could encircle Europe, China, India, New Zealand, the United States, and Argentina. Her borders are the Atlantic Ocean (west), Mediterranean Sea (north), Red Sea (northeast), Indian Ocean (southeast), and offshore islands. She contains four major lakes, notably 4,600-mile Victoria; thirteen rivers, including the Nile, the world's longest river; a few mountains, including Mt. Kilimanjaro; minerals (copper, diamonds, oil, uranium); plants; and wildlife. There are five climate zones: Mediterranean, northern shore to the Cape of Good Hope; Desert, the Sahara (world's largest), Namid, and Kalahari deserts; Sub-Desert or Sahel, a semiarid region below the Sahara between Cape Verde and the Red Sea; Savanna, flat grasslands from Senegal to Ethiopia (largest zone, it includes a tourist reserve); and Tropical Rain Forest, so-called "jungles" across West-Central Africa and Madagascar. Climate sustains fishing, hunting-and-gathering, farming, and herding livelihoods. Agricultural economies, mining, and service industries emerged ca. 1885–1990. Industrialization, including mass migrations to cities, has expanded since 1945. Casablanca (Morocco), Kinshasa (Zaire), Cairo (Egypt), and Lagos (Nigeria), respectively, report 4 to 21 million inhabitants today. Farming is the main pursuit of rural dwellers.

The current population (1.69 billion) is diverse, especially by race (color) and ethnicity (language, religion). Ethnic groups or tribes share a common ancestry, homeland, and livelihood. Aboriginals or blacks comprise a 70 percent majority. Blacks constitute 800 ethnicities and speak 1,000 languages, most of them unwritten. Arabic, Amharic, Malagasy, and Swahili are spoken and written. Africans also have embraced European and other settler languages. Native linguistic areas are North Africa (Afro-Asiatic), Niger River bend to East Africa (Nilo-Saharan), West Africa (Niger Congo), Central Africa (Kordofonian); South Africa (Khoisian), and Madagascar (Austronesian). Africans honor ancestors, gods, and the land but differ in familial, religious, artistic, and political customs. They currently live in sixty-two nations and territories, composing 24 percent of the geographical regions represented in the United Nations. Theirs is "'a continent in crisis'" and they use varied strategies to combat disease, hunger, war, and genocide.

Africa is central in human history. Anthropologists have found the oldest human remains (5.8 to 1.7 million years) in East Africa's Great Rift Valley. They believe that humans first lived there before migrating internally and to the Near East, Europe, Asia, and the Western Hemisphere. Users of fire, natives created bone, stone, bronze, and iron weapons for survival while domesticating animals and plants. They fished, hunted, grew barley or herded sheep, and participated in trans-Saharan trade. After 2500 BC the Sahara began to dry up, thus gradually isolating sub-Saharan peoples.

However, between 4000 BC and 750 AD, native peoples forged states, armies, and civilizations. A crossroads of races and cultures, including Arab and Greek, Egypt developed horticulture, architecture, and hieroglyphic writing. Until the Greek conquest in 332 BC, Egypt's pharaohs controlled an empire from the Upper Nile to the Iberian Peninsula. Kush, Ethiopia, and Nubia mastered the Lower Nile, where tribal faiths, Judaism, Christianity, and Islam coexisted. In the northwest, Carthage advanced its economy and dictated much of Euro-African commerce; it fell to Rome in 202 BC.

Wars raged in the Medieval (500–1500 AD) and Modern (post-1500) periods, as firearms increasingly were used. By 733 Muslims dominated large parts of the Near East, North Africa, and Spain. Muslim empires (Morocco, Algiers, Egypt) eventually invaded the "Land of the Blacks." Ghana, Mali, and Songhay, the land's respective rulers, accommodated Muslims in the western Sudan. Great Zimbabwe ruled southern Africa. Despite the presence of Islam, Judaism, and Christianity, black religions endured. These combined faith in a High God (creator of mankind), animism (lesser deities or spirits in nature), and ancestor worship. Slaves mostly were war prisoners and aliens, held in service but allowed some rights. A second-generation bondman could not be sold, except as a penalty for a serious crime. A member of his master's family, he could marry, receive part of the harvest, and rise to familial or tribal leadership.

Slavery persisted. The Arab-driven Saharan Slave Trade (650–1500) and East African Slave Trade (900–1600) delivered an estimated 17 million blacks to North Africa, the Middle East, and Asia. The European-run Atlantic Slave Trade (1502–1888) transported 12 million blacks to the Caribbean and Americas. This trade paved the way for colonialism (1885–1980) as Belgium, England, France, Germany, Italy, Portugal, and Spain conquered, partitioned, and governed Africa by force. They instituted slave labor, segregation, and white supremacy. Nevertheless, black resistance led to decolonization (1945–1995), independence, international sanctions, and the abolition of apartheid.

Sub-Saharan West Africa was home to most African American forebears, who largely occupied coastal and inlands from Senegal to Angola. Three million were carried across the Atlantic, called the Middle Passage, to the British Caribbean and North America in the eighteenth and nineteenth centuries alone. Captured at age eleven in Nigeria, Olaudah Equiano (1745–1797) was one of fifteen known survivors who wrote of captives' suffering on the crossing, publishing his account in 1789. Of 12 million overall, the Congo-Angola subregion shipped 25% of them (Bakongo, Mbundi, Tio); Bight of Biafra 23% (Yoruba, Fon, Igbo); Gold Coast 16% (Akan, Ewe); Senegambia 13% (Wolof); Sierra Leone (Mende) 6%; Bight of Benin (Aja) 4%; Mozambique (Sena) and Madagascar (Merina) 2%. Many spoke "'Bantu languages'" such as Yoruba, Kongo, Swahili, and Zulu. Griots (oral historians) conserved tribes' memories in proverbs, songs, and tales. Peoples lived in villages of communal subsistence as well as economies based on a barter or monetary system.

Before their New World diaspora, West Africans pursued a variety of occupations. Fishing was the primary means of subsistence among coastal dwellers. Savanna inhabitants were hunters, herdsmen (cattle, goats), and farmers. Using a hoe or spade, they harvested crops such as cotton, millet, and rice. To wit, every adult Ashanti labored in the fields. Dahomey assigned fieldwork only to women, who represented households' wealth as wives, co-wives, child bearers, and workers. Frequently, women were withheld from slave buyers. Although the Yoruba required fieldwork of everyone, men cleared the fields and broke the soil. Education, training (particularly artisans), and commercial life flourished in towns. Niani, capital of Mali, had Arabic schools after 1300. By 1415 Songhay boasted the city of Timbuktu, site of the University of Sankore, a hub of Muslim scholarship. Timbuktu, Gao, and Jenne were intercontinental markets. Besides farm produce and slaves, exports consisted of artisans' wares in basketry, ivory, metallurgy, pottery, textiles, or wood carvings. Yoruba craftsmen and women influenced town councils. Economic activity was comparable to that of Mesopotamia, China, India, Mexico, or Peru.

West African societies valued ideals of kinship, hierarchy, and interdependence. Every community, district, and nation contained interlinked social classes. These included People of Authority (chiefs, elders, captains, kings, nobles, and royal families); Merchants; the Common People; Servants and Slaves; Women; Children; and Occupational Castes (priests, blacksmiths, doctors, griots, or musicians). The king, sometimes advised by a queen mother, exercised absolute authority. He could enslave, exile, or execute any subject for murder, adultery, rebellion, or idolatry. His will prevailed in the judiciary, military, taxation, and trade spheres.

Communalism was the basis of society. Communities allotted land to a kin group or lineage by means of its ancestry of fathers (patrilineal) or mothers (matrilineal). Lineages comprised a clan, its members inhabiting "extended family" or multigenerational households of married and unmarried adults and children. Members had kinship obligations. Spirits of the dead guided the eldest Dahomean male, for example, who supervised the family's fields, granaries, burials, and plural marriages. When he died, his next oldest brother or son succeeded him. Slaves helped account for a household's size, production, and social status. Bondwomen were favored over bondmen, but a household valued both. Slaves' sons could emerge to be heads of households or state authorities. Human sacrifice occurred in sacred rituals, but not universally. Offerings of goats or chickens were customary. The harvest or the naming of a newborn child marked an occasion for drumming, singing, and dancing "in a broken counter-clockwise circle" (Stuckey, 1987, p. 12).

[*See also* Afro-American Studies; Family; Slavery.]

Reference

Stuckey, Sterling. *Slave Culture: Nationalist Theory and the Foundations of Black America*. New York: Oxford University Press, 1987, p. 12.

Further Reading

Collins, Robert O., and James McDonald Burns. *A History of Sub-Saharan Africa*. New York: Cambridge University Press, 2013.

Handler, Jerome S. "Survivors of the Middle Passage: Life Histories of Enslaved Africans in British America." *Slavery & Abolition*, 23 (April 2002): 25–56.

Smallwood, Arwin D., with Jeffrey M. Elliot. *The Atlas of African-American History and Politics: From the Slave Trade to Modern Times*. New York: McGraw-Hill, 1998.

AFRICAN BLOOD BROTHERHOOD (ABB)

Responding to race riots and lynchings during the Red Summer of 1919, Harlem activist and journalist Cyril V. Briggs founded the African Blood Brotherhood for African Liberation and Redemption (ABB), a radical group.

ABB not only advocated armed self-defense and self-determination but also coalesced with the Communist Party USA, fusing black nationalism and communism. With never more than 3,000 members, many of them Caribbean nationals, it boasted a core of intellectuals, including

Jamaica-born writer Claude McKay. Until its demise in the 1920s, ABB was a paramilitary organization. Locally based affiliates, known as posts, received orders from and reported to a central command or Supreme Council in New York City. Posts helped protect and uplift their northern, southern, and West Indian communities.

[*See also* Black nationalism.]

Further Reading

Kuykendall, Ronald A. "African Blood Brotherhood, Independent Marxist During the Harlem Renaissance." *Western Journal of Black Studies* 26 (2002): 16–21.

James, Winston. *Holding Aloft the Banner of Ethiopia: Caribbean Radicalism in Early Twentieth-Century America.* New York: Verso, 1998.

AFRO-AMERICAN STUDIES

Covering African, Africana, and African American subjects, Afro-American Studies comprise research and education in black history and culture. It evolved from the Negro history movement (early 1900s), notably historian Carter G. Woodson's work. Its chief promoters include the Woodson-created Association for the Study of Negro Life and History (1915), African Heritage Studies Association (1969), and National Council for Black Studies (1975). The council seeks "to establish standards of excellence and provide development guidance" (www.ncbsonline.org/about_ncbs) for colleges and universities' programs. San Francisco State College launched the first nonblack college program in 1968.

Subjects and instruction span the humanities and behavioral and social sciences. Slavery examines slave systems beside slaves' experiences and freedom struggles in Africa and the African diaspora. Cultural studies examine Africanisms (African cultural survivals), including Ebonics (black English), Afro-Christianity, and music. Also examined are anti-black racism, plus blacks' economic, political, religious, and social institutions, organizations, and movements. Many researchers and teachers advocate Afrocentrism or study and teaching from and African-centered perspective. Programs rather than departments are the norm at the 400 colleges and universities now offering majors and minors in the field. One hundred and forty of them award the bachelor's degree, twenty-four the master's degree, and five the doctoral degree.

[*See also* Education; Scholarship; Woodson, Carter G.]

Further Reading

Rojas, Fabio. *From Black Power to Black Studies: How a Radical Social Movement Became an Academic Discipline.* Baltimore: Johns Hopkins University Press, 2007.
Rooks, Noliwe M. *White Money/Black Power: The Surprising History of African American Studies and the Crisis of Race in Higher Education.* Boston: Beacon Press, 2006.

AGRICULTURE

A mirror to African American history, agriculture reflects the long struggle for racial and economic equality.

For two and one-half centuries, most African and Afro-American slaves worked in fields. Among them were rice and tobacco cultivators; fishers, hunters, trappers, and animal herders; and forest cutters and other forestry workers. They produced staple crops (tobacco, rice, indigo, wheat, corn, peanuts) and forged families. Some were permitted to have garden plots and barter their produce, thus earning money to purchase freedom and property. Gradual abolition in the post-Revolutionary North saw many ex-slaves buying farms and creating livelihoods, even as "King Cotton" rose in the South. Most free blacks also lived in plantation areas. Treated as "slaves without masters," they survived as farmhands and tenants. Sometimes they acquired land and livestock; a small propertied elite held servants and slaves. Slavery, class privilege, and white racism developed side by side.

In the wake of the Civil War and emancipation, ex-slaves equated freedom with self and land ownership and literacy. Thousands earned wages as Union laborers; their children attended missionary-run schools; and freed communities evolved. Tens of thousands of freedpeople farmed family plots at Roanoke Island, North Carolina, Port Royal, South Carolina, and other government farms. But these opportunities ended when Congress authorized the Freedmen's Bureau (1865) and restored abandoned lands to ex-Rebel owners. Freedpeople still hoped for "40 acres and a mule," or leases on homesteads elsewhere. But most signed Bureau-supervised contracts with cash-strapped landlords, usually as sharecroppers. A sharecropper contributed his labor and half the fertilizer to earn half of the crop. Landlords exacted high interest and often cheated. Sharecroppers who resisted landlords' rules risked expulsion, whipping, and sometimes death.

Sharecropping mirrored the crop-lien system, which kept farmers and tenants in a vicious cycle of debt. With consignment goods from northern mercantile firms, merchants "furnished" food and supplies; buyers used cash or their crops for credit. Every item in the store had two prices, one for cash and another, higher price for "time" customers who paid interest rates from 25 to 50 percent. Once he agreed to his first crop lien, a farmer of tenant rarely could "pay out."

Racial violence shadowed blacks' search for opportunity. In the "Exodus" of 1879 some 60,000 croppers migrated to Kansas, Oklahoma, and Indiana, where they suffered but also built towns and a foundation for progress. Black southerners reported 120,738 farms in 1890, amid farmers' growing protest against the government's pro-business policies. The 1.5 million-member Colored Farmers' Alliance (1890), alongside the white Southern Farmers' Alliance, joined the People's Party (1891) or the Populist Party. Their move challenged Democrats' control and fueled white campaigns of intimidation, murder, disfranchisement, and segregation. Nevertheless, blacks persevered. In 1910 they owned 218,972 farms totaling nearly 15,000,000 acres.

Interregional migrations continued (7 million southern blacks migrated circa 1914–70). Many nonmigrants, heeding Back to the Farm advocates, acquired farms, homes, and economic autonomy. Devastated by boll weevils, low prices, and the Depression-era collapse of cotton tenancy, most blacks embraced relief programs, such as the Agricultural Adjustment Administration, as thousands organized. A biracial Southern Tenant Farmers' Union enrolled 30,000 members in six states between 1934 and 1940 alone. More and more blacks participated in community co-ops and NAACP branches. Churches, schools, fraternal, and women's groups helped sustain a safety net for families and communities. Seven churches (six Baptist, one Holiness) and six Rosenwald Schools crucially sustained Tillery, North Carolina before the Resettlement Administration started a demonstration project there in 1934. Known as the Tillery Farms Project, it included 325 farms across 17,000 acres; 350 frame family houses with electricity and septic tanks; and 1,500 residents. The co-op owned a social center, grist mill, blacksmith shop, potato curing house, storage shed, and farm equipment. Residents chartered the Lower Halifax County NAACP in 1954.

Communities such as Tillery revealed the conditions plaguing rural blacks under Jim Crow as well as during the Civil Rights Movement, War on Poverty, and Urban Crisis (1945–80s). Land loss was a persistent problem. Black-owned acres aggregated 6,000,000 (40 percent of its 1910 total) by 1969 and 3,100,000 (21 percent of its 1910 total) in 1982. Blacks also lost much acreage in the 1960s as the Farmers Home Administration (FmHA), the loan agency of the US Department of Agriculture (USDA), rejected black applicants who joined the NAACP, registered to vote, enrolled their children in white schools, or assisted civil rights organizers. Agribusiness expansion, tax arrearage, and legal theft resulted in losses, too. Created in 1967, the Federation of Southern Cooperatives/Land Assistance Fund helped black farm owners to pay back taxes, follow heir-property laws, and secure FmHA loans. Nonetheless, the National Black Farmers Association, representing 1,000 signers, filed a $3.5 billion discrimination suit in 1969. USDA agreed to settle in 1999 by a Memorandum of Understanding, but its agreement of $50,000 per farmer dragged on until 2010.

[*See also* Business; Labor; Sharecropping.]

Further Reading

Black Farming & History. Retrieved from www.pbs.org/homecoming/history4 .html.

Daniel, Pete. *Dispossession: Discrimination against African American Farmers in the Age of Civil Rights*. Chapel Hill: University of North Carolina Press, 2013.

Ficara, John Francis. *Black Farmers in America*. Lexington: University Press of America, 2006.

AIDS

In 1995 more than 500,000 US residents had tested positive for the human immunodeficiency virus (HIV), the acquired immune deficiency syndrome (AIDS) virus, with 40,000 to 80,000 acquiring it annually.

Low-income racial minorities and women comprised the majority of new infections. Blacks comprised 12 percent of the population and accounted for 30 percent of infectious cases in 1992 alone; Latinos comprised 9 percent of the population and accounted for 17 percent of the cases. Those groups constituted 46 percent of all cases and 54 percent of deaths from AIDS that year. Policy experts are hard put to explain such disparities. Many point to risky behaviors in an underclass predisposed to drugs, sexual promiscuity, and violent crime. AIDS advocates, by contrast, point to discrimination in prevention, treatment, and law enforcement, such as targeting people of color for drug arrests.

[*See also* Poverty.]

Further Reading

Cohen, Cathy J. *The Boundaries of Blackness: AIDS and the Breakdown of Black Politics.* Chicago: University of Chicago Press, 1999.
Geary, Adam M. *Antiblack Racism and the AIDS Epidemic: State Intimacies.* New York: Palgrave Macmillan, 2014.

ALI, MUHAMMAD   PRO BOXER

Born: January 17, 1942, Louisville, KY
Education: Louisville Central High School, graduated 1960

A three-time heavyweight champion, Ali successfully defended that title nineteen times. Many observers called him "the greatest" boxer of the twentieth century.

Ali's emergence paralleled the Civil Rights Revolution and Vietnam War. Popular in Black America, especially among inner-city youth, his flamboyance and trash-talking influenced black culture and race relations. His membership in the Nation of Islam and link to Malcolm X, who preached armed self-defense and liberation "by any means necessary," however, angered many. It fueled a backlash from the boxing and political establishments. But he was defiant: "I don't have to be what you want me to be. I'm free to be what I want" (www.theinnerseed.com/?s=Muhammad+Ali). He became a conscientious objector and antiwar advocate. Boxing revoked his championship in 1967, but the Supreme Court restored it in 1971. He retired in 1981.

Ali's cultural image is different today, partly reflecting public response to his struggles with Parkinson's disease. His calls for racial-ethnic tolerance and peace also are respected. He traveled to Iraq in 1990, hoping to prevent the Persian Gulf War by lobbying American and Iraqi leaders. Honored by the International Olympic Committee, Ali lit the torch to open its 1996 Atlanta Games. He received the Presidential Medal of Freedom in 2005.

Further Reading

Early, Gerald L. *This Is Where I Came In: Black America in the 1960s.* Lincoln: University of Nebraska Press, 2003.
Michael, Ezra. *Muhammad Ali: The Making of an Icon.* Philadelphia: Temple University Press, 2009.

ALLEN, RICHARD   MINISTER

Born: February 14, 1760, Philadelphia, PA
Education: Self-educated
Died: March 26, 1831, Philadelphia, PA

Born a slave, Allen came of age during the American Revolution, whose "created equal" ideal inspired emergent Christian denominations. Self-taught, he and coworker Absalom Jones joined St. George's Methodist Episcopal Church in Philadelphia as well as the black freedom struggle. As blacks faced separation and disrespect at St. George's, Allen and Jones led their walkout and organized the Free African Society (FAS) in 1787. FAS eventually formed a congregation and chose affiliation with the Protestant Episcopal Church. Devoted to Methodism, Allen departed and founded Bethel African Methodist Episcopal Church (AME) in 1794.

Bethel reflected the spread of black Methodists in northern states. They created an AME denomination and elected Allen bishop in 1816. He urged congregants to embrace faith and liberty, to resist enslavement and racial oppression. He established the Bethel Benevolent Society and African Society for the Education of Youth, which espoused black literacy, morality, pride, self-help, and solidarity. An outspoken abolitionist, Allen decried the American Colonization Society (ACS), which would relocate freed blacks to Africa and further secure US slavery. He preached: "We will never separate ourselves voluntarily from the slave population" (www.aaregistry.org/historic_events/view/richard-allen-bishop-ames-first-leader). His opposition to ACS moved him to convene the first Negro National Convention at Bethel in 1830.

Further Reading

Newman, Richard S. *Freedom's Prophet: Bishop Richard Allen, the AME Church, and the Black Founding Fathers.* New York: New York University Press, 2008.

Owens, A. Nevell. *Formation of the African Methodist Episcopal Church in the Nineteenth Century.* New York: Palgrave Macmillan, 2013.

AMERICAN REVOLUTION

The revolutionary era witnessed the American War of Independence (1775–83) and emancipation in the North. The colonial population of 2.8 million included 700,000 blacks, 90 percent of them enslaved.

Inspired by the "created equal" ideal of the war, blacks fought on both the American and British sides. Early on, blacks petitioned Massachusetts to abolish slavery. Virginia's deposed royal governor proclaimed all servants and slaves "free, that are able and willing to bear arms" for the Crown. Only black freemen could join the Continental army but a manpower shortage forced slave conscriptions;

so 5,000 enslaved and free blacks, promised freedom and pensions, were Patriot laborers, sailors, and soldiers. About 1,000 slaves became Crown soldiers; thousands escaped and labored for Britain, which freed and evacuated more than 30,000 of them in 1783. Perhaps 100,000 found refuge in the woods and among Indians. Meantime, slavery was declining in the North, where war had disrupted the economy and energized antislavery. Slavery was abolished in all states north of Maryland between 1777 and 1846, a milestone African Americans helped to reach.

[*See also* Military.]

Further Reading

Gilbert, Alan. *Black Patriots and Loyalists: Fighting for Emancipation in the War for Independence.* Chicago: University of Chicago Press, 2012.

Holton, Woody. *Black Americans in the Revolutionary Era: A Brief History with Documents.* Boston: Bedford/St. Martin's, 2009.

ANDERSON, MARIAN   CONCERT SINGER

Born: February 27, 1897, Philadelphia, PA
Education: Philadelphia High School for Girls, graduated 1921
Died: April 8, 1993, Portland, OR

Anderson was one of the great concert singers of the twentieth century. A contralto, she sang Negro spirituals as well as songs in German, Italian, and French.

She started in Philadelphia church choirs. Rejected by a white music school, she received free instruction from a black teacher and church-paid lessons from an Italian coach. By the 1930s she often performed abroad. After her rendition of *"Ave Maria"* in Austria, conductor Arturo Toscanini exclaimed: "Yours is a voice one hears once in a hundred years."

When she returned to America in 1935, however, mainstream venues ignored her. In 1938 she pursued singing at Constitution Hall but its owners, Daughters of the American Revolution, refused. This stirred black protest. First Lady Eleanor Roosevelt intervened and the Secretary of the Interior arranged Anderson's recital before a live and radio audience from the Lincoln Memorial on Easter in 1939. Probably 75,000 people attended; millions tuned in. She accepted the NAACP Spingarn

Award that year and became the first black singer at the New York Metropolitan Opera in 1955. A soloist at the March on Washington and a Presidential Medal of Freedom recipient (1963), she sang at presidential inaugurations and internationally as a Goodwill Ambassador. She also earned a Grammy Award for Lifetime Achievement (1991).

Further Reading

Arsenault, Raymond. *The Sound of Freedom: Marian Anderson, the Lincoln Memorial, and the Concert that Awakened America.* New York: Bloomsbury Press, 2009.

Freedman, Russell. *The Voice that Challenged a Nation: Marian Anderson and the Struggle for Equal Rights.* New York: Clarion Books, 2004.

ANGELOU, MAYA   WRITER

Born: April 4, 1928, St. Louis, MO
Education: Mission High School, Stamps, Arkansas, graduated 1944
Died: May 28, 2014, Winston-Salem, NC

Distinguished writer Angelou recited her poem "On the Pulse of Morning" at the 1993 presidential inauguration. "History, despite its wrenching pain, Cannot be unlived but if faced With courage, need not be lived again," she declared. "Lift up your eyes upon this day breaking for you. Give birth again To the dream."

Courage, hope, and resilience were central in her career. In a childhood buffeted by divorce, rape, and Jim Crow, she instilled love and self-esteem from her grandmother. At school and church, Angelou learned to value poetry and music. She pursued drama but personal crises landed her in a chorus line. After a 1954–55 overseas tour with *Porgy and Bess*, she cosponsored a benefit concert for the Southern Christian Leadership Conference and embraced the Civil Rights Movement. She also joined the Harlem Writers' Guild, which inspired her acting, writing, and teaching, the latter as an endowed professor at Wake Forest University.

Angelou's more than twenty nonfiction and fiction books, famously *I Know Why the Caged Bird Sings* (1970), foreground black feminism and the self through narrative and poetic voices. She evokes the lived experience of being black and female in intersecting contexts of anti-black racism and male sexism, while revealing the indomitable human spirit.

Further Reading

Burr, Zoila. *Of Women, Poetry, and Power: Strategies of Address in Dickinson, Miles, Brooks, Lorde, and Angelou.* Urbana: University of Illinois Press, 2002.

Gillespie, Marcia Ann, Rosa Johnson Butler, and Richard A. Long. *Maya Angelou: A Glorious Celebration.* New York: Doubleday, 2008.

ANTICOMMUNISM

US opposition to communism as a menace to capitalism, democracy, and freedom spread in the wake of Russia's Communist Revolution (1917).

Official anticommunism endured. In the Red Scare (1917–20), the Justice Department monitored, raided, and arrested thousands of communist, socialist, antiwar, civil rights, and labor activists. Red-baiting during the Depression, New Deal, and Cold War (1945–89) was abetted by white and black conservatives, liberals, and leftists, including politicians, journalists, academics, and unionists. Congressman Martin Dies (D–TX) and Senator Joseph McCarthy (R–WI) chaired infamous anticommunist committees. Meantime, FBI witch-hunts targeted federal departments, the army, and civil rights organizations.

[*See also* Cold War.]

Further Reading

Schrecker, Ellen. *The Age of McCarthyism: A Brief History with Documents.* Boston: Bedford/St. Martin's, 2002.

Lieberman, Robbie, and Clarence Lang, eds. *Anticommunism and the African American Freedom Movement: "Another Side of the Story".* New York: Palgrave Macmillan, 2009.

ANTILYNCHING CAMPAIGN

Lynching, the illegal killing of a person accused of a crime, victimized racial minorities as well as whites. But 72.7 percent of its reported 4,743 victims from 1882 to 1968 were black and mostly men. Lynchings clustered in southern and border states, and usually were perpetrated by white mobs or groups like the Ku Klux Klan. Victims were hanged, shot, and burned, their corpses often mutilated. During Reconstruction and afterward, the freedmen's state conventions, Negro National Convention, National Association of Colored Women, and black press decried lynching and demanded "the equal protection of the laws." John Mitchell, Jr. of the Richmond *Planet* and Ida B. Wells of the Memphis *Free Speech* called for the arrest, prosecution, and punishment of lynchers. Wells, who moved to New York City after receiving death threats, disproved that rape of white women explained most lynchings of black men.

In the first half of the twentieth century, the movement pursued a federal antilynching law. It enlisted an interracial coalition of the NAACP, which started a fund "to stamp out lynching" in 1916; the southern Commission on Interracial Cooperation; and black churches. Joining them were the National Council of Negro Women, Association of Southern Women for the Prevention of Lynching, and leftist International Labor Defense. Southern white liberals stressed local and state steps such as white–black dialogue and jail security for prisoners. But the NAACP led in lobbying the New Deal Administration for antilynching legislation. Although this took time, its activism advanced public opinion on the protection of life. Sixteen states passed laws against mob violence between the 1890s and early 1940s; the US House enacted bills in 1922, 1937, and 1940, but the Senate defeated them. Antilynching sanctions finally came with Civil and Voting Rights acts in 1957, 1960, 1964, and 1965, enforced by the Civil Rights Division of the Department of Justice.

[*See also* Civil rights movement; Interracial relations; Ku Klux Klan (KKK); Violence, racial; Segregation.]

Further Reading

Bay, Mia. *To Tell the Truth Freely: The Life of Ida B. Wells*. New York: Hill and Wang, 2009.
Zangrando, Robert L. *The NAACP Crusade Against Lynching, 1909–1950*. Philadelphia: Temple University Press, 1980.

ANTISLAVERY MOVEMENT

The antislavery movement paved the way for slavery's demise in America. It evolved through reform groups – religious and secular, white and black, during the colonial and Revolutionary eras, as "all men are created equal" became a national creed.

Circa 1780–1846, when every state north of Maryland gradually abolished bondage, many ex-slaves, Quakers, and some evangelical bodies opposed the American Colonization Society's program to emancipate slaves and relocate them to Africa. Black churches, which organized separate Baptist, Methodist, and other denominations, formed the vanguard of anticolonization and freedom struggles. They supported newspapers such as *Freedom's Journal*; maintained Vigilance Committees to assist runaway slaves; and presented petitions to Congress seeking termination of foreign and domestic slave trading. Prior to and after the suppression of slave conspiracies and revolts in Richmond, Virginia (1800); Charleston, South Carolina (1822); and Southampton, Virginia (1831), black and white churches and women's associations helped preserve the Underground Railroad.

Their activism vitalized interracial abolitionism, prodded southern secession, and grounded the Civil War. Frederick Douglass and Sojourner Truth joined white activists such as William Lloyd Garrison and Lydia Maria Child in the American Anti-Slavery Society, whose local chapters had small memberships. Chapters were forthright but not monolithic. Differences in their ideologies and strategies, for instance, peaceful protest versus electoral politics, divided Garrisonians and political abolitionists by 1840, when the latter group formed the Liberty Party. The party enlisted a coalition of moderates, militants, and radicals such as John Brown, who believed armed revolution was necessary for abolition. The war brought it, ending the "Peculiar Institution" and causing a "new birth of freedom."

[*See also* Slavery.]

Further Reading

Mitchell, Beverly E. *Black Abolitionism: A Quest for Human Dignity*. Maryknoll, NY: Orbis Books, 2005.

LaRoche, Cheryl Jennifer. *Free Black Communities and the Underground Railroad: The Geography of Resistance*. Urbana: University of Illinois Press, 2014.

ANTITERROR WARS

After the 9/11 aerial attacks on the World Trade Center and Pentagon killed 3,000 people, 19 al-Queda hijackers among them, the United States and "a Coalition of the Willing" launched a Global War on Terror (currently Overseas Contingency Operation) against terrorist states and organizations, including Afghanistan's Taliban regime and al-Queda (2001–2014) and Iraq (2003–2011).

These wars fueled not only political controversy but also high costs in blood and treasure. By 2011, in the War in Afghanistan there were 10,960 to 49,600 Afghan deaths and 22,291 injuries; 3,075 coalition deaths and 5,757 injuries; 1,933 US deaths and 16,854 injuries. In the same year, The War in Iraq saw 62,570 to 1,124,000 Iraqi deaths and an estimated equal number of injuries; 4,799 coalition deaths and more than 100,000 injuries; 3,988 US deaths and 25,819 injuries. US military and civilian expenditures totaled $2.7 trillion. Many observers feared that federal antiterrorist policies were undermining civil liberties and the human rights of enemy combatants.

[*See also* Military.]

Further Reading

Brown, Seyon, and Robert H. Scales, eds. *US Policy in Afghanistan and Iraq: Lessons and Legacies*. Boulder, CO: Lynne Rienner, 2012.

Katz, Mark N. *Leaving Without Losing: The War on Terror after Iraq and Afghanistan*. Baltimore: Johns Hopkins University Press, 2012.

APARTHEID

Like southern Jim Crow, apartheid or racial separation was official in the Union of South Africa. Enacted by the National Party in 1948 to maintain the power of the white minority, it endured until 1994.

Apartheid not only separated the white, black (Bantu), colored (mixed-race), and Indian races but also excluded native blacks (whose ten tribes constituted the majority population) from education, suffrage, skilled jobs, and decent housing. Blacks lived on less than 8 percent of the land in separate tribal homelands, where crowding and rebelliousness caused police crackdowns and forced removals. After killing many protesters at Sharpeville in 1960, authorities banned the African National Congress (ANC). Established in 1912 for black liberation and suppressed by the government, it carried out armed struggles that helped support increasing homeland protests, the international antiapartheid movement, and abolition of the system. Authorities killed thousands of blacks and relocated more than 3 million during apartheid's forty-six-year reign.

[*See also* TransAfrica; Segregation.]

Further Reading

Louw, P. Eric. *The Rise, Fall, and Legacy of Apartheid*. Westport, CT: Praeger, 2004.

Nesbitt, Francis Njubi. *Race for Sanctions: African Americans against Apartheid, 1946–1994*. Bloomington: Indiana University Press, 2004.

ARCHITECTURE

Afro-American architecture developed from colonial times in the Caribbean and the Americas, where slave and free black artisans created building designs based on West African forms. On farms and plantations, slaves built housing of mud, straw, and thatch in the form of a village hut, a narrow rectangular habitat with an arched doorway, stucco walls, and a thatched roof. Slaves added shuttered windows and doors to foster privacy and togetherness. They frequently arranged houses in the "basic bubble diagram" of an African tribal compound. Houses had gabled roofs, which allowed air inside and provided covers for porches, as well as conical roofs supported by posts. A "shotgun house," from the African word shogun or "God's house," was a linear wooden structure of two rooms and a gabled front porch. Alongside planning and constructing plantation mansions, blacks helped to design and construct public structures and sites throughout the nation. Free-born Benjamin Banneker assisted with the 1791 site assessment for the District of Columbia. Bondman Horace King, who was granted freedom, designed river bridges in Georgia and South Carolina. After the Civil War, shotgun houses sheltered millions of all races. Black architects emerged in the South as freedmen and women pooled their resources to build homes, churches, schools, lodge halls, and community centers. Negro colleges, for example, soon began programs to train draftsmen, probably the earliest being an "architecture certificate" program at Tuskegee Institute in 1892. Hampton Institute and Howard University followed suit after 1900. Tuskegee's students planned and constructed more than forty campus auditoriums and dormitories by 1915. They drew blueprints for the Carnegie Libraries Project and Rosenwald School Building Program. In the meantime, the graduates contracted other notable projects.

Architecture graduates advanced little by little. Tuskegee graduate Jewel V. W. Tandy became New York State's first black licensed architect in 1908. The next year he opened Tandy & Foster, Architects in New York City. The all-white American Institute of Architects (AIA) barred black membership, but Tandy and others formed parallel associations, including the National Builders Association (1923) and the National Technical Association (1929).

Such groups inspired and paralleled a number of African American firsts. Urban designer Robert R. Taylor graduated valedictorian from the Massachusetts Institute of Technology School of Architecture in 1892. As chairman of Tuskegee's mechanical industries department, he defied segregation by earning an Alabama architect's license in 1931. Black architect-educators dubbed Taylor the "dean." Philadelphia-based Julian F. Abele was one of "the early twentieth century's most adept designers of revival buildings." Finishing the University of Pennsylvania in 1902, he participated in major exhibits and attended the École des Beaux Arts, Paris. By 1910 he was a partner with Horace Trumbauer, Architect, of Philadelphia. Abele led the firm from 1938 until his death in 1950, adopting a low profile in hope of deflecting white racism. His most famous creations include the Museum of Art, Philadelphia; Widener Library, Harvard University; and the campuses of Duke University. Norma M. Sklarek won New York State certification and became the first black female licensed architect in 1954. AIA elected her the first female fellow in 1966.

[*See also* Abele, Julian F.; Art.]

Further Reading

Mitchell, Melvin L. *The Crisis of the African American Architect: Conflicting Cultures of Architecture and (Black) Power*. Lincoln, NE: iUniverse, 2002.

Vlach, John Michael. *Back of the Big House: The Architecture of Plantation Slavery*. Chapel Hill: University of North Carolina Press, 1993.

Weiss, Ellen. *Robert R. Taylor and Tuskegee: An African American Architect Designs for Booker T. Washington*. Montgomery, AL: NewSouth Books, 2011.

ART

Afro-American art includes painting, sculpture, graphic arts, crafts, architecture, and other visual productions of blacks in the Americas. Art "played a central role in birth, life, and death" (Driskell, 1995, p. 7) among Africans from slavery to freedom. They invented human and animal figures in wood and metal to honor tribal ancestors and gods or to celebrate religious rituals. Carvings of plants and weapons in ivory and bone honored nature or tribal warriors. African pottery, weaving, and surface designs in line and color reinvented ancient decorative traditions, which influenced slave and free black artisans in America. Black builders, cabinet-makers, ironsmiths, painters, sculptors, and printmakers composed artworks utilizing West and Central African forms. They built plantation mansions showing Africanist balconies and porches of iron supports and ornaments. Black sign painters, portrait limners, and engravers also produced work using Western European motifs and styles. Free-born Joshua Johnston, based in Baltimore, painted highly regarded portraits of white patrons. Johnston, the first black painter to gain public recognition, was followed by New York freeman and engraver Patrick Reason, whose stills were acclaimed.

Others gained wide respect, if not justice, after emancipation in 1865. Seeking refuge from the antiblack racism of the post-Reconstruction era, Henry Ossawa Tanner moved to Paris, where he earned international acclaim for paintings of biblical scenes. He painted mostly Euro-American subjects, unlike his famous "The Banjo Lesson" (1893). The latter portrays an old black man teaching a boy how to play the banjo, an African instrument. This memorable image appears in sidebars of history books. Black sculptress Metta Vaux Warrick Fuller depicted "the hopes and sufferings of her people." Her most important work, "The Awakening of Ethiopia" (ca. 1914), shows an Egyptian woman freeing herself from mummy-like bandages and standing up, foreshadowing the "New Negro Arts Movement."

That movement, also called the Harlem Renaissance and fed by a mass out-migration of rural southern blacks, ushered in the modern, urban period in black artistic expression. Woodcut printer, illustrator, and muralist Aaron Douglas was easily Harlem's major artist. Using stylized silhouettes, earth colors, and sharp angles, he fashioned evocative images of the Afro-American past and jazz music. He created illustrations for magazines and books, and murals such as "Dance Magic" (1930) for the ballroom of Chicago's Sherman Hotel. As the first president of the Harlem Artists Guild in 1935, Douglas persuaded the William E. Harmon Foundation of New York and the Federal Works Progress Administration to fund opportunities for young artists such as Augusta Savage (sculptor) and Jacob A. Lawrence (muralist). Creator of famed narrative series, Lawrence is best known for his sixty paintings in *The Migration Series* (1940–41). Between 1937 and 1966, Douglas created and chaired the department of art at Fisk University, becoming a central figure in establishing artistic studies at historically black colleges and universities. Those institutions significantly conserved the African American visual legacy of dignity and hope for equality; they also trained artists who would help to create "Black Is Beautiful" visuals in the 1960s and the multiethnic art of the post–civil rights years.

[*See also* Architecture; Johnson, Sargent; Lewis, Edmonia.]

Reference

Driskell, David C., ed. *African American Aesthetics: A Postmodernist View.* Washington, DC: Smithsonian Institution Press, 1995, p. 7.

Further Reading

Bernier, Celeste-Marie. *African American Visual Arts: From Slavery to the Present.* Chapel Hill: University of North Carolina Press, 2008.

Collins, Lisa Gail. *The Art of History: African American Women Artists Engage the Past.* New Brunswick, NJ: Rutgers University Press, 2002.

Powell, Richard J., and Virginia M. Mecklenburg with Marcia Battle. *African American Art: Harlem Renaissance, Civil Rights Era, and Beyond.* Washington, DC: Smithsonian American Art Museum, 2012.

ASHE, ARTHUR R.   PRO TENNIS PLAYER

Born: July 10, 1943, Richmond, VA
Education: UCLA, B.A., 1966
Died: February 6, 1993, New York, NY

The first black winner of the men's US Open (1968), Australian Open (1970), and Wimbledon (1975), the latter ranking him Number One in the World, Ashe was inducted to the International Tennis Hall of Fame (1985). "Arthur grew up in segregated Virginia, and that set the tone for his passion," his widow said. "It was not just that people should be the best they could be. It was also going back and helping communities ... move forward and be able to succeed" (*New York Daily News*, 2003).

Ashe embraced civil rights activism. When a heart disorder forced him to retire from tennis in 1979, he contracted HIV through surgery. Still, he achieved distinction as an author and lecturer; advocate of social justice and world peace; and activist in campaigns to end South African apartheid, American racism, sexism, and poverty. He donated a major share of his income to inner-city school programs as well as to AIDS research and education. A large sculpted statue of Ashe today stands on Richmond's Monument Avenue, which is reserved for Confederate war heroes. The statue's location sparked political controversy, but it was not relocated. It honors Ashe's "fight against racism in sports" and struggles for an integrated society.

Reference

"Ashe Legacy Opens in Harlem." *New York Daily News*, August 21, 2003.

Further Reading

Djata, Sundiata A. *Blacks at the Net: Black Achievement in the History of Tennis.* Syracuse, NY: Syracuse University Press, 2006.

Hall, Eric Allen. *Arthur Ashe: Tennis and Justice in the Civil Rights Era.* Baltimore: Johns Hopkins University Press, 2014.

ASSOCIATED NEGRO PRESS (ANP)

Based in Chicago, ANP was the oldest black newspaper service. Founded in 1919 by Claude A. Barnett, who remained its director until his death, it served an increasing number of newspapers.

ANP claimed about 114 subscribers, mostly weeklies, by 1935. Besides news stories and opinion articles, it provided essays as well as book and movie reviews. It also supplied by-lined columns on race relations from key journalists, including William L. Pickens (1881–1954), field secretary of the NAACP. Their contributions articulated African American dignity and demands for civil rights and economic justice. Barnett contributed pieces on the plight of tenant farmers.

[*See also* Journalism.]

Further Reading

Hogan, Lawrence D. *A Black National News Service: The Associated Negro Press and Claude Barnett*. Haworth, NJ: St. Johann Press, 2002.

Washburn, Patrick Scott. *The African American Newspaper: Voice of Freedom*. Evanston, IL: Northwestern University Press, 2006.

ATLANTA COMPROMISE (1895)

The Atlanta Cotton States Exposition address in September 1895 elevated Booker T. Washington to national prominence and recognition as the leader of Afro-America. His audience included the South's most powerful whites; blacks sat in a segregated section. Using his hand and fingers to capture the moment, he adeptly explained how black–white interdependence, notwithstanding segregation, could build a New South.

Did he renounce civil rights as his critics claim? Or did Washington eschew black grievances to invoke a larger vision? The cotton states, miscalculating Union military might, had lost the Civil War. Losing again to northern industrial capitalists, surely they needed black labor. He would leverage it in return for white tolerance, black education, and ultimately racial equality. Washington's long-term strategy put him at the center of Afro-American life and struggle.

Further Reading

Bieze, Michael Scott, and Marybeth Gasman, eds. *Booker T. Washington Reconsidered*. Baltimore: Johns Hopkins University Press, 2012.

Smock, Raymond W. *Booker T. Washington: Black Leadership in the Age of Jim Crow*. Chicago: Ivan R. Dee, 2009.

BACK-TO-AFRICA MOVEMENT

African repatriation for ex-slaves and free blacks from North America and other Western societies began during the eighteenth century. For example, Job Ben Solomon of Senegal was captured, sold to a slave trader, and shipped to Maryland. Literate in Arabic, Job wrote a letter to his father that fell into the hands of a white official, who had it translated. He then helped to buy and liberate Job, who returned to his homeland in 1734. Approximately 1,200 slaves, among the thousands who were emancipated and evacuated by the British after the Revolutionary War, repatriated to Sierra Leone in 1791.

Black emigration to Africa grew in the wake of northern slave emancipation (1780–1846). Free black Boston shipowner Paul Cuffee transported 38 ex-slaves to Sierra Leone in 1815, which foreshadowed a meeting of Presbyterian ministers in Philadelphia the next year. They organized the American Colonization Society (ACS), whose wealthy members included southern masters who pushed to relocate freed blacks. Black opposition to and support for ACS increased. ACS received a $100,000 federal subsidy and founded the African colony of Liberia (1821). It resettled probably 13,000 blacks prior to the Civil War and a total of 20,000 by its closing in 1910. Blacks also emigrated by means of independent black programs despite slavery and post–Civil War segregation. Vital to emigrationism ca. 1900–1945 were Pan-African congresses and the Universal Negro Improvement Association, pursuing Back-to-Africa, freedom, independence, and justice for blacks in Africa and its Diaspora. Many civil rights and Black Power activists later pursued the same goals.

[*See also* Pan-African movement, Universal Negro Improvement Association (UNIA).]

Further Reading

Burin, Eric. *Slavery and the Peculiar Solution: A History of the American Colonization Society.* Gainesville: University Press of Florida, 2005.

Lapsansky-Werner, Emma J. et al., eds. *Back to Africa: Benjamin Coates and the Colonization Movement in America, 1848–1800.* University Park: Pennsylvania State University Press, 2005.

BAKER, ELLA J.   CIVIL RIGHTS ACTIVIST

Born: December 13, 1903, Norfolk, VA
Education: Shaw University, B.A. valedictorian, 1927
Died: December 13, 1986, New York, NY

Cofounder of the Mississippi Freedom Democratic Party, Baker delivered a great speech at its 1964 convention. "Until the killing of black mothers' sons becomes as important as the killing of white mothers' sons," she declared, "we who believe in freedom cannot rest." An activist in "the long civil rights movement" from the 1930s, she also devoted her post-movement years to progressive politics. She never rested.

Fundi: The Story of Ella Baker (1981), a prize-winning documentary, sums up her activism. In its native Swahili, *fundi* means one who masters an art and transmits it, the leader, storyteller, or teacher whose strength and wisdom are shared by the full community. Student organizers called her the *fundi*, as she challenged and guided them in promoting literacy, practical life skills, the right to vote, citizenship, and empowerment among ordinary people. As an organizer, Baker promoted "group-centered leadership rather than a leadership centered group" (Grant, 2001, p. 40), a freedom struggle much larger than that of a leader like Martin Luther King, Jr. This reflected Baker's experience in grassroots movements for justice. She honed her antiracist and freedom strategies organizing workers and women during the Great Depression and as NAACP Director of Branches, 1940–46.

Reference

Grant, Joanne. "Godmother of the Student Movement." *Crisis*, 108, July–August 2001, p. 40.

Further Reading

Moye, J. Todd. *Ella Baker: Community Organizer of the Civil Rights Movement.* Lanham, MD: Rowman & Littlefield, 2013.
Ransby, Barbara. *Ella Baker & the Black Freedom Movement: A Radical Democratic Vision.* Chapel Hill: University of North Carolina Press, 2003.

BAKER V. CARR (1962)

In this significant decision, the US Supreme Court established jurisdiction for federal courts in cases on reapportionment of state legislatures, repealing its 1946 ruling that only elected officials could determine apportionment.

Baker addressed the clear disparity in the number of voters within Tennessee's legislative districts. Voters in lesser populated rural districts had more political power; those in larger urban districts thus incurred vote dilution and a denial of equal protection. The Court apportioned the size of Tennessee electorates for all elective offices by establishing the principle of "one person, one vote." Its decision also enlarged the doorway to black voter representation in southern legislatures.

[*See also* Voting Rights Act of 1965.]

Further Reading

Hasen, Richard L. *The Supreme Court and Election Law: Judging Equality from Baker v. Carr to Bush v. Gore.* New York: New York University Press, 2003.

Smith, J. Douglas. *On Democracy's Doorstep: The Inside Story of How the Supreme Court Brought "One Person, One Vote" to the United States.* New York: Hill and Wang, 2014.

BAKKE V. BOARD OF REGENTS OF CALIFORNIA (1978)

Affirmative action in education was increasingly contested by the 1970s, when the US Supreme Court raised the requirement of standing: the right to sue. A plaintiff had to establish "injury in fact" within Article III of the Constitution and that the laws in question were intended to protect him. The burden of proof tended to discourage minorities from suing. However, if a vital public interest interfaced the plaintiff's suit for relief, the Court sometimes made an exception.

The University of California–Davis Medical School twice rejected Allan Bakke, a white applicant. He claimed the school wrongfully denied him admission "to make room for minority applicants with inferior records of academic achievement" (*Education Commission*, 2002, p. 2) using its regular admissions process along with its minority quota program. The university argued that he lacked standing and should exhaust all administrative remedies before pursuing a lawsuit. But the Court ruled in his favor. It struck down the use of racial quotas in admissions as a violation of the 1964 Civil Rights Act, "but allowed race to be considered as one factor among several for the specific purpose of achieving student body diversity" (*Education Commission*, 2002, p. 3). *Bakke* thus produced a series of conflicting lower-court orders that weakened affirmative-action policies in education and employment.

[*See also* Affirmative Action.]

Reference

"Affirmative Action." *Education Commission of the States Policy Brief*, January 2002.

Further Reading

Ball, Howard. *The Bakke Case: Race, Education, and Affirmative Action.* Lawrence: University Press of Kansas, 2000.

Johnson, John W., and Robert P. Green, Jr. *Affirmative Action.* Santa Barbara, CA: Greenwood Press/ABC-CLIO, 2009.

BALDWIN, JAMES   WRITER

Born: August 2, 1924, Harlem, NY
Education: DeWitt Clinton High School, graduated 1942
Died: December 1, 1987, St. Paul-de-Vence, France

Baldwin grew up poor and ambitious in Harlem. The combined influences of reading, a storefront church, and a student literary club (advised by poet Countee Cullen) put him on a path to writing. After finishing high school, he worked odd jobs and settled in Greenwich Village, where Richard Wright became his role model and mentor. But his 1949 and 1951 essays attacking Wright's *Native Son* irreparably alienated them.

Baldwin went on to an outstanding literary career, spending much of it among American intellectual and political exiles in Paris. A first-rate essayist, he authored six novels. *Giovanni's Room* (1956), using white characters, unveiled homoerotic relationships. He also wrote short stories, plays, and children's books, and reached his artistic summit in explorations of white racism, black protest, and civil rights. His was a powerful voice in the black freedom movement; he joined nonviolent protests and published critical race pieces, many of them reprinted in *Nobody Knows My Name* (1961) and *The Fire Next Time* (1963), the latter coinciding with the March on Washington for jobs and freedom. By then, Baldwin had achieved "popularity and acclaim as the 'conscience of the nation,' who brought to racial discourse a passion and honesty that demanded notice" (Smith, 2010, p. 1).

Reference

Smith, Kevin D. "Baldwin, James." In *Encyclopedia of American History,* Vol. IX, New York: Facts On File, Inc., 2010, p. 1.

Further Reading

Baldwin, James. *The Cross of Redemption: Uncollected Writings.* Edited by Randall Kenan. New York: Pantheon Books, 2010.

Campbell, James. *Talking at the Gates: A Life of James Baldwin.* Berkeley: University of California Press, 2002.

BARNETT, CLAUDE A.   JOURNALIST

Born: September 16, 1889, Sanford, FL
Education: Chicago public schools; Tuskegee Institute, graduated 1906
Died: August 2, 1967, Chicago

A pathmaking journalist, Barnett transformed the Afro-American press into a corporate business. In 1919 he enlisted midwestern and western editors to share their advertising and reporting in an Associated Negro Press (ANP). Its logo displayed an owl and scroll over *Progress, Loyalty, Truth*.

Barnett directed ANP for nearly a half-century. He not only brought in member newspapers and syndicated columnists from every region by the 1930s; he also sponsored foreign correspondents during World War II and the Cold War, thus forging a foundation for black newspapers' survival as the Civil Rights Movement and desegregation of journalism reduced their market.

ANP disseminated news releases to newspaper and magazine publishers, advertisers, and organizations. For an initial fee of $25 weekly, even community groups could obtain its services. Its growth caused tension with the *Chicago Defender*, its main local competitor. Poro College, one of the first million-dollar beauty enterprises, was ANP's largest client. Newspaper membership reached 200 in 1941. At its Chicago headquarters, staff journalists worked on regular features and special stories from paid field reporters. Barnett wrote hundreds of columns, usually under a pseudonym. Several noted leaders and writers were columnists, including NAACP secretary William Pickens and writer Langston Hughes.

Further Reading

Green, Adam. *Selling the Race: Culture, Community, and Black Chicago, 1940–1955*. Chicago: University of Chicago Press, 2007.
Tracy, Steven C. *Writers of the Black Chicago Renaissance*. Urbana: University of Illinois Press, 2011.

BATES, DAISY L.   CIVIL RIGHTS ACTIVIST

Born: November 11, 1914, Huttig, AR
Education: Huttig public schools, ninth grade
Died: November 9, 1999, Little Rock, AR

Bates challenged segregation well before the *Brown* decision and Montgomery Bus Boycott catalyzed the Civil Rights Movement. With her husband, she founded the Little Rock *State Press* in 1941 and made it a voice of protest for racial equality.

Bates emerged to be president of the Arkansas State Conference of NAACP Branches in 1952. Eventually protesting state and local noncompliance with *Brown*, she recruited black students, known as "the Little Rock Nine," to apply for school transfers. When the Federal District Court ordered their transfer to Little Rock's all-white Central High School in 1957, the governor sent in the state National Guard to prevent it, many whites taunted them, and they were turned back. But the president intervened, federalized the Guard, and deployed the 101st Airborne Division to enforce the Court's order. Bates and the Nine received the NAACP Spingarn Award in 1958; the *State Press* lost major advertisers and closed in 1959.

Bates remained an activist. In addition to working in staff positions for the Democratic National Committee and antipoverty agencies, she helped transform the poor black neighborhood of Mitchellville, near Little Rock. Thanks to her leadership, residents obtained public water and sewer systems and paved streets. They also sponsored fundraisers for a community center.

Further Reading

Lanier, Carlotta Walls. *A Mighty Long Way: My Journey to Justice at Little Rock Central High School.* New York: One World Ballantine Books, 2009.
Stockley, Grif. *Daisy Bates: Civil Rights Crusader from Arkansas.* Jackson: University Press of Mississippi, 2005.

BETHUNE, MARY MCLEOD   EDUCATOR

Born: July 10, 1875, Mayesville, SC
Education: Scotia Seminary, 1888–95; Moody Bible Institute, 1895
Died: May 18, 1955, Daytona Beach, FL

A child of ex-slaves, Bethune pursued education, studied religion, and became a leader. She founded Bethune-Cookman College (1923), organized the National Council of Negro Women (1935), and directed Negro Affairs in the National Youth Administration (1936–43) during the New Deal. When scholars named Black America's fifty most significant leaders in 1989, she was one of four unanimous selections. Bethune worked to bridge race, class, gender, and political divides. "Let us forget the office each one of us holds," she urged members of the New Deal's black cabinet. "We must think in terms as a 'whole' for the greatest service of our people" (McClusky and Smith, 1999, p. 227).

To the black press, Bethune was "race leader at large." She fought for equal suffrage, economic justice, and international peace. Courageous, she joined the "Jobs for Negroes" picket line of the New Negro Alliance (1939) and the March on Washington Movement (1941). Consequently, the witch-hunting House Committee on Un-American Activities investigated her alleged communist associations, driving some vital donors away from Bethune-Cookman. But she vindicated herself and the institution survived. She attended the first assembly of the United Nations as an advisor to the US delegation, which included First Lady Eleanor Roosevelt, Walter F. White, and W. E. B. Du Bois.

Reference

McCluskey, Audrey Thomas and Elaine M. Smith, eds. *Mary McLeod Bethune: Building a Better World: Essays and Selected Documents*. Bloomington: Indiana University Press, 1999, p. 227.

Further Reading

Bennett, Lerone, Jr. "The 50 Most Important Figures in Black American History: Experts List Men and Women Who Made Indispensable Contributions." *Ebony*, 44 (February 1989): 176–81.
Hanson, Joyce Ann. *Mary McLeod Bethune & Black Women's Political Activism*. Columbia: University of Missouri Press, 2003.

BIRTH OF A NATION, THE (1915)

Racist images of blacks infused silent films, *The Birth of a Nation* being one of the most popular. Based on Thomas F. Dixon, Jr.'s novel *The Clansman* (1905) and produced by D. W. Griffith, it was Hollywood's first special effects film and a pro-southern story of Reconstruction. It showed black politicians leering at white women and depicted the Ku Klux Klan's violent overthrow of Republican rule as heroic. It broke box office records.

Blacks protested. For example, Los Angeles *Eagle* editor Charlotta Bass condemned the film's "prejudice and vainglory." Many NAACP chapters also organized boycotts and pickets of theaters showing it.

[*See also* Film.]

Further Reading

Polgar, Paul. "Fighting Lightning with Fire: Black Boston's Battle against the 'Birth of a Nation.'" *Massachusetts Historical Review*, 10 (2008): 84–113.

Stokes, Melvyn. *D. W. Griffith's* The Birth of a Nation: *A History of "The Most Controversial Motion Picture of All Time"*. New York: Oxford University Press, 2007.

BLACK ARTS MOVEMENT

Many activists and intellectuals, particularly advocates of Black Power, founded institutions and projects in the 1960s–70s to foster black cultural nationalism.

In some northern and midwestern cities, they painted outdoor murals depicting "Black Is Beautiful" or liberation struggles, such as Chicago's *Wall of Respect* (1967). Founded in Chicago, the African Commune of Bad Relevant Artists (1968) promoted black pride through public art. The Negro Ensemble Company and New Lafayette Theatre were centers of artistic radicalism in New York. Black playhouses and workshops in many cities sponsored performances by artists such as poet-playwright Amiri Baraka and poet Nikki Giovanni, a feminist and nationalist.

[*See also* Theatre.]

Further Reading

Fowler, Virginia C. *Nikki Giovanni: A Literary Biography*. Santa Barbara, CA: Praeger, 2013.

Smethurst, James Edward. *The Black Arts Movement: Literary Nationalism in the 1960s and 1970s*. Chapel Hill: University of North Carolina Press, 2005.

BLACK BELT

A black-soil corridor perhaps 25 miles wide, the Black Belt links 623 of the South's 1,104 counties. From southern Virginia into the Carolinas and Georgia, it crisscrosses Alabama, Tennessee, Arkansas, Mississippi, and Louisiana. A hub of cotton in slavery, of sharecropping and Jim Crow after emancipation, it remains largely rural.

Today blacks comprise 27 percent of its population. It evinces some of the highest rates of illiteracy, unemployment, poverty, disease, and infant mortality in the United States. It is known for its violent racism; white and black cultures, including bluegrass, blues, jazz, and gospel music; and out-migrations. Black Belt whites spearheaded "massive resistance" to *Brown* and the civil rights movement.

Further Reading

Jeffries, Hasan Kwame. *Bloody Lowndes: Civil Rights and Black Power in Alabama's Black Belt.* New York: New York University Press, 2009.
Womack, Veronica L. *Abandonment in Dixie: Underdevelopment in the Black Belt.* Macon, GA: Mercer University Press, 2013.

BLACK BOURGEOISIE (1957)

Black Bourgeoisie, by E. Franklin Frazier, exposed a "world of make-believe" among educated and affluent blacks, including their elitism and isolation from white society. He described and criticized how they imitated white elites.

Published during his term as chair of Howard University's Department of Sociology, his book provoked strong criticism. One reviewer called it "a savage demystification of the 'myth of Negro business,'" conveying a "lack of sympathy in its stark objectivity" (Thompson, 2000). It was revealing, all the same. For after the *Brown* decision, African Americans would expand the struggle against segregation in the context of their persistent class divisions.

[*See also* Desegregation.]

Reference

Thompson, Audrey. "E. Franklin Frazier's Life & Works." Howard University School of Social Work, Washington, DC, May 2000. Retrieved from www.howard.edu/schoolsocialwork/centers/frazierbio.htm.

Further Reading

Holloway, Jonathan Scott. *Confronting the Veil: Abram Harris, Jr., E. Franklin Frazier, and Ralph Bunche, 1919–1941.* Chapel Hill: University of North Carolina Press, 2002.
Teele, James E., ed. *E. Franklin Frazier and Black Bourgeoisie.* Columbia, MO: University of Missouri Press, 2002.

BLACK MANIFESTO (1969)

Black Power advocate James Forman, former chair of Student Nonviolent Coordinating Committee (SNCC), interrupted worship at New York

City's Riverside Church on May 4, 1969 and presented a manifesto for reparations to the largely white congregation.

It demanded $500 million from US churches and synagogues for their role in slavery and segregation, "the vast system of controls over black people and their minds" (Forman, 1997, p. 547). The money would support a southern land bank, four television networks, and a university. The document was ratified in April at the Detroit-based National Black Economic Development Conference (NBEDC), which coordinated presentations, dialogues, and compensations. But its plans faltered. SNCC, for example, declined to endorse the manifesto. While churchmen and women involved in civil rights usually endorsed it, Jewish leaders unanimously rejected it. NBEDC channeled most of the half-million dollars ultimately received to organizations such as the National Urban League.

[*See also* Black Power movement.]

Reference

Forman, James. *The Making of Black Revolutionaries*. Seattle: University of Washington Press, 1997, p. 547.

Further Reading

Forman, James. *The Making of Black Revolutionaries*. Seattle: University of Washington Press, 1997.
Kelley, Robin D. G. *Freedom Dreams: The Black Radical Imagination*. Boston: Beacon Press, 2002.

BLACK NATIONALISM

A protean ideology, black nationalism considers blacks to be a "nation within a nation." Black equality, it contends, requires collective self-help, solidarity, and struggle.

Nationalists are not monolithic. Over time, they were divided on strategies but united on central tenets: consciousness of African heritage; race pride; and economic, political, social, and cultural autonomy. Their formations were separate, yet many nationalists joined interracial or multiethnic alliances. In antebellum times they embraced abolitionism, Afro-Christian churches, and black emigration to and colonization in Africa. The period 1865–1920 saw them forging all-black institutions and towns, Back-to-Africa and Pan-African movements, and global unity among African peoples. Preaching the same, the Garvey Movement not only enlisted millions of ordinary followers in the 1920s but also created businesses and auxiliaries to foster independence. Garveyism influenced various groups, notably the Nation of Islam (NOI), which built a business economy and espoused "the idea of an autonomous separate state." Moreover, at home and abroad, black nationalists ca. 1930s–50s fought racism, colonialism, and imperialism.

The 1960s ushered in a nationalist resurgence. Alarmed by violence against southern civil rights workers, Monroe, North Carolina NAACP president Robert Williams and NOI imam Malcolm X called for armed self-defense. They inspired others to create the Revolutionary Action Movement (1963) and advocate Black Power (1966). Black Power nationalists included the Black Panther Party for Self Defense. Panthers carried guns in their public demonstrations as well as financed free breakfast programs and other community services. The African Liberation Support Committee (1972) promoted Pan-Africanism and the antiapartheid movement. Black nationalists' activism, which the FBI and state authorities had widely suppressed by the mid-1970s, continued through organizations like the National Black United Front. Founded in 1980 by delegates from thirty-five states and five countries, it pledged to "struggle for self-determination." It remains a force on issues such as police brutality, Afrocentric schooling, and reparations for slavery and Jim Crow.

[*See also* Black Panther Party (BPP); Black Power movement.]

Further Reading

Carr, Robert, ed. *Black Nationalism in the New World: Reading the African American and West Indian Experience.* Durham, NC: Duke University Press, 2002.

Taylor, James Lance. *Black Nationalism in the United States: From Malcolm X to Barack Obama.* Boulder, CO: Lynne Rienner, 2011.

BLACK PANTHER PARTY (BPP)

Formed in Oakland, California in 1966, the BPP aimed to promote Black Power and self-defense. Its founders, college students Huey Newton and Bobby Seale, urged blacks to resist racist violence "by any means necessary," wore black berets and leather jackets, carried guns, and recruited mostly young urban members. Its official newspaper was *The Black Panther.* By 1968 the party had a national membership of more than 5,000 in 40 chapters and a *Panther* circulation of 250,000.

Panthers were race rebels. Their community work, including free breakfasts for children, was underappreciated. Media focused on their Ten-Point

Program, which included "freedom for all black and oppressed people now held" in prisons and jails, armed rallies, and confrontations with police. State and local authorities monitored them; the FBI also infiltrated the party's operations to create internal strife. Police had killed at least twenty-eight Panthers by 1970, during which time New York State alone sentenced twenty-one of them to prison. BPP declined in the late 1970s.

[*See also* Black Power movement.]

Further Reading

Bloom, Joshua, and Waldo E. Martin, Jr. *Black Against Empire: The History and Politics of the Black Panther Party.* Berkeley: University of California Press, 2013.

Jeffries, Judson L., ed. *On the Ground: The Black Panther Party in Communities across America.* Jackson: University Press of Mississippi, 2010.

BLACK POWER MOVEMENT

The term black power was not new. The writer Richard Wright published *Black Power* (1954) and Harlem congressman Adam Clayton Powell, Jr. occasionally used it before the 1960 sit-ins. During a 1966 summer march "against fear" from Memphis, Tennessee to Jackson, Mississippi, however, the Student Nonviolent Coordinating Committee (SNCC) revitalized its meaning. Chairman Stokely Carmichael began chanting Black Power to exhort black consciousness and leadership in the liberation movement. He and other activists were frustrated with the progress of the southern freedom struggle. They argued that its nonviolent ideology mostly appeased the power structure and white liberalism compromised civil rights organizations. Campaigns of desegregation and voter registration also glossed over structural race and class poverty. Black cultural and political self-determination cried out for development, too.

Black Power had multiple meanings. The first Black Panther Party, founded in Alabama as the Lowndes County Freedom Organization (LCOFO), worked to empower blacks mainly through the ballot, education, and jobs. The Black Panther Party for Self Defense of Oakland, California was known (and vilified in mainstream media) for taking up arms. To a majority of whites, therefore, Black Power meant retaliation with the gun. But armed self-defense was just one in a cluster of empowerment goals, including blacks' economic control of their communities.

Activists convened a number of meetings: from the National Black Power Conference in Newark, New Jersey (1967) to the National Black

Political Convention in Gary, Indiana (1972). Delegates in Gary proposed slavery and Jim Crow reparations, boycotting the military draft, and a black state. At the same time, they advocated affirmative action in education and employment, expanding black-owned businesses, and electing black candidates to office. Although the movement declined in the 1970s, Black Power activists founded the National Black United Front (1980), renewing their "call for Black Nationalism and Pan-Africanism." Its central office in Calumet Park, Illinois works through local chapters. It remains a strong voice on public schools, women's equity, and police–community relations. It is also a leading advocate of African reparations.

[*See also* Black nationalism; Black Panther Party (BPP); Civil rights movement.]

Further Reading

Countryman, Matthew J. *Up South: Civil Rights and Black Power in Philadelphia*. Philadelphia: University of Pennsylvania Press, 2006.

Joseph, Peniel E. *Waiting 'Til the Midnight Hour: A Narrative History of Black Power in America*. New York: Henry Holt, 2006.

BLACK TOWNS

Slaves and free blacks created autonomous settlements and communities before the Civil War. Afterward many freedmen and women lived in black towns. More than 100 formed between Reconstruction and World War I to foster black self-help and uplift.

Some exist today. Princeville, North Carolina was created by ex-slaves as Freedom Hill (1865). Chartered in 1885, it was renamed around 1905. In 1874 a white developer and three blacks founded Nicodemus, Kansas, a destination of southern black Exodusters to Kansas in 1879. Established in 1887, Mound Bayou, Mississippi became a business center and symbol of racial progress in the early 1900s.

[*See also* Business.]

Further Reading

Flamming, Douglas. *African Americans in the West*. Santa Barbara, CA: ABC-CLIO, 2009.

Hamilton, Kenneth Marvin. *Black Towns and Profit: Promotion and Development in the Trans-Appalachian West, 1877–1915*. Urbana: University of Illinois Press, 1991.

BLOODY SUNDAY

Culminating their voter registration campaign in Selma and Dallas County, Alabama and nearby counties, civil rights activists planned to march the fifty-four miles from Selma to Montgomery and rally at the State Capitol.

They began on Sunday, March 7, 1965. Following John Lewis (Student Nonviolent Coordinating Committee [SNCC]) and Hosea Williams (Southern Christian Leadership Conference [SCLC]), 600 marchers made it six blocks to Selma's Pettus Bridge, where they were stopped by state troopers and sheriff deputies. Then, in full view of the media, lawmen rushed them with clubs, tear gas, and whips. Televised images of the attack and bloodied marchers created public outrage and helped compel Congress's passage of the Voting Rights Act.

[*See also* Voting Rights Act of 1965.]

Further Reading

Combs, Barbara. *From Selma to Mongomery: The Long March to Freedom.* New York: Routledge, 2013.
Garrow, David J. *Bearing the Cross Martin Luther King, Jr., and the Southern Christian Leadership Conference.* New York: Quill, 1999.

BOND, HORACE M.   EDUCATOR

Born: November 8, 1904, Nashville, TN
Education: Lincoln University (PA), B.A. 1923; University of Chicago, M.A., 1926, Ph.D. 1936
Died: December 21, 1972, Atlanta, GA

Lincoln University (1854) was "the first institution found anywhere in the world to provide a higher education in the arts and sciences for male youth of African descent" (Green, 2006, p. 49). Bond, an alumnus, became its first black president (1945–57).

He pursued scholarship and racial justice. His seminal *The Education of the Negro in the American Social Order* (1934) concluded that blacks' inferior schools were attributable to color and class segregation. The same year, with research funds from the Rosenwald Fund, Bond and his wife (Julia) studied African American schooling in the Star Creek District of Washington Parish, Louisiana; they unveiled financial neglect, family poverty, and racist violence. Bond's *Negro Education in Alabama: A Study in Cotton and Steele* (1939) demonstrated that Reconstruction seeded universal literacy in America. He promoted black self-help, interracial cooperation, and federal implementation of "equal protection." Cofounder of the United Negro College Fund and Southern Regional Council, both in 1944, he helped to develop the NAACP's brief for *Brown v. Board of Education.* During the 1960s he publicly backed the Atlanta student sit-ins as well as African anticolonial struggles. Bond conducted other studies in support of school desegregation and equal educational opportunity.

Reference

Green, Claude A. *What We Dragged Out of Slavery with Us.* West Conshohocken, PA: Infinity Publishing, 2006, p. 49.

Further Reading

Houck, Davis W., and David E. Dixon, eds. *Rhetoric, Religion and the Civil Rights Movement. 1954–1965.* Waco, TX: Baylor University Press, 2006.
Urban, Wayne J. *Black Scholar: Horace Mann Bond, 1904–1972.* Athens: University of Georgia Press, 1992.

BOND, JULIAN   CIVIL RIGHTS ACTIVIST

Born: January 14, 1940, Nashville, TN
Education: Morehouse College, 1957–60, B.A., 1971
Died: August 15, 2015, Fort Walton Beach, FL

A son of educators Horace M. and Julia Bond, Julian Bond has been a recognized civil rights leader since his Morehouse years.

Inspired in a course on nonviolence taught by Martin Luther King, Jr., he became an activist. Cofounder of the Atlanta Student Movement, which conducted sit-ins at segregated lunch counters, he was also cofounder of the Student Nonviolent Coordinating Committee (SNCC). Its communications director, he edited the *Student Voice* and managed media coverage of SNCC's sit-in, voter registration, and literacy campaigns in the South. Frequently arrested and jailed, he persisted in calling for nonviolent protest, racial integration, and social justice. He won election to the Georgia House (1965), but, rebuking his criticism of the Vietnam War, it refused to seat him. After the Supreme Court overturned the House's refusal (1967), Bond served in the House and Senate until 1986, "elected to office more times than any other black Georgian" (Roady).

His career afterward included public speaking, narrating documentary films, writing, university teaching; chairing the NAACP Board of Directors, and co-hosting *America's Black Forum* for TV One, Silver Spring, Maryland. Launched in 1977, *Forum* is the oldest black talk show on television. It airs nationwide and in more than forty countries.

Reference

Roady, Jennifer. "Julian Bond (b. 1940)." In *New Georgia Encyclopedia*. Retrieved from www.georgiaencyclopedia.org/articles/history-archaeology/julian_bond.

Further Reading

Bond, Julian. "SNCC: What We Did." *Monthly Review*, 52 (October 2000): 14–28.
Murphree, Vanessa. *The Selling of Civil Rights: The Student Nonviolent Coordinating Committee and the Use of Public Relations.* New York: Routledge, 2006.

BOUCHET, EDWARD A.   EDUCATOR

Born: September 15, 1852, New Haven, CT
Education: Yale University, B.S., 1874, Ph.D., 1876, Phi Beta Kappa, 1884
Died: October 28, 1918, New Haven, CT

A son of ex-slaves, Bouchet rests in Evergreen Cemetery, New Haven, Connecticut. In 1988 Yale placed a granite memorial at his grave. An 1874 Yale College graduate, "ranked sixth in a class of 124," he earned a Yale Ph.D. (Physics) in 1876. He was the first black person to earn a doctorate from an American university.

Facing segregation, Bouchet did not pursue research. Black institutions had few resources to do so. He taught chemistry and physics at the Institute for Colored Youth (ICY) in Philadelphia, a Quaker-supported institution. But "the Du Bois-Washington controversy over industrial vs. collegiate education" (www.buffalo.edu/mad/physics/bouchet_edward_alexander.html) escalated in ICY and it closed the college prep program. Bouchet resigned in 1902, afterward becoming a principal or professor at Negro high schools and colleges in Pennsylvania, Missouri, Virginia, Ohio, and Texas.

He was a revered teacher and mentor. However, his "full impact on black education will never be known" (www.buffalo.edu/mad/physics/bouchet_edward_alexander.html). An Ohio black woman considered him larger than life. "Perhaps the most highly educated person in the area," she remembered, "he inspired both black and white young people with hitherto unknown goals" (www.buffalo.edu/mad/physics/bouchet_edward_alexander.html). His numerous students included her brother, who graduated from Bowdoin College in 1913 and became the first black faculty member at Ohio State University.

Further Reading

Mickens, Ronald E., ed. *Edward Bouchet: The First African-American Doctorate.* River Edge, NJ: World Scientific, 2002.
Sammons, Vivian O. *Blacks in Science and Medicine.* New York: Hemisphere, 1990.

BROOKE, EDWARD W.   US SENATOR

Born: October 26, 1919, Washington, DC
Education: Howard University, B.S., 1941; Boston University School of Law, LL.B., 1948
Died: January 3, 2015, Coral Gables, FL

Raised in a middle-class family, Brooke finished Dunbar High School and Howard University in Washington, DC. An army officer and combat hero in World War II, he defended black soldiers in court-martial trials before returning to study and practice law in Boston.

He achieved national recognition. Over time black Bostonians were loyal Democrats, but he became a Republican. Also a liberal, he ran unsuccessfully for the state House in 1950. But an appointment to the city's Finance Commission boosted his electability. Elected attorney general (1962–66), tough on crime and political corruption, he gained much influence and won two US Senate terms (1966–78). The first African American elected to that body since Reconstruction, he served during an era when racial conflict and the Vietnam War divided America.

Seeking to be judged by merit rather than race, Brooke was successful in the Senate. A member of the banking, aeronautical and space sciences committees, and the president's National Advisory Commission on Civil Disorders, he also fought for and retained an open-housing clause in the Civil Rights Act of 1968. His pro-war position alienated many civil rights and peace activists, though he championed policies to aid Third World nations and sanction apartheid in South Africa.

Further Reading

Brooke, Edward W. *Bridging the Divide: My Life*. New Brunswick, NJ: Rutgers
    University Press, 2007.
Nordin, Dennis S. *From Edward Brooke to Barack Obama: African American
    Political Success, 1966–2008*. Columbia: University of Missouri Press, 2012.

BROOKS, GWENDOLYN E.   WRITER

Born: June 17, 1917, Topeka, KN
Education: Wilson Junior College, graduated 1936, poetry workshop,
1940s
Died: December 3, 2000, Chicago, IL

Growing up in Chicago, Brooks emerged as a writer ca. 1920s–60s. She
was inspired by ambitious parents to learn and achieve. James Weldon
Johnson and Langton Hughes were her early mentors. Joining poet Inez
Cunningham Stark's workshop, which trained "Negro would-be poets in
the very buckle of the Black Belt" (Gates and McKay, 1997, p. 1577), she
studied the modernist writers who influenced her acclaimed first book,
A Street in Bronzeville (1945).

   Her poetry, which richly articulated urban realism, juxtaposed objects
and words; controlled rhyme and meter; used formal and thematic irony;
and translated public events into poetic details. *Annie Allen* (1949), her
second book of poems, received a Pulitzer Prize in 1950. She was the first
African American to earn that distinction. Depicting young hustlers in *We
Real Cool* (1960, p. 1591), she wrote: "... We Sing sin. We Thin gin. We
Jazz June. We Die Soon." When she embraced Black Power, Brooks linked
literary generations. Addressing the Second Black Writers' Conference at
Fisk University in 1967, she praised their embrace of blackness. She published fiction and nonfiction works with independent black presses and
urged "all black people" to patronize black arts. Awarded the National
Medal of the Arts (1995), she affirmed the African American woman
as "a person in the world–with wrongs to right, stupidities to outwit,
with her man when possible, on her own when not" (*Black World/Negro
Digest*, 1973, p. 52).

References

Black World/Negro Digest, vol. 22, March 1973, p. 52.
Gates, Jr., Henry Louis, and Nellie Y. McKay, eds. *The Norton Anthology of
    African American Literature*. New York: W. W. Norton, 1997, pp. 1577,
    1591.

Further Reading

Madhubuti, Haki R. *Honoring Genius: Gwendolyn Brooks: The Narrative of Craft, Art, Kindness and Justice.* Chicago: Third World Press, 2011.

Mickle, Mildred R., ed. *Gwendolyn Brooks.* Pasadena, CA: Salem Press, 2010.

BROTHERHOOD OF SLEEPING CAR PORTERS (BSCP)

Founded in 1925 by A. Philip Randolph, the first president, BSCP organized men who assisted passengers for the Pullman Palace Car Company, America's largest employer of blacks. It was the first black union to receive a charter in the American Federation of Labor (AFL). Early on, with just 1,900 of 10,000 porters joining, BSCP endured a company backlash and internal fears. But its AFL membership and NAACP endorsement provided crucial support. That, alongside the Railway Labor Act (1934), compelled Pullman to recognize the porters' right to organize and bargain collectively in 1937.

[*See also* Labor.]

Further Reading

Bates, Beth Tompkins. *Pullman Porters and the Rise of Protest Politics in Black America, 1925–1945.* Chapel Hill: University of North Carolina Press, 2001.

Tye, Larry. *Rising from the Rails: Pullman Porters and the Making of the Black Middle Class.* New York: Henry Holt, 2004.

BROWN, CHARLOTTE HAWKINS   EDUCATOR

Born: June 11, 1883, Henderson, NC
Education: Salem Teachers' College, 1900–01; Wellesley College, B.A., 1928
Died: January 11, 1961, Greensboro, NC

Griffin Davis, the photographer for *Ebony* magazine's story on Palmer Memorial Institute in 1947, called it "the Groton and Exeter of Negro America."

Palmer exemplified Brown's hope. Established in 1902 for industrial training, it became an elite high school using a classical curriculum. During her presidency, from 1902 to 1952, she raised nearly $1.5 million and transformed the lives of more than 1,000 students, usually from middle-class backgrounds. More than 90 percent of them earned diplomas and enrolled in four-year colleges; 64 percent attended graduate schools. Brown urged students to be self-disciplined and excel academically. A role model through her activism in black women's associations and civil rights struggles – state, regional, and national – she joined the fight against lynching and Jim Crow. A popular speaker, she advocated black moral character, dignity, and self-help; interracial cooperation; and educational equality. She also spoke of her life's calling. "I must sing my song. There may be other songs more beautiful than mine," she declared, "but I must sing the song God gave me to sing, and I must sing it until death" (www .nchistoricsites.org/chb/main.htm). Palmer is preserved as the Charlotte Hawkins Brown Memorial State Historic Site (1987). Brown is honored in the North Carolina Association of Educators Hall of Fame (2006).

Further Reading

Crow, Jeffrey J., Paul D. Escott, Flora J. Hatley Wadelington. *A History of African Americans in North Carolina.* Raleigh: North Carolina Office of Archives and History, 2002.

Wadelington, Charles W., and Richard F. Knapp. *Charlotte Hawkins Brown & the Palmer Memorial Institute: What One Young Woman Could Do.* Chapel Hill: University of North Carolina Press, 1999.

BROWN, JAMES N. (JIM)   PRO FOOTBALL PLAYER

Born: February 17, 1936, St. Simons, GA
Education: Manhasset Secondary School, Manhasset, NY; Syracuse University, athletic scholarship, B.A., 1957

Sports Illustrated (1994) called Brown one of America's greatest athletes. A Cleveland Browns draftee (1957), among the pioneer black players in the National Football League (NFL), he is, to some sports writers, the best-ever pro fullback. Brown is honored in the College Football and NFL halls of fame.

He retired from the Browns in 1965, after nine pro-bowl seasons and at the zenith of his career, to pursue acting. He appeared in more than twenty television and Hollywood films, notably westerns such as *Rio Conchos* (1964) and *The Dirty Dozen* (1967). Usually cast as a strong man or running hero, he sometimes played roles involving interaction with white women (then racially sensitive). He also produced a few feature films, but with little success.

Brown believed that African American professional athletes should be role models in and "give back" to their communities. During the Black Power era and afterward, he worked for community development and reform. In 1986 he founded Vital Issues, Plus, which reached out to urban gangs and ex-convicts. Its core mission was to help them finish high school and get jobs. Reorganized as Amer-I-Can in 1989, it served the Los Angeles metropolitan area. Brown hosted workshops for participants at his home.

Further Reading

Coenen, Craig R. *From Sandlots to the Super Bowl: The National Football League, 1920–1967.* Knoxville: University of Tennessee Press, 2005.
Freeman, Michael. *Jim Brown: The Fierce Life of an American Hero.* New York: William Morrow, 2006.

BROWN V. BOARD OF EDUCATION (1954)

Thanks to the NAACP's litigation against racially segregated public schools, the Supreme Court, in 1952, scheduled oral argument on five suits: *Brown v. Board of Education of Topeka* (Kansas); *Bolling v. Sharpe* (District of Columbia); *Briggs v. Elliott* (Clarendon County, South Carolina); *Davis v. County School Board of Prince Edward County* (Virginia); and *Gebhart v. Belton* (New Castle County, Delaware). These cases raised "a common legal question," the Court announced, that would justify a "consolidated opinion" (Bertain, 1955, p. 141).

NAACP counsel Thurgood Marshall and co-counsel prevailed. They argued and showed that racial segregation via "equal, but separate" schooling not only "deprived the plaintiffs of the equal protection of the laws under the Fourteenth Amendment" but also created in them "feelings of inferiority and doubts about personal worth" (Davis, 1973, p. 124). Announcing the Court's unanimous decision in *Brown*, Chief Justice Earl Warren concurred: "We conclude that in the field of public education the doctrine of 'separate but equal' has no place. Separate educational facilities are inherently unequal" (*Brown v. Board of Education of Topeka*, 1954). In the wake of that opinion, black communities and their allies engaged in nonviolent protests for school desegregation and equality.

[*See also* Marshall, Thurgood; *Plessy v. Ferguson (1896)*.]

References

Bertain, Jr., George J. "Racial Segregation in the Public Schools" *Catholic University Law Review*, Vol. 5, 1955, p. 141.
Brown v. Board of Education of Topeka 347 US 483 (1954).
Davis, Abraham L. *The United States Supreme Court and the Uses of Social Science Data*. New York: MSS Information Corp., 1973, p. 124.

Further Reading

Lau, Peter F., ed. *From the Grassroots to the Supreme Court:* Brown v. Board of Education *and American Democracy*. Durham: Duke University Press, 2004.
Patterson, James T. *Brown v. Board of Education: A Civil Rights Milestone and Its Troubled Legacy*. New York: Oxford University Press, 2001.

BUCHANAN V. WARLEY (1917)

Louisville, Kentucky's 1914 ordinance required "the use of separate blocks, for residence ... by white people and colored people, respectively." The Louisville and national NAACP, contesting "the racial zoning movement" (Silver, 1997, p. 25), counseled William Warley, a black postal worker who contracted to buy property in a white area from realtor Charles Buchanan. The state Court of Appeals ruled against Warley.

But the US Supreme Court unanimously rejected that ruling. It judged the ordinance unconstitutional as it "destroyed the right of the individual to acquire, enjoy, and dispose of his property" and avoided the "due process" clause of the Fourteenth Amendment. Reviewing "separate but equal," it concluded that racially segregated residential zones "exceeded the limitations imposed by the Amendment" (*Buchanan v. Warley*, 1917). Residential ordinances segregating blacks, therefore, were not valid. This gave the NAACP a major victory, although restrictive covenants in deeds to segregate housing would follow.

[*See also* Segregation.]

References

Buchanan v. Warley, 245 US 60 (1917).
Silver, Christopher. "The Racial Origins of Zoning in American Cities." In June Manning Thomas and Marsha Ritzdorf, eds. *Urban Planning and the African American Community: In the Shadows*. Thousand Oaks, CA: SAGE Publications, 1997. p. 25.

Further Reading

Bernstein, David E. "Philip Sober Controlling Philip Drunk: *Buchanan v. Warley* in Historical Perspective." *Vanderbilt Law Review*, 51 (May 1998): 797–879.

Hadden, Sally E., and Patricia Hagler Minter, eds. *Signposts: New Directions in Southern Legal History*. Athens: University of Georgia Press, 2013.

BUFFALO SOLDIERS

The post–Civil War military assigned black soldiers to four regular army units: the Ninth and Tenth cavalries, Twenty-fourth and Twenty-fifth infantries. Often they were deployed on the western frontier to protect whites from hostile Indians, who called the woolly-haired blacks "Buffalo soldiers," and whites did not regard them as equals.

From 1869 to 1890 they fought in 200 battles, frequently rescuing white troops. They also guarded the US Mail, railways, and engineers surveying lands or planning roads. Black cavalry and infantrymen were ordered to suppress labor strikes in the 1890s. They earned four Congressional Medals of Honor, nine Certificates of Merit, and twenty-nine Orders of Honorable Mention.

[*See also* Military.]

Further Reading

Leckie, William H., with Shirley A. Leckie. *The Buffalo Soldiers: A Narrative of Black Cavalry in the West*. Norman: University of Oklahoma Press, 2003.

Shellum, Brian. *Black Officer in a Buffalo Soldier Regiment: The Military Career of Colonel Charles Young*. Lincoln: University of Nebraska Press, 2010.

BUNCHE, RALPH J.   SCHOLAR AND DIPLOMAT

Born: August 7, 1904, Detroit, MI
Education: UCLA, B.A. summa cum laude, 1927; Harvard University, Ph.D., 1934
Died: December 9, 1971, New York, NY

The first black recipient of the Nobel Peace Prize (1950), Bunche was a renowned scholar and diplomat. In one interview, he said that his grandmother inspired him to be race proud and pursue education. He earned academic honors at UCLA and Harvard, writing his doctoral thesis on colonialism in Africa. He excelled as a professor at Howard University, where he organized the Department of Political Science, cofounded the National Negro Congress, and, from 1939, assisted the Carnegie-Myrdal Study of the Negro in America.

World War II catapulted him into diplomacy. From the Office of Military Intelligence, he was assigned to the Department of State and monitored African affairs. Joining the United Nations (UN) staff in 1946, he negotiated an Arab-Israeli truce (1949) and won international renown. Appointed undersecretary (1955), he managed UN peacekeeping forces and operations in the world's most dangerous regions during the Cold War. Bunche also attended to civic commitments. President of the American Political Science Association (1953) and a pillar of the NAACP Board of Directors, he helped shape legal strategy for the *Brown* decision and joined Martin Luther King, Jr. on the Selma-to-Montgomery March for voting rights.

Further Reading

Hill, Robert A., and Edmond J. Keller, eds. *Trustee for the Human Community: Ralph J. Bunche, the United Nations, and the Decolonization of Africa*. Athens: Ohio University Press, 2010.

Holloway, Jonathan Scott. *Confronting the Veil: Abram Harris, Jr., E. Franklin Frazier, and Ralph J. Bunche, 1919–1941*. Chapel Hill: University of North Carolina Press, 2002.

BUSINESS

From slavery to the present, business has been and is foundational in black struggles for freedom, citizenship, and equality.

Business began among slaves and free blacks. They forged individual and group efforts to earn money in enterprise while building families; kin support networks; and religious, fraternal, and burial associations. Colonial masters regularly hired out skilled bondmen, such as blacksmiths, for profit. Given a portion of what they earned, hirelings frequently bought themselves. Some opened barber, cabinetmaking, and other shops. A cadre of black freemen obtained land, houses, servants, and slaves. Lower-South slaves used a task system to acquire autonomy and personal property. Finishing assigned tasks by midday, they were allowed to leave the fields and work unsupervised until night. Many fished, hunted, cultivated family garden plots, and sold goods in the marketplace. Black hawkers impressed one foreign visitor in 1784. "There is hardly any trade or craft which has not been learned and is not carried on

by the negroes" (Travelers' Impressions..., 1916, p. 406), he explained.
They continued to produce and barter in the wake of gradual northern abolition and rise of the southern Cotton Kingdom, sustaining Free
African societies; churches; abolitionist, convention, and emigration
movements; masonic orders; and mutual aid groups. Among them, artisans, beauticians, carpenters, dressmakers, and painters were active businesspeople. In 1861, when it seceded from the Union and ignited the Civil
War, the South counted 120,000 artisans, 100,000 of them black. Nine
in ten were slaves.

Following the precepts of slave and quasi-free forebears, freedpeople organized to uplift their race. They endured the backlash of Black
Codes (1865–66). For example, no South Carolina black resident could
undertake "trade, employment or business" without a white reference
and $100 license ($10 for whites). Yet blacks became wage earners and
saved at the Freedmen's Savings and Trust Company, which had branches
in seventeen states and the District of Columbia from 1865 to 1874. It
failed due to "massive fraud among upper management and among the
board of directors" (Hurst) and blacks lost $57 million. Of $1.6 million
in deposits at the bank's closing, only half were returned by 1900. Better
prospects appeared elsewhere. A federal report classified 4–8 percent of
southern blacks as landowners in 1876. Nationally, blacks were increasingly visible as clothing, grocery, and dry-goods retailers; restaurateurs;
blacksmiths; shoemakers; builders; and manufacturers.

Their "emerging lines" after Reconstruction encompassed not only
stores and factories but also banks and insurance firms. Increased
pride, self-help, solidarity, and civil rights efforts inspired progress.
About 20 percent of blacks owned land in 1900 and they held more
than 15 million acres by 1915, the fiftieth anniversary of emancipation.
Rising numbers of black workers and professionals, rural and urban,
promoted initiatives for "economic self-determination." Alongside groceries, restaurants, funeral homes, beauty and barbershops, they saw
an increasing number of cotton mills, real estate and loan associations,
brickyards, and construction companies. A critical market emerged
in black towns, more than a hundred of which were established ca.
1879–1920. Mound Bayou, Mississippi, touted as a model, boasted 500
residents in 1907. Its forty-four establishments included a bank, sawmill,
and three cotton gins.

Businessmen and women persevered despite Jim Crow, white competition, and insufficient capital. The Grand United Order of True Reformers,
of Richmond, Virginia, launched the first bank, True Reformers Bank

(1888). Richmond's Southern Aid Society began black life and industrial insurance in 1893. *The Negro in Business* (1899), by W. E. B. Du Bois, stressed the need to "patronize black business." In 1900 Booker T. Washington created the National Negro Business League (NNBL). It enlisted 40,000 members and 600 branches in 34 states and Africa by 1915. NNBL helped start scores of enterprises: media, notably newspapers; hair and beauty aids industries; and funeral, hotel, realty, transport, banking, and insurance ventures. Nashville, Tennessee had a women's Negro Business League. In 1914 Marcus Garvey chartered the Universal Negro Improvement Association (UNIA), which by 1925 claimed several million followers, with 700 chapters in 38 states, the Caribbean, and Africa. UNIA's Negro Factories Corporation capitalized a *Negro World* newspaper, black doll factory, and Black Star Line ship company.

Progress came gradually. By 1912 blacks reported 64 banks (3 northern) and 134 in 1934, the Depression's worst year. Only 12 survived, 6 to World War II, the oldest being First Tuskegee Bank, Tuskegee, Alabama. Fraternal lodges formed hundreds of insurance federations ca. 1880–1910. By 1946 some 205 agencies existed, 46 of the larger ones joining the National Negro Insurance Association. North Carolina Mutual Life (Durham), Atlanta Life (Atlanta), and Supreme Liberty Life (Chicago) led the industry.

Black patronage, federal programs, and private philanthropy (especially as desegregation reduced market share) sustained black business in the post–World War II era. The "government was not receptive to black businesses bidding on defense contracts." The Small Business Administration awarded fewer loan guarantees to blacks. More assistance followed the Civil Rights Act (1964), which authorized the Office of Economic Opportunity (OEO) "to provide loans and technical assistance" for minority firms. Black businesspeople, including proponents of Black Power, embraced "black capitalism," seeking to retain the black consumer dollar. They pursued grants from foundations such as the Ford Foundation or loans from OEO and the Minority Small Business/Capital Ownership Development Program. The last, under affirmative action policy, provided a fixed "percentage of government contracts" to minorities. Meanwhile, black Muslims (the Nation of Islam) did not seek federal or white corporate subsidies. They espoused racial separatism, raised their own venture capital, and built an $80 million subeconomy.

Small ventures still defined black entrepreneurship, though this was shifting. Retail and service proprietorships comprised 94 percent of black enterprises in 1977 but 70 percent by 1987. Significantly, the 424,165 black firms in 1987 (representing 34.9 percent of minority-owned and 3.1 percent of US firms) totaled receipts of $19.76 billion, a fraction of blacks' $206 billion income. That year's top 100 black companies, all corporations, demonstrated greater diversity by industry: auto dealership, 53; food/beverage, 10; construction, 8; media, 5; hair care/beauty aids, 5; petroleum/energy, 4; computer/information, 4; entertainment, 2; metal, 1; and miscellaneous, 8. Realigning to compete "outside traditional black consumer markets," Black Corporate America faced intractable issues of poverty, racism, and community "economic empowerment." Among the leaders of corporate-community partnerships for education, training, and employment ca. 1990s–2000s were *Black Enterprise* magazine, TLC Beatrice International Foods, Motown Records (New York); and Johnson Publishing Company (Chicago).

[*See also* Black capitalism; Freedmen's Bank.]

References

Hurst, Ryan. "Freedmen's Savings and Trust Company 1865-1874." Retrieved from www.blackpast.org/aah/freedmen-s-savings-and-trust-company-1865-1874.
"Travelers' Impressions of Slavery in America from 1750 to 1800," *The Journal of Negro History*, vol. 1, October 1916, p. 406.

Further Reading

Black Economic Empowerment: The National Negro Business League. Farmington Hills, MI: Gale, 2011.
Fairlie, Robert W., and Alicia M. Robb. *Race and Entrepreneurial Success: Black-, Asian-, and White-Owned Businesses in the United States.* Cambridge, MA: MIT Press, 2008.
Walker, Juliet E. K. *The History of Black Business in America: Capitalism, Race, Entrepreneurship.* Chapel Hill: University of North Carolina Press, 2009.

CAESAR, SHIRLEY   GOSPEL SINGER

Born: October 13, 1938, Durham, NC
Education: North Carolina College, 1956–58; Shaw University, B.A., 1984; Duke Divinity School

Caesar rose from a childhood of familial hardships to international acclaim in gospel music. She began performing as a soloist at age twelve alongside a Virginia evangelist. Singing often on his Portsmouth television show, she soon recorded her first song, "I'd Rather Have Jesus" (1951). She traveled by bus and train to perform in the Jim Crow South. She left college in 1958 to join the Caravans, a Chicago-based female group. Her performance was powerful and dramatic, as she would leave the stage to shake hands with people in the audience. With the hit "Hallelujah, It's Done" (1961) she incorporated periodic sermonizing into the songs. This became a marker of her singing and preaching.

After leaving the Caravans and organizing the Caesar Singers, she produced an array of hits. These included mother-songs such as "Don't Drive Your Mama Away" (1969). Reviewers called her the "Queen of Gospel" and she received a Grammy Award for "Put Your Hand in the Hand of the Man" (1971). "Faded Rose" (1980), which a son places on his mother's grave, topped the charts. After 1980, despite more than 150 concerts annually, she finished college, began her ministry, and served as a Durham councilwoman.

Further Reading

Caesar, Shirley. *The Lady, the Melody, & the Word: The Inspirational Story of the First Lady of Gospel.* Nashville, TN: Thomas Nelson, 1998.
Darden, Robert. *People Get Ready!: A New History of Black Gospel Music.* New York: Continuum, 2004.

CAPITALISM

Responding to calls for "black capitalism" from civil rights and Black Power leaders, the Small Business Administration (SBA) launched the Minority Small Business/Capital Ownership Development Program (1969). It soon pledged "that a certain percentage of government contracts would go to minority-owned businesses" (Walker, 1998, p. 276).

It was needed. Two dozen race riots (1966–67), which conservatives blamed on black radicals, fed white backlash. The Nixon administration winked affirmative action regulations for contractors, but it allowed SBA to assist some inner-city businesses. Nathan Wright, leader of the Black Power Conference in Newark, New Jersey (1967), called for immediate government and corporate assistance, including opportunities for "high management positions." Endorsing the idea of a "separate black economy," former Congress of Racial Equality (CORE) national director Floyd McKissick organized a venture capital firm and sought federal loan guarantees. Black economist and Federal Reserve Board member Andrew Brimmer, however, insisted that African Americans prioritize education, training, and full employment.

[*See also* Business.]

Reference

Walker, Juliet E. K. *The History of Black Business in America: Capitalism, Race, Entrepreneurship.* New York: Macmillan Library Reference, 1998, p. 276.

Further Reading

Marable, Manning. *How Capitalism Underdeveloped Black America: Problems in Race, Political Economy, and Society.* Cambridge, MA: South End Press, 2000.
Very, Ryan. "Black Capitalism: An Economic Program for the Black American Ghetto." *International Journal of Humanities and Social Science*, 2 (November 2012): 53–63.

CARMICHAEL, STOKELY (KWAME TURÉ) CIVIL RIGHTS AND POLITICAL ACTIVIST

Born: July 29, 1941, Port-of-Spain, Trinidad
Education: Howard University, B.A., 1964
Died: November 16, 1998, Conakry, Guinea

Carmichael emerged as one of the civil rights movement's "most fiery and visible leaders of black militancy" (*Jet*, 1998, p. 5). He joined the Freedom Rides (1961) and became a Student Nonviolent Coordinating Committee (SNCC) field secretary in Mississippi.

But by Freedom Summer (1964) he was frustrated, largely because of black-white division on nonviolent strategy; lack of federal protection (four people, including three volunteers, were killed); and defeat of the Mississippi Freedom Democratic Party's challenge for seats at the Democratic' National Convention. Elected SNCC chairman in May

1966, he pursued a black agenda. He called for Black Power in June as the Southern Christian Leadership Conference (SCLC), Congress of Racial Equality (CORE), and SNCC continued the march against fear when a would-be assassin shot James Meredith, its leader.

Carmichael's new slogan split the movement. Mainstream media stressed its race separatism, rejection of white liberalism, and violent connotation. Martin Luther King, Jr. considered it "an unfortunate choice of words." It invoked "race against race," Roy Wilkins declared. "It is a call for black people in this country to unite," Carmichael rebutted, "to recognize their heritage, to build a sense of community" (Carmichael and Hamilton, 1967, p. 44). Black Power also would prioritize voter registration and voting; economic, educational, and political empowerment; self-defense; and joining antiracist movements "to stop the exploitation of nonwhite people around the world."

References

Carmichael, Stokley and Charles V. Hamilton, *Black Power: The Politics of Liberation in America*. New York: Vintage Books, 1967, p. 44.
"Kwame Ture, Civil Rights Leader Who Coined 'Black Power' Dies." *Jet*, Vol. 95, November 30, 1998, p. 5.

Further Reading

Joseph, Peniel E. *Stokely: A Life*. New York: Basic Civitas Books, 2014.
Walters, Ronald W. *Pan Africanism in the African Diaspora: An Analysis of Modern Afrocentric Political Movements*. Detroit: Wayne State University Press, 1993.

CARVER, GEORGE WASHINGTON
SCIENTIST AND EDUCATOR

Born: 1864, Diamond, MO
Education: Simpson College, 1890; Iowa State College, B.S., 1894, M.S., 1896
Died: January 4, 1943, Tuskegee, AL

Carver is a textbook hero and one of the best known figures in American history. Born a slave, he began his higher education at age thirty and was the first black person to earn degrees from Iowa State College. In 1896 he joined the Tuskegee Institute faculty and developed a respected program in agricultural science. He pursued seminal research in botany and plant bacteriology.

Seeking to improve the South's economy and health, he created more than 400 mainly food products from peanuts, pecans, and potatoes. Peanut butter, a Carver creation, is a national staple. From cotton waste and local clay, he made dyes and other useful goods. He attended to depleted farmlands on weekends, teaching black farmers soil conservation, crop diversification, and productive uses of fertilizers. This work resulted in Tuskegee's annual farming institute, which attracted thousands of rural blacks, and its farm extension service.

Carver advanced scientific and racial progress in spite of Jim Crow. He received the Spingarn Award from the NAACP in 1923; the US Postal Service memorialized him on a stamp in 1948. Five years later Congress authorized the Carver National Monument, which it located at his Missouri birthplace and dedicated on July 17, 1960.

Further Reading

Hersey, Mark D. *My Work Is That of Conservation: An Environmental Biography of George Washington Carver.* Athens: University of Georgia Press, 2011.
Perry, John. *Unshakeable Faith: Booker T. Washington & George Washington Carver: A Biography.* Sisters, OR: Multnomah, 1999.

CHESNUTT, CHARLES W.   WRITER

Born: June 20, 1858, Cleveland, OH
Education: Freedmen's School, Fayetteville, NC
Died: November 15, 1932, Cleveland, OH

Best known for short stories, novels, and essays on issues of race, color, and social identity in the post–Civil War South, Chesnutt was the first black author to succeed in mainstream American letters. He was born in Ohio to mixed-race free blacks from Fayetteville, North Carolina, where he grew up and taught school before migrating to Cleveland in 1883. There he became a lawyer, court stenographer, an acclaimed writer, and civil rights activist.

Chesnutt's fiction, which combined historical events and his lived experiences, depicts African American folk culture and realities of the color line. In *The Conjure Woman* (1899) ex-slave Uncle Julius narrates hoodoo tales showing the humanity and self-help of slaves. Chesnutt thus reveals that they were deserving of citizenship and equal opportunity. *The House Behind the Cedars* (1900) and *The Colonel's Dream* (1905) incisively reveal the class and racial dilemmas of elite mulattoes. Pulled between competing identities, many passed as whites. One response to master–slave miscegenation, passing subverted customs and laws against interracial marriage. A story of the bloody Wilmington, North Carolina race riot of 1898, *The Marrow of Tradition* (1901) powerfully unveils the riot's atrocities as well as black–white interdependence behind its scenes.

Further Reading

Izzo, David Garrett, and Maria Orban, eds. *Charles Chesnutt Reappraised: Essays on the First Major African American Fiction Writer*. Jefferson, NC: McFarland & Co., 2009.

McWilliams, Dean. *Charles W. Chesnutt and the Fictions of Race*. Athens: University of Georgia Press, 2002.

CHILDREN'S DEFENSE FUND (CDF)

Founded in 1973 by civil rights attorney Marian Wright Edelman, CDF, through its Washington, DC and regional offices, is the chief "advocate for the rights of children, with special emphasis on ... poor and minority children." It is funded by corporate, foundation, and individual donors.

Its work is crucial. In the 1980s, for example, it campaigned against teen pregnancy. With half of all black children born out of wedlock alone, Edelman warned that future generations could live in poverty. CDF sponsored radio, television, newspaper, and billboard ads informing teens not only on the health risks of sexual relations but also why they must stay in school and graduate. Ads sidestepped abortion politics by stressing prevention. CDF also initiated the Dodd–Miller Act to Leave No Child Behind (2001). Today, its advocacy continues on behalf of Head Start, Healthy Start, Families First, and Freedom Schools, among other programs.

[*See also* Poverty; Welfare.]

Further Reading

Edelman, Marian Wright. *The State of America's Children: A Report*. Boston: Beacon Press, 2000.

McCartney, Kathleen, Hirokazu Yoshikawa, and Laurie B. Forcier, eds. *Improving the Odds for America's Children: Future Directions in Policy and Practice*. Cambridge, MA: Harvard University Press, 2014.

CHISHOLM, SHIRLEY A.   US CONGRESSWOMAN

Born: November 20, 1924, Brooklyn, NY
Education: Brooklyn College, B.A. cum laude, 1946; Columbia University, M.A., 1952
Died: January 1, 2005, Brooklyn, NY.

Chisholm achieved distinction as the first black woman elected to Congress, as well as the first woman to organize a major party bid for president. Her race, gender, and Caribbean heritage found some members of the civil rights and antiwar coalition questioning her capacity to succeed in that arena. But she challenged racism and sexism in the political system while enlarging the doorway of the House (and other federal institutions) to women of color.

Chisholm had a reputation, built in the New York State Assembly, for being unbought and unbossed. An advocate for the struggling African American and Puerto Rican majority of the 12th Congressional District in Brooklyn, she promoted jobs, job training, assisted childcare, and healthcare. She fought for equality of opportunity in education, employment, and housing and opposed the costly Vietnam War. "Our children, our jobless men, our deprived, rejected, and starving fellow citizens must come first," she asserted in 1969. "I intend to vote 'no' on every bill that comes to the floor of this House that provides any funds for the Department of Defense" (Chisholm, 2010, p. 113). Many of her colleagues in the House considered such statements to be "politically unwise."

Reference

Chisholm, Shirley. *Unbought and Unbossed: Expanded Anniversary Edition.* Washington, DC: Take Root Media, 2010, p. 113.

Further Reading

Gill, LaVerne McCain. *African American Women in Congress: Forming and Transforming History.* New Brunswick, NJ: Rutgers University Press, 1997.
Winslow, Barbara. *Shirley Chisholm: Catalyst for Change.* Boulder, CO: Westview Press, 2014.

CITIES

Like plantations, farms, and rural areas, cities significantly defined African American labor, life, and struggle.

In colonial and antebellum times, the city was a significant site of slaves and free blacks' efforts for autonomy and liberty. Slaves, perhaps 5 percent of the population in New England and Middle Colonies by 1750, usually did small farm, domestic, or industrial work and lived in port hubs such as Boston, New York City, and Philadelphia. Frequently, they were hired out, like many bondmen and women in Baltimore, Richmond, and Charleston. Building families, churches, and communities in the North and South, they struggled for liberty by petition, flight, and joining the American or British armies during the Revolutionary War. Gradual abolition of northern slavery and its cotton-driven southern growth saw an increasing number of free and enslaved blacks in urban areas from Providence to New Orleans. They were segregated and exploited, but they built black institutions, embraced abolitionism, and helped execute the Civil War and emancipation.

Cities provided critical spaces for black aspiration and effort from Reconstruction to World War I. Increasingly, as freedmen became sharecroppers, wage workers, and voters, they moved their families cityward. From 1870 to 1890 blacks increased from 13 to 20 percent of the urban population nationally, from 10 to 15 percent in the South (home to 90 percent of all blacks). Blacks in Atlanta, Charleston, Montgomery, Nashville, New Orleans, Raleigh, and Richmond made notable civic and economic progress. They fought for equal citizenship against segregation; inferior housing, jobs and schools; disfranchisement; and lynching. Oppression and shared hope for decent employment fueled blacks' rural–urban migrations within and out of the South.

The Great Migration (1910–70) catalyzed their urbanization. Some 6–7 million reached destinations in the North, Midwest, and West, including Boston, New York, Buffalo, Newark, Philadelphia, Pittsburgh, Cleveland, Toledo, Detroit, Indianapolis, Milwaukee, Chicago, St. Louis, Omaha, San Francisco, Los Angeles, Portland, and Seattle. They lived largely in ghettos. City dwellers rose from 27 to 80 percent of blacks ca. 1910–70, and from 46 to 74 percent for the nation. Unskilled jobs opened for blacks in industries (railway, stockyards, meat packing, steel, automobile, and shipyards). Competition with immigrant and native whites frequently erupted in violence, though comparably few blacks had skilled jobs before the rise of industrial unions in the 1930s. Their urban resources, however, crucially shaped African Americans' freedom movements. The latter included national business, church, education, fraternal, political, and women's organizations, all foundational to the post–World War II Civil Rights Movement.

Urbanization has leveraged change as well as continuity in race relations, especially since the 1960s. Desegregation, affirmative action, anti-poverty programs, and voting rights in the South and nation noticeably reduced black poverty and expanded the black middle class. Yet what followed were the Urban Crisis of Black Power militancy and white backlash; numerous race riots; northern–midwestern factory closings and relocations; mass joblessness and welfare dependency in cities, although blacks were elected mayors of Gary, Cleveland, Atlanta, Detroit, and Los Angeles in 1967–73. Clearly, structural racism, racial and ethnic inequality, and minorities' frustration persisted. The so-called war on drugs and welfare reform disadvantaged inner-city residents of color, invariably the poorest citizens.

[*See also* Civil Rights Movement; Ghetto; Great Migration; Poverty; Welfare.]

Further Reading

Matlin, Daniel. *On the Corner: African American Intellectuals and the Urban Crisis*. Cambridge, MA: Harvard University Press, 2013.

Sugrue, Thomas J. *The Origins of the Urban Crisis: Race and Inequality in Postwar Detroit*. Princeton, NJ: Princeton University Press, 1996.

Wilson, William Julius. *The Truly Disadvantaged: The Inner City, the Underclass, and Public Policy*. Chicago: University of Chicago Press, 2012.

CIVIL RIGHTS ACT OF 1957

Compelled by black protest, Congress passed this measure, the first civil rights statute since Reconstruction. It established the US Commission on Civil Rights and the Civil Rights Division in the Department of Justice and authorized the attorney general to prosecute violations of persons' right to vote in federal elections.

Also, it stipulated trials for violators before federal judges with or without juries. This complicated enforcement in the South, where white resistance to the *Brown* decision was rampant. Still, the commission's public hearings and reports would expose discrimination, segregation, and violence, even as the act legitimized federal intervention to secure equal suffrage.

[*See also* Civil Rights Movement; Desegregation; Segregation.]

Further Reading

Berry, Mary Frances. *And Justice for All: The United States Commission on Civil Rights and the Continuing Struggle for Freedom in America.* New York: Alfred A. Knopf, 2009.

Finley, Keith M. *Delaying the Dream: Southern Senators and the Fight Against Civil Rights, 1938–1965.* Baton Rouge: Louisiana State University Press, 2008.

CIVIL RIGHTS ACT OF 1964

Of its eleven titles, the five below exemplified the act's scope and significance.

Title I banned unequal voter registration requirements. Title II barred racial discrimination by hotels, restaurants, and public accommodations whose "operations affected Interstate Commerce." The attorney general could sue to stop "a pattern or practice" of discriminating. Title IV authorized enforcement of the Supreme Court decision overruling school segregation. Title VI stipulated that federally funded agencies or programs must not discriminate and, if they did so, could forfeit funds. Title VII provided equal employment opportunity; it forbad employers and unions to exclude persons on the basis "of their race, religion, sex, or national origin." It also instituted an Equal Employment Opportunity Commission to investigate and redress employees' grievances; it exempted schools and local governments but later regulated them. Legal desegregation of suffrage, public accommodations, education, and employment, fueled by civil rights activism, forecast historic progress in southern and national race and social relations.

[*See also Katzenbach v. McClung (1964)*; Segregation; Voting Rights Act of 1965.]

Further Reading

Kotz, Nick. *Judgment Days: Lyndon Baines Johnson, Martin Luther King, Jr., and the Laws that Changed America.* Boston: Houghton Mifflin, 2005.

Risen, Clay. *The Bill of the Century: The Epic Battle for the Civil Rights Act.* New York: Bloomsbury Press, 2014.

CIVIL RIGHTS ACT OF 1968

The crucial rights act of 1964 omitted housing. Although its 1968 sequel forbad violating an individual's civil rights and crossing state lines to incite riot, it was called the Fair Housing Act and enforced by the Department of Housing and Urban Development.

It barred discrimination in the sale, rental, advertising, and financing of houses, apartments, and real estate on the basis of race, gender, national origin, religion, or disability. As certain owners were exempted, the law applied probably to 80 percent of the national residential market. Its enforcement depended mainly on individuals who could take legal action. Few state and local governments strongly used it to reduce residential segregation and discriminatory conduct by individual sellers, lessors, banks, and realtors. Effective enforcement, proponents argued, would help eliminate the ghettoized conditions that fomented racial–ethnic violence and integrate more people of color into white suburban communities.

[*See also* Cities; Kerner Report; Weaver, Robert C.]

Further Reading

Chappell, David L. *Walking from the Dream: The Struggle for Civil Rights in the Shadow of Martin Luther King Jr.* New York: Random House, 2014.
Sidney, Mara S. "Images of Race, Class, and Markets: Rethinking the Origin of U.S. Fair Housing Policy." *Journal of Policy History*, 13 (2001): 181–214.

CIVIL RIGHTS MOVEMENT (CRM)

Rooted in race and class struggles for equality, including workers' right to organize, from the 1930s–40s, the modern CRM emerged 1955–68 and subsided ca. 1976. Black-led and southern based, it drew on black communities, especially churches, schools, colleges, and civic and social organizations, along with multiracial coalitions and federal action.

As the United States mobilized and entered World War II, officially to defeat fascism and save democracy, blacks attacked Jim Crow. Black newspapers began a "Double V" campaign, "victory over our enemies at home and victory over our enemies on the battlefields abroad." Blacks planned a mass march on Washington to protest job discrimination in defense industries, but canceled it when the president established a committee on fair employment. Southern black leaders "fundamentally opposed" segregation in their Durham, North Carolina manifesto, challenging liberal white southerners to cooperate. More than 100 race riots and many "sit down" protests at white-only restaurants (later called sit-ins) occurred nationally. Sit-downs attested to the impact of direct action and NAACP "equal protection" lawsuits. One, *Smith v. Allwright*

(1944), resulted in the Supreme Court outlawing the white primary, a major obstacle to black suffrage.

Racial injustice still gripped postwar society, which embarrassed the United States in the Cold War against Communism. Amid the "Red Scare" and persecution of communists, such as the Civil Rights Congress, the battle to abolish "separate but equal" continued. Circa 1943–53 alone blacks undertook eighteen school boycotts and strikes, ten of them in border and southern states. A Farmville, Virginia high school student strike generated one of the NAACP suits contesting segregated schools. Black citizens of Baton Rouge, Louisiana boycotted buses. These enlarging battles catalyzed the president's 1948 order integrating the US Armed Forces and the 1954 *Brown* decision ending separate schooling.

Post-*Brown*, the movement determined to desegregate the South while securing equal citizenship and opportunities for all Americans. Despite "massive resistance," which involved legal subterfuge, intimidation, and sometimes murder, the movement's leadership and followers advocated nonviolence. However, North Carolina NAACP branch president Robert Williams and his members armed to repel the Ku Klux Klan in 1958–59; the National Office expelled him. Activists mainly pursued desegregation of education, public accommodations, employment, and politics, using school transfer petitions, bus boycotts, pickets, sit-ins, Freedom Rides, voter registration, a March on Washington for Jobs and Justice, and Freedom Schools. These actions gained international publicity; so did leaders such as Baptist minister Martin Luther King, Jr. and Black Muslim imam Malcolm X, whose messages of nonviolence and integration, of self-defense and self-determination exposed growing ideological rifts in the freedom struggle. But public grief after President Kennedy's assassination as well as outrage over the beating and killing of activists compelled Congress to enact the broadest civil, economic, and political rights laws since Reconstruction. Such legislation further raised black expectations and fueled white backlash. As the Vietnam War shifted federal priorities, weakening antipoverty and affirmative action programs, many younger blacks called for Black Power. It stressed black consciousness and liberation "by any means necessary," echoing the assassinated Malcolm X. It strained interracial coalitions and stoked whites' fears, as the new ideology also became a media catchall for summer riots, assassinations (such as King's and presidential candidate Robert F. Kennedy's), and FBI suppression of black and antiwar radicals. In the meantime, examples of civil rights and Black Power advocacy were sparking demands for justice from other minorities. These included the League of United Latin American Citizens, American Indian Movement, Council on American-Islamic Relations, and Asian American Legal Defense and Education Fund. Republican and Democratic Administrations (1968–80) did not prioritize enforcement of nondiscrimination policies. Race, ethnic, class, and gender disparities thus persisted. Yet civil and human rights movements were transforming the United States, upholding "liberty and justice for all."

[*See also* Freedom Rides; Black Power Movement; Desegregation; Sit-ins; Student activism.]

Further Reading

Chappell, David L. *Walking from the Dream: The Struggle for Civil Rights in the Shadow of Martin Luther King Jr.* New York: Random House, 2014.
Dudziak, Mary L. *Cold War Civil Rights: Race and the Image of American Democracy.* Princeton, NJ: Princeton University Press, 2000.
Glasrud, Bruce A., and Merline Pitre, eds. *Southern Black Women in the Modern Civil Rights Movement.* College Station: Texas A&M University Press, 2013.

CIVIL WAR

At the start of the Civil War (1861–65), President Lincoln aimed to preserve the Union. But this would require the "defeat of the world's most powerful slaveholding class" and abolition of slavery.

Blacks backed the Union and called for slaves' liberation. In the summer of 1861 bondmen began fleeing to the army at Fortress Monroe, Virginia. Labeled "contrabands" of war, their rising numbers fueled debate on whether to retain and liberate them. Abolitionist Frederick Douglass argued: "A blow struck for the freedom of the slave is equally a blow for the safety and welfare of the country" (Foner, 2000, p. 477). Lincoln hesitated, but early Confederate victories, Union manpower shortages, and his fear that England and France might recognize the Confederacy prodded his Emancipation Proclamation (1863), which freed slaves in Union-controlled areas, exempted border slave states, and approved black military enlistment. Together with the Conscription Act (1863), it shifted the war's goal and stirred racial conflict. New York City, for example, had riots in July. White mobs burned draft offices, federal buildings, and black communities; 105 blacks perished before Union troops restored order.

Still, America embraced Lincoln's "new birth of freedom." When the war ended half of all eligible northerners had served, compared to three-fourths of southerners. The US Colored Troops and Navy had enlisted nearly 200, 000 blacks. The Union had incurred an estimated 360,000 fatalities; the Confederacy, 258,000. More than 4 million slaves were "forever free" as the Thirteenth Amendment abolished slavery.

[*See also* Constitution, US; Military; Violence, racial.]

Reference

Foner, Philip S., ed. *Frederick Douglass: Selected Speeches and Writings.* Chicago: Chicago Review Press, 2000, p. 477.

Further Reading

Burton, Orville Vernon. *The Age of Lincoln.* New York: Hill and Wang, 2007.
Robinson, Armstead L. *Bitter Fruits of Bondage: The Demise of Slavery and the Collapse of the Confederacy, 1861–1865.* Charlottesville: University of Virginia Press, 2005.

CLARK, KENNETH B.   CHILD PSYCHOLOGIST

Born: July 24, 1914, Panama Canal Zone
Education: Howard University, B.A., 1935, M.A., 1936; Columbia University, Ph.D., 1940
Died: May 1, 2005, New York, NY

Inspired by his Howard professors, who "made their students into instruments of change" (Willie and Greenblatt, 1981, p. 155), Clark led student protests against Jim Crow and later earned graduate degrees in psychology. Using social science research to promote social justice, he became a nationally respected expert on child personality and school desegregation.

He and his wife, Dr. Mamie Clark, established Northside Child Development Center in Harlem (1946); their inquiries supported the need for stable black families. Home environment critically impacted learning, they found. Race relations in communities influenced children's self-esteem as well.

Clark was pivotal among the scholars who assisted NAACP counsel in contesting segregated schools. In 1950 the Clarks conducted studies showing that separate schooling harmed the social development of children regardless of race. Counsel argued this in a Charleston, South

Carolina federal court (1951). The Clarks also experimented with a black doll and a white doll, noting the responses of more than 200 black children. Their palpable preference for the white doll revealed a negative self-image. This proved crucial: the Supreme Court's *Brown* decision, stating that it "generates a feeling of inferiority" in Negro children, overturned school segregation. Afterward, Clark worked to implement racial and curricular integration in New York public education.

Reference

Willie, Charles V., and Susan L. Greenblatt. *The Stages in a Scholar's Life.* Washington, DC: National Institute of Education, 1981, p. 115.

Further Reading

Keppel, Ben. *The Work of Democracy: Ralph Bunche, Kenneth B. Clark, Lorraine Hansberry, and the Cultural Politics of Race.* Cambridge, MA: Harvard University Press, 1995.

Klein, Woody, ed. *Toward Humanity and Justice: The Writings of Kenneth B. Clark, Scholar of the 1954* Brown v. Board of Education *Decision.* Westport, CT: Praeger, 2004.

CLARK, SEPTIMA P.
EDUCATOR AND CIVIL RIGHTS ORGANIZER

Born: May 3, 1898, Charleston, SC
Education: Avery Institute, graduated 1916; Benedict College, B.A., 1942; Hampton Institute, 1945
Died: December 15, 1987, Charleston, SC

A courageous teacher in the Jim Crow era, Clark also taught during the King years. Fired in 1956 because of her NAACP affiliation, she sued the Charleston, South Carolina schools and won compensation (1976). A staff member at Highlander Folk School in Tennessee, she adapted her teaching methods from Charleston and Johns Island to create a curriculum for "citizenship schools." It stressed basic literacy and life skills and knowledge of voting rights.

About 897 Citizenship Schools operated in the South ca. 1957–70. Using them to foster voter registration, the Atlanta-based Voter Education Project (1962) trained 10,000 citizenship tutors by 1966. Schools convened in churches, lodge halls, homes, and fields. Like ex-slaves' Sabbath Schools, foundational in their freedom struggle, Citizenship Schools paved the way for Freedom Schools, which Ella Baker and student activists used to enlarge "the grassroots base of the southern wide opposition to segregation" and increase black suffrage. Baker and Clark had been sisters in civil rights struggles since the 1940s.

Further Reading

Ashton, Susanna, and Rhondda Robinson Thomas, eds. *The South Carolina Roots of African American Thought: A Reader*. Columbia: University of South Carolina Press, 2013.

Charron, Katherine Mellen. *Freedom's Teacher: The Life of Septima Clark*. Chapel Hill: University of North Carolina Press, 2009.

CLUBS

Men's and women's clubs were resources in black society from slavery to freedom. Like mutual aid groups, the National Association of Colored Women (1896), Order of Elks (1899), and other associations, reporting "thousands of members throughout the nation," promoted blacks' well-being. They not only mirrored but also bridged class, gender, and cultural divides among blacks in their collective struggle for racial equality.

For example, Links, Inc., a middle-class club, formed to serve the community in 1946. Many elite Philadelphia black women pledged to "link" their friendship, means, and services on behalf of the disadvantaged. Today, Links has 281 chapters in 40 states, Washington, DC; the Bahamas; and Frankfurt, Germany. Chapters administer programs such as *Service to Youth,* which has funded education for "gifted minority youth," along with crime and drug prevention projects, since 1958. Still operating, Project LEAD (Links Erase Alcohol and Drug Abuse) began in 1985.

[*See also* Fraternal orders and lodges; Fraternities; Sororities.]

Further Reading

Cash, Floris Barnett. *African American Women and Social Action: The Clubwomen and Volunteerism from Jim Crow to the New Deal, 1896–1936*. Westport, CT: Greenwood Press, 2001.

Parker, Marjorie H. *A History of the Links, Incorporated*. Washington, DC: National Headquarters of the Links, Inc., 1992.

COLD WAR

Driven by US–Soviet interests and policies, the Cold War (1945–89) intensified the ideological struggle between the United States and the

Soviet Union, polarizing international relations; spawned military conflicts, usually in Third World nations; escalated a nuclear arms race; and produced regional security pacts.

It witnessed anticommunist propaganda and a Second Red Scare in domestic politics. Senate committees chaired by Joseph McCarthy (R–Wisconsin), with the House Committee on Un-American Activities (HUAC), hounded communists and their sympathizers. In televised hearings, they interrogated citizens accused of being Communist Party members or associates. In 1950, when black activist Paul Robeson refused to answer HUAC's questions, authorities revoked his passport. The next year W. E. B. Du Bois was indicted and isolated for his work at the Peace Information Center. Federal courts exonerated Robeson (1958) and Du Bois (1959). Martin Luther King, Jr. warned that witch-hunts and racism could destroy America's soul.

[*See also* Anticommunism.]

Further Reading

Borstelmann, Thomas. *The Cold War and the Color Line: American Race Relations in the Global Arena.* Cambridge, MA: Harvard University Press, 2001.
Plummer, Brenda Gayle. *In Search of Power: African Americans in the Era of Decolonization, 1956–1974.* New York: Cambridge University Press, 2013.

COLONIALISM

Colonialism is the formation and control of colonies in one territory by people of another territory.

For example, British and European settlers colonized Africa. Ostensibly to resolve boundary and trade issues, their Berlin Conference (1884) carved the continent into colonized territories. In 1914, except for Liberia and Ethiopia, Africa remained under whites' rule. They controlled wealth and power as Africans resisted, often violently. After 1945 the United Nations supported their anticolonial and liberation struggles, which helped to forge independence for many nations ca. 1956–74. These developments galvanized African American activists, who viewed US black inequality as "internal colonialism."

[*See also* Africa.]

Further Reading

Anderson, Carol. *Bourgeois Radicals: The NAACP and the Struggle for Colonial Liberation. 1940–1960.* New York: Cambridge University Press, 2015.

Intondi, Vincent J. *African Americans against the Bomb: Nuclear Weapons, Colonialism, and the Black Freedom Movement*. Stanford, CA: Stanford University Press, 2014.

CONGRESS OF RACIAL EQUALITY (CORE)

Created in 1942, CORE evolved from the Quaker-inspired Fellowship of Reconciliation (1914), a catalyst of the Peace Movement. It advocated racial integration and nonviolent protest against Jim Crow. It launched "sit down" protests at segregated restaurants during World War II and a 1947 bus journey to test states' compliance with the Supreme Court decision barring segregation on interstate buses.

In the wake of the 1960 Greensboro, North Carolina sit-ins, CORE achieved national visibility. Its Freedom Rides (1961) greatly expanded student membership. Partnering with the Atlanta-based Voter Education Project, it registered black voters. Its Freedom Highways and Open Cities projects promoted desegregation of public accommodations and employment in North Carolina and Virginia. During Freedom Summer in Mississippi, two of the three murdered civil rights workers were CORE staffers. Racist violence, inadequate federal protection, and CORE's weakening commitment to nonviolence foreshadowed its turn to Black Power in 1966.

[*See also* Civil Rights Movement; Freedom Rides; Journey of Reconciliation.]

Further Reading

De Jong, Greta. *A Different Day: African American Struggles for Justice in Rural Louisiana, 1900–1970*. Chapel Hill: University of North Carolina Press, 2002.

Singler, Joan et al. *Seattle in Black and White: The Congress of Racial Equality and the Fight for Equal Opportunity*. Seattle: University of Washington Press, 2011.

CONSTITUTION, US (1789)

Since its adoption, the Constitution not only has defined the authority of the federal government and states; it also has functioned to "secure the blessings of liberty" for "the people of the United States." Its amendments have rendered the definition of the people more inclusive over time.

From its framing at the Constitutional Convention, delegates preserved slavery. Abolition had begun in the North, but the institution was robust in the South. James Madison of Virginia noted that "States were divided into different interests not by their difference of size, but … principally from the effects of their having or not having slaves." Compromises were hammered out to bridge that divide and assure ratification. Article I, Section 2 counted "three-fifths" of the enslaved with the free population in allocating Congressmen and direct taxes; Section 8 empowered Congress to "suppress insurrections"; and Section 9 forbad outlawing the slave trade before 1808. Article IV, Section 2 provided for the return of fugitive slaves.

Meantime, pressured by Anti-Federalist demands for individual liberties, Congress adopted the first ten amendments or "the Bill of Rights" (1791). The Amendment I prohibits establishment of religion or barring its free exercise; abridging freedom of speech, the press, assembly, and right to petition the government for redress. II authorizes a militia for securing the people's right to keep and bear arms. III bars the arbitrary quartering of troops. IV bars unreasonable search and seizure. Similarly, V ensures a person accused of a felony "due process of law," including immunity from double jeopardy and self-incrimination. VI establishes the right to counsel for defense, to face accusing witnesses, to a public and timely jury trial. VII provides for a civil jury trial. VIII disallows excessive bail and cruel and unusual punishment. IX protects rights "retained by the people" with those enumerated in the Constitution. X reserves to the states powers not delegated to the United States.

Constitutional inclusion evolved after the Civil War. Amendment XIII (1865) abolished slavery. XIV (1868) made "all persons born or naturalized" in the United States citizens, entitling them to "due process of law" and "equal protection of the laws." XV (1870) guaranteed citizens' right to vote regardless of "race, color, or previous condition of servitude." African Americans, among other groups formerly excluded, struggled for equal citizenship. Seeking "due process" and "equal protection," they protested and sued against racial discrimination, segregation, and violence. Black, interracial, and women's struggles for civil rights and social justice helped create Amendments XIX (1920) securing women's suffrage; XXIV (1964) eliminating the poll tax in federal elections; and XXVI (1971) granting suffrage to citizens 18 years old.

[*See also* Civil Rights Movement; Voting Rights Act of 1965; Feminism.]

Further Reading

Carter, Robert L. *A Matter of Law: A Memoir of Struggle in the Cause of Equal Rights*. New York: The New Press, 2005.

Franklin, John Hope, and Genna Rae McNeil, eds. *African Americans and the Living Constitution*. Washington, DC: Smithsonian Institution Press, 1995.

CONVENTIONS, NATIONAL NEGRO

Between 1830 and 1893, mostly non-southern freemen and post–Civil War freedmen held state and national conventions on their concerns. Chaired by educated leaders, the conclaves reflected black strategies for freedom and justice.

Antebellum delegates convened amid slavery, racism, and violence. They embraced the antislavery movement; they espoused liberty, literacy, racial pride, and economic self-help. African emigration and colonization polarized them. Emigration, said opponents, the majority, would mean forsaking slaves; to proponents, it promised independence. Both sides endorsed tactics of moral suasion and political action.

The postwar Freedmen's Conventions, National Equal Rights League, Citizens' Equal Rights Association, and Afro-American League (1890) continued the struggle. Delegates called for Thirteenth, Fourteenth, and Fifteenth Amendment rights; antilynching; education; suffrage; and equality of opportunity. "We are full-grown, native-born citizens ... All we desire is equal right, equal punishment, equal protection, equal chance, no more," they declared, foreshadowing twentieth century African American protest.

[*See also* Antislavery movement; Back-to-Africa movement; Religion.]

Further Reading

Ernest, John. *A Nation within a Nation: Organizing African-American Communities Before the Civil War*. Chicago: Ivan R. Dee, 2011.
Foner, Philip S., and George E. Walker, eds. *Proceedings of the Black National and State Conventions, 1865–1900*. Vol. I. Philadelphia: Temple University Press, 1986.

CONVICT-LEASE SYSTEM

Reinventing the Black Codes, which incarcerated and hired out ex-slaves for vagrancy before Congress repealed the codes in 1866–67, convict leasing evolved as Democrats overthrew Reconstruction and "committed to using black convicts for internal southern development" (Cohen, 1991, p. 222).

Leasing became the New Slavery. Operating in an environment of limited tax revenues, states allowed private and public contractors to lease convicts. This helped reduce the cost of state and county prisons, collect revenue, and maintain white control. Planters and industrialists usually leased black prisoners, men and women. Lessees had sole custody of prisoners' rations, hours in the fields or mines, and health. Abuses were rampant. Many inmates died from brutality, exposure, and illness, or in work accidents and escape attempts. They also served longer sentences for insubordination, ensuring that imprisoned laborers always would be available. State officials contended that habitually criminal blacks deserved their lot. Civil rights and penal reformers challenged that argument in the early twentieth century.

[*See also* Segregation.]

Reference

Cohen, William. At Freedom's Edge: Black Mobility and the Southern White Quest for Racial Control, 1861–1915. Baton Rouge: Louisiana State University Press, 1991, p. 222.

Further Reading

Blackmon, Douglas A. *Slavery by Another Name: The Re-Enslavement of Black People in America from the Civil War to World War II*. New York: Doubleday, 2008.

Curtin, Mary Ellen. *Black Prisoners and Their World, Alabama, 1865–1900*. Charlottesville: University Press of Virginia, 2000.

COOPER, ANNA JULIA
EDUCATOR AND ACTIVIST

Born: August 10, 1858, Raleigh, NC
Education: St. Augustine's Normal School, 1867–77; Oberlin College, A.B., 1884, M.A., 1887; Université de Paris (Sorbonne), Ph.D., 1925
Died: February 27, 1964, Washington, DC

Born in slavery, Cooper became one of the first post-emancipation college graduates and a leading race, women's rights, and education activist.

During the Nadir (1877–1901), as blacks debated the mission of and curricula in black schools, training hands versus minds, she campaigned for a curriculum of English, Latin, arithmetic, history, and few vocational courses. In short, she pursued literacy and higher learning for all regardless of class or gender, urging the inclusion of females. She also urged the "education of neglected people," creating her night and prep school and community college models to reach them.

Cooper faced and resisted Jim Crow, including its ideologies of white supremacy and black inferiority. She defended and demonstrated the capacity of blacks, "just twenty-one years removed from the conception and experience of a chattel" (Cooper, 2000, p. 61), to learn, achieve progress, and live as equal citizens. Black equality turned crucially on educating black women. "Let our girls feel that we expect something more of them than that they merely look pretty and appear well in society," she declared. "Teach them that there is a race with special needs that they and only they can help." Their role in freedom was indispensable.

[*See also Scholarship.*]

Reference

Cooper, Anna J. *The Voice of Anna Julia Cooper: Including a Voice from the South and Other Important Essays, Papers, and Letters.* Lanham, MD: Rowman & Littlefield, 2000, p. 61.

Further Reading

Johnson, Karen Ann. *Uplifting the Women and the Race: The Educational Philosophies and Social Activism of Anna Julia Cooper and Nannie Helen Burroughs.* New York: Garland, 2000.

May, Vivian M. *Anna Julia Cooper, Visionary Black Feminist: A Critical Introduction.* New York: Routledge, 2007.

COSBY, WILLIAM H. (BILL)　　　ENTERTAINER AND PHILANTHROPIST

Born: July 12, 1937, Philadelphia, PA
Education: Temple University, 1961–62, B.A., 1971; University of Massachusetts, M. Ed., 1972, Ed. D., 1976

Cosby rose from humble conditions, joined the navy, and found a niche in comedy. His talent, egalitarian vision, and business savvy catapulted him to fame.

The Cosby Show, which attracted and retained a racially diverse audience, was an important contribution. It portrayed Cliff Huxtable, a physician; Mrs. Huxtable, an attorney; and their five intelligent children. Dialogue involved humor but dealt with normal familial relations and crises. Critics applauded the show's positive images of the black family. Some said it idealized middle-class blacks while ignoring the poor.

As the show thrived, Cosby battled racial bias in television. He demanded and won major input into production, from hiring writers and directors to selecting performers and professionals for guest appearances. A black psychiatrist advised the cast and Cosby displayed black art on the set. This, plus Cosby's educational programs for inner-city children and philanthropy, made him an icon. But his criticisms of low-income blacks in comments marking the fiftieth anniversary of *Brown v. Board of Education* clearly backfired. Challenging them to embrace *Brown*'s legacy of learning, he criticized "their spending habits, speech patterns, and parenting." Public opinion divided over whether he was unfair.

Also divided is public response to Cosby's 2005–2006 court-released deposition, excerpted by *The New York Times* (July 20, 2015), in which he admitted to drugging and having sex with a number of women without their knowledge and consent.

Further Reading

Whitaker, Matthew C., ed. *Incons of Black America: Breaking Barriers and Crossing Boundaries*. Santa Barbara, CA: Greenwood, 2011.

Mohamed, Theresa A., ed. *Essays in Response to Bill Cosby's Comments about African American Failure*. Lewiston, NY: Edwin Mellen Press, 2006.

DANCE

Blacks already were at the cutting edge of American dance in 1988, when Philadelphia Dance Company hosted the First International Conference on Black Dance Companies and the American Dance Festival, Durham, North Carolina, celebrated The Black Tradition in American Modern Dance. That visibility honored black dance's creators and performers from Africa and slavery to contemporary times.

Slaves created enduring dances. For example, the ring-shout was sacred; worshipers sang, shuffled, stomped, and clapped, moving counterclockwise in a circle. Among secular dances, one utilized flat foot dragging, gliding, and shuffling along. Another used crouched movements, bending waist and knees. Some imitated buzzard, chicken, and other animal steps; others moved rhythmically, showing physicality and feeling. Many involved pelvic moves, thrusting outward from the hips in a swinging manner. African rhythm emphasized the second and fourth beats on the musical bar, as if to answer the first and third beats. This tradition displayed dancers' "polyrhythm in body movements" (Borross). They would move their heads and feet in alternate rhythms, representing motion and harmony.

Black vernacular dancing mirrored racial and social realities. Drumming was colonial slaves' major accompaniment, but slave resistance resulted in laws against and punishment for using drums. The banjo, fiddle, and tambourine thus evolved as customary accompaniments, alongside hand clapping and foot stomping. Dance remained central in religious faith and practice. Worshipers would sing, clap, or shuffle until they were "possessed" by the spirit. Ring-shouts marked birth, marriage, death, or the cotton harvest. Secular dances, such as the Buzzard Lope or Turkey Trot, continued imitating animals. Others celebrated pastimes such as Jonkonnu, a Christmastime festival, or a Saturday night ending the work week. Bondmen and women often did the Cakewalk, a strut mocking the stiff upper bodies of whites at plantation and town balls. Bondfolk also would congregate and dance publicly, as in Congo Square of New Orleans. Free black William Henry Lane clogged and tap danced in the Irish pubs of New York City and performed with the white Ethiopian Minstrels around the world. Known as "Master Juba," he was "considered the most influential performer in nineteenth-century American dance." Also, white minstrels began donning blackface to mimic slaves, including the fictive slave "Jim Crow."

Yet the black dancer was a symbol of cultural pluralism. New Orleans blues, creations of bond and freedpeople alike, influenced the new ragtime and jazz music of the 1890s. Blues soon made the Turkey Trot and Monkey Glide common in popular and ballroom dancing. Bill "Bojangles" Robinson trotted and glided in his performances to rave reviews. He rose from poverty in Richmond, Virginia to be "King of the Tap Dancers," a star in Europe and America. In 1911 the Lafayette Theatre of Harlem premiered *Darktown Follies*, including the Cakewalk, Ballin' the Jack, and Texas Tommy. Enjoying such so-called "primitivism" on stage, whites flocked uptown. The Broadway musical *Shuffle Along* (1922) showcased sexy chorus girls. *Runnin' Wild* (1924) introduced the Charleston. Black dance energized the Harlem Renaissance and Jazz Age.

Black bands played "swing music" and couples sweated it out on ballroom floors. A couple dance, Swing entailed fast and sharp footwork. The tour de force was the Lindy Hop, which popularized Charles Lindbergh's 1927 transatlantic flight. Linking the Texas Tommy and Charleston, it vitalized cabaret and theater dance ca. 1930s–60s and arguably longer. It utilized a crouching position and hand holding, with a couple pulling and pushing. Their special feature was the breakaway, letting go only to improvise. They would then do individual displays of the Susie Q, Boogie Woogie, and Trucking, which paved the way for the Bop, Twist, Moonwalk, and Hip Hop.

Black theatrical dance achieved a transnational audience. Choreographers Katherine Dunham, Pearl Primus, and Alvin Ailey were its trailblazers. An anthropologist and troupe and school creator, Dunham linked African and Caribbean folklore in Broadway ballets such as *Tropical Revue* (1943). She directed *Aida* at the Metropolitan Opera in 1963–64, becoming the Met's first black director. Also trained in anthropology, Primus fused black themes in *African Ceremonial* (1943) and *The Negro Speaks of Rivers* (1944). She organized a dance company in 1946 and later unveiled *Michael Row Your Boat Ashore* (1978), celebrating freedom. Ailey explored southern black life in *Blues Suite* (1958), the year he started a repertory theater. His *Revelations* (1960) interpreted race and spiritual struggles, and he choreographed Leonard Bernstein's *Mass* (1971).

[*See also* Music.]

Reference

Borross, Bob. "Image of Perfection: The Freestyle Dance of Matt Mattox." Retrieved from www.theatredance.com/mhist01.html.

Further Reading

Aschenbrenner, Joyce. *Katherine Dunham: Dancing a Life*. Urbana: University of Illinois Press, 2002.

DeFrantz, Thomas F., ed. *Dancing Many Drums: Excavations in African American Dance*. Madison: University of Wisconsin Press, 2002.

Gottschild, Brenda Dixon. *The Black Dancing Body: A Geography from Coon to Cool*. New York: Palgrave Macmillan, 2003.

DAVIS, ANGELA Y.
POLITICAL ACTIVIST AND SCHOLAR

Born: January 26, 1944, Birmingham, AL
Education: Brandeis University, B.A. magna cum laude, Phi Beta Kappa, 1965; University of California San Diego, M.A., 1969; Humboldt University of Berlin, Ph.D.

Davis is one of the most influential political activists of the twentieth century. While a graduate student, she was active in the Student Nonviolent Coordinating Committee (SNCC) and the Black Panther and Communist Parties. She taught philosophy at UCLA (1969–70). Fired for being a communist, she sued and stayed until her contract ended.

But she earned international respect. She proved crucial in the Panthers' efforts to liberate "black political prisoners" such as the "Soledad Brothers," one of whom was George Jackson. George's brother Jonathan, not incarcerated and using Davis's registered guns, attempted to free two black convicts at the Marin County courthouse in August 1970. He and three others, including the judge, were killed. Guards fatally shot George Jackson, allegedly attempting to escape, in 1971. Charged as a co-conspirator, Davis fled. Arrested by October in New York and extradited to California, she was held without bail until a February 1972 trial. Meanwhile, the National Committee to Free Angela Davis and All Political Prisoners, a multiracial coalition, organized "Free Angela" rallies internationally. The jury acquitted her. Afterward, she founded the National Alliance against Racism and Political Repression, which helped secure federal antihate crime laws. A public intellectual, Davis remains outspoken on civil and human rights.

Further Reading

Aptheker, Bettina. *The Morning Breaks: The Trial of Angela Davis*. Ithaca, NY: Cornell University Press, 1999.

Perkins, Margo V. *Autobiography as Activism: Three Black Women of the 1960s.* Jackson: University Press of Mississippi, 2000.

DAVIS, W. ALLISON
EDUCATIONAL ANTHROPOLOGIST

Born: October 14, 1902, Washington, DC
Education: Williams College, B.A. valedictorian, 1924; Harvard University, M.A. (Comparative Literature), 1925, M.A. (Anthropology), 1932; University of Chicago, Ph.D., 1942
Died: November 21, 1983, Chicago, IL

The first black person to be appointed a professor at the University of Chicago (1946) and to earn tenure in a research university, Davis was a distinguished scholar-educator.

His career mirrored liberalism and racism in higher education. Owing to the "Chicago School" of sociology, a partner of the American Council on Relations, the university enjoyed a liberal reputation. Yet the Rosenwald Fund leveraged Davis's faculty appointment by underwriting his salary. Still, he could not buy a house in university-owned Hyde Park. The color-caste system, which he analyzed in several seminal books, stalked him.

Davis's *Intelligence and Cultural Differences* (1951) was pathbreaking. It discredited using intelligence tests to assess the learning ability and personality development of lower-class black and other minority children. "This study had the most practical effect of any of my work," he recalled years later. "It led to the abolition of the use of intelligence tests in New York, Chicago, Detroit, San Francisco, and other cities" (http://davis-center.williams.edu/daviscenter//allison-davis/). In 1953 he introduced the Davis-Ellis elementary school test to weigh children's abilities with respect to their racial, ethnic, and socioeconomic differences. Davis also advised NAACP counsel on child-centered arguments in briefs for *Brown v. Board of Education.*

Further Reading

Fish, Jefferson M., ed. *Race and Intelligence: Separating Science from Myth.* Mahwah, NJ: Lawrence Erlbaum, 2002.
Harrison, Ita E., and Faye V. Harrison, eds. *African American Pioneers in Anthropology.* Urbana: University of Illinois Press, 1999.

DEATH PENALTY

Racial inequality persists in the administration of the death penalty. To wit, blacks are convicted and executed more than whites for capital crimes.

An aggregate 3,859 executions, including 32 women, occurred from 1930 (when federal officials began recording execution by race) to 1967. Blacks comprised 54, whites 45, and other races 1 percent of the executed. Three in five died in southern states. Black men totaled 399 of 446 or 89.5 percent of deaths for rape. Civil rights groups protested. Citing "the arbitrary nature with which death sentences have been imposed, often indicating a racial bias against black defendants," the Supreme Court declared in *Furman v. Georgia* (1972) that death constituted "cruel and unusual punishment" and barred its use. States resumed using it in 1977. But the *Furman* decision and five-year moratorium energized the growing movement for abolition of the death penalty.

[*See also* Department of Justice, US; Law enforcement.]

Further Reading

Foerster, Barrett J. *Race, Rape, and Injustice: Documenting and Challenging Death Penalty Cases in the Civil Rights Era*. Knoxville: University of Tennessee, 2012.
Ogletree, Charles J. Jr., and Austin Sarat, eds. *From Lynch Mobs to the Killing State: Race and the Death Penalty in America*. New York: New York University Press, 2006.

DELANY, MARTIN R.   ACTIVIST AND LEADER

Born: May 6, 1812, Charles Town, VA
Education: Chambersburg, PA public schools; Harvard Medical School, 1850–51
Died: June 24, 1885, Wilberforce, OH

Born to an enslaved father and free mother, a literate freeman, Delany became one of the most important nineteenth-century black spokesmen.

He advocated abolition, emigration, and colonization. As editor of the Pittsburgh *Mystery* and coeditor of the Rochester *North Star*, he called for Federal sanctions against the Slave Power. He co-organized National Negro conventions (1840s) and African Emigration conferences (1850s). His books and other writings promoted African American resistance, self-help, and an independent black nation in the Caribbean or Africa. Delany also criticized white abolitionists for their racism and they denounced his colonizing ventures. A major in the Union army, he served as its highest ranked black officer in the Civil War. He excelled in recruiting and commanding US Colored Troops. In leadership and influence, he was second to none, except Frederick Douglass. African Methodist Episcopal Church (AME) Bishop Daniel A. Payne deemed him "too intensely African to be popular," adding that "had his love for humanity been as great as his love for his race" (Sellman, 2005, p. 354) he would be Douglass's equal. Influential in Republican politics during Reconstruction, Delany remained at the forefront of struggles for equal citizenship.

Reference

Sellman, James. "Delany, Martin Robison 1812-1885." In *Africana: The Encyclopedia of the African and African American Experience.* New York: Oxford University Press, 2005, p. 354.

Further Reading

Dixon, Chris. *African America and Haiti: Emigration and Black Nationalism in the Nineteenth Century.* Westport, CT: Greenwood Press, 2000.
Tunde, Adeleke. *Without Regard to Race: The Other Martin Robison Delany.* Jackson: University Press of Mississippi, 2003.

DEPRIEST, OSCAR S.   U.S. CONGRESSMAN

Born: March 9, 1871, Florence, AL
Education: Normal school, Salina, KN, graduated 1889
Died: May 12, 1951, Chicago, IL

The son of ex-slaves, DePriest became a businessman and respected Republican politician. First elected a Cook County commissioner, he won election as Chicago's first black alderman in 1915. His victory was attributable to the party's Second Ward machine and loyalty of African American women, who comprised 25 percent of black voters. They obtained suffrage by the State Woman Suffrage Amendment of 1913. Leading clubwoman Frances Barrier Williams (1855–1944) said that DePriest's triumph would provide "an effective weapon with which to combat prejudice and discrimination of all kinds" (Hendricks, 1998, p. 96).

DePriest made her assertion his mission and pursued it in Washington. Elected to the US House in 1928, the first African American congressman since 1901, he authored several key but failing offender protection and antilynching bills. The latter included fines and imprisonment for officials who allowed mobs to harm prisoners and, in cases of lynching, state-financed survivor compensations. He drafted a bill prohibiting racial discrimination in the Civilian Conservation Corps, a major source of black jobs during the Depression. Moreover, he increased Howard University's budget appropriations and nominated black cadets to US military academies. In spite of death threats, he also spoke to southern black audiences on the right to vote.

Reference

Hendricks, Wanda A. *Gender, Race, and Politics in the Midwest: Black Club Women in Illinois*. Bloomington: Indiana University Press, 1998, p. 96.

Further Reading

Hendricks, Wanda A. "'Vote for the Advantage of Ourselves and Our Race': The Election of the First Black Alderman of Chicago." *Illinois Historical Journal*, 87 (Autumn 1994): 171–84.

Reed, Christopher Robert. *The Rise of Black Chicago's Metropolis, 1920–1929*. Urbana: University of Illinois Press, 2011.

DESEGREGATION

Frequently called *integration* by its observers, desegregation originated before World War II and continued with mixed progress through the Second Reconstruction (1945–1982) to the present. Black activism, which prodded federal steps to end "separate but equal" in law and practice," evinced four stages: early, emergence, expansion, and impasse.

Early challenges to Jim Crow included the antilynching, voting rights, and equalization campaigns. NAACP suits to equalize schools, teachers' salaries, graduate and professional school, suffrage, and economic opportunity (1930–44) mirrored ongoing African American movements against lynching, disfranchisement, job discrimination, and unequal education. A black applicant won admission to the all-white University of Maryland Law School (1936) and another to the University of Missouri Law School (1938). Executive Order 8802 created the Fair Employment Practices Committee (1941), averting blacks' march on Washington for jobs and freedom. Black churches and organizations mobilized to support

Smith v. Allwright (1944), the Texas case in which the Supreme Court outlawed the "white primary" election.

In the wake of *Smith*, more than a million southern blacks registered to vote and the movement for racial justice emerged (1945–54). It influenced the President's Committee on Civil Rights, whose 1947 report proposed laws repealing the poll tax, lynching, and segregated transportation. The president also issued an order to desegregate US Armed Forces (1948). Black applicants were admitted to seven state universities by Federal Court orders and to two voluntarily (1948–51). Segregated school cases culminated in *Brown v. Board of Education* (1954), which declared "separate educational facilities ... inherently unequal."

Brown leveraged civil rights. The Montgomery Bus Boycott (1955) and Little Rock School Crisis (1957) reflected the movement's push to open society. Using nonviolent direct action, black activists and their allies struggled to desegregate education, employment, public accommodations, and more. The shameful international publicity resulting from racist violence during sit-ins, Freedom Rides, and the Birmingham and Selma protests pressured Congress to pass the Civil Rights Act (1964) and Voting Rights Act (1965). At the time, only 2.3 percent of black children attended former white schools and 55 percent of blacks were poor.

Desegregation proceeded, but conservative opposition slowed it. While the Federal Courts in 1968 disallowed freedom-of-choice plans to end school segregation and, by 1971, ordered busing students, "white flight" produced private schools, suburban school districts, and anti-busing politics. Simultaneously, educational and family assistance programs of the War on Poverty helped to reduce African American poverty to 30.3 percent by 1974. Affirmative action in college admissions, corporate and government hiring, political participation, and other areas also saw more and more blacks, expanding the black middle class. But powerful white interests, which opposed busing, affirmative action, and welfare, unduly influenced the Supreme Court, which retreated from *Brown*. For example, in *Milliken v. Bradley* (1974) it rejected a lower court's order to bus students from a majority-white suburban district to desegregate Detroit's schools. Although in *Bakke v. University of California* (1978) the Court narrowly approved the use of race as a factor in recruiting a diverse class, opponents dubbed it "reverse discrimination." In short, desegregation would be glacial in post–civil rights America.

[*See also* Affirmative Action; Civil Rights Movement; Resegregation; Segregation.]

Further Reading

Brown-Nagin, Tomiko. *Courage to Dissent: Atlanta and the Long History of the Civil Rights Movement*. New York: Oxford University Press, 2011.

Klarman, Michael J. *From Jim Crow to Civil Rights: The Supreme Court and the Struggle for Racial Equality*. New York: Oxford University Press, 2003.

Kluger, Richard. *Simple Justice: The History of Brown v. Board of Education and Black America's Struggle for Equality*. New York: Vintage Books, 2004.

DIVINE, FATHER (GEORGE BAKER)   MINISTER

Born: ca. 1880, Rockville, VA
Education: Self-educated
Died: September 10, 1965, Philadelphia, PA

Born to ex-slaves, Baker grew up in poverty in Virginia but outmigrated and became a prominent minister. He attended the 1906 Azuma Street Revival in Los Angeles, birthplace of modern Pentecostalism. Azuma's racial inclusion inspired him to become Major J. Divine. By 1914 he was forging his Pentecostal and interracial Peace Mission Movement in New York City.

Divine recruited the poor and working classes. He preached of New Thought, or positive thinking, and Heavens, or homes offering afford-able meals and lodging. Membership increased and the Mission moved to Long Island, where police arrested Divine in 1931 for causing a public nuisance. When the judge who imprisoned him died suddenly, followers began calling him "Father Divine."

Relocating to Harlem, he expanded the movement. During the Depression it bought empty hotels and remade them into Mission Heavens. The Mission required new members to pay off all debt, cancel life insurance, and buy everything in cash. They had to abstain from alco-holic drink and sexual intercourse. Divine also preached racial equality and integration. He married a white Canadian (Mother Divine) in 1946. In the postwar era, no urban black religious group was better known than Divine's. In 1982 its assets included four hotels and eleven Missions.

Further Reading

Jenkins, Philip. *Mystics and Messiahs: Cults and New Religions in American History*. New York: Oxford University Press, 2000.

Mabee, Carlton. *Promised Land: Father Divine's Interracial Communities in Ulster County, New York*. Fleischmanns, NY: Purple Mountain Press, 2008.

DOUGLASS, FREDERICK   ABOLITIONIST, LEADER

Born: February 1818, Talbot County, MD
Education: Self-educated
Died: February 20, 1895, Washington, DC

When historian Carter G. Woodson launched Negro History Week in February 1926, he chose the month of President Abraham Lincoln and Douglass's birthdays. Both men were crucial in the nation's "new birth of freedom." When the Civil War broke out, Douglass canceled a trip to Haiti and vowed to help recruit "a liberating army."

He was a strong enemy of race slavery and injustice. Born a slave, at age seven his owner took him to Baltimore, where luckily he attained literacy, observed free blacks moving about, and determined to be autonomous. He escaped in 1838 and, through an 1841 speech to the Massachusetts Anti-Slavery Society, began his pivotal career. In 1845 he published the first of three autobiographies, selling 5,000 copies within four months and 30,000 by 1850. Publisher of the *North Star, Frederick Douglass' Paper*, and *Douglass' Monthly*, he championed abolitionism, women's rights, and social justice. Active in the Underground Railroad, he aided more than 400 runaway slaves at his Rochester, New York home ca. 1847–57. The war helped achieve black emancipation and freedom, but persistent racism stymied blacks' aspirations and efforts toward equal citizenship. Douglass struggled for racial equality until his death.

Further Reading

Blight, David W. *Race and Reunion: The Civil War in American Memory.* Cambridge, MA: Harvard University Press, 2001.
Zimmerman, Dwight Jon. *The Hammer and the Anvil: Frederick Douglass, Abraham Lincoln, and the End of Slavery in America.* New York: Hill and Wang, 2012.

DRED SCOTT V. SANDFORD (1857)

Using antislavery counsel, Scott petitioned his Missouri owner for freedom in 1846; he served her late husband in free territory. A state court freed him in 1850, but Missouri's Supreme Court overruled it.

Scott sued his new owner, John Sandford, in Federal Court as a citizen of Missouri (1854). But the Court ruled that he was a slave and could not sue. On appeal, the Supreme Court concurred. It declared the Missouri Compromise unconstitutional, that blacks were not citizens, and "had no rights that the white man was bound to respect." Abolitionists decried its decision, which exacerbated North–South conflict over slavery.

[*See also* John Brown's raid.]

Further Reading

Konig, David Thomas, Paul Finkelman, and Christopher Alan Bracey, eds. *The Dred Scott Case: Historical and Contemporary Perspectives on Race and Law.* Athens: Ohio University Press, 2010.

Maltz, Earl M. *Dred Scott and the Politics of Slavery.* Lawrence: University Press of Kansas, 2007.

DREW, CHARLES R.   HEMATOLOGIST

Born: June 23, 1904, Washington, DC
Education: Amherst College, B.A., 1926; McGill University, M.D., C.M., 1933; Columbia University, D. Sc., 1940
Died: April 1, 1950, Burlington, NC

During an internship in New York City's Presbyterian Hospital and doctoral studies at Columbia University, Drew made original discoveries on blood plasma, including that it could be preserved and used for transfusions. He coined his "blood bank" concept in 1940.

During World War II he created the first bank in the Blood for Britain Program and the second for the American Red Cross. Maintaining segregation, however, the War Department declared that "it is not advisable to collect and mix Caucasian and Negro blood" (www.aaregistry.org/historic_events/view/dr-charles-drew-was-lifesaver-through-his-blood-plasma-discoveries). Drew objected and resigned or was fired. "The blood of individual human beings may differ by blood groupings, but there is absolutely no scientific basis to indicate any differences according to race" (Love, 1997, p. 321), he protested. The Jim Crow policy lasted until 1949.

Segregation surrounded Drew's death. His car crashed on the highway from Durham to Greensboro, North Carolina. An ambulance took him to white-only Alamance County Hospital. Two emergency room doctors were treating Drew when he died on the operating table. But a rumor spread that the hospital refused to treat him because of his race and it persisted, especially among southern blacks. Exclusion and death involving segregated hospitals, after all, reflected their lived experiences.

Reference

Love, Spencie. *One Blood: The Death and Resurrection of Charles R. Drew.* Chapel Hill: University of North Carolina Press, 1997, p. 321.

Further Reading

Love, Spencie. *One Blood: The Death and Resurrection of Charles R. Drew.* Chapel Hill: University of North Carolina Press, 1996.
Thomas, Karen Kruse. *Deluxe Jim Crow: Civil Rights and American Health Policy, 1935–1954.* Athens: University of Georgia Press, 2011.

DU BOIS, W. E. B.　　SCHOLAR AND LEADER

Born: February 23, 1868, Great Barrington, MA
Education: Fisk University, B.A., 1888; Harvard University, B. A. cum laude, second place Boylston orator, 1890, M.A., 1891, Ph.D., 1895
Died: August 27, 1963, Accra, Ghana

Du Bois was one of the foremost black leaders ca. 1890–1950s. Despite his critics' labels (elitist, nationalist, separatist, communist), he emerged as African Americans' premier public intellectual. "The problem of the twentieth century is the problem of the color-line," he declared in *The Souls of Black Folk* (1903, p. 32).

Du Bois became an uncompromising critic of Booker T. Washington and his program of industrial education. He said that Washington "apologizes for injustice ... and opposes the higher training and ambition of our brighter minds" (DuBois, 2007, p. 44). Liberal arts colleges were indispensable for the training of a "Talented Tenth," he argued, whose leadership not only promised to create a "superior" culture "within the Veil" but also help educate and advance the masses of "the Race." A free people must value dignity, learning, and progress.

Du Bois left the NAACP in 1934, as his call for blacks' separate development undercut its interracialism. He returned to research, teaching, and civil and human rights struggles. The government prosecuted him unsuccessfully as a Communist Party agent in 1951 but revoked his passport until 1959. He departed the next year to live and die in Ghana, West Africa.

[*See also* Scholarship.]

Reference

Du Bois, W. E. B. *The Souls of Black Folk.* 1903. New York: Oxford University Press, 2007, p. 44.

Further Reading

Appiah, Anthony Kwame. *W. E. B. Du Bois and the Emergence of Identity.* Cambridge, MA: Harvard University Press, 2014.
Lewis, David L. *W. E. B. Du Bois – The Fight for Equality and the American Century, 1919–1963.* New York: Henry Holt, 2000.

DURHAM MANIFESTO (1942)

Southern black leaders publicly renounced Jim Crow and made demands "of the postwar South and nation" when fifty-nine of them, including three women, caucused at North Carolina College in 1942.

The conference statement, called the Durham Manifesto, was unprecedented. Not only were the participants "fundamentally opposed to the principle and practice of compulsory segregation." They also assessed "current problems of racial discrimination and neglect," demanding justice in political and civil rights, industry and labor, service occupations, education, agriculture, armed forces, social welfare, and health. Racial moderates, active in organizations such as the Commission on Interracial Cooperation, NAACP, Urban League, and National Council of Negro Women, they challenged liberal white southerners, who met in Atlanta the next year and pledged to cooperate. The manifesto thus began a dialogue that created the Southern Regional Council in 1944; it also inspired grassroots struggles for equal citizenship such as "efforts at voter registration that formed the principal core of black activism in the South through the 1950s" (Robinson and Sullivan, 1991, p. 212).

[*See also* Civil Rights Movement; Segregation.]

Reference

Robinson, Armstead L. and Patricia Sullivan, eds., *New Directions in Civil Rights Studies.* Charlottesville: University of Virginia Press, 1991. p. 212.

Further Reading

Logan, Rayford W., ed. *What the Negro Wants.* Notre Dame, IN: University of Notre Dame Press, 2001.
Robinson, Armstead L., and Patricia Sullivan, eds. *New Directions in Civil Rights Studies.* Charlottesville: University Press of Virginia, 1991.

EDUCATION

Forged in slavery, education is the bellwether of African American aspirations and struggles for dignity, freedom, and equality.

Both enslaved and free blacks faced firm barriers to education. Laws barred educating slaves; free blacks had little or no opportunity to learn. There were a few "catechizing schools for Negroes," begun in 1704, where clergy from the Society for the Propagation of the Gospel in Foreign Parts taught English and Bible. Clergy also conducted worship on plantations, if masters agreed. During the Great Awakening revival (1730s–70s), some blacks received baptism and instruction in Sabbath or mission schools of Moravians, Quakers, Methodists, Baptists, and others. Slavery abolition in the post-Revolutionary North witnessed blacks forming separate churches, Sunday and Free African Schools, as many white schools excluded black children. Black teachers in African schools attended white colleges such as Oberlin (1832) or all-black Lincoln (1854) and Wilberforce (1856) universities. Nationally, by the Civil War, more than 90 percent of slaves and 50 percent of free blacks were illiterate.

The "first crusade" for black schools in the South began during the war. So-called "contraband" slaves fled to Union lines in large numbers, gaining aid, wage-labor, freedom, and military enlistment. Ex-slaves acquired spelling books and Bibles. formed Sabbath schools, and flocked to missionary teachers. Black teacher Mary Peake opened a school at Fort Monroe, Virginia in 1861; white missionaries Laura Towne and Ellen Murray started Penn School on St. Helena Island, South Carolina in 1862. As the Thirteenth Amendment ended bondage and Freedmen's Bureau aided ex-slaves and white refugees, black schooling expanded. The Bureau oversaw hospitals, courts, landlord–tenant transactions, schools, as well as volunteers from charities, churches, and philanthropies. In 1868 alone the African Methodist Episcopal Church reported 40,000 Sabbath School pupils. The Bureau operated 3,000 schools before closing its operations in 1869. Reconstruction terminated in 1877 and states operated former Bureau Schools, which they neglected. So, sympathetic northern and southern whites helped provide Negro elementary, normal, and trade schools, besides collegiate institutions such as Atlanta, Fisk, and Howard Universities and Hampton Institute, to train ministers, teachers, and skilled workers.

From 1877 to 1901, blacks endured the nadir, "the lowest point in the quest for equal rights," testing their capacity to sustain schools. Black educators advocated self-help while soliciting federal and philanthropic support, particularly appealing to northern philanthropists. While the New England classical curriculum (reading, writing, arithmetic) saw affluent donors, the "Hampton-Tuskegee Idea" of industrial education attracted more of them. In 1881, emulating his mentor, Hampton founder Samuel C. Armstrong, Booker T. Washington founded Tuskegee Institute as a vocational school in rural Macon County, Alabama. On campus and publicly, he stressed knowledge, moral character, thrift, and accommodating to segregation. Through racial pride, solidarity, job skills, and acquiring wealth, blacks ultimately would achieve civil rights. He gained the confidence of capitalists such as steelmaker Andrew Carnegie, who donated to "Tuskegee its first major endowment in 1903."

Southern blacks' "second crusade" (Anderson, 1988, p. 91) (1900–1935), paralleling the Great Migration and de facto segregated schools in the North, was part of a national black educational strategy. Chief spokesman for equality was W. E. B. Du Bois, Atlanta University professor and cofounder of the NAACP. He rebuked Washington's silence on Jim Crow and his trade school philosophy. Classical education must be the race's priority, he argued, with precollege curricula and liberal arts colleges to prepare the Talented Tenth, namely leaders in uplifting the race. However, blacks embraced and fused both Du Bois and Washington's ideas. To obtain Rosenwald Fund school-building matching grants, for example, applicants had to offer academic and industrial courses. Thus the fund assisted the construction of 5,000 black schools in the South (1914–32) and the NAACP fought school inequality nationally.

Teachers were critical in that long fight. By 1930 four-fifths of African American children age ten and older were reading. In median years of school, black boys had 6.5 and girls 7.5 in 1940, compared to white boys' 10.5 and girls' 10.9 years. Black students' progress owed much to teachers who instilled values of literacy and self-esteem. Many [teachers] were Boy and Girl Scout mentors and YMCA and YWCA counselors. State Negro teacher associations created the American Teachers' Association (ATA) in 1939 within the biracial structure of the National Education Association (NEA) and promptly enlisted NEA's assistance in equalizing schools for black students. A joint committee proposed an NEA–ATA merger in 1945, but the NEA declined. The *Brown* decision of 1954 revived the proposal and merger came in 1966. Segregated affiliates completed their mergers by 1968, when North Carolinian Elizabeth D. Koontz became NEA's first African American president. In 1973 NEA was the world's largest professional organization; it currently reports more than 3.2 million members.

Southern massive resistance slowed slowed desegregation, but the Supreme Court ordered stronger remedies. In *Swann v. Charlotte-Mecklenburg County Board of Education* (1971), it required North Carolina's second largest district to desegregate by busing students. A requirement beyond the South, too, busing fueled "white flight" and was invalidated in 1973. But it increased the number of integrated school districts.

In 2004, *Brown*'s fiftieth anniversary, scholars concluded that "substantial progress has been made toward the provision of educational resources to blacks" (Jaynes and Williams, 1989, p. 19). Yet they criticized racial and class disparities in student achievement due to poverty among minorities, racial discrimination, unequal opportunities, and weak affirmative action. Desegregation evinced an overall strong black performance, reducing the black–white gap in median years of schooling: 12.6 black and 13 white by 1980. More blacks pursued higher education: 1,106,800 (1980); 2,164,700 (2004); and 2,975,045 (2011), when blacks comprised 5.4 percent of higher education faculty. "Despite the increasing enrollment of blacks in predominantly white colleges and universities," observed one report, "historically black institutions account for a disproportionate share of the black B.A. pool" (Jaynes and Williams, 1989, pp. 345–346). In addition, the United Negro College Fund (1944) and the National Association for Equal Opportunity in Higher Education (1969) continued to promote "the interests of historically and predominantly black colleges and universities." Some 3,111,000 blacks, including 46.5 percent of those aged twenty to twenty-one (compared to 53.5 percent of whites) were enrolled at higher educational institutions in 2013.

[*See also* Freedmen's Bureau; Historically Black Colleges and Universities (HBCUs); United Negro College Fund (UNCF)].

References

Anderson, James D. *The Education of Blacks in the South, 1860–1935.* Chapel Hill: University of North Carolina Press, 1988, p. 91.

Jaynes, Gerald David and Robin M. Williams, Jr., eds. *A Common Destiny: Blacks and American Society.* Washington, DC: National Academies Press, 1989, pp. 19, 345–346.

Further Reading

Anderson, James D. *The Education of Blacks in the South, 1860–1935.* Chapel Hill: University of North Carolina Press, 1988.

Fairclough, Adam. *A Class of Their Own: Black Teachers in the Segregated South.* Cambridge, MA: Harvard University Press, 2007.
National Education Association. "American Teachers Association: The Story of the ATA and the NEA." http://www.nea.org/events/ATA.htm1#merger (2004).

ELLISON, RALPH   WRITER

Born: March 1, 1914, Oklahoma City, OK
Education: Tuskegee Institute, 1933–36
Died: April 16, 1994, New York, NY

A grandson of slaves, Ellison became one of the most significant writers in America. His *Invisible Man* earned the 1953 National Book Award. In 1965 a *Book Week Magazine* poll of 200 critics declared it "the most distinguished American novel written since World War II."

Ellison's road to that achievement began in a poverty-stricken childhood. A bookish boy who hoped to study music, he achieved scholastically and won a state scholarship to Tuskegee Institute, where he studied literature and sculpture in addition to music. Dispirited by tuition problems and Jim Crow, he withdrew and moved to New York City. There he found work and met Richard Wright, who encouraged him to write. He then published dozens of articles and stories. He also joined the Merchant Marine and, once while out on sick leave, wrote a single sentence: "I am an invisible man." Seven years later he had written his landmark story of a young black man facing a hostile and indifferent society. It follows the unnamed protagonist from the South to the North, from youth to adulthood, and from racial naiveté to self-consciousness, ultimately understanding that he had allowed himself to be defined by a world that segregated and devalued him.

Further Reading

Posnock, Ross, ed. *The Cambridge Companion to Ralph Ellison.* New York: Cambridge University Press, 2005.
Rampersad, Arnold. *Ralph Ellison: A Biography.* New York: Alfred A. Knopf, 2007.

EMANCIPATION

While the Emancipation Proclamation (1863) prioritized Rebel states, exempted loyal border slave states (Delaware, Kentucky, Maryland, and Missouri), Tennessee, and Union-controlled areas of Virginia and

Louisiana, it confirmed black military enrollment and forecast the general emancipation. Believing the Union's victory would liberate them, slaves fled by thousands to Union lines and hurt Rebel manpower. As workers and soldiers, they helped catalyze abolition. The US Colored Troops and Navy enlisted 200,000 enslaved and free blacks. Many fought in key battles or campaigns, which liberated slave families and communities. The Thirteenth Amendment (1865) abolished slavery. Congress required seceded states to ratify it, along with the Fourteenth and Fifteenth amendments, during Reconstruction.

African Americans celebrated freedom. "I didn't know what 'free' meant, and I askes Mrs. Harris if I was free," a freedwoman stated. "She says I was free but was goin' to repent of it. But she told me she wasn't going to whip me anymore; and she never did, cose my father came and took me away" (Berlin, Favreau, and Miller, 1988, p. 215). Freedmen and women reclaimed family members. They also created annual celebrations, like Emancipation Day in North Carolina or Juneteenth in Texas, throughout the country.

[*See also* Civil War.]

Reference

Berlin, Ira, Marc Favreau, and Steven F. Miller, eds. *Remembering Slavery: African Americans Talk About Their Personal Experiences of Slavery and Emancipation.* New York: The New Press, 1988, p. 215.

Further Reading

Kachun, Mitchell A. *Festivals of Freedom: Memory and Meaning in African American Emancipation Celebrations, 1808–1915.* Amherst: University of Massachusetts Press, 2003.

Vorenberg, Michael. *Final Freedom: The Civil War, the Abolition of Slavery, and the Thirteenth Amendment.* New York: Cambridge University Press, 2001.

EQUAL EMPLOYMENT OPPORTUNITY COMMISSION (EEOC)

Established by Title VII of the 1964 Civil Rights Act, EEOC receives and investigates charges of employment discrimination based on race, color, sex, national origin, religion, age, disability, or gender identity. Besides its commissioners and staff, it consists of state and local Fair Employment Practices Agencies. It monitors workplaces with twenty-five or more employees, including labor unions, educational institutions, and governments. It can recommend that the Department of Justice file anti-discrimination suits. Clifford L. Alexander, its first black chairman, was appointed in 1967.

[*See also* Affirmative Action.]

Further Reading

Overcoming the Past, Focusing on the Future: An Assessment of the U.S. Equal Employment Opportunity Commission's Enforcement Efforts. Washington, DC: US Commission on Civil Rights, 2000.

Smith, Robert Samuel. *Race, Labor & Civil Rights: Griggs versus Duke Power and the Struggle for Equal Employment Opportunity*. Baton Rouge: Louisiana State University Press, 2008.

EVERS, MEDGAR W.   CIVIL RIGHTS ORGANIZER

Born: July 2, 1925, Decatur, MS
Education: Alcorn A & M College, B.A., 1952
Died: June 12, 1963, Jackson, MS

Evers was shot fatally on the portal of his Jackson, Mississippi home in 1963. The assassin was not convicted and imprisoned for life until 1994.

Evers became NAACP state field secretary in 1954. He recruited members, organized local chapters, led pickets against gas stations denying restrooms to blacks, and investigated racial atrocities. He publicized the murders of Emmett Till (age fourteen) in 1955 and Charles Mack Parker (age twenty-three) in 1959, blaming the Ku Klux Klan. He urged blacks to demand civil rights.

His leadership inspired others. When students from Tougaloo College and Jackson State University began the Jackson sit-ins in 1961, he spearheaded a boycott of white merchants. This move, along with arrivals of CORE-sponsored Freedom Riders, attracted media to the city. He also insisted that Ole Miss admit James Meredith, whose admission would require the federal marshals he had been requesting for years. In the meantime, Klansmen escalated their attempts to kill him. They threw a dynamite bomb into his garage, which failed to explode, only weeks before his assassination. Evers's shameful death fueled international publicity on the black freedom struggle in the South and the nation.

Further Reading

DeLaughter, Bobby. *Never Too Late: A Prosecutor's Story of Justice in the Medgar Evers Case*. New York: Scribner, 2001.
Williams, Michael Vinson. *Medgar Evers: Mississippi Martyr*. Fayetteville: University of Arkansas Press, 2011.

EXECUTIVE ORDER 9981 (1948)

On July 26, 1948, President Harry Truman ordered "that there shall be equality of treatment and opportunity for all persons in the armed services without regard to race, color, religion, or national origin." His order "shook the Defense Department to its foundations" and southern segregationists in Congress would organize as Dixiecrats to oppose his civil rights program.

But the president faced racial realities at home and abroad. More than a million blacks had served in the segregated military during World War II, more than half of them overseas. Further segregation tainted the international image of American democracy in the Cold War. Civil rights groups were protesting for equal education, employment, and the right to vote, as the black press, March on Washington Movement, veterans, and others partnered to turn out Democratic voters. Black, labor, and liberal votes indeed helped Truman to win the November presidential election.

[*See also* Military.]

Further Reading

Colley, David. *Blood for Dignity: The Story of the First Integrated Combat Unit in the U. S. Army*. New York: St. Martin's, 2003.
Taylor, Jon E. *Freedom to Serve: Truman, Civil Rights, and Executive Order 9981*. New York: Routledge, 2013.

EXODUSTERS

Between 20,000 and 40,000 poor blacks mainly from Border and Deep South states migrated to Kansas, a land of opportunity, in 1879. This "Exoduster Movement," by foot, wagon, train, and river boat, helped transform Kansas society.

The movement reflected a quest for freedom and economic independence. Democrats opposed "the Exodus," spreading rumors of Republican-paid transportation and aid for migrants. But its primary organizer, ex-slave Benjamin "Pap" Singleton of Tennessee, had eyed Kansas as a refuge from oppression and place to own land since 1869. He had led a group of 300 there in 1875. Churches and protective societies in migrants' hometowns and the National Emigrant Aid Society provided temporary housing, food, and medical supplies. Exodusters endured poverty, illness, and white backlash, yet during the first few years they acquired more than 20,000 acres, built churches and 300 homes, and formed social organizations.

[*See also* Migration.]

Further Reading

Jack, Bryan M. *The St. Louis African American Community and the Exodusters.* Columbia: University of Missouri Press, 2007.

Mjagkij, Nina, ed. *Portraits of African American Life since 1865.* Wilmington, DE: SR Books, 2003.

FAMILY

The contemporary status of black families is inseparable from the history of slavery, segregation, and desegregation. Buffeted by white racism over time, they remained markedly uneducated or undereducated and poor. Though the Civil Rights Movement, War on Poverty (WOP), and post–civil rights social programs helped to improve their life chances, persistent racial discrimination especially hurt them.

Enslaved and free blacks laid black familial foundations. When the master agreed, slaves could cohabit or marry. Many masters had bond mistresses, promoted slave breeding, and broke up slaves' families for sale. Yet, by adopting African customs, such as naming children after days of the week or for kin, the enslaved preserved the memory of those lost at auction or in death. For mutual support, they created an extended family: a father, mother, and children; grandparents, aunts, uncles; free kinfolk; and frequently children of deceased or sold friends. Children on large plantations lived with both parents; on smaller ones, mostly with mothers. The free black minority often had two-parent families. Blacks increasingly converted to Christianity, a source of freedom and togetherness. They urged missionaries to implore Christian masters to keep their families together. Black churches, in the meantime, fostered monogamous marriage, marital fidelity, and solidarity among blacks in the South and the nation.

Families survived. Freedmen and women legitimated slave marriages and children, sustained two-parent households, and took in displaced relatives, while they and their posterity faced sharecropping, Jim Crow, and penury. They undertook rural-to-urban migrations for better livelihoods. Circa 1880–1925 "the typical Afro-American family was lower class in status and headed by two parents" (Gutman, 1976, p. 456). High black male mortality, however, produced a larger percentage of female-headed households for blacks than whites before and during the Great Depression. Still, in 1940 three-fourths of black families with a child younger than eighteen included the husband and wife, a trend to 1960.

Racial and economic reforms in the 1960s underlaid blacks' mobility into the middle class and safety net for all. The WOP initiated Medicare and Medicaid. It also revitalized Aid to Families with Dependent Children and launched the Comprehensive Employment and Training Act (1973), which established the Job Corps, altogether funding food stamps, job training, and jobs for the disadvantaged, and the Head Start Program for early childhood education. But the Vietnam War's rising costs cut antipoverty funds. This, amidst a growing information-based economy and factory closings, hit blacks hard. Their education, employment, and income levels already were lower (out-of-wedlock births and male incarcerated populations were far higher) than for whites. In addition, between 1960 and 1985, the proportion of black female-headed families doubled from 22 to 44 percent, while female-headed white families rose from 10 to13 percent. In 1986 husband–wife families constituted 51 percent of black families and earned 70 percent of black income. Female-headed families earned 25 percent of black income; 52 percent of them and 67 percent of their children lived in poverty, as did 43 percent of all black children. To help, since the 1980s the Children's Defense Fund has sustained campaigns to advance schooling, decrease teen pregnancy, and increase funding for Head Start, challenging America to put "families first" and "to leave no child behind."

[*See also* Children's Defense Fund; Cities; Great Migration; Welfare.]

Reference

Gutman, Herbert G. *The Black Family in Slavery and Freedom 1750–1925.* New York: Vintage Books, 1976, p. 456.

Further Reading

Hymowitz, Kay. *Marriage and Caste in America: Separate and Unequal Families in a Post-Marital Age.* Chicago: Ivan R. Dee, 2006.

McAdoo, Harriette Pipes, ed. *Black Families.* Thousand Oaks, CA: SAGE, 2007.

Wilson, William Julius. *More Than Just Race: Being Black and Poor in the Inner City.* New York: W. W. Norton, 2009.

FARMER, JAMES L.   CIVIL RIGHTS LEADER

Born: January 12, 1920, Marshall, TX
Education: Wiley College, B.A., 1938; Howard University School of Religion, B.D., 1941
Died: July 9, 1999, Fredericksburg, VA

The Congress of Racial Equality (CORE), which Farmer cofounded in 1942, advocated pacifism, nonviolent protest, and racial integration. He helped organize its freedom ride, a bus Journey of Reconciliation (1947), to test southern states' compliance with the Supreme Court decision barring segregation on interstate buses. It was the forerunner of Freedom Rides (1961), which energized demonstrations to desegregate public accommodations, education, employment, housing, and voting. As CORE national director (1961–66), he created Freedom Highways and Open Cities projects and spoke at the March on Washington.

CORE's ideological crisis disheartened him. When many activists, notably Mississippi Freedom Summer volunteers, espoused black control of leadership, expelling whites, rejecting nonviolence and integration, and demanding Black Power, he resigned. Afterward consulting and teaching, he ran for a New York congressional seat. He also joined the Department of Health Education and Welfare (HEW), where segregationists blocked his efforts to integrate staff, expand Head Start, and recruit minorities into HEW's fellowship program. He left to be a policy consultant and visiting professor at Mary Washington College. His *Lay Bare the Heart: An Autobiography of the Civil Rights Movement* (1985) defends the movement's quest for an integrated society.

Further Reading

Jakoubek, Robert E. *James Farmer and the Freedom Rides.* Brookfield, CT: Millbrook Press, 1994.

Purnell, Brian. *Fighting Jim Crow in the County of Kings: The Congress of Racial Equality in Brooklyn.* Lexington: University Press of Kentucky, 2013.

FARRAKHAN, LOUIS A.   RELIGIOUS LEADER

Born: May 17, 1933, Bronx, NY
Education: Boston English high school, honors graduate, Winston-Salem Teachers College, 1951–53

Imam of the Nation of Islam (NOI), Farrakhan is one of the most influential black religious leaders. For blacks to secure "freedom, justice and equality," he advocates Islam, black nationalism, and self-determination.

Farrakhan became captain of NOI's security force and minister of Temple No. 11 in Boston by the late 1950s. He rose to national spokesman when Malcolm X left NOI (1964) but not to imam after Elijah Muhammad died in 1975. Muhammad's son Warith succeeded him, reinvented NOI as the American Society of Muslims, which embraced orthodoxy and racial inclusion. Leading a large splinter group, Farrakhan reclaimed NOI's name, properties, and teachings.

By 1981 he had reopened 130 mosques and rebuilt membership to tens of thousands. He received wide publicity through NOI's antidrug project, a *Time* cover story, and television, including *Sixty Minutes*. But mainstream media attacked him when, as a supporter of Jesse Jackson's 1984 presidential campaign, he made anti-Semitic statements. Still, the NAACP invited him to its Black Leadership Summit; he remained outspoken on race, religion, and politics. He also co-organized the Million Man March for atonement and responsibility (1995), then the largest black demonstration in American history.

[*See also* Nation of Islam (NOI); Religion.]

Further Reading

Magida, Arthur J. *Prophet of Rage: A Life of Louis Farrakhan and His Nation.* New York: Basic Books, 1996.

Walker, Dennis. *Islam and the Search for African American Nationhood: Elijah Muhammad, Louis Farrakhan, and the Nation of Islam.* Atlanta: Clarity Press, 2005.

FEMINISM

Black feminism, if sometimes sidelined in the US feminist movement, emerged beside Black Power. Resisting institutionalized racism, sexism, and class oppression, it pursued equality for black and all women.

Black feminists embraced freedom struggle. Indeed, slave and free black women were essential in creating families, support networks, and churches, which grounded black survival and resistance. Many joined the women's rights and abolitionist movements. Post–Civil War, they led efforts for equal citizenship in groups such as the National Association of Colored Women, a catalyst of women's suffrage. They partnered in campaigns against Jim Crow, including disfranchisement, lynching, inferior education, and employment, and helped bring desegregation. But men usually dictated 1960s–70s progressive agendas, as the Women's Liberation or Gay Liberation agenda isolated black women. Yet, they championed the antipoverty campaign and were strong supporters of the Equal Rights Amendment (1972), namely that "Equality of rights shall not be denied or abridged ... on account of sex." It failed to achieve ratification.

Black feminists' organizing quickened, however. One of them asserted: "What if more of us had decided to build multi-issued grass-roots organizations in our own communities that dealt with Black women's basic survival issues and at the same time did not back away from raising issues of sexual politics?" (Marable, Frazier, and Campbell, 2013, p. 110). For example, the National Black Feminist Organization (1973) charged affiliates in New York, Chicago, and other cities to uphold "positive self-images" of black women, as well as fight racism and sexism. Boston based and important in the Northeast, the Combahee River Collective (1974) adopted an anticapitalist, antiracist, and anti-sexist agenda. It sponsored retreats to plan protests against homophobia, poverty, domestic violence, or sterilization abuse of black and poor women in America and the Third World.

Their struggles continued. In the 1980s, while joining antiapartheid demonstrations at the South African Embassy, black feminist educators spearheaded the development of courses, research, and publishing on black women's experiences in Africa, America, and the Caribbean. Books such as *All the Women Are White, All the Blacks Are Men, But Some of Us Are Brave: Black Women's Studies* (1982) did much to integrate the study and teaching of race, ethnicity, gender, and sexuality, expanding knowledge of women and men from diverse cultural backgrounds. Also, after televised Senate confirmation hearings for black Supreme Court nominee Clarence Thomas, black feminists protested. Black professor Anita Hill's testimony on how Thomas had sexually harassed her notwithstanding, senators confirmed him. Thus they solicited more than 1,600 signatures and donations to sponsor a full-page ad in *The New York Times* and several black newspapers on November 17, 1991. Entitled "African American Women in Defense of Ourselves," it denounced senators' "racist and sexist treatment" of Hill, who was "maligned, castigated, and slandered for daring to come forward and tell." It also tied Thomas to the Republican Party and the Court's rollback of affirmative action and social programs. Elsewhere, black feminists defended the civil and human rights of all, regardless of skin color or sex orientation. They participated in Philadelphia's Million Woman March (1997) and remain active in the Black Coalition for AIDS Prevention and World Conference Against Racism.

[*See also* National Association of Colored Women (NACW); National Council of Negro Women.]

Reference

Marable, Manning, Nishani Frazier, and John Campbell MacMillan, eds. *Freedom on My Mind: The Columbia Documentary History of the African American Experience*. New York: Columbia University Press, 2013, p. 110.

Further Reading

Collins, Patricia Hill. *Black Feminist Thought: Knowledge, Consciousness, and the Politics of Empowerment*. New York: Routledge, 2000.

James, Stanlie M., Frances Smith Foster, Beverly Guy-Sheftall, eds. *Still Brave: The Evolution of Black Women's Studies*. New York: Feminist Press, 2009.

Springer, Kimberly. *Living for the Revolution: Black Feminist Organizations, 1968–1980*. Durham, NC: Duke University Press, 2005.

FILM

Although negative images of black people pervaded the early New York and Hollywood motion picture industry, blacks contested racism in film. Silent movies invariably depicted a dumb, silly, and subservient Negro. Depicting that character was *The Birth of a Nation* (1915); a three-hour melodrama of the Civil War and Reconstruction, it glorified slavery and the Ku Klux Klan and set box office records. Race caricatures infused sound pictures such as *The Jazz Singer* (1927). *Gone with the Wind* (1939) featured plantations with "crooning darkies and mint juleps." Television followed suit in the late 1940s. *Amos' n' Andy* (1950), a popular black comedy on CBS, presented lowbrow characters. Black newspapers and civil rights organizations, led by the NAACP, had begun protesting antiblack films in 1915.

Their struggle against "unfair representation" continued. Editorializing, picketing, and creating black cinema, they prodded Hollywood toward fairness. Caught in the crossfire of protests were actors such as Lincoln Perry, who played the minstrel Stepin Fetchit, and Hattie McDaniel, the first black Academy Award winner. She won Best Supporting Actress "as a strong and resolute Mammy" in *Gone with the Wind*. Also, from 1915 to 1945, blacks produced more than 200 "race movies," featuring doctors, lawyers, ministers, soldiers, cowboys, or gangsters. Oscar Micheaux made more than thirty, including *The Symbol of the Unconquered* (1921), which condemned lynching, and *Birthright* (1939), starring a northern college graduate who confronted southern Jim Crow.

Black casting changed. In 1942 Lena Horne signed a long-term contract with Metro-Goldwyn-Mayer. Unprecedented, it stipulated "that she would not be cast in stereotypical black roles." Horne appeared in *Stormy Weather* (1943), singing her hit song of the same name. A speaking role in *Meet Me in Las Vegas* (1956) raised her profile and helped dignify the black female image. Between *The Negro Soldier* (1943), a government-backed documentary, and *Lilies of the Field* (1963), featuring

Sidney Poitier and a racially mixed cast, blacks began appearing in dignified roles. Poitier received the 1963 Academy Award for Best Actor, the
first for a black actor.

Change persisted. Films such as *Guess Who's Coming to Dinner*
(1968), which starred Poitier as a highly accomplished doctor and
showed "blacks as working and middle-class people in normal, loving
relationships," saw a growing audience. The NAACP initiated its Image
Awards (1969) to recognize the progress. Still, *Sweet Sweetback's Baad
Asssss Song* (1971) and *Superfly* (1972) typified so-called "blaxploitation
films," glamorizing sex, drugs, and crime in the inner city. Many independent black filmmakers, however, presented "more positive" castings.
Notable among independents is Spike Lee, producer of the acclaimed
Malcolm X (1992). In the meantime, Black Entertainment Television
(1980) pursued "plans to produce films for the African American market" as the NAACP rededicated the Image Awards to "wider representa-
tions of African-American life."

[*See also* Music; Theatre.]

Further Reading

Cripps, Thomas. *Slow Fade to Black: The Negro in American Film, 1900–1942.*
New York: Oxford University Press, 1993.
Mask, Mia. *Divas on Screen: Black Women in American Film.* Urbana: University
of Illinois Press, 2009.
Reid, Mark A. *Black Lenses, Black Voices: African American Film Now.* Lanham,
MD: Rowman & Littlefield, 2005.

FISHER, MILES MARK   MINISTER

Born: October 29, 1899, Atlanta, GA
Education: Morehouse College, B.A., 1918; Northern Baptist Seminary,
B.D., 1922; University of Chicago, M.A., 1922, Ph.D., 1948
Died: December 15, 1970, Richmond, VA

Son of a former slave, Fisher studied religion at Morehouse College
and taught it at Virginia Union and Shaw universities, three institutions founded by the northern-based American Baptist Home Mission
Society. Teaching the theory of evolution, he rejected creationism
and Biblical fundamentalism. He used slave spirituals to show links
between Africans and Afro-Americans' religious and secular worlds.
Fundamentalists in the black Virginia Baptist General Association once

demanded his resignation from Virginia Union. But he stayed and was influential.

He made rich contributions as a scholar and minister. *Negro Slave Songs in the United States* (1953), his pathbreaking book, traced the roots of Afro-Christianity in African slavery, conversion, and freedom struggle. He preached a social gospel at White Rock Baptist Church in Durham, North Carolina (1933–65), creating an outreach ministry and enlisting members (such as North Carolina Mutual Life Insurance Company officers) to help. He established the church's community center, which sponsored a summer softball league, boxing team, table tennis, Boy and Girl Scouts, and guest lecturers. It supported a nursery school, health clinic, and rooms for civic gatherings. Fisher was an outspoken leader in the Durham NAACP, Committee on Negro Affairs, and protests against Jim Crow.

Further Reading

Greene, Christina. *Our Separate Ways: Women and the Black Freedom Movement in Durham, North Carolina.* Chapel Hill: University of North Carolina Press, 2005.
Taylor, Clarence. *Black Religious Intellectuals: The Fight for Equality from Jim Crow to the Twenty-First Century.* New York: Routledge, 2002.

FOREIGN AFFAIRS

Blacks were both objects and subjects in diplomacy from the earliest times. Captives in the African slave trade, slaves producing crops for market, fugitives, abolitionists, emigrants, Unionists, they crucially shaped the domestic and foreign course of slavery and emancipation before, during, and following the Civil War. Probably three blacks, notably Frederick Douglass, were appointed consuls to Haiti and Liberia prior to 1900. Black newspapers largely supported the Spanish-American War but deplored the racist and imperialist attitudes and interests that fueled it.

African Americans simultaneously pursued domestic civil rights and global human rights. They opposed racial and colonial oppression through the Pan-African Congress, NAACP, Universal Negro Improvement Association (UNIA), and other organizations, even as their service in World War I, appeals to the League of Nations, and efforts supporting Africa's self-rule promised a freer world. Black military and civilian contributions to World War II catalyzed desegregation of the armed and diplomatic services, leveraging that promise. So did the fifty-member United Nations, launched in 1945 to foster the peace, security, dignity, and self-determination of all peoples. Ralph Bunche, the first black UN diplomat, negotiated the truce that ended the Arab-Israeli War in 1949. Among "official consultants" to the American UN delegation were NAACP representatives, who soon created a coalition of Third World delegates, nongovernmental organizations, and the black press. During the Cold War, the coalition called for decolonization; nonproliferation of nuclear weapons; prevention of regional wars, like the one in Vietnam; race, ethnic, and religious tolerance; and economic aid to underdeveloped nations. In addition, Amnesty International, despite "the domestic jurisdiction clause," petitioned the UN Commission on Human Rights for intervention to free African American political prisoners. TransAfrica promoted affirmative action to recruit more blacks and other minorities into Foreign Service careers; policies to sanction apartheid and genocide in Africa; and ending the immigration ban for Haitian refugees.

[*See also* Cold War; Military; TransAfrica; Universal Negro Improvement Association (UNIA).]

Further Reading

Anderson, Carol. *Eyes Off the Prize: The United Nations and the African American Struggle for Human Rights, 1944–1955.* New York: Cambridge University Press, 2003.

Ledwidge, Mark. *Race and U.S. Foreign Policy: The African American Foreign Affairs Network.* New York: Routledge, 2012.

"FORTY ACRES AND A MULE"

Hoping to dissuade the thousands of slaves who followed his army in Georgia, General William Sherman and the Secretary of War met their leaders in Savannah, January 12, 1865. The war "is taking us from under the yoke of bondage, and placing us where we could reap the fruit of our own labor," one leader declared. "The way we can best take care of ourselves is to have land, and turn it and till it … until we are able to buy it and make it our own" (Jones, 2009, p. 219).

Four days afterward Sherman issued Special Field Order 15 as a practical and temporary policy. It "set apart" abandoned plantations on Sea Islands of South Carolina and Georgia, thirty miles inland from Charleston to the St. Lawrence River in Florida, for ex-slaves. Families would have "possessory title" to forty-acre farms and use army mules. More than 10,000 families built homes, planted, and "anticipated permanent possession." But in its Freedmen's Bureau bill, Congress did not authorize confiscation of former slaveholders' lands. This aborted general black landowning and helped interests for "more and cheaper cotton." The Bureau oversaw freedpeople's transition into farm tenancy, the vast majority as sharecroppers.

[See *also* Agriculture.]

Reference

Jones, Jacqueline. *Saving Savannah: The City and the Civil War*. New York: Vintage Books, 2009, p. 219.

Further Reading

Baker, Bruce E., and Brian Kelly, eds. *After Slavery: Race, Labor, and Citizenship in the Reconstruction South*. Gainesville: University Press of Florida, 2014.

Cimbala, Paul A. *The Freedmen's Bureau: Reconstructing the American South after the Civil War*. Malabar, FL: Krieger, 2005.

FOUR FREEDOMS

Freedom of speech and worship, freedom from want and fear, in President Roosevelt's 1941 State of the Union Address, framed official American ideology in World War II. Promoted by the government and mainstream press, the four freedoms became a wartime mantra.

Racial and economic inequality divided America; winning a war against the Axis Powers required national unity. Black newspapers pronounced the mantra along with their campaign for a Double-V, victory over fascism abroad and over racial discrimination in America. They served in military and civilian defense, but also fought to abolish segregation and secure civil rights.

[See *also* World War II.]

Further Reading

Bodar, John E. *The "Good War" in American Memory*. Baltimore: Johns Hopkins University Press, 2010.

Wynn, Neil A. *The African American Experience During World War II*. Lanham, MD: Rowman & Littlefield, 2010.

FRANKLIN, ARETHA L.   POP SINGER

Born: March 25, 1942, Memphis, TN
Education: Public high school, Detroit, MI

Franklin's soulful singing began in the choir at New Bethel Baptist Church (Detroit). Her father was the pastor and her mother, a gospel singer. Gospel and popular singers Mahalia Jackson and Sam Cooke were her mentors. She recorded *Precious Lord* (1956) but left the church at age eighteen for a career in pop music.

She succeeded. Her first album, *I Never Loved a Man*, topped the billboard charts, sold a million copies, and had two number-one hit singles, "I Never" and "Respect." Singing about love, sex, pain, pride, and dignity in an emotional and gospel-inflected voice, she became the top soul vocalist of the civil rights–Black Power years. With four other million-sellers between 1967 and 1969, while earning four Grammy Awards, she became the "Queen of Soul." Even as "Respect" expressed women's and black liberation, Aretha also sang to collective hope for nonviolence, racial integration, and equality of opportunity, particularly during the nationally televised funeral of Martin Luther King, Jr. Helping to generate equal opportunities and outcomes for others, she gives generously to Mothers Against Drunk Driving, sickle cell anemia research, the NAACP, and United Negro College Fund, among many recipients of her philanthropy.

Further Reading

Martin, Waldo E., Jr. *No Coward Soldiers: Black Cultural Politics in Postwar America*. Cambridge, MA: Harvard University Press, 2005.
Ritz, David. *Respect: The Life of Aretha Franklin*. New York: Little, Brown and Company, 2014.

FRANKLIN, JOHN HOPE   HISTORIAN

Born: January 2, 1915, Rentiesville, OK
Education: Fisk University, A.B. honors, 1936; Harvard University, M.A., 1937, Ph.D., 1942

Author and editor of more than twenty books, Franklin is best known for *From Slavery to Freedom: A History of African Americans* (1947,

9th ed. 2011); sales are more than 3 million. He came of age, finished college, and began teaching at black colleges in the Jim Crow South. His career saw distinguished professorships at Chicago and Duke; learned society presidencies; and academic and civic awards and honors, including the Presidential Medal of Freedom (1995).

Franklin determined to integrate American life and history. He wrote memoranda on the Fourteenth Amendment for the *Brown v. Board of Education* legal team; marched with Martin Luther King, Jr. for voting rights; urged affirmative action in education, employment, and politics; and chaired the advisory board of the President's Race Commission (1996). His scholarship not only integrated the black experience into the national narrative; it also interpreted how black–white relations crucially defined American ideas and institutions on race, ethnicity, gender, and class. Stressing those points in Race Commission forums across the country, he argued that they could inform public policies to end racial discrimination. *One America in the 21st Century: Forging a New Future* (1998), the Commission's final report, restated his argument and hope.

[*See also* Scholarship.]

Further Reading

Franklin, John Hope. *Mirror to America: The Autobiography of John Hope Franklin*. New York: Farrar, Straus and Giroux, 2005.
Rutland, Robert Allen, ed. *Clio's Favorites: Leading Historians of the United States, 1945–2000*. Columbia: University of Missouri Press, 2000.

FRATERNAL ORDERS AND LODGES

African Baptist, Methodist, and other black churchmen established fraternal orders, lodges, and "voluntary associations" for racial uplift before and after the Civil War. Newport, Rhode Island blacks formed the African Union Society (1780). Their brethren in Philadelphia founded the Free African Society (1787), when lay leader Prince Hall chartered Boston's African Lodge No. 459 for Negro Masons. Grand United Order of Odd Fellows (1843) began in New York, as did Grand United Order of Galilean Fishermen (1856) and Knights of Pythias 1864) in Washington, DC, and Knights of Tabor (1872) in Independence, Missouri. All had women's auxiliaries, such as Daughters of the Eastern Star with Masons.

Fraternal groups helped communities. They fostered literacy and thrift, "the most far-reaching economic influence" among former slave patrons of the Freedmen's Bank. Orders and mutual benefit societies seeded the growth of fifty-five black banks ca. 1887–1908; they also founded insurance companies such as North Carolina Mutual Life Insurance Company (1898) and Atlanta Life Insurance Company (1905). They promoted "'Negro support of Negro business.'"

[*See also* Clubs; Fraternities; Freedmen's Bank; Sororities.]

Further Reading

Hackett, David G. "The Prince Hall Masons and the African American Church: The Labors of Grand Master and Bishop James Walker Hood, 1831–1918." *Church History*, 69 (December 2000): 770–802.

Lynch, Katherine A., ed. *African American Fraternal Associations and the History of Civil Society in the United States. Social Science History*, 28(3) (September 2004).

FRATERNITIES

Perhaps the first black male groups at Historically Black Colleges and Universities and a few white universities, black fraternities are among the largest African American organizations. They comprise an undergraduate, graduate, and alumni membership of more than 500,000 today. African and West Indian alumni of US colleges, black students abroad, and military personnel frequently join chapters in United Kingdom, Germany, Africa, South Korea, and the Caribbean. Black Greeks include Alpha Phi Alpha (1906) and Kappa Alpha Psi (1911), begun at Cornell and Indiana universities, respectively. Howard University men founded Omega Psi Phi (1911) and Phi Beta Sigma (1914).

Fraternities play vital roles. On campus they provide academic assistance and social support. In addition to sponsoring dances and other socials, they engage in community service, including voter education and registration. They also donate to the United Negro College Fund. In the 1950–60s, Alphas donated generously to brother Martin Luther King Jr.'s nonviolent civil rights and poor people's campaigns. Meantime, Kappas funded a national program of student financial aid and help for the elderly.

[*See also* Clubs; Sororities.]

Further Reading

Jones, Ricky L. *Black Haze: Violence, Sacrifice, and Manhood in Black Greek-Letter Fraternities*. Albany: State University of New York Press, 2004.

Kimbrough, Walter M. *Black Greek 101: The Culture, Customs, and Challenges of Black Fraternities and Sororities*. Teaneck, NJ: Fairleigh Dickinson University Press, 2003.

FREE AFRICAN SOCIETY (FAS)

Led by former slaves Richard Allen and Absalom Jones (1746–1818) in 1787, blacks withdrew from St. George's Methodist Church (Philadelphia) where they were segregated. They founded FAS, "perhaps the first autonomous organization of free blacks in the United States."

The society gained supporters among white Quakers, Methodists, and abolitionists. It worshiped in a storehouse and later at a Quaker-sponsored Free African School. FAS opposed African colonization, aided the poor, and practiced self-help. When it pursued a denominational affiliation, Allen advocated Methodism. But a majority of the members, led by Jones, chose the Episcopal Church. Allen departed; he established Bethel African Methodist Episcopal (AME) Church (1794) and cofounded the AME denomination (1816).

[*See also* Temperance movement.]

Further Reading

Mitchell, Henry H. *Black Church Beginnings: The Long-Hidden Realities of the First Years*. Grand Rapids, MI: Eerdmans, 2004.
Nash, Gary B. "New Light on Richard Allen: The Early Years of Freedom." *William and Mary Quarterly*, 46 (April 1989): 332–40.

FREE BLACKS

Slaveholding colonies (containing some slaves), slave colonies (at least 20 percent slaves), and states evolved in America. The proportion of free blacks was small.

In 1750 free black people comprised less than 2 percent of all blacks. They were mainly artisans, farmers, farmhands, and domestic workers. Slaves could attain freedom by birth to a free-black mother, self-purchase, manumission, or escape. Those methods and gradual abolition of northern slavery increased the free black population from 60,000 or 2 percent of blacks (1790) to 500,000 or 9 percent (1860). More than half lived in the South. Maryland (83,942), Virginia (58,042), Pennsylvania (56,949), and New York (49 005) reported the largest numbers.

They struggled. Segregated in the North and considered "slaves without masters" in the South, they developed families and communities.

Black churches, schools, charities, and social networks enabled them to affirm and help themselves. Intragroup differences in color, literacy, and economic status, however, strained racial solidarity. For example, elite light-skin free blacks tended to be educated and owned much property, including slaves. The vast majority of free blacks remained illiterate and poor. Manumitted, owning little, and usually living near slave kin, they closed ranks with their enslaved brethren in an ongoing freedom struggle.

[*See also* Slavery.]

Further Reading

Berlin, Ira. *Slaves without Masters: The Free Negro in the Antebellum South.* New York: The New Press, 1992.
King, Wilma. *The Essence of Liberty: Free Black Women during the Slave Era.* Columbia: University of Missouri Press, 2006.

FREEDMEN'S BANK

Established by Congress (1865), the Freedmen's Savings and Trust Company exemplified black thrift. It opened thirty-seven branches in seventeen states and the District of Columbia during its operation. It reported more than 70,000 depositors and total deposits of $57,000,000. Black churches, fraternal orders, and schools maintained accounts. Many blacks served as cashiers and on branch boards. But directors approved bad investments in Washington, DC real estate and New York interests devastated by the Panic of 1873. Congress closed the bank in 1874. Frederick Douglass was its last president. Half of the depositors received partial reimbursement; half lost everything.

[*See also* Business.]

Further Reading

Osthaus, Carl R. *Freedmen, Philanthropy, and Fraud: A History of the Freedman's Savings Bank.* Urbana: University of Illinois Press, 1976.
Levy, Jonathan. *Freaks of Fortune: The Emerging World of Capitalism and Risk in America.* Cambridge, MA: Harvard University Press, 2012.

FREEDMEN'S BUREAU

Congress established the Bureau of Refugees, Freedmen, and Abandoned Lands (1865); it was unprecedented.

Its national commissioner, state commissioners, and local officials would manage the South's transition from slavery to freedom. They were to create a system of free labor, courts, and schools; uphold racial peace; and protect missionary teachers, who included blacks. Agents mediated landlord–tenant disputes, many over sharecropper contracts, and used military patrols to safeguard freedpeople from ex-Confederate violence. Blacks embraced northern missionaries and the Republican-run Union Leagues, becoming voters and officeholders. Confederate diehards waged war against the Bureau. It closed in 1869 but continued its school program until 1872.

[*See also* Reconstruction.]

Further Reading

Cimbala, Paul A., and Randall M. Miller, eds. *The Freedmen's Bureau and Reconstruction: Reconsiderations*. New York: Fordham University Press, 1999.

Farmer-Kaiser, Mary. *Freedwomen and the Freedmen's Bureau: Race Gender, and Public Policy in the Age of Emancipation*. New York: Fordham University Press, 2010.

FREEDOM RIDES

After *Boynton v. Virginia* (1960) banned segregated accommodations in interstate travel, Congress of Racial Equality (CORE) initiated Freedom Rides to test compliance with that Supreme Court decision.

On May 4, 1961, boarding two Greyhound buses from Washington, DC, fifteen black and white riders hoped to integrate waiting rooms, restaurants, and restrooms along the route to New Orleans, Louisiana. Near Anniston, Alabama a white mob attacked, burned one bus, and brutally beat a number of Freedom Riders. The attack made international news, embarrassed America, and forced the attorney general to order police protection. Riders also were assaulted, arrested, and sometimes incarcerated in Birmingham, Montgomery, and Jackson, Mississippi, where many others, particularly college students, joined them. The rides continued through the summer and energized the civil rights struggle.

[*See also* Congress of Racial Equality (CORE); Journey of Reconciliation.]

Further Reading

Arsenault, Raymond. *Freedom Riders: 1961 and the Struggle for Racial Justice*. New York: Oxford University Press, 2006.

Niven, David. *The Politics of Injustice: The Kennedys, the Freedom Rides, and the Electoral Consequences of a Moral Compromise.* Knoxville: University of Tennessee Press, 2003.

FREEDOM SUMMER

Over 1,000 out-of-state volunteers, mostly northern white college students, hundreds of healthcare and other providers, and thousands of local blacks joined the 1964 Mississippi Summer Project. Organized by Robert Moses, the Student Nonviolent Coordinating Committee (SNCC)'s Mississippi Project director, and sponsored by the Council of Federated Organizations (NAACP, Congress of Racial Equality [CORE], Southern Christian Leadership Conference [SCLC], Student Nonviolent Coordinating Committee [SNCC]), the project conducted "Freedom Schools" and a voter-registration campaign.

It was crucial. Schools stressed literacy, black history, and life skills. Voter registration challenged black disfranchisement and helped create the Mississippi Freedom Democratic Party. Segregationists struck back: 67 black churches, homes, and businesses were bombed and burned; 1,000 fieldworkers were arrested, 80 beaten, 4 severely injured, and 3 murdered. That summer's events not only focused international media on racial atrocities in the South but also pushed the civil rights movement to the forefront of American politics.

[*See also* Mississippi Freedom Democratic Party (MFDP).]

Further Reading

King, Ed, Rev., and Trent Watts. *Ed King's Mississippi: Behind the Scenes of Freedom Summer.* Jackson: University Press of Mississippi, 2014.

Watson, Bruce. *Freedom Summer: The Savage Season that Made Mississippi Burn and Made America a Democracy.* New York: Viking, 2010.

FREEDOM TRAIN

Created by the American Heritage Foundation to foster democracy and patriotism, the Freedom Train toured in 1947–49, early Cold War years.

Ironically, the tour exposed racial segregation. The streamliner locomotive (red, white, and blue locomotive with a 1776 logo) carried the Bill of Rights and other documents on liberty for public viewings. It traveled more than 33,000 miles, stopping in every state. Business and civic leaders, its main boosters, popularized the slogan "Freedom Is

Everybody's Job." At some stops, notably in southern states, Jim Crow was the rule. But many black communities protested. Poet Langston Hughes captured their protests in "Freedom Train" (1947), stating "What shall I tell my children? ... You tell me–Cause freedom ain't freedom when a man ain't free."

[*See also* Cold War.]

Further Reading

Coleman, Evelyn. *Freedom Train*. New York: McElderry Books, 2008.
Fried, Richard M. *The Russians Are Coming! The Russians are Coming!: Pageantry and Patriotism in Cold-War America*. New York: Oxford University Press, 1998.

FUGITIVE SLAVE ACT (1850)

A pillar of the Compromise of 1850, which preserved the Union until 1861, this act guaranteed federal enforcement of the constitutional provision for reclaiming runaway slaves or servants.

The statute required US marshals and deputies to help slaveowners reclaim human property; it levied a fine of $1,000 if they refused. Citizens could be deputized to assist the capture of fugitives. Criminal charges could be imposed for harboring them or obstructing capture. Free states sometimes enacted personal liberty laws to block compliance. Black and white abolitionists sued in state courts to protect runaways while supporting an underground network for their escape.

[*See also* Underground Railroad.]

Further Reading

Finkelman, Paul, and Donald R. Kennon, eds. *Congress and the Crisis of the 1850s*. Athens: Ohio University Press, 2012.
Maltz, Earl M. *Fugitive Slave on Trial: The Anthony Burns Case and Abolitionist Outrage*. Lawrence: University Press of Kansas, 2010.

GARVEY, MARCUS M.   PAN-AFRICAN LEADER

Born: August 7, 1887, St. Ann's Bay, Jamaica
Education: St. Ann's Bay Common School
Died: June 10, 1940, London, England

Vendors still sell pictures of a regally attired Garvey in New York City, where he appealed to black pride like no others. He founded the Universal Negro Improvement Association (UNIA) in Kingston, Jamaica (1914) and its Harlem headquarters (1917). Urging blacks to be proud of their color and history, build black enterprises, and even go "Back-to-Africa," Garvey enlisted thousands of Caribbean emigrants and southern black migrants in UNIA. It formed hundreds of chapters in the North, South, and West Indies. Membership rose to several million by the 1920s. Many observers called Garvey the "Black Moses" of his people.

Black nationalism is the foundation of Africa's liberation and of self-determination in America, he preached, rejecting the NAACP's pursuit of civil rights and racial integration. W. E. B. Du Bois, A. Philip Randolph, and others denounced him as a misleader. But he continued to oppose them and recruit members. His arrest for mail fraud involving Black Star Line ships, incarceration, and deportation (1925) hurt his movement. Garvey's ideology persisted not only in UNIA but also among black nationalists such as black Muslims.

Further Reading

Dagnini, Jeremie Kroubo. "Marcus Garvey: A Controversial Figure in the History of Pan Africanism." *The Journal of Pan African Studies*, 2 (March 2008): 198–208.

Grant, Colin. *Negro with a Hat: The Rise and Fall of Marcus Garvey and His Dream of Mother Africa*. London: Jonathan Cape, 2008.

GHETTO

The geographically continuous and separate black residential and social space, usually in cities, is termed a ghetto. It evolved with slavery; free blacks and slaves clustered in antebellum urban enclaves. After the Civil War, freedpeople increasingly migrated to them.

Black ghettoization grew during the Great Migration of southern blacks (ca. 1914–70) to northern, midwestern, and western industrial centers. More than 4 million left the South from 1940 to 1970 alone. Facing racial discrimination in education, employment, and housing, many inner-city blacks evidenced what sociologists term a "tangle of pathology," including high rates of illiteracy, joblessness, poverty, crime, and out-of-wedlock births. But that sociological label underappreciates the community institutions that nurture race pride and resilience, forging a Harlem Renaissance or a civil rights movement.

[*See also* Poverty.]

Further Reading

Polikoff, Alexander. *Waitng for Gautreaux: A Story of Segregation, Housing, and the Black Ghetto.* Evanston, IL: Northwestern University Press, 2006.
Rainwater, Lee. *Behind Ghetto Walls: Black Families in a Federal Slum.* New Brunswick, NJ: Transaction Publishers, 2006.

G. I. BILL (1944)

The Servicemen's Readjustment Act was "a bill of rights for G. I. Joe and G. I. Jane," providing opportunities for more than 16 million men and women, including over a million blacks, who served in the US military.

The act allowed payments covering tuition, books, and subsistence for up to four years of college or vocational education. It granted home mortgages at low interest, farm or business loans, and a $20 weekly "readjustment allowance" as veterans searched for employment.

The bill critically influenced postwar America. By 1956 about 10 million GIs had used benefits to earn degrees or enter skilled jobs. Black veterans' dollars helped sustain many Negro colleges and increase African American literacy. Owning farms and businesses, they leveraged families, communities, and a black growing middle class. They were vital in the emerging civil rights movement.

[*See also* Historically Black Colleges and Universities (HBCUs); United Negro College Fund (UNCF).]

Further Reading

Humes, Edward. "How the G.I. Bill Shunted Blacks into Vocational Training." *The Journal of Blacks in Higher Education*, 53 (Autumn 2006): 92–104.
Katznelson, Ira. *When Affirmative Action Was White: An Untold History of Racial Inequality in Twentieth-Century America.* New York: W. W. Norton, 2005.

GIBSON, ALTHEA   TENNIS PRO

Born: August 25, 1927, Silver, SC
Education: Florida A & M College, athletic scholarship, B.A., 1953
Died: September 28, 2003, East Orange, NJ

Recalling her career, Gibson declared: "I tried to feel responsibilities to Negroes, but that was a burden on my shoulders" (Schwartz). From segregation to civil rights, however, she shouldered it.

Her experience reflected core values of learning, pride, and uplift. Raised in Harlem, she dominated tennis play in the Police Athletic League before relocating to Wilmington, North Carolina. There physician Hubert Eaton coached her to ten American Tennis Association girls' singles championships. College competition and teamwork prepared Gibson to face racism and win with dignity. She used those lessons at US competitions when "she often had to find her own lodging, because hotels willing to host white players refused to accommodate Negroes."

Gibson was pro "tennis' own Jackie Robinson." The first black player in the National Indoor Tournament, as well as the first to enter and win the French Open, Wimbledon, and US Open tournaments, she integrated women's golf tours (1963). Although never a big money winner, she paved the way for multimillion dollar black stars such as Arthur Ashe, Serena Williams, and Venus Williams. After her retirement, she supervised New Jersey state education and recreation programs for children. Her foundation also focused on disadvantaged minority youths.

Reference

Schwartz, Larry. "Althea Gibson Broke Barriers." Retrieved from https://espn .go.com/sportscentury/features/00014035.html

Further Reading

Gray, Frances Clayton, and Yanick Rice Lamb. *Born to Win: The Authorized Biography of Althea Gibson*. Hoboken, NJ: John Wiley & Sons, 2004.
Schoenfeld, Bruce. *The Match: Althea Gibson and Angela Buxton: How Two Outsiders–One Black, the Other Jewish–Forged a Friendship and Made Sports History*. New York: Amistad, 2004.

GOSPEL OF FREEDOM

Hope for freedom was deeply rooted in slavery and Afro-Christianity. In the twilight of the Civil War and general emancipation black churches invoked that hope. African Methodist Episcopal (AME), Baptist, and other preachers "proclaimed a new Gospel of Freedom." For example, AME bishop Daniel A. Payne said that freedmen and -women must embrace Christian character, education, self-help, and racial solidarity to cope with the injuries of slavery and raise their voices for justice.

[*See also* Religion.]

Further Reading

Hildebrand, Reginald F. *The Times Were Strange and Stirring: Methodist Preachers and the Crisis of Emancipation.* Durham, NC: Duke University Press, 1995.

Strobert, Nelson T. *Daniel Alexander Payne: The Venerable Preceptor of the African Methodist Episcopal Church.* Lanham, MD: University Press of America, 2012.

GRAVES, EARL G.   ENTREPRENEUR

Born: January 9, 1935, Brooklyn, NY
Education: Morgan State University, B.A., 1958

A leading spokesman and publisher on black business, Graves created a conglomerate of market research, broadcast, and beverage corporations.

He pursued opportunities. Raised in Brooklyn, he reached adulthood during the civil rights struggle, terming it "the beginning of the end of a system that pushed African Americans to make the shots but refused to let us call them" (www.thefreelibrary.com/Putting+together+the+Top+50+blacks+in+sports.a0129169811). College prepared him for key jobs: army officer, treasury agent, and member of Senator Robert F. Kennedy's staff. After the senator's assassination, he used a grant and Small Business Administration (SBA) loan to start what became a $53 million media empire by 2002.

Its hub is *Black Enterprise* (BE), the premier magazine about black-owned businesses and market activity. It has 475,000 subscribers and an international readership of more than 4 million. Readers include 100,000 members of religious, civic, and economic organizations, including the NAACP, National Urban League, and National Bankers Association. *BE* annually ranks the top-100 black companies and analyzes policy issues facing the Minority Advisory Council of SBA. It reports consumer income and spending trends by race, class, gender, and region. Its growing network of supporters includes *Fortune* 500 corporate executives, social philanthropists, sports figures, and others who help to underwrite "equality of opportunity."

Further Reading

Clarke, Caroline V., ed. "Inside View: Earl G. Graves on the Record." *Black Enterprise-Silver Anniversary Commemorative,* 26 (August 1995): 13–14, 54–62.

Jalloh, Alusine, and Toyin Falola, eds. *Black Business and Economic Power.* Rochester, NY: Universityof Rochester Press, 2002.

GREAT DEPRESSION

The stock market crash of 1929 fueled America's worst depression, which lasted until the World War II recovery.

As commercial, industrial, retail, and service companies failed or cut production, unemployment spiraled upward. Masses of the unemployed joined bread lines; racial and ethnic minorities faced much discrimination. When the Roosevelt Administration began the New Deal (1932), median family income was half its pre-crash level and one in four breadwinners had no income. Black joblessness exceeded 50 percent in large cities. Three in ten black families were destitute.

Like business, industry, and labor, blacks lobbied the government. They sought equity in federal relief and jobs programs, but reform was slow. Social security benefits, for example, did not include sharecroppers and tenant farmers, the supermajority of black workers. Also, under the Agricultural Adjustment Administration's crop reduction program, farmowners signed contracts and received cash payments to reduce planting acreage as much as 40 percent, resulting in rampant black evictions. Some evicted families secured low-interest loans to buy farms via the Farm Security Administration. Its Subsistence Homestead Program resettled many of them in rural communities. It also subsidized migrant farm worker camps. The Civilian Conservation Corps (CCC) segregated black youths, who flocked to CCC educational, public works, and residential sites. The National Recovery Administration's wage codes were the lowest for blacks in all occupations.

Blacks pushed for equality nonetheless. Black voters consistently supported President Roosevelt, who appointed a Federal Council on Negro Affairs, known as the "Black Cabinet." Led by National Youth Administration director Mary M. Bethune, members coalesced with the NAACP and Urban League to pursue civil rights and equal opportunities. At the same time, more and more elite and ordinary blacks enlisted in civic organizations and labor unions (along with white liberals, socialists, and communists) to launch protests against race and economic inequality.

[*See also* Agriculture; Labor.]

Further Reading

Ferguson, Karen. *Black Politics in New Deal Atlanta*. Chapel Hill: University of North Carolina Press, 2002.

Sitkoff, Harvard. *A New Deal for Blacks: The Emergence of Civil Rights as a National Issue: The Depression Decade*. New York: Oxford University Press, 2009.

GREAT MIGRATION

African American migration from the South began surging when immigration restrictions created an industrial labor shortage. Pulled by decent job prospects and pushed by the Jim Crow system as America mobilized for World War I, sharecroppers, farmhands, and domestics, among others, migrated to southern and northern cities, including Atlanta, Nashville, Chicago, and New York. Circa 1910–30 an estimated 1.75 million moved to the North. They filled factory jobs, forged communities, and pursued equal citizenship, using their churches, fraternal groups, the NAACP, and the Urban League.

Between 1940 and 1970, more than 5 million black southerners went to urban centers in the North, Midwest, and West. In the "Promised Land" black migrants faced de facto segregation, job and union discrimination, racial hatred, and riots. But they found higher pay, more freedom to vote, and better education for their children. Their economic and political progress helped sustain the long civil rights movement and desegregate society.

[*See also* Cities.]

Further Reading

Berlin, Ira. *The Making of African America: The Four Great Migrations.* New York: Viking, 2010.

Wilkerson, Isabel. *The Warmth of Other Suns: The Epic Story of America's Great Migration.* New York: Random House, 2010.

HAITIAN REVOLUTION

In the wake of the French Revolution, slaves on St. Domingue, France's sugar-rich Caribbean island, rose in 1791, burning plantations and killing 2,000 slaveowners. Their leader, Toussaint L' Ouverture (1744–1803), forged an army that defeated all invading forces – French, British, Spanish – and abolished slavery in 1794.

Fear permeated societies across the region. France captured L' Ouverture (1802) and he died in captivity. Jean-Jacques Dessalines (1758–1806) took command, masterminded final victory, and led the liberated colony. Renamed Haiti in 1804, it was the first black and second republic in the Western Hemisphere. Its revolution inspired slave rebellions in the United States and throughout the Atlantic World.

[*See also* Slavery.]

Further Reading

Dubois, Laurent. *Slave Revolution in the Caribbean: A Brief History with Documents*. New York: Palgrave Macmillan, 2006.

Jackson, Maurice, and Jacqueline Bacon, eds. *African Americans and the Haitian Revolution: Selected Essays and Historical Documents*. New York: Routledge, 2010.

HALL, PRINCE   MASONIC LEADER

Born: ca. 1735
Education: Self-taught
Died: December 4, 1807, Boston, MA

Called "the most famous black in the Boston area during the American Revolution and through the turn of the nineteenth century," Hall was a pioneer. According to *The Official History of Freemasonry among the Colored People in North America* (1903), a Boston leather-dresser owned him in the 1740s. He learned his master's craft, joined the Congregational church, and taught himself to read and write. His master emancipated him in 1770 for his "steadfast service." Hall probably mustered in the Continental Army, but this is uncertain. Still, he married, opened a leather shop, and opposed slavery. He urged free blacks to lead in liberating and uplifting their race.

Hall stressed a need for "beneficial endeavors" alongside black churches. In 1775 the St. John's Lodge of Freemasons refused him membership on racial grounds. But a British Army local lodge allowed Hall and fourteen others to create African Lodge No. 1, officially chartered in 1787. As the Grand Master of colored masonry, Hall prioritized black freedom, entreating fellow masons to embrace abolition, literacy, religious salvation, and thrift. In 1808, honoring his pioneering leadership, northern Negro masons renamed themselves Prince Hall Masons.

Further Reading

Uzzel, Robert L. *Prince Hall Freemasonry in the Lone Star State: From Cuney to Curtis, 1875–2003.* Austin, TX: Sunbelt Eakin Press, 2004.
Walker, Corey D. B. *A Noble Fight: African American Freemasonry and the Struggle for Democracy in America.* Urbana: University of Illinois Press, 2008.

HAMER, FANNIE LOU   CIVIL RIGHTS LEADER

Born: October 6, 1917, Montgomery County, MS
Education: Sunflower County elementary school
Died: March 14, 1977, Ruleville, MS

Documentaries often capture Mrs. Hamer singing "This Little Light of Mine" at the Democratic National Convention (1964). Cofounder of the Mississippi Freedom Democratic Party (MFDP), she testified in a nationally televised hearing on its challenge for official seats. Such images depict the activism that underlay her induction to the National Women's Hall of Fame (1993).

The Student Nonviolent Coordinating Committee (SNCC) recruited Hamer from a plantation timekeeping job to register black voters. "Nobody never come out into the country and talked to real farmers" before SNCC came, she stated. Yet "it was these kids what broke a lot of this down. They treated us like we were special and we loved 'em... We trusted 'em" (Jones-Brown, Frazier, and Brooks, 2014, p. 539).

Enlarging the trust, Hamer pursued blacks' right to vote, for which she was shot at and beaten; engaged in electoral politics through MFDP; ran for Congress; cofounded the National Women's Political Caucus (1971); and established Freedom Farm (1969–74), a nonprofit venture to provide food, social services, educational assistance, and job training. Despite suffering with cancer during her final years, she remained active in civil, human, and women's rights causes. Indeed, she represented the long struggle for human dignity and social justice in America.

Reference

Jones-Brown, Delores D., Beverly D. Frazier, and Marvie Brooks, eds. *African Americans and Criminal Justice: An Encyclopedia.* Santa Barbara: ABC-CLIO, 2014, p. 539.

Further Reading

Asch, Christopher Myers. *The Senator and the Sharecropper: The Freedom Struggles of James O. Eastland and Fannie Lou Hamer.* New York: The New Press, 2008.
Lee, Chana Kai. *For Freedom's Sake: The Life of Fannie Lou Hamer.* Urbana: University of Illinois Press, 1999.

HAMPTON–TUSKEGEE IDEA

Samuel C. Armstrong, who founded Hampton Institute (1868), believed that a vocational course of study would instill self-discipline, practical knowledge, and Christian character. He also saw industrial education and ordinary labor as the best vehicles for teaching former slaves to accept a subordinate place in post-emancipation economy and society. Thus he concurred with Virginia Conservatives who, besides ignoring racial terror, perpetrated laws to control blacks, including denial of suffrage and segregation. He anticipated correctly that his principles would be instilled by Hampton-trained educators such as Booker T. Washington, an honor graduate and founder of Tuskegee Institute; county training schools; and major northern philanthropies.

Efforts to institute the Hampton–Tuskegee idea generated strong opposition in schools and communities from W. E. B. Du Bois and advocates of classical learning. Both sides in the Washington–Du Bois debate closed ranks and criticized the other. Washington, in short, stressed uplift by training black hands; Du Bois by educating black minds.

[*See also* Education.]

Further Reading

Engs, Robert Francis. *Educating the Disfranchised and Disinherited: Samuel Chapman Armstrong and Hampton Institute, 1839–1893.* Knoxville: University of Tennessee Press, 1999.
Wukovits, John F. *Booker T, Washington and Education.* Detroit: Lucent Books, 2008.

HANCOCK, GORDON B.   EDUCATOR, MINISTER

Born: June 23, 1884, Ninety-Six, SC
Education: Benedict College, A.B., 1911, B.D., 1912; Colgate University, A.B., 1919, B.D., 1920; Harvard University, M.A., 1921
Died: July 24, 1970, Richmond, VA

"This world must be brotherized or it will be brutalized," Hancock, a Virginia Union University sociologist and Richmond pastor, told the 1939 World Baptist Alliance in Atlanta. Unless the Christian church renounced racism, it would "seal its own damnation."

He grappled with the color line. "The problem of race relations is crucial if American democracy is to survive," he taught. His course on "Race Relations," one of the first in a Negro college, studied racial and ethnic groups; their contact, conflict, cooperation, and commingling. In his Associated Negro Press column, carried by 114 newspapers, he urged black empowerment through education, jobholding, thrift, moral uplift, voting, and patronizing "race" enterprises. Invited to speak at white colleges, he invoked tolerance, fairness, and justice, once declaring: "Segregation means death to the Negro race. It is a form of elimination that must be terminated if the Negro is to survive."

Hancock worked for an integrated South and nation. For example, he co-organized the Durham Conference of southern black leaders (1942). Their "Durham manifesto" declared that "We are fundamentally opposed to the principle and practice of segregation in our American society." It challenged sympathetic whites to stand with them and helped catalyze post–World War II civil rights activism.

Further Reading

Egerton, John. *Speak Now Against the Day: The Generation before the Civil Rights Movement in the South.* New York: Alfred A. Knopf, 1994.
Robbins, Richard. *Sidelines Activist: Charles S. Johnson and the Struggle for Civil Rights.* Jackson: University Press of Mississippi, 1996.

HANDY, WILLIAM C. (W.C.)   MUSICIAN

Born: November 16, 1873, Florence, AL
Education: High school, Florence, AL, graduated 1893
Died: March 28, 1958, New York, NY

A son of ex-slaves and high school graduate, Handy began playing the guitar, organ, and trumpet in rural Alabama. He became a teacher and string quartet and band director and played the minstrel circuit, performing alongside blacks who sang "the weirdest music I'd ever heard." Called the blues, it expressed the realities of their lives. It also afforded him rich material for arrangements and compositions.

Handy would become "Father of the Blues," not because he was the creator but rather its great innovator. "Composer, orchestra leader, trumpeter, astute business entrepreneur, and articulate spokesman for his people–particularly in regard to music," he catapulted the blues into mainstream popular culture. With his first published song, "Mr. Crump," reissued as "The Memphis Blues," he won popularity; then came "St. Louis Blues," one of the most recorded songs of all time, earning him recognition with the best known composers. Moreover, his records on the Columbia label (1917) were among the earliest made by blacks, foreshadowing the blues–jazz craze of the 1920s and the rise of vocalists and instrumentalists such as Bessie Smith, Duke Ellington, and Louis Armstrong. NBC's all-Handy special (1940) was the first radio program to showcase the music of an African American composer.

Further Reading

Brooks, Tim. *Lost Sounds: Blacks and the Birth of the Recording Industry, 1890–1919*. Urbana: University of Illinois Press, 2004.

Robertson, David. *W. C. Handy: The Life and Times of the Man Who Made the Blues*. New York: Alfred A. Knopf, 2009.

HARLEM RENAISSANCE

During the 1920s, Harlem, New York saw a "dramatic upsurge of creativity in literature, music, and art within black America" (Rampersad, 1992, p. ix). It was attributable to World War I and the Great Migration, which landed 1.75 million southern and Caribbean blacks in northern cities between 1915 and 1930 alone.

Many blacks in the arts migrated to Harlem seeking opportunities. They were young, usually college-educated, and voiced the "New Negro." Their promoters included magazine editors Charles S. Johnson (*Opportunity*) and W. E. B. Du Bois (*Crisis*), and white patrons such as philanthropist Charlotte O. Mason and photographer-writer Carl Van Vechten, who provided financial and media support. Cultural artists expressed the race pride and dignity of ordinary and elite blacks alike. Band leader Fletcher Henderson and others did so through music. Harlem's nightlife high-lighted the chic Cotton Club, with black chorus girls and a mostly white clientele, as well as "rent parties" among migrants in the tenements.

A landmark of the renaissance was *The New Negro* (1925), edited by Alain Locke, "dean of the movement" and professor of philosophy at Howard University. In the anthology, he showcased emerging talents, including Jean Toomer and Zora Neale Hurston in fiction and Claude McKay and Langston Hughes in poetry. In short stories, novels, paint-ings, and poems, they celebrated black history and life, blues and jazz music, popular song and dance, and hope for black civil rights and self-determination.

[*See also* Literature; New Negro movement.]

Reference

Rampersad, Arnold. "Introduction." *The New Negro*. New York: Macmillan, 1992, p. ix.

Further Reading

Huggins, Nathan Irvin. *Harlem Renaissance*. New York: Oxford University Press, 2007.
Mitchell, Verner D., and Cynthia Davis. *Literary Sisters: Dorothy West and Her Circle: A Biography of the Harlem Renaissance*. New Brunswick, NJ: Rutgers University Press, 2012.

HARRIS, ABRAM L.   ECONOMIST

Born: January 17, 1899, Richmond, VA
Education: Virginia Union University, B.A., 1922; University of Pittsburgh, M.A., 1924; Columbia University, Ph.D., 1930
Died: November 16, 1963, Chicago, IL

Influenced by his professors at Virginia Union, Harris earned graduate degrees and became a distinguished economist. His research and advo-cacy helped define problems of race and class in labor relations and eco-nomic thought.

While teaching at Howard University, he embraced Marxist analysis. He and Sterling Spero did in *The Black Worker: The Negro and The Labor Movement* (1931). A seminal study of "the relation of the domi-nant section of the working class to the segregated, circumscribed, and restricted Negro minority" (Review of *The Black Worker*, 1932, p. 128), the book argued that an interracial working-class struggle would be needed to end racial segregation in unions and the workforce. Harris restated that argument to the NAACP's Amenia Conference (1933). In his 1935 report to the NAACP Board of Directors, never adopted, he urged a labor-organizing rather than legal strategy against Jim Crow. He co-created Howard's conference on blacks in the Depression (1933), resulting in its Social Science Division, the National Negro Congress, and his *The Negro as Capitalist: A Study of Banking and Business among American Negroes* (1936). Harris left for the University of Chicago (1945), its second black professor, where he achieved scholarly distinction in economics.

Reference

Review of *The Black Worker* in *Journal of the Royal Statistical Society*, Vol. 95, 1932, p. 128.

Further Reading

Holloway, Jonathan Scott. *Confronting the Veil: Abram L. Harris, Jr., E. Franklin Frazier, and Ralph Bunche, 1919–1941*. Chapel Hill: University of North Carolina Press, 2002.

Wilson, Francille Rusan. *The Segregated Scholars: Black Social Scientists and the Creation of Black Labor Studies, 1890–1950*. Charlottesville: University of Virginia Press, 2006.

HASTIE, WILLIAM H.   ATTORNEY, FEDERAL JUDGE

Born: November 17, 1904, Knoxville, TN
Education: Amherst College, B.A. valedictorian, 1925, Harvard Law School, LL.B., 1930, S.J.D., 1933
Died: April 14, 1976, Philadelphia, PA

Hastie "was considered one of the best legal minds in twentieth century jurisprudence," wrote his colleague Robert Weaver. He grew up in Jim Crow Washington, DC and taught at Howard Law School, where he helped mentor the greatest generation of civil rights lawyers. Pursuing "equal protection," he breached the color line as NAACP counsel, federal judge (1937–39, 1949–71), civilian aide to the secretary of war (1940–43), and governor of the Virgin Islands (1946–49).

Hastie's battle began years earlier. As leader of the "young Turks" in the Washington NAACP, he organized a "Jobs for Negroes" campaign and lobbied Federal departments to hire qualified blacks. Litigating NAACP cases, he argued *Hocutt v. Wilson* (1933), representing a black male applicant to the Pharmacy School at the University of North Carolina. He lost that case, but it was the NAACP's first challenge to segregated higher education and the "genesis" of *Brown v. Board of Education*. After he resigned from the War Department to protest racism, Hastie helped win Supreme Court victories in *Smith v. Allwright* (1944), eliminating the white primary election, and *Morgan v. Virginia* (1946), prohibiting segregation on interstate buses.

Further Reading

Rawn, James. *The Double V: How Wars, Protest, and Harry Truman Desegregated America's Military.* New York: Bloomsbury Press, 2013.
Ware, Gilbert. *William Hastie: Grace under Pressure.* New York: Oxford University Press, 1984.

HEIGHT, DOROTHY I.
WOMEN'S, CIVIL RIGHTS ACTIVIST

Born: March 24, 1912, Richmond, VA
Education: NYU, B.A., 1932, M.A., 1933
Died: April 20, 2010, Washington, DC

A "'godmother' of the American Civil Rights Movement," Height was president of the National Council of Negro Women (NCNW) from 1957 to 88. With headquarters in Washington, DC and more than four million members, it is one of the largest black organizations. She spearheaded efforts to foster civil and human rights; equality for women; and interracial, ethnic, and international cooperation.

Her leadership mirrored the twentieth century African American freedom struggle. Growing up and pursuing education during Jim Crow, she instilled strong values of racial pride and self-help, inspiring her activism for social justice. Height fought against race, class, and gender discrimination as a New York City caseworker, YWCA officer, and sorority leader. She not only marched in Times Square to protest southern lynching and disfranchisement, but also organized rallies on behalf of the women's and peace movements. Moreover, she had a voice in civil rights strategy, including Martin Luther King, Jr. and other leaders' tense sessions before the March on Washington (1963), urging them to bridge differences and create a united front. Height managed the formation of the Mary McLeod Bethune Memorial Museum and National Archives for Black Women's History (1970s) and initiated projects to fight illiteracy, poverty, and AIDS. She received the Presidential Medal of Freedom (1994) and Congressional Gold Medal (2004).

Further Reading

Height, Dorothy. *Open Wide the Freedom Gates: A Memoir*. New York: Public Affairs, 2003.
Springer, Kimberely, ed. *Still Lifting, Still Climbing: Contemporary African American Women's Activism*. New York: New York University Press, 1999.

HIGGINBOTHAM, A. LEON
ATTORNEY, FEDERAL JUDGE

Born: February 25, 1928, Trenton, NJ
Education: Antioch College, B.A. 1949, Yale Law School, LL.B., 1952
Died: December 14, 1998, Boston, MA

Author of award-winning books on race and the law, Higginbotham was one of the most important black attorneys and jurists of the twentieth century.

Pursuing equality, he continued the quest of William Hastie, Charles Houston, Thurgood Marshall, and "that small cadre of other lawyers associated with them, who laid the groundwork for success in the twentieth-century racial civil rights cases" (Jackson, 1998). A private and state attorney, Federal Trade commissioner, law professor, and federal judge (1964–93), writing more than 650 opinions, Higginbotham upheld "equal protection of the laws." Finding "cruel and unusual punishment," for example, he ordered Allegheny County, Pennsylvania (1990) to end crowding its prisoners.

After his federal retirement, he taught at Harvard's Kennedy School of Government and helped litigate suits for affirmative action and diversity, congressional redistricting and minority representation, and equity to dependent families and children. In addition, the NAACP Legal Defense and Educational Fund and the Lawyers' Committee for Civil Rights Under Law enlisted him to be an expert witness in litigation challenging black vote dilution, job discrimination, and school resegregation. An official observer of South Africa's historic presidential election (1994), he received the Presidential Medal of Freedom (1995) and NAACP Spingarn Award (1996).

Reference

Jackson, Derrick Z. "Higginbotham's History Lesson." *The Boston Globe*, December 20, 1998.

Further Reading

Birnbaum, Jonathan, and Clarence Taylor, eds. *Civil Rights since 1787: A Reader on the Black Struggle.* New York: New York University Press, 2000.
Higginbotham, A. Leon, Jr. *Shades of Freedom: Racial Politics and Presumptions of the American Legal Process.* New York: Oxford University Press, 1996.

HISTORICALLY BLACK COLLEGES
AND UNIVERSITIES (HBCUS)

Higher education for blacks evolved in the shadow of slavery. Cheyney (1837), Lincoln (1854) and Wilberforce (1856) paved the way. During and after Reconstruction, the federal government, major philanthropies, and blacks combined to found black institutions of higher learning. Virginia Union University started in a former slave jail, Atlanta University in a train car, and Spelman College in a church basement. Mary McLeod Bethune founded Bethune-Cookman College with $1.50 and dumped furniture. Today there are, in nineteen states, Washington, DC, and US Virgin Islands, 106 private and public HBCUs. Alumni include W. E. B. Du Bois, Martin Luther King, Jr., and Toni Morrison.

Racial integration will define their future. Constituting 3 percent of US colleges and universities, they yield 25 percent of bachelor's degrees earned by blacks. Enrollment increased by 45 percent between 1976 and 2011, from 223,000 to 324,000. They enroll 16.4 percent of 1.4 million black collegians today and are more diverse than white schools. At HBCUs 11 percent of college and 31 percent of graduate and professional students are white. At white-majority schools 6 percent of college and 4 percent of graduate and professional students are black. Kentucky State and Lincoln, Bluefield State and West Virginia State are now more than half white. Immigrants comprise 6 percent of HBCU students. Asian Americans, Latinos, and Native Americans comprise 2 percent of HBCU students.

[*See also* Education; Scholarship.]

Further Reading

Lovett, Bobby L. *America's Historically Black Colleges: A Narrative History, 1837–2009.* Macon, GA: Mercer University Press, 2011.
Newkirk, Vann R., ed. *New Life for Historically Black Colleges and Universities: A 21st Century Perspective.* Jefferson, NC: McFarland & Co., 2012.

HOPE, JOHN   EDUCATOR

Born: June 21, 1868, Augusta, GA
Education: Worcester Academy honors, 1890; Brown University honors, 1894
Died: February 20, 1936, Atlanta, GA

The first black president of Morehouse College for men, Hope immersed it in liberal arts despite philanthropic support for industrial arts. Cofounding the Commission on Interracial Cooperation (CIC, 1918), he founded the Atlanta University Center (1929) and became one of the most important black educators of the twentieth century.

Hope prioritized higher education. Deeming it essential to full freedom, he joined W. E. B. Du Bois in the Niagara Movement (1905), protesting disfranchisement and Jim Crow and advocating college training. Hope walked a tightrope. Publicly, in the NAACP and Commission on Interracial Cooperation (CIC), he fought against lynching and discrimination. But he opposed segregation by "moderating his 'militant' stance" to accommodate the "separate but equal" ideology of some philanthropists. He espoused interracial cooperation to equalize schools, employment, and housing, even as he advised teachers to pursue equal-salary lawsuits, which increased NAACP membership. By enabling black educators and their institutions to survive, Hope helped pave the way for the modern civil rights movement.

Further Reading

Avery, Vida A. *Philanthropy in Black Higher Education: A Fateful Hour Creating the Atlanta University System.* New York: Palgrave Macmillan, 2013.
Davis, Leroy. *A Clashing of the Soul: John Hope and the Dilemma of African American Leadership and Black Higher Education in the Early Twentieth Century.* Athens: University of Georgia Press, 1998.

HORNE, LENA M.
ACTRESS, SINGER, AND DANCER

Born: June 30, 1917, Brooklyn, NY
Education: Attended high school
Died: May 9, 2010, New York City

Touted for her beauty and talent, Horne performed on Broadway, in Hollywood and television films, and was a leading black performer.

She persevered. Raised by her paternal grandmother, a civil rights activist, she instilled values of freedom and race pride. Leaving school at sixteen because of financial hardship, Horne secured a job dancing and singing at Harlem's Cotton Club. Gifted with a "sultry voice," she soon starred "as a popular singer of the blues." She also linked art and politics by joining the struggle for civil rights. Her long-term contract with Metro-Goldwyn-Mayer (1942), the first between a black actor and major studio, stipulated that she would not perform in servile roles. Resisting racial stereotypes, she helped change blacks' roles. Publicly supporting antiracist campaigns of the NAACP and actor Paul Robeson, she entered a "controversial interracial marriage" in 1947 and was "blacklisted for several years" by movie studios. Still, she performed at nightclubs, recorded songs, and performed in musicals. A supporter of the March on Washington (1963), Horne received the NAACP Spingarn Award (1983) and Image Award (1984), Kennedy Center Award for Lifetime Achievement in Arts (1984), and Grammy Award for Lifetime Achievement (1989).

Further Reading

Gavin, James. *Stormy Weather: The Life of Lena Horne*. New York: Atria Books, 2009.

Klotman, Phyllis R. *African Americans in Cinema: The First Half Century*. Champaign, IL: University of Illinois Press, 2003.

HOUSTON, CHARLES H.
ATTORNEY AND NAACP COUNSEL

Born: September 3, 1895, Washington, DC
Education: Amherst College, B.A. Phi Beta Kappa, 1915; Harvard Law School (HLS), first black member of *Harvard Law Review*, LL.B. cum laude, 1922, D. Jur., 1923, University of Madrid, D.C.L., 1924
Died: April 22, 1950, Bethesda, MD

Raised in a middle-class family and studious, Houston faced isolation but not persecution at "white Amherst." As a World War I army enlistee and first lieutenant trained in a Jim Crow camp at Des Moines, Iowa, he and others endured racist bigotry. "'I felt damned glad I had not lost my life fighting for this country'" (Andrews, 2014, p. 95), he said. Honorably discharged in 1919, he was "an impatient and bitter young man."

Injustice compelled him to study and use law in the struggle for racial equality. During his Harvard studies, lawyering, and work as a dean and teacher at Howard Law School, he defined constitutional principles and strategies for justice. Appointed NAACP general counsel (1935), Houston helped build a foundation of the civil rights movement. Howard-trained lawyers ("social engineers") used his "due process" and "equal protection" arguments to win the *Brown* decision overruling school segregation. It was Houston who first breached segregated public education in *Murray v. Maryland* (1936), filmed the inequality of southern black schools, and sued for equal salaries for teachers. He paved the way in 1940s litigation for the right of suffrage, fair employment, and collective bargaining as well. He received the NAACP Spingarn Award (1950).

Reference

Andrews, Gordon. *Undoing Plessy: Charles Hamilton Houston, Race, Labor, and the Law, 1895–1950*. Newcastle, UK: Cambridge Scholars, 2014, p. 95.

Further Reading

McNeil, Genna Rae. *Groundwork: Charles Hamilton Houston and the Struggle for Civil Rights*. Philadelphia: University of Pennsylvania Press, 1983.
Rawn, James. *Root and Branch: Charles Hamilton Houston, Thurgood Marshall, and the Struggle to End Segregation*. New York: Bloomsbury Press, 2009.

HUGHES, LANGSTON   POET AND WRITER

Born: February 1, 1902, Joplin, MO
Education: Columbia University, 1921–22; Lincoln University (PA), B.A., 1929
Died: May 22, 1967, New York, NY

Called "the Negro Poet Laureate," Hughes emerged in the Harlem Renaissance and became one of the leading American writers. He wrote novels, short stories, children's stories, plays, magazine and newspaper series, nonfiction books, essays, and more. Generations of schoolchildren learned about his first poem, "The Negro Speaks of Rivers" (1921), published in *The Crisis*.

Hughes advocated black consciousness and pride, civil and human rights, and justice for all. "We younger Negro artists who create now intend to express our individual dark-skinned selves without fear or shame" (Lewis, 1997, p. 191), he stated in 1926. His play *Don't You Want to Be Free?* (1938) thrived in Harlem, Chicago, and Los Angeles black theaters, which he founded with support from the Federal Theatre Project. Moreover, he joined communist-led protests to free the "Scottsboro Boys," Alabama youths falsely accused of raping two white women, and to gain workers' right to organize. Using poetry, prose, and protest, whether on behalf the NAACP, Congress of Industrial Organizations, or the United Nations, he spoke out and acted for racial, ethnic, and economic equality; integration; and peace. He also recognized the risk of democratic dissent: "Don't say it– because you might be declared subversive– *but we want freedom*" (Hughes and De Santis, 2001, p. 198).

References

Hughes, Langston, and Christopher C. De Santis, eds. *Fight for Freedom and Other Writings on Civil Rights*. Columbia: University of Missouri Press, 2001, p. 198.
Lewis, David Levering. *When Harlem Was in Vogue*. New York: Penguin Books, 1997, p. 191.

Further Reading

Miller, R. Baxter, ed. *Langston Hughes*. Ipswich, MA: Salem Press, 2013.
Rampersad, Arnold. *The Life of Langston Hughes*. New York: Oxford University Press, 2002.

HUMPHREY–HAWKINS BILL (1976)

Enacted as the Full Employment and Balanced Growth Act, Humphrey–Hawkins resulted largely from lobbying by a coalition of black and multiethnic organizations, socialists, democratic leftists, labor unions, Cold War liberals, Senator Hubert Humphrey of Minnesota, and black Representative Augustus Hawkins of California.

In its original form, the bill provided that all able and working adults be guaranteed equal opportunities for useful paid work at fair wages. It declared that the federal government must "meet human and national needs," including day care, transportation, and housing subsidies. Also, reflecting the crucial need for jobs, it created a Job Guarantee Office to ensure "the right of all … to a job."

The act prioritized disadvantaged racial and ethnic minorities such as African American women and children; two-thirds of the latter lived in poverty. Crafted to implement the promise of the Great Society, it was the "most significant employment legislation to appear in the United States in thirty years" (Marable, 2007, p. 168). Even so, House and Senate conservatives strongly opposed it and President Carter "did not battle aggressively for" it. It passed, though in a watered down form, revealing the federal retreat from social programs.

[*See also* Family.]

Reference

Marable, Manning. *Race, Reform, and Rebellion: The Second Reconstruction and Beyond in Black America, 1945–2006.* Jackson: University Press of Mississippi, 2007, p. 168.

Further Reading

Chappell, Marisa. *The War on Welfare: Family, Poverty, and Politics in Modern America.* Philadelphia: University of Pennsylvania Press, 2010.
Mink, Gwendolyn, and Rickie Solinger, eds. *Welfare: A Documentary History of U.S. Policy and Politics.* New York: New York University Press, 2003.

IMMIGRATION

Black immigration is a rich source of US cultural pluralism; it evolved from racial slavery and discrimination.

Europeans imported more than 12 million African blacks to the Western Hemisphere as slaves ca. 1502–1888, with British North American colonies importing 6.45 percent of them. Congress made only whites eligible for citizenship in 1790 and, from 1865 to 1965, when it abolished "quotas based on national origin," denied alien status to Africans.

African, Caribbean, and South American immigrants arrived in large numbers post-1965. Seeking asylum and jobs, they helped increase the foreign-born black population sevenfold between 1960 and 1980. Foreign-born blacks increased from 125,000 (1980) to 2,815,000 (2005), most immigrating after 1990. One-third originated in Africa and two-thirds in the Caribbean and Latin America. Ten countries, notably Nigeria and Ethiopia, accounted for 70 percent of black African immigrants. They tended to settle in densely populated cities such as Washington, DC and New York City. A majority of Caribbean blacks and Latinos came from Jamaica, Haiti, Trinidad and Tobago, Guyana, and the Dominican Republic; two-thirds of their total number settled in the New York and Miami metropolitan areas. About a million black-immigrant Africans, plus 3 million West Indians and Latinos of African descent, live in the United States today.

[*See also* Afro-American studies.]

Further Reading

Kent, Mary Mederios. "Immigration and America's Black Population." *Population Bulletin*, 62 (December 2007): 3–16.

Shaw-Taylor, Yoku, and Steven A. Tuch, eds. *The Other African Americans: Contemporary African and Caribbean Immigrants in the United States.* Lanham, MD: Rowman & Littlefield, 2007.

INDENTURED SERVITUDE

A contract system, indentured servitude provided mainly white labor to European colonies. To repay their travel and subsistence costs, laborers assented to indentures or contracts as servants, usually seven years. White servitude evolved in the Western Hemisphere along with Indian and African slavery. It is estimated that between one-half and two-thirds of all white immigrants in British America (1630s–1770s) came via indenturing.

They also faced difficult conditions, one witness stating that they were "treated like slaves, with great cruelty." While it lessened as black bondage expanded widely, the servant system lingered to the 1840s or later.

[*See also* Slavery.]

Further Reading

Morgan, Edmund S. *American Slavery, American Freedom: The Ordeal of Colonial Virginia.* New York: W. W. Norton, 2003.

Morgan, Kenneth. *Slavery and Servitude in North America, 1607–1800.* Edinburgh: Edinburgh University Press, 2000.

INDIAN WARS

Between the rise of British and European colonization (1600s) and the end of the western frontier (1890s), colonial, state, and federal governments conducted wars against native peoples of many tribal nations. In the main, along with countless casualties on both sides, those conflicts led to Indians' defeat and loss of homelands and forced their removal to reservations.

As colonies and states determined to open and expand territories for white settlement, Indians resisted. Powhatan tribes did so at Jamestown, Virginia in 1622, fueling the intermittent battles that reduced Virginia's Indian population to fewer than 1,000 by 1680.

Blacks and Indians struggled as enemies and allies. Slave and free black militiamen fought beside whites in King William's War (1689–97) and in the French and Indian War (1754–63). But a black-Indian alliance sustained the First (1817–18), Second (1835–42), and Third (1855–58) Seminole Wars. Runaway slaves and rebel Creek (Seminole) Indians countered the federal invasion of Florida, but they finally lost. In the Civil War, Seminoles backed the Union; Cherokees helped the Confederacy. About fifty "Seminole Indian Scouts," removed from Florida in 1858, became Buffalo Soldiers in the postwar West. When the Colorado Utes virtually wiped out the US cavalry post in 1879, black and Indian soldiers rescued the survivors.

[*See also* Military.]

Further Reading

Leonard, Elizabeth D. *Men of Color to Arms!: Black Soldiers, Indian Wars, and the Quest for Equality.* New York: W. W. Norton, 2010.

Schubert, Frank N., ed. *Voices of the Buffalo Soldier: Records, Reports, and Recollections of Military Life and Service in the West.* Albuquerque: University of New Mexico Press, 2003.

INSTITUTE OF THE BLACK WORLD (IBW)

After King's assassination, black intellectuals formed IBW in Atlanta, Georgia. An independent institute promoting research, analysis, and activism, it grew from conversations on Black Studies between Vincent Harding, chair of History and Sociology at Spelman College, and Stephen Henderson, chair of English at Morehouse College.

IBW was active as well as influential circa 1969–80. Its staff consisted of Harding, Henderson, an anthropologist, a musicologist, a political scientist, and a sociologist, advocates of Black Power. They worked to integrate the black experience in public school, college, and university curricula and published major studies such as *IBW and Education for Liberation* (1973).

[*See also* Afro-American Studies.]

Further Reading

Hall, Perry A. *In the Vineyard: Working in African American Studies.* Knoxville: University of Tennessee Press, 1999.

White, Derrick E. *The Challenge of Blackness: The Institute of the Black World and Political Activism in the 1970s.* Gainesville: University Press of Florida, 2011.

INTERRACIAL RELATIONS

Race relations have been central in Americans' pursuit of democracy and equality over time.

Rooted in post-slavery social reform, organized efforts to foster racial justice emerged during the twentieth century. Using litigation and protest, the NAACP challenged the Jim Crow system; the National Urban League battled economic injustice. The Anti-Defamation League of B'nai B'rith fought anti-Semitism and racism while forging a Jewish–black alliance; fostering peace, the American Friends Service Committee created alternatives to military service for conscientious objectors. Fostering dialogue, the American Council on Race Relations funded "race relations committees," "human relations councils," and "civic unity councils," even as the American Civil Liberties Union furnished legal help regardless of color. The southern Commission on Interracial Cooperation promoted white–black dialogue; reorganized as the Southern Regional Council, it also espoused desegregation (1951). However, from its founding (1938), the Southern Conference for Human Welfare renounced segregation; its successor, the Southern Conference Educational Fund, partnered in nonviolent demonstrations against segregated schools, public accommodations, and employment. Supported by the Leadership Conference on Civil Rights, such antiracist dissent sustained the national interracial coalition that helped win passage of post-1954 federal civil rights laws. Desegregation and affirmative action, for example, have seen both progress and polarization, including much violence, in racial-ethnic interactions since the 1960s. Accordingly, the Southern Poverty Law Center (1971) initiated projects to promote tolerance and monitor "hate groups" such as the Ku Klux Klan, which attacked Asians as well as blacks. Moreover, the President's Initiative on Race (1997) held town hall forums to advocate racial understanding.

[*See also* Immigration; Labels, race; Minorities, racial and ethnic.]

Further Reading

Pathways to One America in the 21st Century: Promising Practices for Racial Reconciliation. Washington, DC: The President's Initiative on Race, 1999.
Takaki, Ronald. *Iron Cages: Race and Culture in 19th-Century America.* New York: Oxford University Press, 2000.

JACKSON, JESSE L.
CIVIL RIGHTS AND POLITICAL LEADER

Born: October 8, 1941, Greenville, SC
Education: NC A & T College, B.A., 1964; Chicago Theological Seminary, 1965–66

Circa the 1980s–90s blacks demanded Democratic Party reforms, including racially diverse primary candidates, campaign staffs, convention delegates, and a transparent presidential nomination. A little known candidate for president had to bypass party operatives and win enough primaries to be the nominee. Jackson attempted that in 1984 and 1988, pursuing "equal opportunity for political office."

A leader in the civil rights movement and a charismatic figure, he remains both respected and reviled. Many centrist Democrats, seeking suburban and blue-collar white votes, shunned the "liberal" label. Jackson embraced it and its vision of democracy. His campaigns prioritized the plight of ordinary Americans, notably the poor. Keynoting the Democratic National Convention (1988), Jackson rebutted "all these experts on subculture, underclass, I got my life degree in subculture. Looked down on. Rejected. Low expectations. Told you can't make it. I was born in the slum, but the slum was not born in me." Invoking human dignity and equality, he appealed to a broad constituency and recruited millions of new voters. Racial and ethnic minorities, immigrants, women, gays, and workers were active in his National Rainbow Coalition (1986). He called for education, affirmative action, justice for drug offenders, and statehood for Washington, DC, inclusive if not election-winning issues.

Further Reading

Frady, Marshall. *Jesse: The Life and Pilgrimage of Jesse Jackson.* New York: Simon & Schuster, 2006.
Persons, Georgia A., ed. *Contours of African American Politics.* New Brunswick, NJ: Transaction, 2012.

JACKSON, LUTHER P.   HISTORIAN AND ACTIVIST

Born: July 11, 1892, Lexington, KY
Education: Fisk University, B.A., 1914, M.A., 1916; Columbia University, M.A., 1922; University of Chicago, Ph.D., 1937
Died: April 20, 1950, Petersburg, VA

A Virginia State College professor, Jackson led freedom struggles in the segregated South.

He promoted learning and teaching Negro history as well as political participation. His research pursued slaves and free blacks' religious, social, and economic life and post-slavery progress, resulting in seminal books. He visited schools, churches, and civic groups to promote citizenship education, especially the right to vote. In his Norfolk *Journal and Guide* weekly column, he called on blacks to resist Jim Crow "by voting, by organizing political parties, by maintaining pressure groups … by the lobby, and by such common everyday devices as the letter, the telegram, or the personal interview with office holders."

Partnering with the Virginia NAACP and State Teachers Association, he recruited and remade the Petersburg League of Negro Voters as the statewide Virginia Voters League. During World War II he crusaded for the "double b": "By the bullet our soldiers and civilians may help to win the present war against fascism, but a permanent democracy can only be achieved by the ballot" (Gavins, 1993, p. 111). Jackson helped organize the Durham, North Carolina conference of southern black leaders (1942) whose statement "fundamentally opposed" segregation. He also joined postwar campaigns to abolish the poll tax.

[*See also* Scholarship.]

Reference

Gavins, Raymond. *The Perils and Prospects of Southern Black Leadership: Gordon Blaine Hancock, 1884–1970*. Durham, NC: Duke University Press, 1993, p. 111.

Further Reading

Dennis, Michael. *Luther P. Jackson and a Life for Civil Rights*. Gainesville: University Press of Florida, 2004.

Smith, J. Douglass. *Managing White Supremacy: Race, Politics, and Citizenship in Jim Crow Virginia*. Chapel Hill: University of North Carolina Press, 2003.

JACKSON, MAHALIA   GOSPEL SINGER

Born: October 6, 1911, New Orleans, LA
Education: McDonough School No. 24, grade 8; Scott Institute of Beauty Culture, Chicago, 1927
Died: January 27, 1972, Chicago, IL

One observer called Jackson "the greatest gospel singer ever to live," with the "stage presence and spiritual intensity" of a blues singer.

Growing up poor, migrating to Chicago, and singing in Baptist church choirs shaped Jackson's path to fame. Her discography includes thirty albums, some still best-sellers, but many of her early records are forgotten. The first was "God's Gonna Separate the Wheat from the Tares" (1937). After recording "Move on Up a Little Higher" (1948), "the best-selling gospel record of all time," she became an international diva with a "cult following." Some reviewers said that she reminded audiences of the great blueswoman Bessie Smith. "I Can Put My Trust in Jesus" (1952) earned her a French Academy Award for artistic achievement and a sold-out European tour. She hosted her own CBS-TV show (1954–55), which enjoyed a large crossover audience; recorded the hit single "Rusty Old Halo" (1954); and appeared on the Dinah Shore and Ed Sullivan TV shows. She played the role of the funeral soloist in the noted film *Imitation of Life* (1959) and sang for both President John F. Kennedy's inauguration and Martin Luther King, Jr.'s funeral. Many music critics applauded her 1971 farewell concert in Germany as a triumph.

[*See also* Music.]

Further Reading

Darden, Robert. *People Get Ready!: A New History of Black Gospel Music.* New York: Continuum, 2004.
Schwerin, Jules Victor. *Got to Tell It: Mahalia Jackson, Queen of Gospel.* New York: Oxford University Press, 1992.

JACKSON, MICHAEL J.   POP SINGER

Born: August 29, 1958, Gary, IN
Education: Gary public schools
Died: June 25, 2009, Los Angeles, CA

Jackson was one of nine children in a working-class and musically talented Gary, Indiana family. The youngest of five boys, he became lead singer of the Jackson 5, who signed with Motown Records of Detroit in 1969. They had four hit singles in 1970 and Michael began his solo career in 1971. Three more of the brothers left Motown to become the Jacksons in 1975.

Michael emerged as America's leading pop music figure in the 1980s. His best songs included "Got to Be There" (1971), "Rockin' Robin"

(1972), and "Ben" (1972), theme song of a noted movie about a boy and his pet rat. Songs in another film, *The Wiz* (1978), the African American version of *The Wizard of Oz*, were sophisticated and versatile. "Off the Wall" (1979) made him an international cross-over icon. As "Thriller" (1982) topped the charts, he earned American Music awards and was the black trailblazer on music-television. Critics acclaimed him the "King of Pop." His philanthropy supported many causes, notably disadvantaged children. He also faced business and personal crises, such as prosecution for and acquittal of child sexual abuse in 2005. Michael died unexpectedly on the verge of a planned comeback tour. He received eighteen Grammy Awards.

[*See also* Music.]

Further Reading

Jackson, Michael. *Moonwalk*. New York: Harmony Books, 2009.
Vogel, Joseph. *Man in the Music: The Creative Life and Work of Michael Jackson*. New York: Sterling, 2011.

JACOBS, HARRIET A.   SLAVE NARRATOR

Born: ca. 1813, Edenton, NC
Education: Taught as a slave
Died: March 7, 1897

Jacobs's Edenton, North Carolina mistress taught her to read and write. Her master's sexual harassment later forced her to escape and write *Incidents in Life of a Slave Girl: Written by Herself* (1861), the first published narrative of a black bondwoman.

Using pseudonyms, Jacobs related a "harrowing and sensational story," which many scholars assumed a white person had written. But historian Jean Yellin confirmed her authorship in 1987. Jacobs aimed "to arouse the women of the North to a realizing sense of the condition of the two millions of women at the South, still in bondage, suffering what I suffered, and most of them far worse" (*Incidents in the Life of a Slave Girl*, 1987, p. 1).

Thus Linda resisted the advances of her master, Dr. Flint. Her grandmother Martha, a freedwoman and homeowner, provided refuge, as did Sawyer, a white neighbor, who fathered Linda's two children. Hoping that her absence ultimately would force Flint to sell them to their father, she hid in the crawl space of her grandmother's attic for seven years.

In 1842, aided by the antislavery underground, she escaped to Boston. Antislavery women furnished material and moral support and helped purchase the children's freedom. Linda's female employer paid for and freed her in 1853.

Reference

Incidents in the Life of a Slave Girl: Written by Herself, ed. by Jean Fagan Yellin. Cambridge, MA: Harvard University Press, 1987, p. 1.

Further Reading

McKay, Nellie Y., and Frances Smith Foster, eds., *Incidents in the Life of a Slave Girl: Contexts, Criticisms.* New York: W. W. Norton, 2001.
Yellin, Jean Fagan. *Harriet Jacobs: A Life.* New York: Basic Civitas Books, 2004.

JEMISON, MAE C.   ASTRONAUT

Born: October 17, 1956, Decatur, AL
Education: Stanford University, B.S., 1977; Cornell University, M.D., 1981

Jemison's parents instilled their three children with values of self-esteem, achievement, and service, which she exemplifies.

Hers is an exemplary career. Entering Stanford at sixteen, she had a double major (Chemical Engineering, African & Afro-American Studies) and participated in modern black dance. Earning an M.D., she joined the Peace Corps in 1983 and became a medical officer, fighting disease and poverty in West Africa to 1985. She continued similar work in under-served communities of Los Angeles until joining the National Aeronautics and Space Administration (NASA). A mission specialist 1987–93, she did research in material and life sciences, including bone cell research. When the shuttle *Endeavor* lifted off in 1992, observers heralded her as "the first woman of color to go into space."

Since NASA she has embraced advocacy, mentoring, and teaching. She founded both the Jemison Group (1993) to promote the advancement of science and technology and the Jemison Institute for Advancing Technology in Developing Countries (1995). She is also founder and chair of The Earth We Share (1994), a four-week summer project for teens. In its science-based courses, they seek to develop critical thinking and problem solving skills. Jemison is an inductee of the National Women's Hall of Fame (2003)

Further Reading

Gubert, Betty Kaplan et al. *Distinguished African Americans in Aviation and Space Science.* Westport, CT: Oryx Press, 2002.
Jemison, Mae C. *Find Where the Wind Goes: Moments from My Life.* New York: Scholastic, 2001.

JOBS CAMPAIGNS

Also known as "Don't Buy Where You Can't Work," jobs campaigns drew on calls for the "Double-Duty-Dollar" (1925) and to "Spend Your Money Where You Can Work." Black self-support would build independence and press white employers for fair hiring. Thus blacks initiated boycotts and pickets against businesses or industries refusing to hire them.

Job demands heightened with blacks' urban migrations. Churches, schools, newspapers, and social and civic organizations endorsed and joined in nonviolent direct action to leverage black employment. Between 1929 and 1941, thirty-six cities, eleven of them southern, witnessed such protests. These foreshadowed the postwar civil rights movement.

[*See also* Segregation.]

Further Reading

Greenberg, Cheryl Lynn. *To Ask for an Equal Chance: African Americans in the Great Depression.* Lanham, MD: Rowman & Littlefield, 2009.
Ezra, Michael, ed. *The Economic Civil Rights Movement: African Americans and the Struggle for Economic Power.* New York: Routledge, 2013.

JOHN BROWN'S RAID

John Brown (1800–59) is both martyr and murderer in American memory. A radical abolitionist, he harbored runaway slaves and formed a biracial group to assist them. In 1856 he spearheaded a massacre of five pro-slavery settlers in Pottawatomie, Kansas. He also convinced the Secret Six (wealthy northern abolitionists) to support his plan for black freedom.

Brown planned to seize the federal armory at Harpers Ferry, Virginia and incite a slave insurrection. He recruited twenty-two men, seventeen whites (among them his four sons) and five blacks, including North Carolinian and former Oberlin College student John A. Copeland. The group obtained and stockpiled steel pikes for slaves' weapons. They raided the armory in October 1859, but US army troops defeated them.

Ten of the men died; seven escaped. Brown, Copeland, and three others were captured, tried, and eventually hanged. The event fueled slaveholders' fears, southern secession, and the Civil War.

[*See also* Antislavery movement.]

Further Reading

McGinty, Brian. *John Brown's Trial*. Cambridge, MA: Harvard University Press, 2009.
Quarles, Benjamin. *Allies for Freedom & Blacks on John Brown*. Cambridge, MA: Da Capo, 2001.

JOHN HENRYISM

An eight-foot bronze statue of John Henry stands in the park above Big Bend Tunnel near Tulka, West Virginia. Ex-slave railroad workers, including Henry, built Big Bend ca. 1870s. According to a legend, he engaged in a rock-drilling competition against the tunnel company's steam drill. "He won, but died of exhaustion, his life cut short by his own superhuman effort" (http://sandbox.npr.org/programs/morning/features/patc/johnhenry/index.html). John Henryism, a term coined by epidemiologist Sherman A. James, negatively affects African Americans' health. Their heroic efforts to cope with stressors of racial prejudice and discrimination contribute to high death rates from hypertension and cardiovascular disease, especially for African American men.

[*See also* Medicine.]

Further Reading

James, Sherman A. "John Henryism and the Health of African-Americans." *Culture, Medicine and Psychiatry*, 18 (June 1994): 163–82.
Nelson, Scott Reynolds. *Steel Drivin' Man: John Henry, the Untold Story of an American Legend*. New York: Oxford University Press, 2006.

JOHNSON, JOHN A. (JACK)　　　PRO BOXER

Born: March 31, 1878, Galveston, TX
Education: Galveston public schools, grade 5
Died: June 10, 1946, Raleigh, NC

Up from poverty, at 6' 1" and 195 pounds, Johnson became the most powerful boxer in the world.

He became the first black heavyweight champion. In 1903 he boasted fifty-four wins and two losses, but his status was unofficial and white heavyweights would not box him. He won the official title in Sydney, Australia (1908) by a fourteenth round knockout of his white opponent. His skill and power in the ring made him a black folk hero. Courageously, he defied Jim Crow, among other transgressions, by dating and marrying white women.

However, the color line derailed his fighting career. For example, he co-starred in "the fight of the century" at Reno (1910). Jim Jeffries, touted as "the Great White Hope," came out of retirement to stop him. But he defeated Jeffries with a left hook "full on the face" and ignited many racist attacks on blacks. In 1913 Johnson was convicted for violating the Mann Act (1910), which prohibited transporting women across state lines for "immoral purposes." He fled to France; performed in vaudeville shows; and lost his title in Havana, Cuba (1915). He went to federal prison (1920), after which he did boxing exhibitions, wrote his memoir, and faded into history.

Further Reading

Hietala, Thomas R. *The Fight of the Century: Jack Johnson, Joe Louis, and the Struggle for Racial Equality.* Armonk, NY: M. E. Sharpe, 2002.
Ward, Geoffrey C. *Unforgivable Blackness: The Rise and Fall of Jack Johnson.* New York: Alfred A. Knopf, 2004.

JOHNSON, JOHN H.   ENTREPRENEUR

Born: January 19, 1918, Arkansas City, AR
Education: Du Sable High School, graduated 1936; University of Chicago part-time, 1936–39
Died: August 8, 2005, Evanston, IL

Johnson came of age in Jim Crow Arkansas and rose to be wealthy and internationally influential.

He built a media empire. While attending college in Chicago and editing *The Guardian*, Supreme Life Company's organ, he started *Negro Digest.* "Within eight months, we were selling 50,000 copies a month nationally," he recalled. "We never looked back." Circulation soared to 100,000 by late 1943, thus underwriting *Ebony* (1945), modeled after *Life* magazine and courting the black middle class. He also founded Johnson Publishing Company (1949), which promoted blacks' aspirations for an integrated society.

"The first black listed on the *Forbes* 400," Johnson became eminent in publishing, beauty products, and philanthropy. In 1951 he launched *Jet*, intended for a mass readership, and a book publishing division. *Jet's* September 1955 feature story included a photo of the "horribly mangled body" of Emmett Till, age fourteen, a black Chicagoan killed in Mississippi allegedly for flirting with a white woman. The issue sold out and helped "to traumatize Black America and prepare the way for the Freedom Movement" (www.slideshare.net/kirkcody/emmett-till-case-powerpoint-8118774), which Johnson reporters followed. Moreover, Johnson's cosmetics and *Ebony Fashion Fair* influenced African American identity, even as his generous donations buoyed philanthropic support for corporate–community partnerships and organizations promoting affirmative action.

Further Reading

Johnson, John H., with Lerone Bennett, Jr. *Succeeding Against the Odds.* New York: Warner Books, 1989.

Weems, Robert E. *Business in Black and White: American Presidents & Black Entrepreneurs in the Twentieth Century.* New York: New York University Press, 2009.

JOHNSON, SARGENT C.   SCULPTOR

Born: October 7, 1887, Boston, MA
Education: West Art School, San Francisco, 1915; California School of Arts, 1919–23; California School of Fine Arts, 1940–42
Died: October 10, 1967, San Francisco, CA

Sculptor, ceramist, and printmaker, Johnson produced African American figures of telling beauty and reserve. One of the most inventive artists of the Harlem Renaissance era, he sculpted human figures and still objects in plaster, bronze, and earthenware. "It is the pure American Negro I am concerned with, aiming to show the natural beauty and dignity in that characteristic lip and that characteristic hair, bearing and manner," he said, "and I wish to show that beauty not so much to the white man as to the Negro himself" (Wintz and Glasrud, 2012, p. 106).

His busts, like "*Negro* Woman" (1933), and public creations have lasted. For the Federal Arts Project (1930s) in the San Francisco Bay Area, he built a large redwood organ screen in the chapel of California School for the Blind. He created entrance reliefs and mosaic murals for the walking deck to the Maritime Museum in Aquatic Park and two 8-foot Inca Indians, seated on llamas, depict native heritage. Johnson's cast stone frieze decorates the athletic field of the George Washington Carver High School. In 1947 he started constructing massive panels of porcelain on steel. Over the next two decades he received commissions for them, including a 78-by-39 feet panel for a Reno casino.

Reference

Wintz, Cary D., and Bruce A. Glasrud. *The Harlem Renaissance in the American West: The New Negro's Western Experience.* New York: Routledge, 2012, p. 106.

Further Reading

Jordan, Denise. *Harlem Renaissance Artists.* Chicago: Heinemann Library, 2003.
LaFalle-Collins, Lizetta, and Judith Wilson. *Sargent Johnson: African-American Modernist.* San Francisco: San Francisco Museum of Modern Art, 1998.

JORDAN, BARBARA C.   U.S. CONGRESSWOMAN

Born: July 9, 1936, Houston, TX
Education: Texas Southern University, B.A. magna cum laude, 1956; Boston University, J.D., 1959
Died: January 17, 1996, Austin, TX

Embracing strong values on education and service, Jordan challenged race, class, and gender injustice in Texas. The first black person elected to the state Senate since Reconstruction, she rose to national political distinction. Her career reflected black Democrats' growing power after the reapportionment of electoral districts under the Civil Rights Act of 1964. Elected in a majority black and Latino district, she not only championed workers' rights but also pushed for the Texas Fair Employment Practices Commission and a minimum wage bill.

The pioneer black congresswoman from the South, Jordan won election to the US House of Representatives in 1972. She gained respect and influence as a voice of inclusion, civil rights, and equal justice to all. "I am neither a black politician nor a female politician, just a politician," Jordan declared once (*Texas Monthly*, March, 1996). The press particularly noted her contributions on the Judiciary Committee, where, by using the Voting Rights Act of 1965, she fought successfully to sustain her black and Latino coalition. Democratic colleagues touted Jordan for her vote and inspired words at the impeachment hearings for President

Richard M. Nixon (1974). Voting aye to impeach, she stated: "My faith in the Constitution is whole, it is complete, it is total" (*The New York Times*, January 18, 1996).

Further Reading

Rogers, Mary Beth. *Barbara Jordan: American Hero*. New York: Bantam Books, 1998.
Sherman, Max, ed. *Barbara Jordan: Speaking the Truth with Eloquent Thunder*. Austin: University of Texas Press, 2007.

JORDAN, MICHAEL J.
PRO BASKETBALL PLAYER

Born: February 17, 1963, Brooklyn, NY
Education: Laney High School, Wilmington, NC, 1981; University of North Carolina–Chapel Hill, athletic scholarship, 1981–84

The National Basketball Association (NBA) represents the model of its game; it recruits basketball players from all over the world. Basketball is played professionally in more than twenty countries. Consisting of twenty-nine US and Canadian teams, the NBA is basketball's premier professional league.

Many analysts rank Jordan, who is destined for the NBA Hall of Fame, as the best player in league history. Epitome of athleticism and skill on the court, a peerless competitor and winner, he remains a global sports and cultural icon. To his fans, he was "Superman," "Last Shot," or "Air Jordan." He earned $30.1 million from commercial endorsements in 1994 alone. In the wake of his father's death that year, he left the Chicago Bulls to play baseball for the Chicago White Sox's farm team. But he rejoined the Bulls (1995), which led to their sixth NBA Championship (1998) and his fifth season and sixth final Most Valuable Player awards.

Jordan became co-owner of the Washington Wizards in 2000. Also a part-time player, he donated his salary to victims of the September 11, 2001 attacks on the World Trade Center and Pentagon. Yet the Wizards did not make the playoffs, fueling criticism of him; he soon resigned.

Further Reading

Andrews, David L., ed. *Michael Jordan, Inc.: Corporate Sport, Media Culture, and Late Modern America*. Albany: State University of New York Press, 2001.
Lazenby, Roland. *Michael Jordan: The Life*. New York: Little, Brown, 2014.

JOURNALISM

More than 133 years elapsed between New York–based *Freedom's Journal* (1827) and the freedom struggles of the 1960s. Indeed, from slavery to desegregation, Afro-American journalists were drum majors for justice. The civil rights movement gained publicity in the national press, but this gain had costs. Large black newspapers (such as *Chicago Defender*, New York *Amsterdam News*, Baltimore *Afro-American*, and *Pittsburgh Courier*) saw a serious decline in circulation. Their news agency, the Associated Negro Press, declined too. Black journalism survived, if mostly through religious, fraternal, academic, and local venues. The owners not only revitalized the National Newspaper Publishers Association (1940) but also launched the National Association of Black Journalists in 1975.

White magazines, newspapers, radio and television networks, in the meantime, gradually hired black journalists. One of the older reporters to accompany *Life* photojournalist Gordon Parks in breaking barriers was Malvin R. Goode (1908–95). Since 1948 he had been with the *Pittsburgh Courier* and co-anchor at a black radio station. Joining ABC in 1962, he became the first African American television network reporter and an inductee to the National Association of Radio and TV News Directors. Parks and Goode reported on the southern freedom movement.

As it fueled demands for racial integration in newsrooms, some younger blacks achieved distinction. Among them was Charlayne Hunter-Gault (b. 1942), a South Carolinian. When she and Hamilton E. Holmes (1942–95) breached the University of Georgia's color line in 1961, the National Guard had to quell a race riot. After graduate study at Washington University, Hunter-Gault joined the staff of *Trans-Action* and was an evening anchor at WRC-TV in Washington, DC. She covered the metro news for the *New York Times* from 1968 and the *MacNeil/ Lehrer Report* from 1978. She went to South Africa as chief of National Public Radio's African Bureau in 1997.

Black reporters struggled with a sense of racial isolation. Pamela Newkirk held positions at four news organizations in a single decade and co-won a Pulitzer Prize for spot reports at New York *Newsday*. Still, she quit in 1993 because "I felt constricted by the narrow scope … of reporting on African Americans. I found that our sensibilities, attitudes and experiences were often viewed with skepticism or alarm, and were left out." It is estimated that 550 "journalists of color" were recruited by major news organizations between 1994 and 2000; however, 400 of them resigned. Thus the Freedom Forum, which sponsors media centers at Columbia and Vanderbilt universities, "pledged $5 million toward increasing newsroom diversity" (*The Washington Post*, September 24, 2000).

[*See also* Film; Television.]

Further Reading

Broussard, Jinx C. *Giving Voice to the Voiceless: Four Pioneering Black Women Journalists.* New York: Routledge, 2004.

Mellinger, Gwyneth. *Chasing Newsroom Diversity: From Jim Crow to Affirmative Action.* Urbana: University of Illinois Press, 2013.

Newkirk, Pamela. *Within the Veil: Black Journalists, White Media.* New York: New York University Press, 2000.

JOURNEY OF RECONCILIATION (1947)

After the Supreme Court outlawed segregation on interstate buses in *Morgan v. Virginia* (1946), the Congress of Racial Equality (CORE) organized a bus ride from Washington, DC into the Upper South to test compliance. The riders consisted of sixteen men (eight white and eight black), including co-organizer Bayard Rustin. Twelve were pacifists. All occupied front seats and rode in biracial pairs. Churches, colleges, and NAACP chapters held rallies along the route.

CORE challenged southern Jim Crow. Clearly, states and localities did not comply with the *Morgan* decision. Riders incurred twelve arrests for violating separate seat laws. Four were arrested in Chapel Hill, North Carolina, where one suffered a serious beating and two received death threats. A local white minister arranged their bail and safe passage to Greensboro. A court later convicted them and they served a month on the state chain gang. CORE's journey prefigured the Freedom Rides of 1961.

[*See also* Freedom Rides.]

Further Reading

Catsam, Derek Charles. *Freedom's Main Line: The Journey of Reconciliation and the Freedom Rides.* Lexington: University Press of Kentucky, 2009.

Podair, Jerald. *Bayard Rustin: American Dreamer.* Lanham, MD: Rowman & Littlefield, 2009.

JUST, ERNEST E.   BIOLOGIST AND EDUCATOR

Born: August 14, 1883, Charleston, SC
Education: Dartmouth College, B.S. magna cum laude, 1907, University of Chicago, Ph.D. magna cum laude, 1916
Died: October 27, 1941, Washington, DC

Just rose from humble beginnings in the segregated South to become an internationally recognized and respected scientist.

He was a wunderkind. Finishing Dartmouth College with high honors, he taught at Howard University for more than thirty years. In 1911 he helped Howard men to organize Omega Psi Phi, a black fraternity. Earning his doctorate, he pursued research on the fertilization in marine animal eggs. His book, *The Biology of the Cell Surface* (1939), largely established experimental embryology.

Just clearly challenged the limits of Jim Crow. Though he declared that blacks should study and excel in science for its discipline and objectivity, he understood that they would do so in a racist society. Thus he found opportunities to teach and write in Europe where white racism seemed less pervasive. Still, Howard's deans chafed at his frequent leaves of absence between 1929 and 1940. Philanthropic foundations eagerly supported his European work and authorities in Nazi-occupied France once detained him. He returned home, resumed teaching, and had begun to mend fences at Howard before his illness and untimely death. One colleague said that "an element of tragedy ran through all Just's scientific career due to the limitations imposed by being a Negro in America" (Manning, 1983, p. 329).

Reference

Manning, Kenneth R. *Black Apollo of Science: The Life of Ernest Everett Just.* New York: Oxford University Press, 1983, p. 329.

Further Reading

Byrnes, W. Malcolm, and William R. Eckberg. "Ernest Everett Just (1883–1941)-An Early Ecological Developmental Biologist." *Developmental Biology,* 296 (August 2006): 1–11.

Manning, Kenneth P. *Black Apollo of Science: The Life of Ernest Everett Just.* New York: Oxford University Press, 1984.

JUSTICE, US DEPARTMENT OF

Evolving from the Judiciary Act of 1789, which designated the attorney general (AG) as legal advisor to Congress and the president, the Department of Justice (DOJ) crystallized in 1870. It included a solicitor general (SG) to represent the government before the Supreme Court, began enforcing civil liberties and rights, interstate commerce, and immigration statutes and, by 1872, administering federal prisons. It expanded in the twentieth century, adding a deputy and an associate AG; eight divisions, for example the Civil Rights Division (CRD); seven police affiliates, among them the Federal Bureau of Investigation (FBI); thirty-five offices such as the Office of Tribal Justice; and five special agencies such as the National Drug Intelligence Center. Today DOJ is one of the largest departments, employing more than 30,000 people.

Civil and human rights advocates look to CRD; it enforces laws banning discrimination based on race, ethnicity, gender, religion, language, disability, and sexual orientation. Formerly the Civil Liberties Unit (1939) and Civil Rights Section (1941), it became CRD by the Civil Rights Act of 1957, which added an assistant AG and advisory US Commission on Civil Rights. The black freedom movement and southern white backlash tested the Division, as did enforcement of the Civil and Voting Rights Acts of 1960, 1964, and 1965. The crucial 1964 act not only barred unequal voter registration criteria, segregated schools and accommodations, and employment bias, but also instituted the Community Relations Service (CRS) to assist state, local, and school officials in resolving disputes. Racial riots, fueled by tensions over desegregation or injustices such as police brutality, broke out in 314 cities ca. 1963–67. By request, CRS sends conciliators into communities. Moreover, CRD implements the Fair Housing Act (1968), Equal Credit Opportunity Act (1974), Americans with Disabilities Act (1990), and Voting Rights Act (renewed a fourth time in 2006). It protects absentee, aged, and disabled voters; "institutionalized persons"; equal access to public clinics; victims of police misconduct; and immigrants.

CRS helps citizens negotiate their differences and develop mechanisms to defuse racial-ethnic tensions, as well as promote tolerance, diversity, and inclusion. In 2007, after a cross burned on the front lawn of a Cortlandt, New York black family, creating fear, CRS facilitated dialogue between law enforcement, schools, city officials, and civic leaders that restored calm. Also, thanks to CRS mediation, the Charlottesville, Virginia Police Department and University of Virginia Chapter of the

NAACP signed an agreement to end police–minority student discord and improve race relations.

[*See also* Civil Rights Movement; Interracial relations.]

Further Reading

Axelrod, Alan. *Minority Rights in America.* Washington, DC: CQ Press, 2002.

Levine, Bertram J. *Resolving Racial Conflict: The Community Relations Service and Civil Rights, 1964–1989.* Columbia: University of Missouri Press, 2005.

Voting Rights Enforcement and Reauthorization: The Department of Justice's Record of Enforcing the Temporary Voting Rights Act Provisions. Washington, DC: U.S. Commission on Civil Rights, 2006.

KATZENBACH V. MCCLUNG (1964)

Activists sat in or picketed segregated facilities, where they were harassed, often beaten, and arrested. Their protests gained vital support from the Civil Rights Act of 1964, notably Title II, which prohibited racial discrimination by "hotels, motels, restaurants, theaters, and all other public accommodations engaged in interstate commerce." It also authorized the attorney general to enforce nondiscrimination by lawsuit. Soon the Birmingham Restaurant Association (BRA) challenged Title II's constitutional validity.

BRA's counsel recruited Ollie's Barbecue, owned by lay Presbyterian minister Ollie McClung and his son, to challenge the law on behalf of restaurants. The McClungs, grossing $350,000 annually, "served large numbers of local customers," 90 percent of them black. But their dining room was for whites only. Counsel argued that, if forced to desegregate, "plaintiffs would suffer serious and irreparable injury." His argument convinced the US District Court for the Northern District of Alabama, as it issued an injunction against enforcing Title II at Ollie's. However, the Justice Department won a stay on that order and filed an accelerated appeal to the US Supreme Court. The Court upheld Title II, noting "the adverse effects on commerce produced by restaurant segregation." Thus overruling the District Court, its *McClung* decision reinforced desegregation.

[*See also* Civil Rights Act of 1964.]

Further Reading

Cortner, Richard C. *Civil Rights and Public Accommodations: The Heart of Atlanta Motel and McClung Cases.* Lawrence: University Press of Kansas, 2001.

Grofman, Bernard, ed. *Legacies of the 1964 Civil Rights Act.* Charlottesville: University Press of Virginia, 2000.

KERNER REPORT

As Congress considered the civil rights bill, racial violence swept America. Rochester, Jersey City, and Philadelphia erupted in 1964. The Watts riot (Los Angeles) killed 34 in 1965. Riots engulfed 25 major cities in 1967–68. Detroit's left 43 dead and 2,000 injured. The president appointed the National Advisory Commission on Civil Disorders (Illinois Governor Otto Kerner chair) to investigate and make recommendations.

Many testified at commission hearings. For example, Martin Luther King, Jr. attributed the riots to "the greater crimes of white society," including race and class poverty, discrimination, and unemployment. He strongly applauded the commission's report, issued only weeks before his assassination. "This is our basic conclusion: Our nation is moving toward two societies, one black, one white–separate and unequal," it stated. Poverty and racism created in the "ghetto a destructive environment totally unknown to most white Americans." It recommended "unprecedented levels of funding" for education, training, and employment programs.

[*See also* Cities.]

Further Reading

Harris, Fred R., and Roger W. Wilkins, eds. *Quiet Riots: Race and Poverty in the United States. The Kerner Report Twenty Years Later.* New York: Pantheon Books, 1988.

McLaughlin, Malcolm. *The Long, Hot Summer of 1967: Urban Rebellion in America.* New York: Palgrave Macmillan, 2014.

KING, MARTIN LUTHER, JR.
CIVIL AND HUMAN RIGHTS LEADER

Born: January 15, 1929, Atlanta, GA
Education: Morehouse College, B.A., 1948; Crozer Theological Seminary, B.D. valedictorian, 1951; Boston University, Ph.D., 1955
Died: April 4, 1968, Memphis, TN

The civil rights movement made King. Perhaps its most influential leader, King also helped make the movement. Espousing nonviolent protest against racial segregation, he pursued "liberty and justice for all."

He instilled humane values. His family, Ebenezer Baptist Church, and teachers nurtured his reverence for learning, religion, and service. College and seminary professors introduced him to social gospel theology and Mohandas Gandhi's teachings on nonviolence. Like other fellow seminarians who joined the Fellowship of Reconciliation and Congress of Racial Equality, he applied Gandhian ideas to social struggles for race and economic equality and peace. Nonviolence sustained his moral purpose and action in the Montgomery bus boycott and subsequent campaigns to end segregation.

King powerfully influenced the movement's priorities, including desegregation, voting rights, and fair employment, from Montgomery to the

1968 sanitation workers' strike in Memphis, where he was assassinated. Southern Christian Leadership Conference raised funds and mobilized through black clergy, congregations, and communities as well as national Protestant, Catholic, and Jewish bodies. White supremacists and the FBI harassed him along the way, but he remained outspoken. He rejected both Black Power and the Vietnam War, hoping to redeem the soul of America from the injustice of racism, militarism, and poverty.

Further Reading

Burns, Stewart. *To the Mountaintop: Martin Luther King Jr.'s Sacred Mission to Save America 1955–1968*. New York: HarperSanFrancisco, 2004

Garrow, David J. *Bearing the Cross: Martin Luther King, Jr., and the Southern Christian Leadership Conference*. New York: Vintage Books, 1988.

KOREAN WAR

This war (1950–53) ignited when USSR- and China-supported North Korea invaded South Korea. An UN resolution formed a twenty-one-nation coalition, South Korea joining, to repel the North under US command. The death toll approximated 1.2 million on all sides, including 54,000 Americans.

The United States assigned black soldiers to desegregated units. The move had begun in draftee training programs (1950) and gradually moved to combat operations. The army also received the vast majority of African American drafted and enlisted men. Army field commanders incurring manpower shortages, therefore, tended to assign more and more blacks to racially mixed platoons or squads. Their fatality rate thus doubled that of whites. Even so, morale elevated among black personnel as desegregation gained traction. By 1951 officials reported the integration of black and white troops in the Far East. More than 90 percent of all black soldiers served in newly integrated companies, battalions, and regiments in 1953.

[*See also* Cold War; Executive Order 9981 (1948).]

Further Reading

Edgerton, Robert B. *Hidden Heroism: Black Soldiers in America's Wars*. Boulder, CO: Westview Press, 2001.

Woods, Naurice Frank. *A History of African Americans in the Segregated United States Military: From America's War of Independence to the Korean War*. New York: Edwin Mellen Press, 2013.

KU KLUX KLAN (KKK)

Formed in 1865 as a "secret lodge" by former Confederates in Pulaski, Tennessee, the Invisible Empire or Ku Klux Klan (KKK) has been and remains committed to white supremacy in America.

Klansmen, beside other diehard groups, violently resisted Reconstruction. Still defending the South, they fought Union Army occupation, Republican governments, and blacks' freedom. Donning hoods and using secret titles, they took an oath to defend Christianity, the Constitution, and the white race, especially their women's purity. Loyal to the Democratic Party, the Klan enlisted men and women from all classes. Targeting Union Leagues (freedmen's political clubs), night riders harassed and often killed black and Republican voters and officeholders, burned black churches and schools, intimidated teachers, and stole elections. In the 1868 elections, alongside Knights of the White Camellia, they murdered 1,000 black and white Republicans in Louisiana alone. After its investigation, Congress passed the Ku Klux Act (1871). But undermanned Union garrisons rarely stopped the Klan's plunder. Its terrorism during the election of 1876 hastened Reconstruction's end.

Between 1877 and 1910 the KKK fueled Democrats' push to establish one-party rule and Jim Crow. A coalition of Democrats, Klansmen, Red Shirts, Rifle Clubs, and White Leagues targeted freedmen and their allies, utilizing ballot fraud, intimidation, and murder. Some 1,751 blacks were lynched in southern and border states ca. 1882–1900 as black and white farmers' alliances and the Populist Party coalesced for reform. Defeat of populists by ballot-rigging and terror enabled Democrats, as the Supreme Court instituted the "separate but equal" rule, to enact Jim Crow. The system disfranchised and terrorized blacks; it also persecuted Jews, Catholics, and nonwhite immigrants.

Klan people promoted white racism in the twentieth century. Early on they enlisted members with *The Birth of a Nation* (1915), a film glorifying the Klan's bloody defeat of Reconstruction. By the mid-1920s, the second KKK claimed several million members in more than a dozen states. Affiliates were strong in the Midwest (being more anti-Catholic and anti-immigrant there) than in the South. State and local Klans frequently attacked progressives prior to the Civil Rights Act of 1957, which ensured the right to vote. Its passage signaled the danger of a third KKK in the post-*Brown* South. Although dozens of civil rights activists died in 1960s and later Klan murders, authorities arrested and

prosecuted relatively few of the perpetrators. However, KKK membership has declined as more and more citizens reject racial and ethnic
violence. For example, Klansmen's fatal shooting of five anti-Klan
marchers in Greensboro, North Carolina (1979) outraged the public,
reinforced federal surveillance, and vitiated KKK recruitment. Even so,
KKK affiliates now are coalescing or disbanding and reinventing themselves in a broader antigovernment, Patriot militia, and white nationalist movement.

[*See also* Civil Rights Movement; Segregation.]

Further Reading

Cunningham, David. *Klansville, U.S.A.: The Rise and Fall of the Civil Rights-Era
Ku Klux Klan*. New York: Oxford University Press, 2013.
MacLean, Nancy. *Behind the Mask of Chivalry: The Making of the Second Ku
Klux Klan*. New York: Oxford University Press, 1994.
Trealease, Alen W. *White Terror: The Ku Klux Klan Conspiracy and Southern
Reconstruction*. Baton Rouge: Louisiana State University Press, 1995.

KWANZAA

In Swahili *kwanzaa* means gathering first fruits. Kwanzaa thus is the
annual festival celebrating African American heritage based on African
harvest rituals. Created in 1966 by black nationalist Maulana Karenga, it
is observed December 26–January 1.

It includes family, community, church, club, or school gatherings.
These include candle-lighting, recitation, gifts, food, and drink, honoring
seven principles: *umoja* (unity), *kujichangulia* (self-determination), *ujima*
(collective work and responsibility), *ujamaa* (cooperative economics), *nia*
(purpose), *kuumba* (creativity), and *imani* (faith). Its observance endures.
According to a market survey in 2001, one in seven African Americans
celebrated kwanzaa as a spiritual, cultural, or commercial complement
to Christmas.

[*See also* Afro-American studies.]

Further Reading

Asante, Molefi Kete. *Maulana Karenga: An Intellectual Portrait*. Malden,
MA: Polity, 2009.
Riley, Dorothy Winbush. *The Complete Kwanzaa: Celebrating Our Cultural
Harvest*. New York: HarperCollins, 1995.

LABOR

Workplace equity underpins blacks' efforts for equality. The Committee on the Status of Black Americans (1989), judging black life from 1944, concurred. Black median family income was 57 percent of white median family income in 1986, it reported. Moreover, 32 percent of black families and 15 percent of white families earned subpoverty incomes; and 22.6 percent of employed blacks, compared to 16.3 percent of whites, were union members. Racial inequality persisted.

Just as slaves and free blacks subsisted normally by helping themselves, freedpeople created guilds, protective associations, and cooperatives to subsist and earn livelihoods. They also established black auxiliaries of white labor organizations. Excluded by the National Labor Union (1866), blacks formed the Colored National Labor Union (1869) for "'the opportunity to work and rise.'" National Negro Conventions promoted schooling; fairness to tenant farmers, sharecroppers, and urban laborers; and co-ops to buy farm supplies and land. Blacks also took direct action. In 1881 washerwomen of Atlanta, Georgia founded the Washing Society, a citywide secret group, and went on strike for higher pay. Similarly, many blacks joined the white-led Noble Order of the Knights of Labor (1869). Blacks accounted for 10 percent (60,000) of Knights' local assemblies in 1886, as black Texans began the Colored Farmers' Alliance. In face of segregation, disfranchisement, and lynching, the alliance enlisted 1, 250, 000 southern members, joined cotton pickers' strikes, and supported the Populist Party. Locals of the American Federation of Labor (AFL, 1886) usually were for "white only." Yet some unions, such as the United Mine Workers of America (UMW, 1886), recruited large numbers of blacks. So did the Industrial Workers of the World (IWW, 1905); its socialist founders pledged to organize workers of every color, ethnicity, class, gender, occupation, and skill.

Union organizing prior to the 1930s, paralleling "the massive migration of rural southern Negroes to northern cities and to new modes of employment and living," forecast the Wagner Act (1935), which ensured the right of collective bargaining. Critical early unions – biracial as well as black – included the National Association of Afro-American Gas Engineers and Skilled Laborers (1900), recognized by its parent body soon after, and the Colored Men's Locomotive Firemen's Association (1902), which spawned several colored railway brotherhoods. After the Railway Mail Association excluded them, black mail clerks organized the National Alliance of Postal Employees (1913), "the pre-World War I union with the longest career." The International Longshoremen's Association (1917) absorbed pioneer black longshoremen. Founded by A. Philip Randolph, the all-black Brotherhood of Sleeping Car Porters (BSCP, 1925) fought until 1934 to gain recognition from its powerful employer, the Pullman Palace Car Company. BSCP signed its first contract in 1937 and spearheaded the March on Washington Movement (1940), which won executive orders for fair employment in 1941 and military desegregation in 1948, when the NAACP hired Herbert Hill (1924–2004) at the National Office. Named labor secretary in 1951, he pursued strategies to enlarge membership among workers and combat union segregation.

Unions expanded in the wake of the Wagner Act. Formed by activists, including New Deal liberals and communists, the Congress of Industrial Organizations (CIO, 1935), unlike the AFL, organized skilled and unskilled workers. CIO eyed the steel, automotive, textile, tobacco, and other mass production industries. In 1937 it consisted of 32 unions with 4 million members, including 1.25 million African Americans. The United Automobile Workers (UAW, 1935) had 400,000 members, mostly in Detroit, which had several majority-black locals. Blacks embraced the vision of interracial solidarity and job security "to support their families ... to educate their children." More than 30,000 employers accepted CIO-negotiated contracts to increase wages and improve working conditions. Even so, organizers faced racist and anti-union violence, notably in the wartime and postwar South. Among other unions, the Southern Tenant Farmers' Union (1935) and United Cannery, Agricultural, Packing, and Affiliated Workers of America (1937) sponsored black union organizers.

In the meantime, blacks pushed for "civil rights unionism" and opposed the Taft–Hartley Act (1947), which forbade the union shop and work stoppages. Following the AFL-CIO merger (1955) the body elected Randolph vice president, making him leader of the "Black-Labor Alliance." The alliance challenged racial, economic, ethnic, and gender discrimination in employment during the Cold War, for example, co-sponsoring the March on Washington for Jobs and Freedom (1963) and supporting the United Farm Workers (UFW). Organized in 1962 by César E. Chávez (1927–93) and majority-Chicano, UFW used nonviolent tactics to leverage its demands. Leading a 300-mile march from Delano to Sacramento, California in 1966, Chávez unveiled the plight of grape pickers to the nation.

Furthermore, the black–labor alliance leveraged labor reforms. It backed Herbert Hill's steps to expose and abolish segregation in the apprenticeship and seniority systems of trade and industrial unions. With liberals, progressives, and civil rights activists, it lobbied successfully for Congressional legislation against segregated public facilities, education, employment, suffrage, and housing. Prioritizing work and civil and voting rights issues, black unionists drew upon ideologies of integration, Black Power, and affirmative action, whether on behalf of the integrated Hospital Workers' Union, 1199 (1937) or League of Revolutionary Black Workers (1969). In addition, since the 1980s, the largest African American memberships have been those of UAW; American Federation of State, County, and Municipal Employees (1936); Hospital Workers' Union, 1199; and Service Employees International Union (1968). Labor's rank and file helped to propel the global antiapartheid movement; Jesse Jackson's 1984 and 1988 campaigns for the Democratic presidential nomination; and the ongoing struggle for equal citizenship, justice, and opportunity regardless of race.

[*See also* Agriculture; Business.]

Further Reading

Arnesen, Eric. *Brotherhoods of Color: Black Railroad Workers and the Struggle for Equality.* Cambridge, MA: Harvard University Press, 2001.

Cobble, Dorothy Sue. *The Other Women's Movement: Workplace Justice and Social Rights in Modern America.* Princeton, NJ: Princeton University Press, 2004.

Frymer, Paul. *Black and Blue: African Americans, the Labor Movement, and the Decline of the Democratic Party.* Princeton, NJ: Princeton University Press, 2008.

LAW ENFORCEMENT

The Constitution ensures "equal protection of the laws." Federal, state, and local governments and agencies are charged to enforce them. But race and class discrimination over time vitiated "justice under law."

Discrimination troubled Raymond P. Alexander (1897–1974), Senior Judge of the Court of Common Pleas No. 4, Philadelphia. "There is still active and virulent discrimination in employment, in housing, in education and in many other areas," he declared in 1969. "So, too, the law has not dealt adequately with the problem of de facto discrimination — that discrimination which is inherent in Ghetto living" (Alexander, 1969, p. 95).

Injustices against blacks have endured since slavery and emancipation. Slaves and free black people, the US Chief Justice said in 1857, were "so far inferior, that they had no rights which the white man was bound to respect." In the Reconstruction South, home of nine in ten African Americans, an Army-staffed judiciary sought to protect black workers and voters while settling black-white disputes. Governing by 1877, ex-Confederates quickened purges of blacks from jury and voter rolls. Arbitrarily and repeatedly, they arrested, prosecuted, and imprisoned blacks to be leased laborers. In 1896, when the Supreme Court declared its "equal, but separate" ruling, black southerners faced not only legal disfranchisement and segregation but also rampant "Lynch Law." De facto race separation and injustice spread nationwide.

Blacks fought for equality. For example, the NAACP's fight to end lynching and litigate civil and criminal cases enlisted black churches and women's, civic, fraternal, labor, and interracial organizations. Its litigation won Court decisions securing black citizens' right to counsel, to trial by juries of their peers, and to vote, while overruling segregated housing and schools. It lobbied for and helped win passage of the 1957, 1960, 1964, and 1965 civil and voting rights acts.

But inequities persisted. Racial profiling, used in the War on Drugs (1970), and police brutality fueled massive riots in Miami (1980) and Los Angeles (1992). Assessing drug, alcohol, and handgun crimes from 1944, the Committee on the Status of Black Americans (1989) reported "overt bias in arrests, trials, and sentencing." In capital prosecutions, the skin color of the victim clearly shaped "the odds of a murderer's receiving the death penalty." Not surprising, the National Black Police Association, with locals in thirty-five major cities, called for community policing, narcotics interdiction, and gun control.

In short, the committee recommended major reforms. Educating and employing "more black policemen, prosecutors, judges, jurors, and other decision makers" would integrate and help promote fairness in institutions of law enforcement. Blacks constituted 3,000 or just 1 percent of 300,000 lawyers in 1970 alone. At the same time, blacks made up 27 to 63 percent of residents in Detroit, Atlanta, Chicago, and Washington, DC, but only 5 to 21 percent of those cities' police forces. Calling for diversity and equity since the committee's report is the National Conference of Black Lawyers, "an activist legal organization," seeking to secure the equal "rights of black people specifically and of people of color, the poor, and the disadvantaged generally."

[*See also* Death penalty; Department of Justice, US.]

Reference

Alexander, Raymond Pace. "Civil Rights, the Negro Protest and the War on Poverty: Efforts to Cure America's Social Ills." *New York State Bar Journal*, Vol. 41, February 1969, p. 95.

Further Reading

Alexander, Michelle. *The New Jim Crow: Mass Incarceration in the Age of Color Blindness*. New York: The New Press, 2010.
Jackson, L. Jesse, Sr., et al. *Legal Lynching: The Death Penalty and America's Future*. New York: The New Press, 2001.
Nelson, Jill, ed. *Police Brutality: An Anthology*. New York: W. W. Norton, 2000.

LAWSON, JAMES M.
CIVIL AND HUMAN RIGHTS LEADER

Born: September 22, 1928, Uniontown, PA
Education: Baldwin-Wallace College, 1947–52, B.A.; Oberlin School of Theology, 1956–58; Vanderbilt Divinity School, 1958–60; Boston University, S.T.M., 1960

Lawson instilled strong familial values on justice. Joining the Fellowship of Reconciliation (FOR) and Congress of Racial Equality in college, he resisted the draft, was imprisoned (1949–52), and studied Gandhian nonviolence while a Methodist missionary to India.

During graduate study at Oberlin, he met Martin Luther King, Jr., who urged him to join the southern freedom movement. "We don't have anyone like you down there," King said, adding "Come as quickly as you can. We really need you."

Lawson moved to Nashville and Vanderbilt. He launched civil disobedience workshops, which led to the Nashville Student Movement, sit-ins against segregation, and his expulsion from divinity school. Still, he mentored many civil rights student activists, including Diane Nash and John Lewis. "Lawson was arming us, preparing us, and planting in us a sense of both rightness and righteousness," Lewis stated. "A soul force that would see us through the ugliness and pain that lay ahead" (Lewis, 1998, p. 78). Cofounder of the Student Nonviolent Coordinating Committee,

Lawson wrote its mission statement. He also joined the Freedom Rides and organized the Southern Christian Leadership Conference's nonviolent campaigns in Albany, Georgia and elsewhere. Deservedly, he served as president of FOR (1994–2000) and Distinguished Visiting Professor at Vanderbilt (2006).

Reference

Lewis, John. *Walking with the Wind: A Memoir of the Movement.* New York: Simon & Schuster, 1998, p. 78.

Further Reading

Burns, Stewart. *To the Mountaintop: Martin Luther King Jr.'s Sacred Mission to Save America.* New York: HarperSanFrancisco, 2004.
Houck, Davis W., and David E. Dixon, eds. *Rhetoric, Religion, and the Civil Rights Movement, 1954–1965.* Waco, TX: Baylor University Press, 2006.

LEE, SHELTON J. (SPIKE)   FILMMAKER

Born: March 20, 1957, Atlanta, GA
Education: Morehouse College, B.A., 1979; New York University, M.F.A., 1983

Noted independent filmmaker, Lee came of age during the civil rights–Black Power era in Brooklyn, New York. Like his grandfather and father, he finished Morehouse College and was knowledgeable in African American history and culture. During the 1980s hip-hop and rap music rage, he began producing black genre films.

Lee's subjects include drugs and sex among blacks as well as racial freedom and violent conflict. *She's Gotta Have It* (1986) depicts a woman who is sexually adventurous, dates three men, and rationalizes her behavior as independence. *School Daze* (1988) shows rivalry between Greek and non-Greek students, reflecting skin-tone and hair-texture divisions, at a southern black college. *Do the Right Thing* (1989) traces rising tensions between an Italian pizzeria and poor blacks that explode in rioting, a black fatality, and the pizzeria's destruction. *Malcolm X* (1992), perhaps his best film, cost $34 million. Denzel Washington, who plays Malcolm, was an Academy Award nominee. By the end of 1994 *Malcolm X* had earned $48 million. *Four Little Girls* (1998) presents their church bomb deaths, premiered on Home Box Office, and received an Academy nomination. The owner of 40 Acres and a Mule Filmworks, Lee also produces musical videos, television specials, and commercials.

Further Reading

Alexander, George. *Why We Make Movies: Black Filmmakers Talk about the Magic of Cinema.* New York: Harlem Moon, 2003.
Vest, Jason P. *Spike Lee: Finding the Story and Forcing the Issue.* Santa Barbara, CA: Praeger, 2014.

LETTER FROM BIRMINGHAM JAIL (1963)

During the Alabama Christian Movement for Human Rights and Southern Christian Leadership Conference's Birmingham campaign (1963), police brutally attacked nonviolent demonstrators, including hundreds of schoolchildren. They used firemen with high-pressure water hoses and attack dogs, as media reported and televised race brutality to the nation and world. Among the protest leaders arrested, King was held in City Jail. A *Post-Herald* statement by eight white clergy criticized him for the civil disorders, which particularly put children at risk.

King answered them. He began drafting a reply in the margins of the newspaper, continued on scraps of paper "supplied by a friendly Negro trusty," and finished "on a pad my attorneys were eventually permitted to leave me." Writing to his critics in the New Testament tradition of the Apostle Paul, King gave biblical and philosophical reasons for why he must "carry the gospel of freedom to all communities and states." He defended the use of nonviolence and direct action, its timing, and its call to justice. King also deplored the moral fence-sitting of "the white moderate" and commended the "still too few" antiracist whites. Finally, he expressed hope "to meet each of you ... as a fellow clergyman and a Christian brother."

[*See also* Southern Christian Leadership Conference (SCLC).]

Further Reading

Bass, S. Jonathan. *Blessed Are the Peacemakers: Martin Luther King, Jr., Eight White Religious Leaders, and the "Letter from Birmingham Jail".* Baton Rouge: Louisiana State University Press, 2001.
Rieder, Jonathan. *Gospel of Freedom: Martin Luther King, Jr.'s Letter from Birmingham Jail and the Struggle that Changed a Nation.* New York: Bloomsbury Press, 2013.

LEWIS, EDMONIA   SCULPTOR

Born: ca. July 14, 1843, near Albany, NY
Education: Oberlin College, 1859–63
Died: September 17, 1907, London, England

Art historians consider Lewis the first major black female artist in America. Born free as Wildfire, the child of an Indian mother and black father, she attended Oberlin College, mastered drawing, and renamed herself Mary Edmonia. She also resisted white racism and, though twice acquitted of fighting racist students, was not allowed to graduate. In 1863 she moved to Boston, where the black painter Edward Bannister tutored her. She created a fine marble "Bust of Colonel Robert Gould Shaw" (1865), leader of the Union's 54th Massachusetts US Colored Regiment, and earned money for apprenticeships in Europe.

European training enriched her art. In Italy she produced "Forever Free," perhaps her best known work. Depicting the Emancipation Proclamation, it presents slaves who are just learning of their freedom. The woman kneels in prayer; the man rests one foot on an iron ball symbolizing slavery and lifts an arm in victory over its broken chain. Lewis won acclaim at the Philadelphia Centennial for "The Death of Cleopatra." Cleopatra is dead, seated on the throne, with a snake that has bitten her right hand, as her left hand hangs lifeless. Sometime in the late nineteenth century Lewis went back to Italy. She later died in London.

Further Reading

Buick, Kirsten Pai. *Child of Fire: Mary Edmonia Lewis and the Problem of Art History's Black and Indian Subject.* Durham, NC: Duke University Press, 2010.
Nelson, Charmaine A. *The Color of Stone: Sculpting the Black Female Body in Nineteenth-Century America.* Minneapolis: University of Minnesota Press, 2007.

LEWIS, JOHN R.
CIVIL RIGHTS LEADER AND US CONGRESSMAN

Born: February 21, 1940, Troy, AL
Education: American Baptist Theological Seminary, S.T.B., 1961; Fisk University, B.A., 1967

Lewis's career mirrors the civil rights movement. In college he emulated James Lawson, who conducted workshops on nonviolent protest. Lewis cofounded the Nashville Student Movement and Student Nonviolent Coordinating Committee (SNCC). During the Freedom Rides, he faced several of many arrests and attacks at the hands of segregationist police and mobs. The chairman of SNCC during its dangerous voter registration campaigns in the Deep South, he also clung to nonviolence and racial integration as many of his colleagues embraced Black Power and self-defense.

Lewis is now one of the most admired and influential members of the Congressional Black Caucus. His rise to Congress began in the 1986 Democratic primary for the 5th Georgia District. It included a close run-off between two old friends and SNCC veterans: Julian Bond, a former Georgia senator, and Lewis, formerly an Atlanta councilman. Lewis's victory, amid media allegations of Bond's drug use, tested their friendship. Lewis won the general election by a wide margin. An influential congressman, he has been Chief Deputy Democratic Whip. He is a member of the Ways and Means Committee and its Subcommittee on Health and Oversight. An outspoken progressive, he strongly supports affirmative action, public education, labor, and social programs.

Further Reading

Barber, Lucy G. *Marching on Washington: The Forging of an American Political Tradition.* Berkeley: University of California Press, 2002.

Lewis, John, with Michael D'Orso. *Walking with the Wind: A Memoir of the Movement.* New York: Simon & Schuster, 1998.

LEWIS, REGINALD F.   ENTREPRENEUR

Born: December 7, 1942, Baltimore, MD
Education: Virginia State College, B.A., 1965; Harvard Law School (HLS), LL.B., 1968
Died: January 19, 1993, New York, NY

One contemporary called Lewis the "Jackie Robinson of Wall Street ... the man who broke the color barrier in large-scale mergers and acquisitions and leveraged buyouts."

Lewis instilled strong values in a household where his mother and grandparents taught him to be hardworking and self-confident. As a Baltimore high school athlete, he learned to play hard and smart. He excelled in college, in law school, and as an entrepreneur.

His career reflected "the third-wave rise of black corporate America." Lewis bought McCall Patterns in 1984 for $23 million, doubled its profits, and sold it in 1987 for $90 million. He managed to buy Beatrice International Foods for $985 million, "the first such acquisition by a black in American business history," which made him CEO of TLC-Beatrice International. The largest African American business, it owned sixty-four companies in thirty-one countries. Beatrice Foods, its center, was the thirty-fifth ranked American corporation. Lewis, who accumulated an estimated $400 million in personal wealth, became one of the 400 richest Americans. A philanthropist, he donated to higher education, historic preservation, black political campaigns, the NAACP, and the Rainbow/Push Coalition. Baltimore's inner-city youth programs and African American Museum are beneficiaries of the Lewis Foundation.

Further Reading

Dingle, Derek T. *Black Enterprise Titans of the B.E. 100s: Black CEOs who Redefined and Conquered American Business*. New York: John Wiley & Sons, 1999.
Lewis, Reginald F., and Blair S. Walker. *Why Should White Guys Have All the Fun?: How Reginald Lewis Created a Billion-Dollar Empire*. Baltimore, MD: Black Classic Press, 2012.

"LIFT EVERY VOICE AND SING"

Inaugurated on February 12, 1900, "Lift Every Voice and Sing" became "The Negro National Anthem." Writer James Weldon Johnson and musician John Rosamond Johnson, his brother, composed its words and music to honor Abraham Lincoln's birthday at the Colored High School in Jacksonville, Florida. It was "sung by schoolchildren–a chorus of five hundred voices."

During the next two decades black institutions and organizations – educational, religious, social, and civic – sang and adopted it. It invoked the African American journey from slavery to freedom. "The song not only epitomizes the history of the race, and its present condition, but voices their hope for the future," the Johnsons declared in 1926, the first year of Negro History Week. Augusta Savage also sculpted "Lift Every Voice and Sing" (1939), a black choir in the form of a harp. The song's lyrics on struggle and aspiration especially resonate in the observance of Black History Month.

Further Reading

Bond, Julian, and Sondra Kathryn Wilson, eds. *Lift Every Voice and Sing: A Celebration of the Negro National Anthem.* New York: Random House, 2000.

Johnson, James Weldon. *Along this Way: The Autobiography of James Weldon Johnson.* New York: Da Capo Press, 2000.

LITERATURE

From its origins in slavery to the present, literature has reflected African American life, thought, and freedom struggle.

Enslaved and free black poets and writers echoed Africans' conversion to Christianity. Slave poet and preacher Jupiter Hammon of New York, in *An Evening Thought, Salvation, by Christ, with Penitential Cries* (1760), celebrated faith and hope. He hailed Christ's redemption of "every nation," even "Ethiopians" like him, and called Boston bondwoman Phillis Wheatley the "Ethiopian Poetess." In *Poems on Various Subjects, Religious and Moral* (1773), the first book published by a black American, Wheatley invoked blacks' humanity, singing "Negros, black as Cain, May be refin'd and join th' angelic train." Comparably, in *The Hope for Liberty, Containing a Number of Poetical Pieces* (1829), North Carolina slave George Moses Horton, voiced slaves' desire to be free. "Along the dismal path" of slavery, Horton sang, freedom's "last beam of hope" guided them. Baltimore freewoman Frances E. W. Harper exposed slavery's cruelty in *Poems on Miscellaneous Subjects* (1854), as in "The Slave Mother."

Slave narratives related experiences of bondage and freedom. Perhaps the best early one was *The Interesting Narrative of the Life of Olaudah Equiano, Written by Himself* (1789), which had a 10th edition before his death. Equiano (1745–97) faced abduction at age eleven, the ordeal of the Middle Passage, slaving in Virginia, on British war ships, and in the Caribbean until 1766, when he bought his liberty and embraced abolitionism. "The abolition of slavery would be in reality an universal good" (Equiano, 2003, p. 336), he stated. *The History of Mary Prince, A West Indian Slave, Related by Herself* (1831), a key female narrative, helped forge support for emancipation in the British West Indies. Thanks to his critical *Narrative of the Life of Frederick Douglass, an American Slave, Written by Himself* (1845), Douglass became American abolition's most respected spokesman. Harriet A. Jacobs, an Edenton, North Carolina fugitive who found refuge in the North, authored *Incidents in the Life of a Slave Girl, Written by Herself* (1861).

Novels also appeared. Noted was Kentucky runaway William Wells Brown's *Clotel, or the President's Daughter: A Narrative of Slave Life in the United States* (1853). In the plot, after the death of President Thomas Jefferson, Clotel, his mulatto daughter is sold. She later commits suicide to find freedom. Freeman Frank J. Webb of Philadelphia disclosed interracial marriage and passing in *The Garies and Their Friends* (1857). The Negro maid Harriet E. Wilson of Milford, New Hampshire created an abused and angry mulatto in *Our Nig; or Sketches from the Life of a Free Black* (1859). Scholars deem Wilson the first black female novelist. Charles Town, Virginia freeman and emigration advocate Martin R. Delany wrote *Blake, or the Huts of America* (1859), the last of his four antebellum novellas. A freeman and radical, Blake rejects the myth of slaves' docility. Thus he travels throughout the South and Cuba, encouraging and plotting a mass slave rebellion.

Emancipation and Reconstruction not only catalyzed blacks' literacy but also inspired their literary production. Former slaves and free blacks, like white citizens, determined to "secure the blessings of liberty to ourselves and our posterity." African American schools and colleges were indispensable for securing the "freedom to work and think ... to love and aspire." In the face of the economic exploitation, Jim Crow, and lynching intended to drive them "back toward slavery," they strived for "the equal protection of the laws."

Black authors revealed that striving. Fiction and nonfiction writings show realities of white racism plus blacks' efforts to survive, resist, and help themselves. For example, in Frances Harper's tale on freedpeople, *Iola Leroy or, Shadows Uplifted* (1892), Iola, an educated mulatto freedwoman, refuses to "pass" for white. She joins "pure African" freedmen in uplifting the black community. Dayton, Ohio's Paul Laurence Dunbar, the leading black poet-writer before the twentieth century, restored the shadow of the plantation in depicting the black masses. Among his works, the best-selling *Lyrics of a Lowly Life* (1896) and *The Strength of Gideon and Other Stories* (1900) depict sharecroppers and ghetto dwellers' folk speech and deep sense of dignity. However, many reviewers criticized Dunbar's use of racial stereotypes.

Others still captured the realism and heroism of the poor. Short story writer Charles W. Chesnutt used former bondman Uncle Julius to express the folklore and pride of the downtrodden in *The Conjure Woman* (1899). Julius pictures slavery as dehumanizing, but its survivors evince resilience and initiative in building their own communities.

Novelist and pastor Sutton E. Griggs from Chatfield, Texas captures black workers' grass roots militancy. In his *Imperium in Imperio* (1899) working-class blacks organize an army for a would-be racial revolution to establish their black nation. W. E. B. Du Bois describes struggles for equality in *The Souls of Black Folk* (1903), arguably the finest set of black essays and stories before 1920. His folk, typically Black Belt farm tenants, strive not only for autonomy and simple justice from "within the Veil." They contend against "poverty, poor land, and low wages."

Black letters have been plentiful and diverse since World War I and the Great Migration, inspiring the Harlem Renaissance (1920s) and writings to present times. At its center, as in earlier periods, stands the relationship of art and writing to politics and power. Race, class, and gender relations, black workers, the underclass, and the meaning of soul remain crucial issues. Writers explore them, displaying empathy as well as rejection, from "The Weary Blues" (1926) by Langston Hughes, "Poet Laureate of the Negro Race," to *Jazz* (1992) by Toni Morrison, the only African American recipient of the Nobel Prize in Literature.

Many writers, among them Richard Wright, Ralph Ellison, James Baldwin, and Alice Walker, were major contributors along the way. In addition, Harlem Renaissance diva Zora Neale Hurston presented southern black folktales and folkways in *Mules and Men* (1935). Creative and enduring, *Mules* yet offers invaluable insights into rural segregation and black aspirations. Similarly, award-winning playwright August Wilson explores a father–son conflict in *Fences* (1987), here representing the contemporary importance of the black family.

[*See also* Harlem Renaissance; New Negro movement; Scholarship.]

Reference

Equiano, Olaudah. *The Interesting Narrative and Other Writings*. New York: Penguin, 2003, p. 336.

Further Reading

King, Lovalerie, and Shirley Moody-Turner, eds. *Contemporary African American Literature: The Living Canon*. Bloomington: Indiana University Press, 2013.
Gates, Henry Louis, Jr., and Nellie Y. McKay, eds., *The Norton Anthology of African American Literature*. New York: W. W. Norton, 2004.
Moore, Steven T. *The Cry of Black Rage in African American Literature from Frederick Douglass to Richard Wright*. Lewiston, NY: Edwin Mellen, 2013.

LITTLE (X), MALCOLM   RELIGIOUS AND
HUMAN RIGHTS LEADER

Born: May 19, 1925, Omaha, NE
Education: Junior high school, Lansing, MI
Died: February 21, 1965, New York, NY

The most influential black nationalist of the 1960s, Malcolm rose from poverty and delinquency. While incarcerated, he joined the Nation of Islam (NOI), was national spokesman until parting with imam Elijah Muhammad, and founded the Muslim Mosque, Inc. and Organization of Afro-American Unity (OAAU) in 1964.

Using *Muhammad Speaks*, mass rallies, or mainstream media, he spoke out. Calling whites devils, Malcolm censured the US "white power structure" for racism, colonialism, and imperialism. He condemned the civil rights movement for black self-hatred, thus seeking racial integration. Rather blacks must disavow a slave mentality and join NOI, which stressed blacks' culture and advancing their businesses, families, schools, and communities. Citing racist attacks on peaceful demonstrators and police brutality, he urged self-defense "by any means necessary."

He was both respected and reviled. Many civil rights activists revered him, some organizing the Revolutionary Action Movement (1963). Others embraced OAAU and, in the wake of his assassination, formed vanguards of the Black Power and Pan-African movements. Still, many in the press considered Malcolm a demagogue who espoused race hate and violence, for example blaming him for riots that engulfed New York and six other cities in 1964. *The Autobiography of Malcolm X* (1965) became a best-selling nonfiction book.

Further Reading

Marable, Manning. *Malcolm X: A Life of Reinvention*. New York: Viking, 2011.
Terrill, Robert E., ed. *The Cambridge Companion to Malcolm X*. New York: Cambridge University Press, 2010.

LITTLE ROCK CRISIS

Advised by the Arkansas NAACP, nine black students (five women, four men) transferred to Little Rock's all-white Central High (1957). It fueled a white backlash and revealed their remarkable courage.

Crisis ensued from opening day. The state National Guard blocked Central's entrance on Governor Orville Faubus's orders as a mob harassed the students. President Dwight Eisenhower urged Faubus to comply; in the meantime guardsmen withdrew and local police became students' protectors. But Faubus was defiant and racial violence escalated. To enforce school desegregation and keep the peace, the president federalized the state Guard and ordered in the 101st Airborne Division. The division remained at Central High for more than two months; Guard units did so until the end of the year. Desegregation then stalled as the city closed its schools in 1958–59.

The "Little Rock Nine" were courageous and empowered. They drew strength from the black community, whose churches and civic and educational groups helped build Arkansas' freedom movement. Melba Pattillo never forgot "the daily insults and abuse at school" but appreciated that "a few white students were trying to reach out to us." Ernest Green, Central High's first black graduate (1958), considered his ordeal to be a victory, adding "I had cracked the wall" of segregation.

[*See also Brown v. Board of Education* (1954); Desegregation; Massive resistance; Student activism.]

Further Reading

Beals, Melba Patillo. *Warriors Don't Cry: A Searing Memoir of the Battle to Integrate Little Rock's Central High.* New York: Pocket Books, 1995.

Jacoway, Elizabeth. *Turn Away Thy Son: Little Rock, the Crisis that Shocked the Nation.* New York: Free Press, 2007.

LOUIS, JOE   PRO BOXER

Born: May 13, 1914, Lafayette, AL
Education: Elementary and trade school, Detroit, MI
Died: April 12, 1981, Las Vegas, NV

When boxing phenom Joseph Louis Barrow debuted, sponsors (black Detroit businessmen) prepped him to avoid ex-champion Jack Johnson's flamboyance.

Thus he became Joe Louis. He took lessons in social graces, table manners, and public speaking. Go for the knock-out, they said; fancy footwork vexed racist judges. He could not smile or boast after winning and, urgently, never be seen alone with a white woman. He must be a race role model, a symbol of equality in America's fight against fascism and Nazism.

Louis was a hero and victim. Knocking out German boxer and former heavyweight champion Max Schmeling (1938), he won the undisputed World Championship and Americans' hearts crossed the color line. Joining the army and unpermitted to defend the title, he performed more than 100 benefit fights, earning only his soldier's pay. However, when he faced financial and personal setbacks after retiring (1949), the government prosecuted and garnisheed him for income tax evasion. To subsist, he returned to the ring as a wrestler and worked as a casino greeter. Still, he helped blaze the trail for Jackie Robinson and other postwar black athletes. In 2005 the International Boxing Research Organization ranked Louis the number one heavyweight of all time.

Further Reading

Erenberg, Lewis A. *The Greatest Fight of Our Generation: Louis vs. Schmeling.* New York: Oxford University Press, 2006.

Mead, Chris. *Joe Louis: Black Champion in White America.* Mineola, NY: Dover Publications, 2010.

LOVING V. VIRGINIA (1967)

Virginia citizens Richard Loving (white) and Mildred Jeter (black) married in Washington, DC in 1958. Their state prohibited interracial marriage by laws dating from slavery and endured during Jim Crow. State authorities arrested, indicted, and convicted the couple in 1959 for violating the Racial Integrity Act (1924). But a judge voided the one-year prison sentence for twenty-five years if they would leave Virginia.

They moved to the District of Columbia and found legal counsel. In 1963 the American Civil Liberties Union filed their petition against Virginia's anti-miscegenation statute. However, after three years of litigation, the Virginia Court of Appeals ruled to sustain it. But the US Supreme Court invalidated that ruling 9–0 in 1967. "Virginia is now one of 16 States which prohibit and punish marriages on the basis of racial classifications," the Court concluded, and it set aside such statutes in all states. It defined marriage as a fundamental right protected by the Fourteenth Amendment.

[*See also* Miscegenation.]

Further Reading

Newbeck, Phyl. *Virginia Hasn't Always Been for Lovers: Interracial Marriage Bans and the Case of Richard and Mildred Loving.* Carbondale: Southern Illinois University Press, 2004.

Wallenstein, Peter. *Tell the Court I Love My Wife: Race, Marriage, and Law: An American History.* New York: Palgrave Macmillan, 2002.

MANDELA, NELSON R.
PRESIDENT OF SOUTH AFRICA

Born: July 18, 1918, Mvezo, South Africa
Education: Healdtown mission school, 1937–39; University College of Fort Hare, 1940–41; University of South Africa, B.A., 1943
Died: December 5, 2013, Johannesburg, South Africa

South Africa's apartheid system, wherein a white minority segregated and ruled a black majority, stirred rising protests in the 1980s. Mandela was a revered hero. Leader of the African National Congress' (ANC) armed freedom struggle, he had been incarcerated more than twenty-seven years when international sanctions pressured state authorities to free him in 1990. Mandela led in building an unsegregated, democratic nation. Co-recipient of the Nobel Peace Prize (1993), he became the first black president of South Africa.

He was a visionary. In 1992 he succeeded Oliver Tambo, his former law partner, as head of ANC, which today advocates peaceful change. At the same time, Mandela and President F. W. De Clerk created a plan for multiracial democracy, signing a *Record of Understanding* that included a new constitution and free elections. In 1994, with blacks voting for the first time and in a great number, ANC outvoted all parties and Mandela won the presidency. President Mandela worked for peace and reform, establishing the Truth and Reconciliation Commission to help heal racial wounds; he mediated African wars. He pursued trade and foreign investment to sustain the economy and finance critical social reforms, including education. After serving one term, he stepped aside in 1999.

Further Reading

Barnard, Rita, ed. *The Cambridge Companion to Nelson Mandela.* New York: Cambridge University Press, 2014.
Scott, Christina. *Nelson Mandela: A Force for Freedom.* London: Andre Deutsch, 2010.

MANUMISSION

Manumission was the act of freeing from slavery. A master could manumit his slave for "meritorious service." By 1750, amid growing slave population and unrest, he needed a colony's and then state's approval.

Northern states abolished slavery in 1780–1843; the South ended manumissions, except by legislatures. South Carolina forbade manumission (1820) and free-black immigration (1822).

[*See also* Emancipation.]

Further Reading

Rose, Willie Lee, ed. *A Documentary History of Slavery in North America.* Athens: University of Georgia Press, 1999.
Newman, Richard S. *The Transformation of American Abolitionism: Fighting Slavery in the Early Republic.* Chapel Hill: University of North Carolina Press, 2002.

MARCH ON WASHINGTON (1963)

As the Civil Rights Bill stalled in Congress, movement leaders caucused to urge its enactment. They also endorsed a plan to March on Washington for Jobs and Freedom revived by AFL-CIO vice president A. Philip Randolph. He first proposed it in 1941.

Plans proceeded; the NAACP and Southern Christian Leadership Conference (SCLC) even set aside a dispute on direct action protest. Civil rights, religious, and social organizations across the country successfully enlisted marchers. Though the Kennedy Administration feared a congressional backlash, the planners reiterated their commitment to nonviolence, racial integration, and equal opportunity.

The march to the Lincoln Memorial was historic. Many accounts note its size (250,000, then the largest in American history) and the great speech by Martin Luther King, Jr. Student Nonviolent Coordinating Committee (SNCC) chair John Lewis had strong criticisms of the Administration in his text. But Randolph persuaded him to omit them, thus reflecting the movement's unity in pressing for Federal legislation. Hope was alive.

[*See also* Civil Rights Movement.]

Further Reading

Euchner, Charles. *Nobody Turn Me Around: A People's History of the 1963 March on Washington.* Boston: Beacon Press, 2010.
Jones, William P. *The March on Washington Movement: Jobs, Freedom, and the Forgotten History of Civil Rights.* New York: W. W. Norton, 2013.

MARCH ON WASHINGTON MOVEMENT (MOWM)

Protesting the segregated Armed Forces and black exclusion from defense industry jobs, A. Philip Randolph and Bayard Rustin formed MOWM (1941–47) "to mobilize five million Negroes into one militant mass for pressure," using "Non-Violent Civil Disobedience and Non-Cooperation."

The movement buoyed civil rights. Randolph, Walter White (NAACP), and T. Arnold Hill (National Urban League), meeting President Roosevelt and his advisers in September 1940, sought desegregation of the military, where more than 1,000,000 blacks would serve, with more and better jobs for blacks in every industry with a federal contract. The administration stalled; so, in January 1941 Randolph proposed a July 1 March on Washington to force action. MOWM chapters organized; their rallies drew 23,500 in New York, 20,000 in Chicago, 15,000 in St. Louis, and thousands elsewhere. The *Amsterdam News* (New York) also reported "100,000 IN MARCH TO CAPITOL." Unsuccessfully, the president sent New York's mayor and Mrs. Roosevelt to dissuade MOWM leaders. On June 25 he signed an order. Providing that "there shall be no racial discrimination in the employment of workers in defense industries or government," it created the Committee on Fair Employment Practice to monitor nondiscrimination by federal and contract-employers. Though cancelling the march, MOWM continued to pursue nonviolent protest.

[*See also* Civil Rights Movement; Desegregation; World War II.]

Further Reading

Barber, Lucy G. *Marching on Washington: The Forging of an American Tradition.* Berkeley: University of California Press, 2002. http://www.blackpast.org/?q=aah/march-washington-movement-1941-1947.

Lucander, David. *Winning the War: The March on Washington Movement, 1941–46.* Urbana: University of Illinois Press, 2014.

MARSHALL, THURGOOD
US SUPREME COURT JUSTICE

Born: July 2, 1908, Baltimore, MD
Education: Lincoln University, B.A. cum laude, 1930; Howard Law School, LL.B. magna cum laude, 1933
Died: January 24, 1993, Bethesda, MD

Marshall made thirty-two final arguments to the Supreme Court before becoming its first black member (1967–91). He won twenty-nine cases, notably *Brown v. Board of Education.*

Utilizing the law, he pursued equality. In one final argument, Justice Felix Frankfurter asked him to define the meaning of "equal." "Equal means getting the same thing, at the same time and in the same place," he declared. His noted tenure on the Court mirrored that definition. In *San Antonio Independent School District v. Rodriguez* (1973), for example, justices ruled 5–4 that a Texas property-tax formula for funding education did not violate "equal protection" of the laws. In dissenting, Marshall rebuked their "acquiescence in a system that deprives children ... of the chance to reach their full potential as citizens."

Marshall's goal was deep rooted. He rose from Charles Houston's assistant and director of the Legal Defense Fund (LDF), which handled NAACP litigation, to the pinnacle of American jurisprudence. LDF's team achieved pathmaking victories, including *Smith v. Allwright* (1944), which overturned the "white primary" election, and *Sweatt v. Painter* (1950), which directed the University of Texas School of Law to admit the black applicant. The latter forecast *Brown* and desegregated education in America.

Further Reading

Tushnet, Mark V. *Making Constitutional Law: Thurgood Marshall and the Supreme Court, 1936–1961.* New York: Oxford University Press, 1997.
Zelden, Charles L. *Thurgood Marshall: Race, Rights, and the Struggle for a More Perfect Union.* New York: Routledge, 2013.

MASSIVE RESISTANCE

Brown (1954) and *Brown II* (1955) disallowed school segregation and ordered desegregation "with all deliberate speed."

Segregationists objected. Senator Harry Byrd (D–VA) invoked "massive resistance to this order" and a hundred congressmen endorsed the Southern Manifesto (1956) defying "judicial encroachment." Five state legislatures amended laws so no white child would be forced to attend a desegregated school; four denied funds to racially mixed schools; and eight adopted resolutions upholding the right to close public schools. Ten enacted statutes banning the NAACP, alleging it was a communist front. Citizens' Councils and the Ku Klux Klan harassed African American parents who signed NAACP petitions for pupil transfers and whose children attended white schools. When a black woman enrolled at the University of Alabama in the fall of 1956, whites rioted. Little Rock, Arkansas became a battleground the next year when the governor defied a Federal Court order to enroll nine black students at all-white Central High School. The president eventually deployed the 101st Airborne Division to protect them. Prince Edward County, Virginia closed its schools (1959–64). Resisters undermined America's reputation abroad and escalated civil rights enforcement. Defiance waned after the Supreme Court overruled states' freedom-of-choice plans (1968) and permitted busing for school integration (1971).

[*See also* Swann v. *Charlotte-Mecklenburg Board of Education* (1971).]

Further Reading

Day, John Kyle. *The Southern Manifesto: Massive Resistance and the Fight to Preserve Segregation.* Jackson: University Press of Mississippi, 2014.

Katagiri, Yasuhiro. *Black Freedom, White Resistance, and Red Menace: Civil Rights and Anticommunism in the Jim Crow South.* Baton Rouge: Louisiana State University Press, 2013.

MAYS, BENJAMIN E.   EDUCATOR AND MINISTER

Born: August 1, 1894, Ninety-Six, SC
Education: Virginia Union University, 1917; Bates College, B.A., 1920; University of Chicago, M.A., 1925, Ph.D., 1935
Died: March 28, 1984, Atlanta, GA

Growing up in the segregated South, Mays hoped "that someday I would be able to do something about a situation that had shadowed my early years and killed the spirit of all too many of my people" (Mays 2003, p. 49). Between the 1930s and 1960s, he became an educator, minister, and civil rights activist of major importance. An institution builder, he helped foster the philosophy and practice of nonviolence. Generations called him "School Master of the Movement."

Education, religion, and equality were his paramount causes. A pillar of the Atlanta NAACP, National Baptist Convention USA, and National Council of Churches, he joined in interwar movements against lynching, the white primary election, job discrimination, and Jim Crow education. He authored seminal books on Christianity and race relations; his autobiography was reissued in 1987 and 2003. He taught seminary and college students, including Martin Luther King, Jr., to excel and challenge segregation through nonviolence. Mays was King's eulogist before an international television audience. King honored him as his "spiritual mentor and my intellectual father." Some Atlanta whites, calling Mays a communist, picketed his residence at Morehouse College. As the chairman of the Atlanta School Board, he led its adoption and execution of a full desegregation policy.

Reference

Mays, Benjamin E. *Born to Rebel: An Autobiography.* Athens: University of Georgia Press, 2003, p. 49.

Further Reading

Jelks, Randal Maurice. *Benjamin Elijah Mays, Schoolmaster of the Movement: A Biography.* Chapel Hill: University of North Carolina Press, 2012.
Roper, John Herbert, Sr. *The Magnificent Mays: A Biography of Benjamin E. Mays.* Columbia: University of South Carolina Press, 2012.

MCCOY, ELIJAH J.   INVENTOR

Born: May 2, 1843, Colchester, CN
Education: Machinist trainee, 1858 ff, Edinburgh, Scotland
Died: October 10, 1929, Eloise, MI

McCoy's parents escaped Kentucky slavery to Canada, but moved to the North. They sacrificed to school their twelve children, including mechanics for fifteen-year-old McCoy in Scotland. This opportunity was not available for northern blacks, who faced rampant job discrimination after the Civil War. Unable to find machinist work when he returned, McCoy became a fireman and oilman for the Michigan Central Railroad. He routinely shoveled coal into his train's engine and oiled engine parts during frequent stops. Oiling would prevent combustible friction. Thus he invented and patented a "lubricating cup" for locomotives in 1872. The cup facilitated "the continuous flow of oil on the gears ... thereby do [ing] away with the necessity of shutting down the engine," he explained.

McCoy's brand won a loyal following. Others tried to reinvent his lubrication device, but the McCoy Graphite Lubricator captured the market and customers always asked "Is this the real McCoy?" Their use of the popular expression reflected a product of high quality. Opening his own shop, McCoy created, obtained patents on, and sold almost six dozen mechanical devices and products, notably an automatic lawn sprinkler and an ironing board. He was inducted to the National Inventors Hall of Fame (2001).

Further Reading

Haber, Louis. *Black Pioneers of Science and Invention.* San Diego: Harcourt Brace Jovanovich/Haber Books, 2007.

Hollar, Sherman, ed. *Pioneers of the Industrial Age: Breakthroughs in Technology.* New York: Britannica Educational Publications with Rosen Educational Services, 2013.

MCKISSICK, FLOYD B.
ATTORNEY AND CIVIL RIGHTS LEADER

Born: March 9, 1922, Asheville, NC
Education: Morehouse College, 1940–41, North Carolina College, A.B., 1947, LL.B., 1951, University of North Carolina Law School, 1951
Died: April 21, 1991, Durham, NC

Congress of Racial Equality (CORE) national director and founder of Soul City, McKissick made critical contributions to desegregation, civil rights, and African American empowerment. His suit, argued in the US Fourth Circuit Court of Appeals (1951), ended white-only admission to the School of Law at the University of North Carolina.

McKissick sought racial and social justice. He joined the NAACP while attending one of North Carolina's few black high schools; he attended Morehouse College but went to the army in 1942. He participated in CORE's 1947 journey testing integration on interstate buses. In the wake of *Brown*, he represented blacks arrested for trespassing at a white Durham ice cream parlor in 1957 and sued to transfer his children to white schools. Sponsoring many workshops on nonviolence, he helped mobilize statewide sit-ins at segregated public accommodations. Director of National CORE (1963–69), he also embraced Black Power, self-defense, and economic independence. To promote the last, he supported Republican presidential candidate Richard M. Nixon in 1968. Troubled by McKissick's rejection of nonviolence and integration, many members departed from CORE. He thus resigned to develop

Soul City, a black industrial community in Warren County, North Carolina, financed via loan guarantees from the Nixon administration.

Further Reading

Fergus, Devin. *Liberalism, Black Power, and the Making of American Politics, 1965–1980.* Athens: University of Georgia Press, 2009.
Strain, Christopher. "Soul City, North Carolina: Black Power, Utopia, and the African American Dream." *Journal of African American History*, 89 (Winter 2004): 57–75.

McKISSICK V. CARMICHAEL (1951)

In 1950 several law students at black North Carolina College, using NAACP counsel, petitioned for admission to the School of Law at the University of North Carolina. A Federal District Court rejected their petition, declaring that "the best interests of the plaintiffs will be served by denying the relief sought."

On appeal, they breached Jim Crow. The lead plaintiff was Floyd McKissick, World War II hero and future leader of CORE. Counsel said petitioners were denied "the equal protection of the laws" and "the Negro School is clearly inferior to the white, and the judgment must therefore be reversed in accordance with the decision in *Sweatt v. Painter*" (*McKissick v. Carmichael, 1951*). The 4th US Court of Appeals concurred, overruled the District Court, and ordered the plaintiffs' enrollment. Five, including McKissick, began classes in the summer of 1951. Their admission affirmed NAACP strategy of "direct attack" on segregated higher education and informed its litigation for *Brown* (1954).

[*See also* Civil Rights Movement; Desegregation; *Sweatt v. Painter* (1950).]

Reference

McKissick v. Carmichael, 187 F. 2d 949 (4th Cir. 1951).

Further Reading

Scott, Wendy B. "*Mckissick v. Carmichael* Revisited: Legal Education in North Carolina through the Lens of desegregation." *North Carolina Central Law Review*, 34 (March 2011): 38–62.
Wallenstein, Peter. "Higher Education and the Civil Rights Movement: Desegregating the University of North Carolina." In Winfred B. Moore Jr. et al., eds. *Warm Ashes: Issues in Southern History at the Dawn of the Twenty-First Century.* Columbia: University of South Carolina Press, 2003.

MEDICINE

Driving to Atlanta in 1931, Fisk University dean of women Juliette Derricotte and three students crashed into a car containing a white couple. As the closest hospital excluded "Negroes," they received aid at a black home. A student died; so did Derricotte the next day, after being driven sixty-six miles to Walden Hospital in Chattanooga. This outraged blacks. Jim Crow reigned, but they fought for dignity and equality.

Black southerners evinced two broad strategies on healthcare. One accommodated to segregation, while securing financial and political concessions from whites and sustaining black institutions. Such was the case for Lincoln Hospital of Durham, North Carolina (1901), which funded three renovations but still lagged behind white Watts Hospital. Watts's assets aggregated $2,800,000 by 1950 whereas Lincoln's approximated $740,000. The second strategy pursued desegregation of medical staffs, employees, patients, and facilities.

Desegregation had major advocates along the way. These included the black National Medical Association (NMA); black caucuses in dentistry, pharmacy, and nursing; and gradually the white American Public Health Association. Founded in 1895 as the National Association of Colored Physicians, Dentists, and Pharmacists by Chicago surgeon Daniel Hale Williams (1856–1931) and others, NMA supported black physicians prior to and after the American Medical Association admitted them in 1950. Williams, who served as NMA vice president, also founded Chicago's Provident Hospital, the oldest African American hospital, where he performed the first successful open-heart operation in 1893. NMA's membership rose from about 50 in 1904 to more than 500 by 1912. In 1920 it had fifty local and state affiliates and its *Journal of the National Medical Association* reported on the research and service of members. Their work provided critical support to black medical schools, hospitals, and clinics, as well as in recruiting blacks into health professions. They worked alongside the NAACP, National Urban League (NUL), and other organizations to challenge and end segregated hospital care.

The NAACP and NUL led the fight, using Harvard Medical School graduate Louis T. Wright (1891–1952). The chair of the NAACP's Health Committee, he enlisted Howard Medical School professor W. Montague Cobb (1904–1990) to conduct a major study of medicine and race. Cobb found "grossly unfair" medical care and education for African Americans. In his related "health and social services" survey for the NUL, Cobb's colleague Paul B. Cornely had similar findings. The "separate but equal provision" in the Hospital Survey and Construction Act of 1946, known as the Hill–Burton Act, was a key barrier. Thus, in the early 1950s, Wright and his associates directly challenged "what is perhaps the greatest of all discriminatory evils, differential treatment with respect to hospital facilities" (Morais, 1967, p. 141).

NAACP counsel filed several "equal protection" suits against Hill–Burton hospitals, eighty-nine of them in the South. For example, Hubert Eaton (1916–91) and others sued for "staff privileges" at Wilmington, North Carolina's white hospital in *Eaton v. Board of Managers of the James Walker Memorial Hospital* (1950). The 4th Circuit Federal Court denied them on grounds that the hospital's "discrimination did not constitute state action." *Eaton*, however, paved the way for *Simkins v. Moses H. Cone Hospital* (1963), wherein Greensboro, North Carolina dentist and NAACP leader George C. Simkins won admission to Cone's residential staff. Moreover, within months Title VI of the Civil Rights Act (1964) ordered nondiscrimination in all federally funded programs. *Simkins* remains the legal breakthrough in integrating the American hospital.

[*See also* Science; Technology.]

Reference

Morais, Herbert Monfrot. *The History of the Negro in Medicine.* Cornwells Heights, PA: Publishers Company, 1967, p. 141.

Further Reading

Reynolds, Preston P. "Dr. Louis T. Wright and the NAACP: Pioneers in Hospital Racial Integration." *American Journal of Public Health*, 90 (June 2000): 883–92.
———. *Durham's Lincoln Hospital.* Charleston, SC: Archdia, 2001.
Thomas, Karen Cruse. *Deluxe Jim Crow: Civil Rights and American Health Policy.* Athens: University of Georgia Press, 2011.

MICHEAUX, OSCAR   FILMMAKER

Born: January 24, Metropolis, IL
Education: Metropolis public schools
Died: March 25, 1951, Charlotte, NC

A pioneer filmmaker, Micheaux produced Race Movies during the Jim Crow era. He left Illinois at seventeen to be a writer, but worked as a Pullman porter and lived on a South Dakota farm.

Eventually, he began writing and self-publishing books and operating a film company, which issued *The Homesteader* (1919). Based on his novel, it showed blacks "in dignified roles" and was the first silent race movie. Micheaux made "44 of the 82 all-Negro pictures" advertised from 1920 to 1950, though most of his are lost. He financed production primarily with book sales, paid previews, and companies in New York City and Chicago, the large movie markets.

Micheaux's films captured the black experience. Some reviewers charged that he glorified elite and ignored poor blacks, but Micheaux exposed lived realities, including blacks' light-skin prejudice and whites' racist violence. A lynching witness inspired *Within Our Gates* (1919), which portrayed the Ku Klux Klan's wartime revival. *Birthright* (1924) depicted a black teacher's successful battle to build a school in the segregated South, while *Body and Soul* (1924) unveiled a hypocritical black preacher. *The Exile* (1931) became the first black sound film. Fittingly, the US Postal Service issued a Micheaux commemorative stamp (2010).

Further Reading

Bowser, Pearl, and Louise Spence. *Writing Himself into History: Oscar Micheaux, His Silent Films, and His Audiences*. New Brunswick, NJ: Rutgers University Press, 2000.
McGilligan, Patrick. *Oscar Micheaux, the Great and Only: The Life of America's First Great Black Filmmaker*. New York: HarperCollins, 2007.

MILITARY

African Americans' service in US Armed Forces parallels their long struggle for liberation, citizenship, and equality. Notwithstanding the nation's purpose for war, they served in the past and today to help defend and make it more inclusive.

Blacks mustered during slavery. Colonial militias used many enslaved and free blacks in Indian wars, allowing some slaves to earn freedom. But growing fear of slaves' rebellion led to black exclusion. Facing manpower needs in the Revolutionary War, the army enlisted slave and free black men from the North. They were mainly laborers, but about 5,000 bore arms. Thousands of bondmen escaped to the British side, there mainly laboring too; perhaps 1,000 engaged in fighting. Both sides promised liberty with land and/or a pension.

The color line endured in America. Northern states had begun gradual emancipation as Congress, in 1792, limited the army to "able-bodied white male citizens between the ages of 18 and 45." In 1798 it excluded "Negroes, mulattos, and Indians" from the marines. Still, while conserving white privilege, the army and navy impressed black quotas in the War of 1812 (1812–15). By 1820 the army banned further black impressment and the navy adopted a 5 percent quota in 1839. Blacks thus were less visible in the Mexican-American War (1846–48) and ordinarily did routine labor. Southern militia companies, now all-white, assisted slave catchers.

Black military participation surged in the Civil War and increased afterward. Slaves fled to Union lines in droves and commanders started keeping them. Called "contraband of war," they became paid workers and scouts before 1863, when the Emancipation Proclamation emancipated slaves of rebel masters and permitted blacks to join the army. Black enrollments, including women, approximated 200,000. Abolitionist Sojourner Truth was a nurse in a field hospital; Harriet Tubman a scout. Each also crusaded for justice during Reconstruction, when the army retained four black units: the 24th and 25th Infantries, 9th and 10th Cavalry Regiments. Whether "Buffalo Soldiers" in Indian Wars or "Smoked Yankees" in the Spanish-American and Philippine wars, they exhibited courage and dignity.

The War Department sustained the "invariable rule" of segregating African Americans. It deployed approximately 750,000 blacks within Jim Crow ranks during World War I, 90 percent of them in labor battalions. Many were assigned to the French army, where they found greater acceptance and received more honors than their brethren with the American Expeditionary Force. Urged by the NAACP, the War Department opened the Colored Officers' Training Camp at Fort Dodge in Des Moines, Iowa. It trained 639 men, less than 1 percent of the officer corps. Racial disparity persisted into World War II, when almost a million black men and women were in the military. Blacks protested racism in defense industries and Armed Forces, gaining a Committee on Fair Employment Practice (1941) and other reforms. Officials created Army Air Corps black units, whose recruits would be the Tuskegee Airmen, marines, Women's Auxiliary Army Corps (WACS), and the navy's Women Accepted for Volunteer Emergency Service (WAVES). With ongoing black protest and the President's Committee on Civil Rights submitting its report, *To Secure These Rights* (1947), Jim Crow policy officially ended. In 1948 the president ordered "that there shall be equality of treatment and opportunity for all persons in the armed services, without regard to race, color, or national origin" (Executive Order 9981). His order initiated military desegregation.

After the official pronouncement, desegregation came little by little. The authors of *The American Soldier* (1949) found higher ratios of positive racial attitudes among soldiers in mixed-race than single-race units. Between 1950 and 1953, when the army began desegregating its basic training and combat operations, one black Korean War soldier described critically what would persist for ensuing decades. Though "blacks and whites fought, slept, and ate together in Korea," he said, the officer corps and advanced programs virtually ignored African Americans. They mostly filled labor, ordnance, and infantry assignments, limiting their options to advance. Frequently, as in the WACS, blacks were confined to domestic and unskilled roles. On and off bases, however, they steadily made demands for unsegregated training, employment, housing, schools, and public accommodations, hereby energizing the civil rights movement. Indeed, the NAACP presented the military's move toward integration and its influence on how other nations viewed the United States in briefs and oral arguments for *Brown v. Board of Education*.

From *Brown* to the present, racial disparities, conspicuously for draftees and officers, have been persistent. Only 1.3 percent of draft board members were black by 1966 and local boards in seven states had none. Draft deferments, notwithstanding, escalated for young white middle- and upper-class men. Black and antiwar activists condemned the Selective Service "for favoring the induction of blacks and the poor." Blacks constituted 12 percent of ground troops but more than 20 percent of fatalities in Vietnam, 1966–69. Authorities agreed that "social and economic injustices in the society itself are at the root of inequities" (Binkin, 1982, p. 33). In 1972, the final year of the draft, blacks aggregated 18 percent of military personnel and 3.9 percent of officers. From 1973, when the All-Volunteer Force was instituted, blacks have been conspicuous in the national military service population. Studies confirm that they are in an overrepresented demographic of racial and ethnic minorities for whom the military services provide the opportunity to overcome economic and educational disadvantages. Blacks composed 20.3% of army, marines, navy, and air force personnel, as opposed to 6.8% of officers, by 1991. They comprised 10.6% of combat troops in the Persian Gulf War, compared to 20% of the casualties. Nationally, African Americans represented 13% of the military serving population in 1996. At the same time, they accounted for 30.2% of army, 18.5% of navy, 17.1% of marines, and 16.8% of air force personnel. So, black servicemen and women remain highly visible. Aggregate military membership in 2000 incorporated 34.4% minorities: 20.1% black, 7.9% Hispanic, and 6.3% others.

In 2010 service members were 14.4% female and 86.4% male, 70% of them white and 30% minorities: 17% black, 10.8% Hispanic, and 2.2% others. Such demographics mirror not only minorities' integration into the military but also inequalities in education and life chances that compel them to embrace it.

[*See also* Antiterror, Afghanistan, and Iraq Wars; Buffalo Soldiers; Civil War; Executive Order 9981 (1948); Indian Wars; Korean War; Persian Gulf War; Port Chicago Mutiny (1944); Revolutionary War; Spanish-American War; Vietnam War; World War I; World War II.]

References

Binkin, Martin. *Blacks and the Military.* Washington, DC: Brookings Institution Press, 1982, p. 33.
Executive Order 9981. Retrieved from www.trumanlibrary.org/9981a.htm

Further Reading

Buckley, Gail Lumet. *American Patriots: The Story of Blacks in the Military from the Revolution to Desert Storm.* New York: Random House, 2001.
Defense, U.S. Department of. *Demographics 2010 Profile of the Military Community.* (http://www.icfi.com/markets/defense/campaigns/workforce-research).
Evans, Rhonda. *A History of the Service of Ethnic Minorities in the U.S. Armed Forces.* Santa Barbara, CA: Center for the Study of Sexual Minorities in the Military, 2003.

MILLIKEN V. BRADLEY (1974)

US Supreme Court post-1954 school rulings gradually shifted. Between 1954 and 1972 the Court focused its decisions, including *Swann* (1971), on legally segregated schools. In *Keyes v. School District of Denver* (1973), however, it let stand a distinction between de jure or legal and de facto segregation in a northern school district.

Thus the Court narrowed its orders to desegregate northern schools. Black second-grader Ronald Bradley's parents sued Detroit Public Schools, which put him in a kindergarten class that was 97 percent black. Black pupils were 70 percent of Detroit's pupil population at the time. For plaintiffs' relief, a Federal District Court ordered an interdistrict desegregation plan, linking Detroit and fifty-three white suburban districts in a busing order desegregating inner-city and suburban schools. Its ruling fueled anti-busing sentiment among whites, who protested and litigated against the plan, but the Federal Appellate Court for the 6th Circuit sustained it. Yet, on appeal the Supreme Court majority found no solid evidence that segregation in Detroit was caused by discriminatory actions of outlying districts and struck down a metropolitan remedy. *Milliken* signaled a retreat. In his strong dissent, Justice Thurgood Marshall declared that white parents' fears had undermined the Court's *Brown* decision.

[*See also* Desegregation.]

Further Reading

Baugh, Joyce A. *The Detroit School Busing Case: Milliken v. Bradley and the Controversy over Desegregation.* Lawrence: University of Kansas Press, 2011.
Steinberg, Stephen. *Turning Back: The Retreat from Racial Justice in American Thought and Policy.* Boston: Beacon Press, 2001.

MINORITIES, RACIAL AND ETHNIC

Nonwhite minorities stand at the cutting edge of contemporary social history, including how their differences and experiences reflect majority group power and privilege. Minorities are largely nonnative, most as involuntary or voluntary immigrants. They aggregated 281.4 million, or 30 percent of the US population, in 2000. Judging aggregate nonwhite immigration and birth ratios, the Census Bureau estimates non-Hispanic whites will decline from a majority to 40 percent of Americans by 2100.

Minorities are American Indian and Alaska Native, Asian American, Black or African American, Hispanic or Latino, and Native Hawaiian and Other Pacific Islander. A sixth category, Multiracial American (6.8 million or 2.4%) was included tentatively in 2000. Blacks (12% or 35 million) and Latinos (12.5% or over 35 million) were the largest, compared to Asian Americans (3.6% or 10 million), American Indians (0.9% or 2.5 million), and Pacific Islanders (0.1% or 400,000). All contribute to the nation, whether culturally or economically, yet face racial or ethnic discrimination. Thus they evince disparities in education, employment, income, housing, health, and political participation. Blacks and Latinos remain in the forefront of debate and policy on race, class, and gender poverty; public welfare; criminal justice; and electoral politics.

[*See also* Interracial relations.]

Further Reading

Kivisto, Peter. *Race and Ethnicity: The Basics.* New York, Routledge, 2012.
McClain, Paula D., and Joseph Stewart Jr. *"Can We All Get Along": Racial and Ethnic Minorities in American Politics.* Boulder, CO: Westview Press, 2010.

MISCEGENATION

Derived from *genus* and *miscere*, Latin for race and mix, miscegenation historically evoked white fear. Democrats, charging Republicans with "the sexual mixing of races, particularly of whites and blacks," perpetrated anti-miscegenation laws in at least twenty, mostly southern states, from the end of the Civil War to *Loving v. Virginia* (1967). Anti-miscegenation ideology also fueled collective terror, such as black lynching, against "interracial domestic relationships." *Loving* overruled Virginia and all states' statutes banning white–black marriage.

Comparatively few interracial unions have occurred since that decision. For every 100,000 married couples in 1960, there were 126 white–black marriages and 396 by 1990. But attitudes were changing. In the mid-1990s, only 18 percent of whites said yes to this National Research Opinion Center query: "Do you think there should be laws against marriages between Blacks and Whites?" In addition, 97 and 99 percent of black men and women, respectively, preferred marriage in their racial group.

[*See also Loving v. Virginia* (1967).]

Further Reading

Lemire, Elise. *"Miscegenation": Making Race in America*. Philadelphia: University of Pennsylvania Press, 2002.
Robinson, Charles F. II. *Dangerous Liaisons: Sex and Love in the Segregated South*. Fayetteville, AR: University of Arkansas Press, 2003.

MISSISSIPPI FREEDOM DEMOCRATIC PARTY (MFDP)

Mississippi Democrats legally disfranchised blacks, a demographic and Republican majority, in 1890. They maintained one-party rule by law and terror.

In 1964 Student Nonviolent Coordinating Committee (SNCC), Congress of Racial Equality (CORE), and NAACP activists formed MFDP to register and empower black voters. Its integrated delegation challenged Mississippi's all-white delegates to be seated at the Democratic National Convention in Atlantic City, here refusing a brokered deal for two nonvoting seats. Thus, after exposing the state's racism in the nationally televised testimony of party leader Fannie Lou Hamer, MFDP walked out of the convention. It mobilized locally and statewide back home, increasing voter education, registration, voting, and empowerment.

[*See also* Freedom Summer.]

Further Reading

Collier-Thomas, Bettye, and V. P. Franklin, eds. *Sisters in the Struggle: African American Women in the Civil Rights and Black Power Movement.* New York: New York University Press, 2001.

Payne, Charles M. *I've Got the Light of Freedom: The Organizing Tradition and the Mississippi Freedom Struggle.* Berkeley: University of California Press, 2007.

MITCHELL, CLARENCE M.   NAACP DIRECTOR

Born: March 8, 1911, Baltimore, MD
Education: Lincoln University (PA), B.A., 1932; University of Maryland Law School, LL.B. 1962
Died: March 18, 1984, Washington, DC

Director of the NAACP's Legislative Bureau in Washington, DC, Mitchell was its lobbyist on Capitol Hill. Known as "the 101st Senator of the United States," he helped broker modern civil rights laws. After the passage of the Fair Housing Act (1968), the Congressional Quarterly Service stated that he "was the catalyst who organized and kept together the forces that passed the bill."

He emerged during the post–World War II struggle against Jim Crow. As NAACP labor liaison, he founded the Leadership Conference on Civil Rights (1950), including more than fifty civic, religious, and social organizations. While pursuing the conference's legislative priorities, he cultivated supporters in Congress, Democratic and Republican. A critical breakthrough came with the Civil Rights Act (1957). The first such law since 1875, it formed the US Commission on Civil Rights to advise and report to Congress and the Civil Rights Division in the Department of Justice to investigate or prosecute violations of civil liberties and rights. With segregated public accommodations and violent attacks on southern nonviolent activists rampant in the early 1960s, Mitchell lobbied tirelessly for protection. The Presidential Medal of Freedom (1980) honored him for helping to pass the Civil Rights Act (1964) and Voting Rights Act (1965).

Further Reading

Grofman, Bernard, ed. *Legacies of the 1964 Civil Rights Act.* Charlottesville: University Press of Virginia, 2000.

Watson, Denton L. *Lion in the Lobby: Clarence Mitchell, Jr.'s Struggle for the Passage of Civil Rights Laws.* Lanham, MD: University Press of America, 2002.

MONTGOMERY BUS BOYCOTT

Rosa Parks's arrest, 1 December 1955, for refusing to give her seat to a white passenger inspired a 381-day protest in Montgomery, Alabama. It not only involved nonviolence and a US Supreme Court decision against bus segregation; it also meant international press coverage for civil rights and Martin Luther King, Jr.'s leadership.

The black community sustained the boycott, set by the Women's Political Council for December 5, when Parks, local NAACP secretary, went on trial. After her conviction, civic groups and churches formed the Montgomery Improvement Association (MIA), elected King of Dexter Avenue Baptist president, and called a mass meeting to continue the effort. MIA sued in Federal Court and negotiated with city authorities, as blacks walked, used taxicabs, and car pooled. Facing police harassment, legal injunctions, arbitrary arrests, and racist violence, which brought them publicity as well as allies, they used, in King's words, "a new and powerful weapon–nonviolent resistance."

[*See also* Civil Rights Movement; Southern Christian Leadership Conference.]

Further Reading

Burns, Stewart, ed. *Daybreak of Freedom: The Montgomery Bus Boycott*. Chapel Hill: University of North Carolina Press, 1997.
King, Martin Luther, Jr. *Stride Toward Freedom: The Montgomery Story*. Boston: Beacon Press, 2010.

MOORE, HARRY T.
TEACHER AND CIVIL RIGHTS ACTIVIST

Born: November 18, 1905, Houston, FL
Education: Florida Memorial High School, graduated 1925; Florida Normal Institute, Bethune-Cookman College, A.A., 1936, B.S., 1951
Died: December 25, 1951, Tallahassee, FL

A bomb demolished the Florida home of Harry and Harriette Moore, parents, teachers, and civil rights activists, Christmas night in 1951. He died then; hospitalized, she died January 3. Pressed by the NAACP, the FBI investigated the Ku Klux Klan to no avail. The killers remain unknown.

The Moores reflected the activism of many black teachers in the segregated South. Founders of the Brevard County (1934) and Florida State (1941) NAACP, they fought segregation, initiating teachers' equal salary suit and seeking the right to vote. "A Voteless Citizen Is a Voiceless Citizen" was the motto of the Progressive Voters League, which Harry founded (1945). That year alone, it boosted statewide voter registration from 5 to 37 percent of voting age blacks. Retaliating, Brevard County's school board fired the couple in 1946. After, as state NAACP executive director (1946–51), Harry protested to stop police brutality against blacks. Conceding ground, Brevard County hired the state's first black deputy sheriff (1950) and even allowed him to arrest whites. In addition, Harry pursued the prosecution of Lake County's sheriff for shooting two black men, both in handcuffs. But he and his wife soon were killed. The National NAACP honored them as Civil Rights Martyrs (1952).

Further Reading

Emmons, Caroline. "'Somebody Has Got to Do that Work': Harry T. Moore and the Struggle for African-American Voting Rights in Florida." *Journal of Negro History*, 82 (Spring 1997): 232–43.
Green, Ben. *Before His Time: The Untold Story of Harry T. Moore, America's First Civil Rights Martyr*. Gainesville: University Press of Florida, 2005.

MORGAN V. VIRGINIA (1946)

Irene Morgan, a black Virginian, was on a packed Greyhound bus en route to Baltimore, Maryland in July 1944. Ordered by the driver to give up her seat in the "colored" section to a white passenger, she not only refused but also resisted. She was arrested, convicted, and fined.

Morgan secured counsel. Richmond NAACP attorney Spottswood W. Robinson (1916–98) filed her case. However, the Virginia Supreme Court of Appeals upheld the fine. Robinson appealed its decision and the US Supreme Court consented to review it. He, Thurgood Marshall, and William Hastie presented the oral argument. They argued that Virginia's separate seating statute was an illegal burden on American commerce. Segregation laws also differed by state, so varying racial restrictions would be imposed. By a 7–2 majority the Court concurred, ruled for Morgan, and disallowed segregation on interstate buses. The Fellowship of Reconciliation launched a 1947 interracial journey to test compliance with *Morgan*.

[*See also* Journey of Reconciliation (1947).]

Further Reading

Barnes, Catherine A. *Journey from Jim Crow: The Desegregation of Southern Transit*. New York: Columbia University Press, 1983.

Catsam, Derek C. and Brendan Wolfe. "*Morgan v. Virginia* (1946)." Encyclopedia
Virginia. Virginia Foundation for the Humanities, July 2, 2014. Online July 27, 2014.
Retrieved from www.encyclopediavirginia.org/Morgan_v_Virginia#start_entry

MORRISON, TONI   WRITER

Born: February 13, 1931, Lorain, OH
Education: Howard University, B.A., 1953; Cornell University, M.A.,
1955

One of the most influential contemporary writers, Morrison is the
first African American to receive the Nobel Prize in Literature (1993).
Instilling family stories, reading at preschool age, she became an excellent
student. Graduate school and teaching literature inspired her to pursue
writing. She explains: "The search for love and identity runs through
most everything I write."

Her most uncommon characters seek to affirm themselves in communities or overcome barriers. *Sula* depicts the close friendship of Nel
Wright and Sula Peace and life in a midwestern community, The Bottom,
between the 1920s and 1940s. *The Bluest Eye* presents a black girl who
prays for blue eyes, believing such would ensure her acceptance by people in a 1940s Ohio town. The main character in *Song of Solomon* is
Milkman Dead, an Ohioan. He goes to the South to learn of his ancestors, whose folklore honored escaped slaves who flew back to Africa.
Tar Baby, which uses whites as key actors, portrays race, class, and gender conflict on a Caribbean island. *Beloved* unveils the ideal and reality
of freedom. The slave Sethe escapes with her infant and, to elude capture, kills the child. Thus, though freeing herself, she becomes an outcast
among the freedpeople.

Further Reading

Furman, Jan. *Toni Morrison's Fiction.* Columbia: University of South Carolina
Press, 2014.
Seward, Adrienne Lanier, and Justine Tally, eds. *Toni Morrison: Memory and
Meaning.* Jackson: University Press of Mississippi, 2014.

MOSELEY-BRAUN, CAROL   US SENATOR

Born: August 16, 1947, Chicago, IL
Education: University of Illinois, Chicago, B.A., 1967; University of
Chicago Law School, 1972

Moseley-Braun was the first black female elected to the US Senate. Her journey to it began when Illinois' incumbent Democratic senator voted aye to confirm Judge Clarence Thomas, accused of sexual harassment, as associate justice of the Supreme Court. Outraged feminists, blacks, and liberals urged her, "a rising star in Democratic circles," to challenge his reelection bid. Running an underfunded campaign but garnering the vast majority of blacks and women's votes, she won the primary and election (1992).

Some political observers labeled Moseley-Braun a "symbolic senator." Her campaign, following an investigation, faced a misconduct charge. She also received harsh criticism from Democrats for her trip to Nigeria, whose military president had been censured for human rights violations. Blacks were upset by Moseley-Braun's support for prosecuting teen offenders as adults and her refusal to endorse a black candidate for Chicago mayor. Still, she earned wide respect. For example, many liberal and progressive activists praised her speech opposing a Senate bill to renew the flag label of the United Daughters of the Confederacy. "This vote is about race ... and the single most painful episode in American history," she said (Smith, 1992–2003, p. 484). She served as the US Ambassador to New Zealand (1999–2001).

Reference

Smith, Jessie Carney, ed., *Notable Black American Women*, Book 2. Detroit: Gale Research, 1992-2003, p. 484.

Further Reading

Gill, LaVerne McCain. *African American Women in Congress: Forming and Transforming History*. New Brunswick, NJ: Rutgers University Press, 1997.
Kenney, David, and Robert E. Hartley. *An Uncertain Tradition: U.S. Senators from Illinois, 1818–2003*. Carbondale: Southern Illinois University Press, 2003.

MOTLEY, CONSTANCE BAKER ATTORNEY
AND FEDERAL JUDGE

Born: September 14, 1921, New Haven, CT
Education: Fisk University, 1941; New York University, A.B., 1943; Columbia Law School, LL.B., 1946
Died: September 28, 2005, New York, NY

NAACP Legal Defense Fund (LDF) lawyer, Motley argued major desegregation cases and earned distinction in public service.

She rose by means of ability. Daughter of West Indian immigrants and the ninth of twelve children, she instilled values of education and hard work. Thanks to a New Haven, Connecticut philanthropist, Motley finished college. She then earned a law degree and clerked for LDF.

By 1950 she had become a superb litigator, mainly assisting Robert Carter with school segregation cases. She co-wrote the initial brief in *Brown* and, by 1957, represented the nine black students who integrated Little Rock, Arkansas' Central High School. She presented ten oral arguments to the US Supreme Court and won nine, desegregating schools and the universities of Alabama, Georgia, Mississippi, and Clemson University. *Meredith v. Fair* (1962) resulted not only in James Meredith's enrollment at Ole Miss but also in deadly rioting on the campus.

Appointed and elected to the New York State Senate (1964), Motley was its first black female senator. Other firsts included her term as Manhattan Borough president (1965), the best-paid position ever held by a black woman, and a federal judgeship (1966). Inducted to the National Women's Hall of Fame, she also received the Presidential Citizens Medal (2001).

Further Reading

Motley, Constance Baker. *Equal Justice under Law: An Autobiography.* New York: Farrar, Straus and Giroux, 1998.

Salkin, Patricia E., ed. *Pioneering Women Lawyers: From Kate Stoneman to the Present.* Albany, NY: Albany Law School, 2008.

MOYNIHAN REPORT

Economist and assistant secretary of Labor Daniel Patrick Moynihan's *The Negro Family: The Case for National Action* (1965) stirred controversy.

Moynihan detailed African American familial disorganization. Too many children, mostly born out of wedlock, forced their parents to quit school. Parents' low educational levels, in turn, meant inadequate income, thus depriving children of opportunities. Women headed 25 percent of households, where girls often became pregnant and boys rarely learned "appropriate" male roles. To disrupt this cycle of family poverty, Moynihan prescribed remedies of education, job training, and military service for young men. Higher rates of employment were essential. More and better jobs would "strengthen the Negro family so as to enable it to raise and support its members as do other families" (Shinkin and Frate, 1978, p. 174).

Many black leaders and scholars roundly criticized the report. Their basic critique was that it over-blamed the victims. They urged measures to end racial discrimination and educate blacks and the poor.

[*See also* Poverty; Welfare.]

Reference

Shimkin, Edith M., and Dennis A. Frate, eds., *Extended Family in Black Societies.* Chicago: Aldine, 1978, p. 174.

Further Reading

Geary, Daniel. "Racial Liberalism, the Moynihan Report, and the Daedalus Project on the 'Negro American.'" *Daedalus*, 140 (Winter 2011): 53–66.

Patterson, James T. *Freedom Is Not Enough: The Moynihan Report and America's Struggle over Black Family Life from LBJ to Obama.* New York: Basic Books, 2010.

MUHAMMAD, ELIJAH   RELIGIOUS LEADER

Born: October 1897, Sandersville, GA
Education: Eighth grade
Died: February 25, 1975, Chicago, IL

Poole "had seen enough of the white man's brutality in Georgia to last me 26,000 years" (Pitre, 2007, p. 3) and said America would never ensure "freedom, justice, and equality" to descendants of her slaves.

He migrated and worked for a Detroit automaker. But he was jobless in 1931, when Wallace Fard recruited him to the year-old Temple No. 1, Nation of Islam (NOI). Formerly in the Moorish Science Temple, Fard taught the Koran. Elijah, given the surname Muhammad, was Fard's chief aide. Yet internal conflict, violence, and federal surveillance ensued. Muhammad relocated to Chicago, founded Temple No. 2, and rose to imam after Fard disappeared in 1934.

Honored by the NOI faithful as the Messenger of Allah, Muhammad became a powerful advocate of Islam, black pride, and self-determination. Rejecting nonviolence, integration, and dependence on the white man (his characterization of the civil rights leadership), he preached and promoted racial separatism, economic independence, and Muslim doctrine. Blacks flocked to the Nation by tens of thousands, notably in large urban areas, when Malcolm X served as its national spokesman. Its prison education and antidrug programs transformed many African Americans. When the

Messenger died, NOI had an estimated 120,000 members, 75 temples, and more than $40 million in assets.

Reference

Pitre, Abul. *The Educational Philosophy of Elijah Muhammad: Education for a New World*. Lanham, MD: University Press of America, 2007, p. 3.

Further Reading

Berg, Herbert. *Elijah Muhammad and Islam*. New York: New York University Press, 2009.
Clegg, Claude Andrew III. *The Life and Times of Elijah Muhammad*. Chapel Hill: University of North Carolina Press, 2014.

MULTICULTURALISM

Intended to foster cultural diversity and understanding, multiculturalism is vital in contemporary education.

It promotes knowledge of and respect for diverse cultures, Western and non-Western. Proponents argue that instruction and study about different experiences, whether shaped by race, ethnicity, religion, oppression, or privilege, could facilitate interaction and acceptance between individuals or groups with varied backgrounds. They also emphasize the use of instructional materials exploring racial and ethnic relations; immigration; or African American, Latino, and women's histories. Informing students' appreciation of differences, such learning promises to decrease group stereotypes, increase social interactions, and instill values of tolerance.

Extensively instituted in K–12 curricula, the multicultural approach strongly influences postsecondary minority, women's, and international studies. It also intersects objectives of the *National History Standards* (1996), which many opponents charged with undermining Western culture. Multicultural perspectives are well represented by Teaching Tolerance, a school project of the Southern Poverty Law Center in Montgomery, Alabama.

[*See also* Feminism; Interracial Relations.]

Further Reading

Schramm-Pate, Susan, and Rhonda B. Jeffries, eds. *Grappling with Diversity: Readings on Civil Rights Pedagogy and Critical Multiculturalism*. Albany: State University of New York Press, 2008.
Zimmerman, Jonathan. *Whose America? Culture Wars in the Public Schools*. Cambridge, MA: Harvard University Press, 2002.

MURRAY, PAULI
WOMEN'S AND CIVIL RIGHTS LEADER

Born: November 20, 1910, Baltimore, MD
Education: Hunter College, B.A., 1933; Howard Law School, LL.B., 1944; University of California–Berkeley, LL.M., 1945; Yale University, S.J.D., 1965; General Theological Seminary, M. Div., 1976
Died: July 1, 1985, Pittsburgh, PA

Murray is revered for *Proud Shoes: The Story of an American Family* (1956), which traces her family's contributions to education, service, and citizenship ca. 1860s–1950s. Activist and scholar, she resisted race, class, and gender injustice. Her *States' Laws on Race and Color* (1951), said Thurgood Marshall, was the bible for the NAACP's strategy of "direct attack" on segregation. Cofounder of the National Organization for Women (1966), she became the first black woman priest in the Episcopal Church (1977). Elected to sainthood, she is profiled in *Holy Women, Holy Men* (2012).

She fought Jim Crow. Her best known challenge built on the NAACP's unsuccessful suit (1933) of a black applicant to the University of North Carolina Pharmacy School. Motivated by that case, she applied to its graduate school in 1938. In his rejection letter, the dean reminded her that "members of your race are not admitted to the University." Elsewhere, she engaged in nonviolent protest against the color line. Virginia police arrested Murray for violating the state's segregated seat law on a Greyhound bus in 1940. As a Howard Law School student during World War II, she not only challenged sexism in her classes but also helped organize sit-down protests at white-only restaurants.

Further Reading

Azaransky, Sarah. *The Dream Is Freedom: Pauli Murray and American Democratic Faith.* New York: Oxford University Press, 2011.
O'Dell, Darlene. *Sites of Southern Memory: The Autobiographies of Katharine Du Pre Lumpkin, Lillian Smith, and Pauli Murray.* Charlottesville: University Press of Virginia, 2001.

MUSIC

The black musical tradition has enriched American culture and society. In 1903 W. E. B. Du Bois stated that "by fateful chance the Negro folk song – the rhythmic cry of the slave – stands today not simply as the sole

American music, but as the most beautiful expression of human experience born this side of the seas" (Blight and Gooding, 1997, p. 186). It "remains as the singular spiritual heritage of the nation," he added, "and the greatest gift of the Negro people."

Its creators came mostly from West and Central Africa. There, prior to and during the Atlantic slave trade, music-making was customary. To wit, singers were vital in ancestor worship and ceremonies for marriage, birth, death, hunting, and the harvest. Music evinced improvisation (instrumental and vocal) and repetition. A core feature was polyphony (two or more melodic lines or parts). Instruments and voices together effected harmonic exchanges. Tribes, clans, and nations customarily sang by a method of call-and-response. After a lead singer or canter began a holler or chant, then others answered in a choral refrain. He led via varying pitches: yodels, falsettos, screams, slides, or raspy sounds. Drums (with wood, gourd, or clay bodies), clapsticks, bells, and rattles provided percussion. The common string instruments were the bow, harp, and lute, forerunner of the American banjo. Traditional wind instruments included the flute, animal horn-trumpet, and oboe.

In the face of New World slavery and oppression, Africans retained and reinvented many of their religious and musical customs. Gradually accepting Catholicism and Protestantism, but retaining elements of indigenous African religions, including Islam, slaves created Afro-Christianity. Converts modified tribal traditions of "sacrifice, drumming, singing, and [spirit] possession." Slaves also assembled the West African "circle and [used] its counterclockwise direction" or "ring-shout" in worship services

Bondmen and women were creative vocalists. This is not surprising, given their roots in oral cultures. Their learning to read and write was strictly forbidden. Antebellum art shows slaves playing banjos and dancing; slave gatherings also had singing and storytelling. They engaged in "lining out" hymns in church service, where maybe only one was literate. The leader recited a line of the song and the congregants would sing it. In the "invisible institution" of slave and free black churches, worshipers normally lined out their hymns. In 1801 ex-slave and Methodist minister Richard Allen published a hymnal for the African Methodist Episcopal Church denomination, which he founded in 1816. Rural black Methodists and Baptists regularly praised God with a holy ring-shout or "shuffle step" at camp meetings and revivals. Slave "hush harbors" resonated with spirituals of sorrow, consolation, and hope for freedom.

Folk music evolved as well. During the 1830s white minstrel Thomas "Daddy" Rice performed a "shuffling Sambo" routine as the slave Jim

Crow. Meantime, slaves simply made up songs to relieve the stress of toil or affirm themselves. Their dances often imitated animal movements, as in the "Turkey Trot." Some feigned "cake walks" to mimic the stiff ballroom dancing of white people. Others were "camper downs," "patting juba," as well as jumps and scampers, hand clapping, knee and shoulder tapping, and shuffles.

Post-emancipation black musicians hoped for the opportunity to perform with dignity. Black minstrels sometimes put "darky" dialect in their lyrics. The black Georgia Minstrels sang ditties such as "All Coons Look Alike to Me." Black songwriter James A. Bland wrote more than 700 songs and his "Carry Me Back to Old Virginny" (1878) later became Virginia's state song. Before long, itinerant black pianists in bordellos and saloons were turning to syncopated tunes and piano rags. Ragtime soon captivated the honky-tonk and vaudeville circuits, gaining an international following ca. 1890s–1910. Its premier composer was Scott Joplin, whose "Harlem Rag" (1897) energized the spirit of those times. Black churches and colleges, moreover, promoted religious music. Among the best college vocalists were the Fisk Jubilee Singers and Hampton Singers; both groups modernized the Negro spiritual. Atlanta University graduates James Weldon and John Rosamond Johnson composed "Lift Every Voice and Sing" (1900), by the 1920s sung everywhere as "the Negro National Anthem."

Improvisation endured as a distinctive aspect of black music in the twentieth century. Prior to the mid-century, emerging radio, recording, and motion picture industries were segregated, thus sustaining a black "race market." During the 1960s, while still prioritizing their "race" audience, more and more African American musicians entered mainstream entertainment and recreated black musicality.

Every musical genre exhibited creativity. Concert music demonstrated it in spirituals such as "A Balm in Gilead "and folk songs such as "Ol' Man River." These were the stock-in-trade for black concert artists such as Roland Hayes, Paul Robeson, and Marian Anderson. They sang and recorded in English, French, German, and Italian, as did more recent black opera stars Leontyne Price, Jessye Norman, and Laurence R. Albert. Blues, rooted in slave field hollers, work songs, and spirituals, developed in three key forms. Country or Down-Home Blues usually involved a performer, self-accompanied on guitar, singing about personal setbacks. Charley Patton, a creator of Delta Blues, represented that form. Picking while talking or "signifying," Patton produced several popular records between 1929 and 1934. W. C. Handy, "Father of the Blues," invented the second format by employing a twelve-bar structure, as in his famous "Memphis Blues" (1912), a first in sheet music. Cabaret diva Mamie Smith personified the third form, Classic or City Blues, using an ensemble accompaniment. "You Can't Keep a Good Man Down" (1920), among other hits, made her "Empress of the Blues." Starting with "I Cried for You" (1936), Billie Holiday attracted a large white following and enjoyed "crossover" fame.

Jazz took the Harlem Renaissance and Swing Era (1920s–30s) by storm, forging many subgenres or styles. Drawing on ragtime and blues, Dixieland or New Orleans jazz combined big band and orchestra modes, featuring a five to eight-instrument combo for melody (trombone, clarinet, cornet) and rhythm (guitar, piano, trap drum set, tuba). One of its best practitioners was cornetist Joseph "King" Oliver. Writers touted Oliver's Chicago orchestra for its dance jazz and showcasing New Orleans–born trumpeter Louis "Satchmo" Armstrong, widely acclaimed for his solos, playing against or behind the beat, and "scat singing." Pianist, composer, and conductor Edward "Duke" Ellington propelled boogie-woogie and swing-jazz. His band, the attraction of Harlem's elite Cotton Club ca. 1920s–40s, subsequently performed overseas on Department of State "cultural diplomacy" tours in the Cold War era. His discography, fusing classical and jazz motifs, includes more than 2,000 songs, "Take the A Train" (1941) being one of the most memorable.

The 1940s ushered in Bebop, displaying quick tempos, interlocking rhythms, and small combos. Beboppers, such as saxophonist Charlie "Yardbird" Parker and trumpeter John "Dizzy" Gillespie, transformed jazz into a "musician's music." Bebop cofounder Thelonious Monk, who riffed in "irregular rhythms and jarring harmonies," boasted an international fan base. His album *Brilliant Corners* (1956) is recognized as an artistic treasure. Jazz pianist and vocalist Nat "King" Cole, by contrast, embraced melodies, producing hit ballads like "Unforgettable" (1950). Bebop's style inspired free jazz and avant-garde jazz, giving performers more latitude (as in John Coltrane's riffs), and jazz fusion, which interfaced jazz and rock (as did trumpeter Miles Davis). At the same time, gospel, rhythm & blues, and rock 'n' roll emerged. Blues people incorporated electric guitars into their routines, including pioneers B. B. King and Chuck Berry, and gained black and white audiences. Actor-singer Harry Belafonte debuted Caribbean popular and calypso songs in *Calypso* (1956), among the earliest black million-copy sellers.

Gospel music increased its popularity. Former bluesman Thomas Dorsey was the "Father of Gospel Music." Debuting with "If You See My Saviour, Tell Him That You Saw Me" (1928), he recorded more than 400 songs. He organized the National Convention of Gospel Choirs and Choruses in 1933. Mentor to Mahalia Jackson, Rosetta Tharpe, and James Cleveland, Dorsey anchored the Golden Age of Gospel (1940s–60s) and introduced gospel-based songs in the Civil Rights Movement. Critics called Dorsey protégée Jackson, creator of 30 albums and 12 million-selling singles, the "World's Greatest Gospel Singer." Cleveland probably was gospel's most innovative artist. His "Peace Be Still" (1963) "sold over 800,000 copies and set the standard for modern gospel choir recordings" (www.encyclopedia.com/topic/ James_Cleveland.aspx).

Consistently creative, black music grew in demand and reached a broad public. Black musicians boosted record sales of major companies, even as some recorded on their own and other black labels. Ex-gospelers Ray Charles, Sam Cook, and James Brown remade rhythm and blues and rock with powerful rhythms, deep melodies, and social messages. Brown, known for his passion in dance and song, was also a creator of funk, "a heavily rhythmic, dance-oriented music," disco, and hip-hop (or rap) music. Black-owned Motown Records of Detroit became the leading producer of soul music. It signed Aretha Franklin, who topped the charts with "Respect" (1967). Eventually, she "had more million-selling records than any other woman in music history" (www.rollingstone .com/music/artists/aretha-franklin/biography). Michael Jackson, leader of Motown's Jackson Five, launched his solo career in 1971, released major best-sellers like "Bad" (1987), and reigned as "the world's most popular contemporary musician." Beside Motown's stars stood musical artists such as trumpeter Wynton Marsalis, internationally famous "for both jazz and classical music recordings," and gospel icon Shirley Caesar, who combines singing and talking. Rhythmic talk spawned hip-hop (1970s) as deejays "began speaking to the rhythm of the music." It surged with "Rapper's Delight" (1979). Rap thrives in the present; it expresses the frustrations and hopes of urban black and other youths of color.

[*See also* Dance; Film; Theatre.]

Reference

Blight, David W., and Robert Gooding-Williams, eds., *The Souls of Black Folk by W. E. B. Du Bois*. Boston: Bedford/St. Martin's, 1997, p. 186.

Further Reading

Jackson, Jerma A. *Singing in My Soul: Black Gospel Music in a Secular Age.* Chapel Hill: University of North Carolina Press, 2004.

Peretti, Burton W. *Lift Every Voice: The History of African American Music.* Lanham, MD: Rowman & Littlefield, 2009.

Von Eschen, Penny M. *Satchmo Blows Up the World: Jazz Ambassadors Play the Cold War.* Cambridge: Harvard University Press, 2004.

NATION OF ISLAM (NOI)

Founded in Detroit (1930), NOI is the largest body of unorthodox US black Muslims.

Relocating it to Chicago, Elijah Muhammad was imam from 1934 to 75. He oversaw construction of its home mosque and headquarters while preaching Islam, racial separatism, and black self-sufficiency. He converted Malcolm X in 1952, appointed him national spokesman, and opened dozens of mosques. Alongside the Clara Muhammad Schools (honoring his wife) and *Muhammad Speaks*, the official newspaper, NOI owned businesses, farms, and real estate in America and abroad. Muhammad rejected the civil rights movement and racial integration as "self-destruction, death, and nothing else." Echoing that message, Malcolm X stressed black nationalism and armed self-defense before resigning in 1964.

By 1975 NOI had an estimated 120,000 members, 75 mosques, and assets of $40 million. Its prison education and antidrug programs transformed the lives of countless blacks. Rejecting its orthodox Islam affiliation, which followed Muhammad's death, Louis Farrakhan became imam of a walkout membership (20,000–50,000) in 1978. Restoring NOI's name and separatist and nationalist traditions, and publishing *The Final Call*, he has made NOI a controversial force in politics.

[*See also* Farrakhan, Louis; Malcolm X; Muhammad, Elijah; Religion.]

Further Reading

Curtis, Edward E. *Black Muslim Religion in the Nation of Islam, 1960–1975*. Chapel Hill: University of North Carolina Press, 2006.
Gibson, Dawn-Marie, and Jamillah Karim. *Women of the Nation: Between Black Protest and Sunni Islam*. New York: New York University Press, 2014.

NATIONAL ASSOCIATION FOR THE ADVANCEMENT OF COLORED PEOPLE (NAACP)

Architect of the *Brown* decision, the NAACP is the oldest, largest, and arguably most significant civil rights organization. Formed in 1909, it joined whites and blacks who opposed racial violence and Booker T. Washington's conciliatory leadership and demanded "the equal protection of the laws." W. E. B. Du Bois, director of publicity and research, edited *The Crisis*. Its New York national office and board of directors oversaw local and state branches and regional offices.

The Legal Committee (1913) shaped the agenda. It included a national campaign against lynching and lawsuits contesting Jim Crow education, suffrage, housing, employment, criminal justice, and military service. In 1917 James Weldon Johnson became field secretary to organize branches and served as the first black executive secretary (1920–30). In 1940 the board established the NAACP Legal Defense and Educational Fund, Inc. (LDF) for litigation. By 1948 there were "734 branches out of 1,123, a percentage of sixty-five percent," in the South. Led by Thurgood Marshall and his staff, with lawyers such as Oliver W. Hill of Virginia, LDF won Supreme Court decisions outlawing the "white primary" election (1944), housing "restrictive covenants" (1948), segregated graduate education (1950), and public school segregation (1954).

Buffeted by challenges since 1954, the NAACP has been resilient and remains a leading force for racial equality. Financial and policy differences led LDF and the parent body to separate in 1956. However, the NAACP Legal Department under Robert Carter successfully litigated school desegregation and voting rights cases. This paralleled the NAACP's support of organizations using nonviolent strategies as well as its lobbying to secure the 1960s Civil and Voting Rights and Fair Housing laws. Advocating integration and criticizing Black Power politics, its more than half-million membership supported crucial reforms, including court-ordered busing; affirmative action programs; electing liberals, blacks, and other minorities to public office; abolishing police brutality; and ending race and class poverty. NAACP members helped sustain the movement to end South Africa's apartheid system, yet its leadership faltered (due partly to misconduct) and finances weakened. Thanks to board, executive officer, and staff policies implemented in 1995, the NAACP has reclaimed its leading position in the freedom struggle.

[*See also Brown v. Board of Education* (1954); Civil Rights Movement.]

Further Reading

Bynum, Thomas L. *NAACP Youth and the Fight for Black Freedom, 1936–1965.* Knoxville: University of Tennessee Press, 2013.
Sullivan, Patricia. *Lift Every Voice: The NAACP and the Making of the Civil Rights Movement.* New York: The New Press, 2009.

NATIONAL ASSOCIATION OF BLACK SOCIAL WORKERS (NABSW)

Founded during the Black Power movement (1968), NABSW has headquarters in Washington, DC, as well as state and local affiliates.

It publishes the *Black Caucus Journal*, which engages race and public policy. It prioritizes equitable human services in and trains advocates for underserved communities of color. Its Office of Student Affairs pursues the recruitment and retention of African American students, along with the study and practice of diversity, in schools of social work. Related initiatives center on policy advocacy and delivery of services, including family adoptions of black children. Affiliates also promote public education, job training, employment opportunity, and political activism.

[*See also* Family.]

Further Reading

Bell, Joyce M. *The Black Power Movement and American Social Work.* New York: Columbia University Press, 2014.
Bent-Goodley, Tricia, ed. *African-American Social Workers and Social Policy.* New York: Haworth Social Work Practice Press, 2003.

NATIONAL ASSOCIATION OF COLORED WOMEN (NACW)

Founded in 1896, the year of the Supreme Court's "equal, but separate" decision, NACW was the first national organization of black women. It united middle-class associations in a strong body.

NACW pursued activism and service. Its 5,000 members in 1897, representing 14 states and the District of Columbia, espoused moral behavior and race uplift. If their motto "Lifting as We Climb" implicated elitism, they prioritized the race's most vulnerable – the uneducated, poor, and suffering – while pursuing civil rights and social justice. Uplifting was a duty regardless of literacy, gender, or class. NACW local affiliates funded, among other initiatives, kindergartens, literary clubs, orphanages, and homes for elders. Many supported the antilynching, women's suffrage, and "Don't Buy Where You Can't Work" campaigns. Membership totaled 100,000 by 1924 but declined considerably during the Great Depression and after the National Council of Negro women formed in 1935 (www .blackpast.org/aah/national-council-negro-women-1935).

[*See also* National Council of Negro Women (NCNW).]

Further Reading

Carle, Susan D. *Defining the Struggle: National Racial Justice Organizing, 1880–1915.* New York: Oxford University Press, 2014.

White, Deborah Gray. *Too Heavy a Load: Black Women in Defense of Themselves, 1894–1994.* New York: W. W. Norton, 1999.

NATIONAL COUNCIL OF NEGRO WOMEN (NCNW)

Founded in 1935, NCNW is one of the largest and most influential black women's organizations worldwide. Its founder, Mary McLeod Bethune, formerly president of the National Association of Colored Women, envisioned a more inclusive and activist organization. A reported twenty-nine church, civic, professional, and sororal groups, elite as well as working class, sent delegates to the founding conference in New York City. Bethune served as president until 1949.

NCNW pursued civil and human rights, black self-help, and community service. Many members joined coalitions in support of federal antilynching legislation. They supported local communities' nonviolent protests against Jim Crow in relief and jobs programs (1930s); defense industries and Armed Forces during World War II; and denial of the right to vote. Their delegation attended the inaugural meeting of the United Nations (1945). Afterward, they contributed crucially to school desegregation, affirmative action, antipoverty programs, and UN humanitarian projects. Today, with an estimated membership of 4 million, NCNW continues its work for social justice.

[*See also* National Association of Colored Women (NACW).]

Further Reading

Knupfer, Anne Meis. *The Chicago Black Renaissance and Women's Activism.* Urbana: University of Illinois Press, 2006.

Smith, Elaine M. *Mary McLeod Bethune and the National Council of Negro Women: Pursuing a True and Unfettered Democracy.* Washington, DC: Alabama State University for the Bethune Council House, National Historic Site, National Park Service, 2003.

NATIONAL URBAN LEAGUE (NUL)

Formed in 1910 as the National League on Urban Conditions Among Negroes, NUL is a major social service and civil rights organization. Today, with more than 100 local affiliates in 35 states, it pursues the well-being of blacks and the disadvantaged regardless of color.

Its motto "Not Alms But Opportunity" guided NUL programs. Black sociologist George E. Haynes, later a Fisk University professor, became the first director (1918); he prioritized equal education, employment, and housing. Affiliates formed in the nation's largest cities. Undertaking research and publishing *Opportunity: A Journal of Negro Life* (1923–48), the league fought racial discrimination in trade and industrial unions, the civil service, and Armed Forces. During the directorship of Whitney M. Young Jr. (1961–71), it helped define federal civil rights policy, the War on Poverty, and affirmative action. After the 1960s Los Angeles and other riots, it won more aid to families with dependent children; job training for high school dropouts; and partnered on job placement, voter registration, and welfare projects. Director Vernon E. Jordan Jr. (1972–81) not only expanded such initiatives and started an annual report, *The State of Black America*; he also obtained significant donations from corporations.

[*See also* Civil Rights Movement.]

Further Reading

Armfield, Felix L. *Eugene Kinckle Jones: The National Urban League and Black Social Work, 1910–1940*. Urbana: University of Illinois Press, 2012.
Reed, Touré F. *Not Alms But Opportunity: The Urban League and the Politics of Racial Uplift, 1910–1950*. Chapel Hill: University of North Carolina Press, 2008.

NÉGRITUDE

Poet and statesman Aimé Césaire of Martinique and his fellow intellectuals in 1930s Paris first used Négritude to affirm "that one is black and proud of it." Similar to earlier ideas, such as the "New Negro," it inspired a literary movement emphasizing black identity and liberation in Africa and the African diaspora.

[*See also* New Negro Movement; Pan-African Movement.]

Further Reading

Césaire, Aimé. *The Original 1939 Notebook of a Return to the Native Land: Bilingual Edition*. Edited by A. James Arnold and Clayton Eshleman. Middletown: Wesleyan University Press, 2013.
King, Richard H. *Race, Culture, and the Intellectuals: 1940–1970*. Washington, DC: Woodrow Wilson Center Press, 2004.

NEGRO HISTORY MOVEMENT

Formal study of the black past followed *History of the Negro Race in America from 1619 to 1880* (1882), by ex-Union soldier and pastor

George Washington Williams, and *A School History of the Negro Race in America, from 1619 to 1890* (1890), by North Carolina educator Edward A. Johnson.

Negro history evolved as a field in the early 1900s. Atlanta University professor W. E. B. Du Bois hosted annual research conferences, publishing sixteen historical and sociological Studies of the Negro Problem (ca. 1899–1910) that inspired much inquiry. Carter G. Woodson, the "Father of Negro History," made recovery of the black experience his lifework. He founded the Association for the Study of Negro Life and History (ASNLH) in 1915 and the *Journal of Negro History* (JNH) in 1916. Woodson critically defined black historiography and mentored its noted researchers and scholars. To promote race pride as well as "to convince all that we have a heritage," he established "Negro History Week" (1926) and the *Negro History Bulletin* for juvenile readers (1937). His scholarly contributions helped lay the groundwork for Black Studies in the 1960s. Afro-American replaced Negro in ASNLH's official name by 1972. African American is used in the names of its *Journal* and *Bulletin* today.

[*See also* Afro-American Studies.]

Further Reading

Dagbovie, Pero Gaglo. *The Early Black History Movement, Carter G. Woodson, and Lorenzo Johnston Greene*. Urbana: University of Illinois Press, 2007.
Meier, August, and Elliott Rudwick. *Black History and the Historical Profession, 1915–1980*. Urbana: University of Illinois Press, 1986.

NEW LEFT

Inspired by the civil rights movement and youth counterculture, centered in academia, New Left ideology framed 1960s radicalism. New leftists moved beyond communist and socialist agendas to articulate a universal vision of human equality. Antiracist, antiwar, feminist, and free-speech activists, among others, confronted Cold War politics and society.

They invoked a democratic and inclusive America. In the *Port Huron Statement* (1962) Students for a Democratic Society (SDS) called for student awareness and political opposition to the military-industrial complex. Also, the Student Nonviolent Coordinating Committee (SNCC) fought against racial segregation and economic injustice by means of sit-ins, voter registration, and "participatory democracy."

[*See also* Student activism.]

Further Reading

Dawson, Michael C. *Blacks In and Out of the Left.* Cambridge, MA: Harvard University Press, 2013.
Goose, Van. *The Movements of the New Left, 1950–1975: A Brief History with Documents.* Boston: Bedford/St. Martin's 2005.

NEW NEGRO MOVEMENT

The black press used "New Negro" as early as 1895, applauding a generation who refused to be kept in the "Negro's place." The term implied opposition to the conciliatory philosophy of Booker T. Washington. During the Great Migration and World War I, when more than 200,000 blacks served in the Armed Forces to save democracy abroad, African American newspapers popularized the image of an "assertive, race-proud New Negro" at home. "We return from the slavery of the uniform which the world's madness demanded us to don to the freedom of civilian garb," W. E. B. Du Bois declared in *The Crisis.* "... We return from fighting. We return fighting" ("Returning Soldiers," 1919, p. 13).

Such appeals to race pride, resistance, and uplift inspired major initiatives, among them the National Urban League migrant aid program, NAACP campaign against lynching, women's suffrage, Garvey movement, and Harlem Renaissance. Blacks determined to fight for dignity and equal citizenship.

[*See also* Harlem Renaissance.]

Reference

"Returning Soldiers," *The Crisis,* XVIII (May 1919), p. 13.

Further Reading

Lamothe, Daphne. *Inventing the New Negro.* Philadelphia: University of Pennsylvania Press, 2008.
Whalan, Mark. *The Great War and the Culture of the New Negro.* Gainesville: University Press of Florida, 2008.

NIAGARA MOVEMENT

Twenty-nine prominent blacks, all but five from the North, met at Niagara Falls, Canada in 1905 to organize their opposition to white racism and violence as well as Booker T. Washington's conciliatory leadership. Led by Atlanta University scholar W. E. B. Du Bois, they vowed to fight for civil rights, including the right to vote; abolition of Jim Crow and lynching; and economic and educational equality.

Their movement echoed that of forerunners such as the Citizens' Equal Rights Association and Afro-American League. It published *The Moon* and *Horizon* newspapers, had 30 branches with about 400 members, convened annual meetings, and remained a strong voice of protest. Du Bois and others cofounded the NAACP in 1909.

[*See also* Civil Rights Movement; National Association for the Advancement of Colored People (NAACP).]

Further Reading

Jones, Angela. *African American Civil Rights: Early Activism and the Niagara Movement.* Santa Barbara, CA: Praeger, 2011.

Marable, Manning. *W. E. B. Du Bois: Black Radical Democrat.* Boulder, CO: Paradigm, 2005.

NORRIS V. ALABAMA (1935)

At the Scottsboro, Alabama Courthouse in April 1931, nine young black men, charged with raping two white women on a freight train, stood trial. Without proper counsel, their trials took only four days and all were found guilty. Eight received a death sentence; the youngest boy life in prison. The NAACP and Communist Party (CP) vied to represent the "Scottsboro Boys," but the CP prevailed.

When Clarence Norris was retried and convicted in 1933, his attorney appealed on grounds that blacks were barred by color from the jury venire. Even so, the Alabama Supreme Court upheld the lower court verdict. However, the US Supreme Court overruled that decision, concluding in *Norris* that when "all persons of the African race are excluded ... as grand jurors in the criminal prosecution of a person of the African race, the equal protection of the laws is denied to him." Norris, still incarcerated, was not paroled until 1943. He received a full pardon in 1977.

[*See also* Segregation.]

Further Reading

Carter, Dan T. *Scottsboro: A Tragedy of the American South.* Baton Rouge: Louisiana State University Press, 2007.

Kinshasa, Kwando Mbiassi. *The Man from Scottsboro: Clarence Norris and the Infamous 1931 Alabama Rape Trial, in His Own Words.* Jefferson, NC: McFarland, 1997.

OBAMA, BARACK H.   US PRESIDENT

Born: August 4, 1961, Honolulu, HI
Education: Columbia University, B.A., 1983; Harvard Law School, J.D. magna cum laude, 1986

The forty-fourth and first black US president, Obama triumphed in 2008, mirroring results of the Voting Rights Act; black, minority, and liberal coalitions; and a more diverse electorate.

The election astonished his opponents. An Illinois Democrat, he was elected to the Illinois State Senate (1996) and US Senate (2004) soon after addressing the Democratic National Convention. Labeled a "political talent with enormous potential," he opposed the Iraq War and invoked change. In the primaries, Obama's advisers adeptly presented his biracial identity, education, experience, and vision. Early on, he polled third of ten candidates and most blacks favored Hillary Clinton. But Obama placed first in the Iowa caucus, John Edwards second, and Clinton third, situating him to lionize blacks, nonwhite minorities, youths, and liberals to win the nomination. The Great Recession, two wars, and race shadowed his and Joe Biden's campaign against Republicans John McCain and Sarah Palin, among others, but he and Biden prevailed. Obama claimed every region by double digits except the South, which McCain took by 9 percent. McCain won whites 55–43 percent, while Obama won African Americans 96–4, Hispanics 67–31, Asians 62–35, and 18–29 age voters 66–32. The elderly backed McCain 53–43. Obama received 365 electoral votes and McCain 173.

Further Reading

Maraniss, David. *Barack Obama: The Story.* New York: Simon & Schuster, 2012.
Plouffe, David. *The Audacity to Win: The Inside Story and Lessons of Barack Obama's Historic Victory.* New York: Viking, 2009.

OPERATION PUSH (PEOPLE UNITED TO SAVE HUMANITY)

Founded in 1971 by Jesse L. Jackson, Chicago director of Southern Christian Leadership Conference's Operation Breadbasket, PUSH pledged to help fulfill Martin Luther King, Jr.'s dream of eliminating poverty and securing racial equality.

From its start PUSH advocated education, job placement, and economic empowerment. It gained support from the business community through negotiations or by demonstrations such as sit-ins or boycotts. Major goals included fair housing and voter registration, which paved the way for the election of Chicago's first black mayor in 1983. As Jackson anticipated his second run for the Democratic presidential nomination, he renamed the organization the National Rainbow/PUSH Coalition in 1985. Racial and ethnic minorities, women, and workers comprised a majority of its supporters.

[*See also* Southern Christian Leadership Conference (SCLC).]

Further Reading

House, Ernest R. *Jesse Jackson & the Politics of Charisma: The Rise and Fall of the PUSH/Excel Program*. Boulder, CO: Westview Press, 1988.

Walters, Ronald W., and Robert C. Smith. *African American Leadership*. Albany: State University of New York Press, 1999.

OWENS, JAMES C. (JESSE)
TRACK AND FIELD HERO

Born: September 13, 1913, Oakville, AL
Education: East Technical High School, Cleveland, OH, graduated 1933; Ohio State University, 1933–36
Died: March 30, 1980, Tucson, AZ

Owens won four gold medals at the Berlin, Germany Olympics (1936). He set an Olympic record, challenged white racism, and was acclaimed internationally.

Jim Crow reigned at home, yet he helped undermine its reign with a strong sense of dignity. "I wasn't invited up to shake hands with Hitler, but I wasn't invited to the White House to shake hands with the president, either," Owens said. Unable to secure decent employment, the track hero raced in vaudeville (against horses, motorcycles, or train engines) for income. He also earned modest honoraria from his occasional speeches. Eventually, he began a public relations firm, barely subsisting, and became an overseas sports consultant. Owens was a moderate on civil rights. Still, when he publicly criticized the Black Power salute at the 1968 Olympics, some black activists called him an Uncle Tom.

Even so, most people respected him. "Despite the many honors, his greatest satisfaction came from his work with you," Owens's wife declared in eulogizing him. His work continues in the Jesse Owens Foundation, which awards scholarships, and in the annual Atlantic Richfield Jesse Owens Games for youth ages 8–15. Annually, the International Amateur Athletic Association selects the best amateur athlete for the Jesse Owens International Trophy Award.

Further Reading

Edmondson, Jacqueline. *Jesse Owens: A Biography*. Westport, CT: Greenwood Press, 2007.

McCrae, Donald. *Heroes without a Country: America's Betrayal of Joe Louis and Jesse Owens*. New York: ECCO, 2002.

PAN-AFRICAN MOVEMENT

Pan-Africanism as a movement concerns efforts of black-skinned peoples in Africa and her black diaspora for self-determination and unity.

In the New World, it evolved in enslaved and free blacks' emigration and colonization, including Africa's Sierra Leone (1787) and Liberia (1821). Liberian emigrant and leader Edward W. Blyden urged Caribbean and US blacks to return, especially after the Civil War as their Back-to-Africa initiatives expanded. The Pan-African Congress in London (1900) and five additional congresses (1919–45) included delegates from Africa; North America, notably W. E. B. Du Bois; and the Caribbean. Marcus Garvey's Universal Negro Improvement Association not only helped sustain Pan-African organizing but also galvanized post-1945 African American freedom struggles.

[*See also* Universal Negro Improvement Association (UNIA).]

Further Reading

Sherwood, Marika. *Pan-African History: Political Figures from Africa and the Diaspora since 1787*. London: Routledge, 2003.
Walters, Ronald W. *Pan Africanism in the African Diaspora: An Analysis of Modern Afrocentric Political Movements*. Detroit: Wayne State University Press, 1993.

PARKS, GORDON   PHOTOGRAPHER

Born: November 30, 1912, Fort Scott, KS
Education: Fort Scott, KS high school
Died: March 7, 2006, New York, NY

Growing up poor with fourteen siblings, Parks struggled to succeed and did so remarkably. The camera "was to become my weapon against poverty and racism," he declared. He took many pictures of everyday life on his train stopovers as a Pullman porter in the mid-1930s. Those photos not only earned him a Rosenwald Foundation Fellowship but also attracted the attention of Eastman Kodak Company, which exhibited them at its store in Chicago.

Parks rose to be an award-winning photographer, writer, and filmmaker. He worked for the Farm Security Administration and the Office of War Information in the 1940s. His photo of black housekeeper Ella Watson, posing with her broom and mop beside the US flag in a federal building, is an American classic. He desegregated the photography staffs of *Vogue* and *Life*, completing more than 300 assignments between 1948 and 1972 for *Life* alone. He photographed racial and social conditions from Harlem to Latin America as well as 1960s civil rights protests and race riots. In its effort to address issues that the rioting bared, the motion picture industry named Parks director of *The Learning Tree* (1969), based on his autobiography (1963) and the first Hollywood film directed by an African American.

Further Reading

Kasher, Steven. *The Civil Rights Movement: A Photographic History, 1954–68.* New York: Abbeville, 2000.
Parks, Gordon. *To Smile in Autumn: A Memoir.* Minneapolis: University of Minnesota Press, 2009.

PARKS, ROSA L.   CIVIL RIGHTS ACTIVIST

Born: February 4, 1913, Tuskegee, AL
Education: Booker T. Washington High School, Montgomery, AL, graduated 1928
Died: October 24, 2005, Detroit, MI

Parks is revered as the "Mother of the Civil Rights Movement." Arrested December 1, 1955 for refusing to give her seat to a white man, she inspired the Montgomery Bus Boycott and ensuing nonviolent demonstrations against Jim Crow.

No ordinary passenger, Parks was a veteran in African Americans' struggle for dignity and equality. Child of a schoolmarm and craftsman, she graduated from Montgomery's Industrial School for Girls, married a barber, and worked as a seamstress. A member of the local NAACP since 1943, she had been secretary, advised the youth, and helped organize a voter registration campaign. Shortly before her arrest, Parks accepted a scholarship to Highlander Folk School, Monteagle, Tennessee, for a workshop on school desegregation and community leadership. She also engaged in women's church and civic clubs, including the Women's Political Council. The council printed more than 52,000 fliers to prepare for a one-day bus strike on December 5, the date of Parks's trial. Found guilty and fined, she gave notice of her appeal. That night black citizens attended a mass meeting at Holt Street Baptist Church, where they established the Montgomery Improvement Association, elected Dexter Avenue pastor Martin Luther King Jr. president, and approved what proved to be a 381-day boycott.

Further Reading

Theoharis, Jeanne. *The Rebellious Life of Mrs. Rosa Parks*. Boston: Beacon Press, 2013.
Thornton, J. Mills, III. *Dividing Lines: Municipal Politics and the Struggle for Civil Rights in Montgomery, Birmingham, and Selma*. Tuscaloosa: University of Alabama Press, 2002.

PERSIAN GULF WAR

After Iraq invaded and occupied Kuwait in August 1990, imperiling a vital Western oil source, the UN adopted resolutions endorsing the liberation of Kuwait and protection of Saudi Arabia and other Gulf states. Desert Storm (January–February 1991) saw UN coalition forces, led by the United States, devastate the Iraqi. They suffered 25,000–65,000 casualties compared to the coalition's nearly 200.

As the war restored the balance of power in the Middle East, it marked racial progress for US Armed Forces. Black army generals Colin L. Powell, chairman of the Joint Chiefs of Staff, and Calvin A. H. Waller (1937–96), Deputy Commander-in-Chief, coordinated strategy and tactics. Although 13 percent of the population, with 50 percent opposing Desert Storm, blacks were 25 percent of US combat personnel. Members of the All-Volunteer Force (AVF), which replaced the draft in 1973, their service helped preserve "liberty and justice for all."

[*See also* Military.]

Further Reading

Bin, Alberto, Richard Hill, and Archer Jones. *Desert Storm: A Forgotten War*. Westport, CT: Praeger, 1998.
DeYoung, Karen. *Soldier: The Life of Colin Powell*. New York: Alfred A. Knopf, 2006.

PHILANTHROPY

A central purpose of philanthropy over time has been African American education.

Public and private philanthropies (religious, secular, white, black) helped educate former slaves and their descendants. Philanthropies included the

Freedmen's Bureau; many church organizations, including the American Baptist Home Mission Society, American Missionary Association, and African Methodist Episcopal Church; the Peabody Educational Fund (1867); Slater Fund (1882); Southern Education Board and General Education Board (1902), both endowed by oil magnate John D. Rockefeller; and the Carnegie Foundation (1905). The Jeanes Fund (1908) and Phelps-Stokes Fund (1910) financed rural schools; the Rosenwald Fund (1912), awarding matching grants, maintained its school construction program; and the Rockefeller Foundation (1913) supported high school and college academic and vocational programs. Foundations operated within the limits of segregation. Yet they assisted blacks' freedom by supporting universal schooling, which enslaved and free blacks pursued long before the Civil War. Literacy empowered blacks. Black denominations, for example, funded twenty-two of the seventy-two private Negro colleges and universities in 1917. Administrators founded the United Negro College Fund (1944) for mutual aid, partly by getting federal, Rockefeller, Ford Foundation (1936), and other assistance. Similar to others, Ford's help preceded the 1954 *Brown* decision and continues today. Contemporary black philanthropists, among them Bill Cosby and Oprah Winfrey, are also vital donors.

[*See also* Education; Historically Black Colleges and Universities (HBCUs); United Negro College Fund (UNCF).]

Further Reading

Anderson, Eric, and Alfred A. Moss, Jr. *Dangerous Donations: Northern Philanthropy and Southern Black Education, 1902–1930.* Columbia, MO: University of Missouri Press, 1999.

Ferguson, Karen. *Top Down: The Ford Foundation, Black Power, and the Reinvention of Racial Liberalism.* Philadelphia: University of Pennsylvania Press, 2013.

PHOTOGRAPHY

Between US slavery and contemporary times, photography has contributed richly to documenting not only race relations but also African American life. From the free black practitioners of the "'new art'" ca. 1840s through their successors who documented the long civil rights movement, black photographers have conserved images of freedom struggle, racial progress, and American society.

The result is a crucial visual record. The pioneers customarily made photographs of prominent individuals, including clerics, white and black abolitionists, or Union army soldiers. In that tradition were photographers C.M. Battey of Tuskegee Institute and Addison N. Scurlock of Howard University. Scurlock's black-and-white photographs of Frederick Douglass, Booker T. Washington, W. E. B. Du Bois, Mary McLeod Bethune, and others still appear in history books. Moreover, Scurlock, who operated his Washington, DC studio ca. 1911–64, photographed events for magazines like *The Crisis*. The 1920 census listed 608 blacks, 101 of them women, in photographic occupations.

Their numbers and opportunities enlarged over time. New York's Harlem Renaissance and black cultural production in urban centers stimulated public demand for studio photography, painters, and artistic designers. The 1930s and 1940s projects of the Farm Security Administration (FSA) and Office of War Information created more federal employment for African Americans; Gordon Parks began his famed career as an FSA photojournalist. Civil rights activism after the *Brown* decision increased the number of blacks among photojournalists working in the South. Also, the 1960s Black Arts Movement brought national attention to black photographers' craft. During the 1980s–90s, the Smithsonian Institution sponsored major exhibitions of their works.

[*See also* Art; Architecture.]

Further Reading

Lewis, David Levering, and Deborah Willis. *A Small Nation of People: Portraits of Progress*. New York: Amistad Press, 2003.

Willis, Deborah. *Reflections in Black: A History of Black Photographers, 1840–1999*. New York: W. W. Norton, 2000.

PLESSY V. FERGUSON (1896)

Homer Plessy, an octoroon or seven-eighths white, belonged to New Orleans's Committee of Citizens. Initiating a committee challenge to the state Separate Car Act (1890), Plessy bought an East Louisiana Railroad first-class ticket, boarded a "whites only" railcar, and was arrested. Suing the railroad for violating his constitutional rights, he lost in state court. His lawyer Albion Tourgée appealed to the US Supreme Court, which affirmed the state's ruling and the act.

Its *Plessy* decision debuted the "separate but equal" doctrine that legalized segregation. Accordingly, the Court approved a presumption of blacks' inferiority that undermined their right to suffrage and allowed states to segregate public accommodations at will. Also consequential was the states' power to define citizens by color. "There is no caste here," Justice John Marshall Harlan wrote in dissent. "Our Constitution is color-blind, and neither knows nor tolerates classes among citizens." Blacks hoped that Harlan's view would prevail someday.

[*See also Brown v. Board of Education* (1954).]

Further Reading

Elliott, Mark. *Color-Blind Justice: Albion Tourgee and the Quest for Racial Equality: From the Civil War to Plessy v. Ferguson*. New York: Oxford University Press, 2006.

Kelley, Blair Murphy. *Right to Ride: Streetcar Boycotts and African American Citizenship in the Era of Plessy v. Ferguson*. Chapel Hill: University of North Carolina Press, 2010.

POLITICS

African American politics concerns aspirations and efforts that have informed struggles for freedom, justice, and equality from slavery to the present. Black ideologies, programs, and strategies mirror not only contexts of white racism but also intrablack differences.

Enslaved and free blacks were political actors. They resisted and affirmed themselves, using African religious, familial, and kin traditions; Christianity; and manumissions. During the Revolutionary War, many bondmen earned liberty by serving in the American and British militaries. Slave rebels and fugitives and black and white abolitionists helped catalyze southern secession, the Civil War, and emancipation. Postwar, the Constitution abolished slavery and granted ex-slaves citizenship and suffrage. Blacks both coalesced with white allies and struggled autonomously, the latter desired by nationalists. Thus postwar generations paved the way for civil rights, desegregation, Black Power, multiethnic politics, and empowerment.

Struggles in the Reconstruction South, home to more than 90 percent of blacks, grounded blacks' civic future. Assisted by the Freedmen's Bureau, Republican Party, missionary societies, Union League, and soldiers, they embraced free labor, mostly as sharecroppers; reunited families; enrolled children in school; and established churches and protective associations. In 1867 more than 700,000 black men voted despite Ku Klux Klan terror. More than 2,000 blacks held elective and appointive offices – local, state, and federal; 1 served briefly as a governor, 14 in the US House, and 2 in the Senate. Most black officeholding ended after

Democrats regained state power and the final Union troops left (1877). The nadir (1877–1901) witnessed Republicans and Populists' isolation; black lynching, disfranchisement, and segregation; and the federal retreat from civil rights. Blacks persevered, even as they pursued freedom movements of varying persuasions: democratic, socialist, nationalist, and interracial.

The right to vote formed the cutting edge of racial battles. In the NAACP's case *Guinn v. Oklahoma* (1915), the US Supreme Court struck down the grandfather clause, which inspired efforts for black and women's suffrage. Black socialists pressed workers' rights; nationalists called for black self-help and unity. A black Republican won election to Congress from Chicago in 1928. During the Depression, many blacks joined the Communist Party and industrial unions. A majority of black voters also spurned Republicans to support liberal Democrats and New Deal reforms. In 1941 growing black protest against discrimination in defense jobs gained a federal committee on fair employment practices and, in NAACP-argued *Smith v. Allwright* (1944), the Court voided the "white primary." Black voter registration thus quickened, foreshadowing the president's order to desegregate Armed Forces (1948), as the Dixiecrats' presidential candidate carried four Deep South states; the 1954 *Brown* decision, which overturned school segregation; and mass nonviolent demonstrations in the South and nation.

Nonviolence, amid anticommunist witch-hunts and segregationist violence, ushered in, among other rights legislation, the Voting Rights Act of 1965 (VRA). Congress has renewed it four times, the most recent a twenty-five-year renewal (2006). VRA reenfranchised southern blacks and galvanized African American voting nationally. Since the 1960s, it is estimated that 90 percent or more of eligible blacks vote for Democrats in federal elections, a legacy of Kennedy–Johnson administration liberalism.

Black representation increased markedly. The Joint Center for Political and Economic Studies reports that black southerners occupied fewer than 25 elective offices in 1964 and 500 in 1970. Nationally, between 1970 and 2001, the number of black state legislators rose from 168 to 567 or 7 percent of all state legislators. Blacks counted 2,973 male and 530 female officeholders by 1975, compared to 5,683 male and 2,332 female officeholders in 1993. Some became mayors of small and large cities in and outside the South, such as Democrats Carl B. Stokes (Cleveland, Ohio, 1967), the first black "mayor of a major and predominately white city"; Johnny L. Ford (Tuskegee, Alabama, 1972); and

Maynard H. Jackson (Atlanta, Georgia, 1973). The thirteen members
of the Congressional Black Caucus (1971) were Democrats, as were
L. Douglas Wilder, elected Virginia and America's first black governor
(1989); Deval L. Patrick, elected governor of Massachusetts (2006)
and reelected (2010); and lieutenant governor David A. Paterson, who
became New York governor (2008–10) after the governor's resignation.
Five black Republicans have been elected to the House since the Black
Caucus formed. Congress seated forty blacks, eleven women included, in
2001, and forty-two, including fourteen women, in 2012. Elected senators were Edward W. Brooke (R–MA 1966, 72); Carol Moseley Braun
(D–IL 1992); Barack H. Obama (D–IL 2004), replaced by Roland Burris
(2009–10); and Timothy E. Scott (R–SC 2012). The Democratic National
Committee appointed a black chairman (1989), as did the Republican
National Committee (2009). Seventeen blacks were named Cabinet secretaries and Supreme Court justices by Democratic and Republican presidents, 1966–2009.

Black activism and debate proceeded apace. Civil rights and Black
Power activists split on armed self-defense but endorsed the War on
Poverty, education, job training, and affirmative action. Riots across
urban America impelled such reforms, as the Voter Education Project,
Mississippi Freedom Democratic Party, and rights organizations registered working-class and poor people to help elect progressives. Activists
called the National Black Political Assembly in 1972 to build unity and
press the Democratic Party to champion equity, register nonwhites, and
recruit minority candidates. Increasingly outspoken black conservatives criticized activists' racial appeals, affirmative action, and welfare,
instead advocating "personal responsibility," a "color blind" society,
and Republican social policy. However, the National Black Independent
Political Party, launched in 1980, pushed race-based policies; so did Jesse
Jackson's campaigns for the Democratic presidential nomination in 1984
and 1988, indicating the need for interethnic coalitions. Organized in
1998, the Black Radical Congress proposed a "freedom agenda" that
prioritized "Black working and poor people." Activism proceeded, helping to produce 9,101 black elected officials (2001) and Senator Barack
Obama's rise to the presidency (2008). Obama received 96% of blacks'
vote, 67% of Hispanics', 62 % of Asians', and 43 % of whites'. Facing
"the Great Recession," the worst economic downturn since the 1930s,
Obama's administration adopted race-neutral measures "that will lift all
boats." By contrast, hard hit peoples of color, notably blacks and Latinos,

urged "a plan to address the rapidly growing unemployment rate in black and Latino communities." They demanded a jobs bill. Democrats finally acted on one in 2011, but Republicans defeated it.

[*See also* Voting Rights Act of 1965.]

Further Reading

Bositis, David A. *Black Elected Officials: A Statistical Summary 2001*. Washington, DC: Joint Center for Political and Economic Studies, 2001.

Harris, Fredrick C. *The Price of the Ticket: Barack Obama and the Rise and Decline of Black Politics*. New York: Oxford University Press, 2012.

Lawson, Steven F. *Running for Freedom: Civil Rights and Black Politics in America since 1941*. Malden, MA: Wiley-Blackwell, 2009.

Lewis, Angela. *Conservatism in the Black Community: To the Right and Misunderstood*. New York: Routledge, 2013.

PORT CHICAGO MUTINY (1944)

Only blacks loaded explosives at the Naval Ammunition Depot in Port Chicago, California, and white officers sometimes raced work crews against each other. On the night of July 17, 1944, an explosion rocked the Bay Area. It razed two anchored ships; killed 320 civilians and servicemen, 202 of them black; and injured more than 400 others. It was the worst home-front disaster of World War II.

The tragedy also caused injustice. Ordered back to work in the same unsafe situation, 258 black sailors refused; 208 were court-martialed for mutiny and dishonorably discharged. Fifty of the men received 8- to 15-year prison terms. Civil rights activists launched protests and the NAACP filed suits. After the war, the navy released those imprisoned without pardons. Later research by Robert Allen, editor and publisher of the *Black Scholar*, resulted in an official review (1994); it did not vacate the convictions. The president pardoned only one of the few survivors (1999).

[*See also* Military.]

Further Reading

Allen, Robert L. *The Port Chicago Mutiny: The Story of the Largest Mass Mutiny Trial in U.S. Naval History*. Berkeley, CA: Heyday Books, 2006.

Wagner, Margaret. E. et al., eds. *The Library of Congress World War II Companion*. New York: Simon & Schuster. 2007.

POVERTY

With roots in slavery and segregation, especially southern sharecropping, black poverty persisted over time. In 1939, amid the Great Depression, 65 and 93 percent of white and black Americans, respectively, lacked income and resources for minimal subsistence. Despite the World War II recovery and broad postwar prosperity, 39.5 million or 22 percent of the people were poor by the late 1950s. The poorest included the elderly, conspicuously women; whites in rural Appalachia; and blacks in the South and inner cities.

Black poverty was disproportionate. Mainly because of federal reforms, it decreased from 55.1 to 30.3 percent between 1959 and 1974, a year when 9 percent of whites were destitute. The black poor faced destitution and racial discrimination; millions of those who worked earned low wages and lived in ghettoes. Between 1980 and the mid-1990s about 12 percent of whites, compared to 30 percent of blacks and Hispanics and 27 percent of Native Americans, were poor. The urban black underclass had higher rates of drug addiction, crime, out of wedlock births, and welfare dependency, which mirrored structural disparities rooted in deindustrialization, blacks' much larger loss of factory work, and a larger proportion of female-headed black households. Unemployment was 22% for black men ages 20–24 in 1980 alone, easily reducing the pool of marriageable men and potential husband–wife families while increasing women and children's dependent status. Poverty was 11.7% nationally in 2002 and blacks had its highest rate at 22.7%. In 2008 some 39.8 million, 13.2% of the population, were impoverished, namely 8.6% of whites, 11.8% of Asians, 23.8% of Hispanics, 24.2% of Native Americans, and 24.7% of blacks.

Antipoverty programs helped maintain the public safety net. These had been expanded and initiated via the Equal Opportunity Act of 1964 and Office of Economic Opportunity (OEO)-led War on Poverty. Fighting "the causes, not just the consequences of poverty," OEO provided aid, education, and training. It furnished cash payments through Aid to Families with Dependent Children, food stamps, and housing subsidies. It instituted Head Start, Job Corps, College Work Study, and local community action programs, the last pledging to enlist the "maximum feasible participation" of the poor. Vitally important was OEO's "program of loans and guarantees" with companies that contracted to train and hire the unemployed. Moreover, civil and human rights organizations, including the Southern Christian Leadership Conference, National Welfare Rights Organization, and Association of Community Organizations for Reform Now, became allies in a diverse and nonviolent antipoverty movement. Women frequently led campaigns, which used community organizing, voter registration, policy advocacy, and mass protest to pursue welfare rights. This struggle continues today.

[*See also* Black Belt; Children's Defense Fund; Cities; Great Migration; Welfare.]

Further Reading

Lang, Kevin. *Poverty and Discrimination*. Princeton, NJ: Princeton University Press, 2007.

Martin, Lori Latrice. *Black Asset Poverty and the Enduring Racial Divide*. Boulder, CO: First Forum Press, 2013.

Orleck, Annelise. *Storming Caesars Palace: How Black Mothers Fought Their Own War on Poverty*. Boston: Beacon Press, 2005.

POWELL, ADAM CLAYTON, JR.   US CONGRESSMAN

Born: November 29, 1908, New Haven, CT
Education: Colgate University, B.A., 1930; Columbia University, M.A., 1932
Died: April 14, 1972, Miami, FL

Pastor of Harlem's Abyssinian Baptist Church, known for saying "'Keep the faith, baby,'" Powell emerged politically following the Harlem Riot (1935). Job discrimination and police brutality against blacks fueled the riot, he preached, soon starting a newspaper column. He eventually won election to New York City Council (1941); co-created the weekly *People's Voice*; and organized black churches and civic organizations' "Don't Buy Where You Can't Work" picket campaign. Powell also led fair employment marches to Harlem Hospital and Con Edison, furthering blacks' demands for jobs and justice. He compelled the attention, respect, and support of Tammany Hall Democrats.

Elected to the House of Representatives in 1945, he was the first black congressman from the northeast and fourth (perhaps the most powerful) in the twentieth century. Powell served until 1970, except for a 1967–69 suspension owing to violations of House rules. The dismissal beclouds his invaluable legislative contributions as chairman of the House Education and Labor Committee (HELC) from 1961. For example, he maneuvered the Kennedy administration's minimum wage bill through a fierce southern opposition and gave the new president a crucial early victory. Indeed, Powell orchestrated fifty-nine other civil rights, education, health, and antipoverty bills of the Kennedy–Johnson administrations to passage.

Further Reading

Hamilton, Charles V. Hamilton. *Adam Clayton Powell, Jr.: The Political Biography of an American Dilemma*. New York: Atheneum, 1991.
McNeil, Genna Rae, et al. *Witness: Two Hundred Years of African-American Faith and Practice at the Abyssinian Baptist Church of Harlem, New York*. Grand Rapids, MI: Eerdmans, 2014.

POWELL, COLIN L.
US ARMY GENERAL AND SECRETARY OF STATE

Born: April 5, 1937, New York, NY
Education: City College of New York, B.A., 1958; Army Command and General Staff College, 1967–68; Georgetown University, M.B.A., 1971; National War College, 1975

Political pundits saw Powell's presidential capital as second to none, arguing that he would be peerless on foreign policy. But he declined to seek the Republican nomination for president in 1996, declaring "that political life requires a calling that I do not hear."

His journey to success evokes the American Dream. A black youth from the East Bronx, he attended City College, won distinction in the Reserve Officers' Training Corps, and graduated second lieutenant. Powell worked hard and excelled, rising through the army's officer ranks to national security advisor, four-star general, and chairman of the Joint Chiefs of Staff. He co-commanded the Persian Gulf War and became the first black secretary of state.

Powell made difficult decisions. His troop deployment to Somalia backfired; another, to the former Yugoslavia, washed out. He opposed President Clinton's move to end exclusion of gays from the Armed Forces and to reduce the military budget. The antigay implications of the "Don't ask, don't tell" policy (a compromise) could have been a future campaign problem for him. He endorsed affirmative action, but remained silent on the Bush administration's support of anti-affirmative action suits against the University of Michigan. Sources argue that he reluctantly supported the Iraq War.

Further Reading

Halberstam, David. *War in a Time of Peace: Bush, Clinton, and the Generals.* New York: Scribner, 2001.

Steins, Richard. *Colin Powell: A Biography.* Westport, CT: Greenwood Press, 2003.

RACE LABELS

From slavery to freedom to the present, whites' power to caricature or negatively label blacks has been a major source of conflict in race relations. Even after *Brown* (1954), which overruled school segregation, our society rarely embraced its racial-ethnic diversity and black stereotypes persisted. For example, the NAACP continued its campaign to remove the stereotypical *Amos 'n' Andy Show* from television; it was removed in 1966. Today, the association lobbies film, television, the press, and other media to present nonracist images and reports as well as to provide equal employment opportunities.

Negative black labels persist. *The Bell Curve: Intelligence and Class Structure in American Life* (1994) and *Nigger: The Strange Career of a Troublesome Word* (2002) include many. Slavery spawned black stereotypes: the docile Sambo, loyal Mammy, lewd Jezebel, and carefree Jim Crow. All were labeled inferior or "lazy and pretentious." Segregation saw little alteration in white perceptions of blacks, largely confining them to servant status. Aunt Jemima, Uncle Mose, and Uncle Ben, the faithful servants, became major money-makers for American advertisers during the first-half of the twentieth century. Their smiling black faces advertised food products, dishware, and varieties of collectibles. Also popular were Jim Dandy, a city slicker, and Sapphire, a bossy "negress." The childlike "negro" image in *Gone With the Wind* (1939), which romanticized the Confederacy and the Ku Klux Klan, was persistent and *Amos 'n' Andy* reinvented it. Many civil and human rights and progressive groups fight against the labeling or profiling of African Americans today.

[*See also* Law enforcement.]

Further Reading

Goings, Kenneth W. *Mammy and Uncle Mose: Black Collectibles and American Stereotyping.* Bloomington: Indiana University Press, 1994.
Kennedy, Randall. *Nigger: The Strange Career of a Troublesome Word.* New York: Pantheon Books, 2002.

RACE MAN/WOMAN

The race man and woman represented a type of black leadership during Jim Crow. Proud of the race, they defended it with dignity. Neither accepting the permanence of segregation nor begging crumbs from whites, they condemned white supremacists and Uncle Toms alike. They advocated black self-help as well as interracial cooperation and peaceful protest for civil rights. Always mindful of the disadvantaged, they urged elite blacks to prioritize economic and educational programs that assist and secure less fortunate blacks. Race women in the National Association of Colored Women not only espoused respectability but also provided childcare and other services, living their motto "Lifting as We Climb."

[*See also* Segregation.]

Further Reading

Alexander, Ann Field. *Race Man: The Rise and Fall of the "Fighting Editor," John Mitchell, Jr.* Charlottesville: University of Virginia Press, 2002.

Horne, Gerald. *Race Woman: The Lives of Shirley Graham Du Bois.* New York: New York University Press, 2000.

RANDOLPH, A. PHILIP
LABOR AND CIVIL RIGHTS LEADER

Born: April 15, 1889, Crescent City, FL
Education: Cookman Institute, graduated 1907; City College of New York, New York University, 1911
Died: May 16, 1979, New York, NY

A major spokesman, Randolph argued that labor organizing and economic empowerment were essential to race and class equality. He and Chandler Owen cofounded *The Messenger* (1917), a socialist magazine, which assailed segregation, lynching, and the draft. It urged union organizing.

Randolph pursued racial and economic justice. He organized the Brotherhood of Sleeping Car Porters (1925), the first recognized black trade union. It gained recognition from the Pullman Palace Car Company, the nation's largest employer of blacks, by 1934. It won its second contract in 1937 and merged with the Brotherhood of Railway and Airline Clerks (1978). As president of the National Negro Congress (1935–40), Randolph pushed civil rights unionism.

In 1941 he organized the March on Washington Movement to fight for black inclusion in national defense jobs and freedom. He canceled its planned mass march when the president ordered the creation of the Committee on Fair Employment Practice. His leadership helped blacks to obtain a presidential order desegregating the military (1948). He became vice president of the American Federation of Labor-Congress of Industrial Organizations (1955). Randolph and his assistant, activist Bayard Rustin, were the architects of the historic March on Washington for Jobs and Freedom (1963). Randolph received the Presidential Medal of Freedom (1964).

Further Reading

Kersten, Andrew E. *A. Philip Randolph, A Life in the Vanguard*. Lanham, MD: Rowman & Littlefield, 2007.
Welky, David. *Marching Across the Color Line: A. Philip Randolph and Civil Rights in the World War II Era*. New York: Oxford University Press, 2013.

RECONSTRUCTION (1865–77)

Abolition of slavery, black citizenship and suffrage, and restoring the Union sorely strained post–Civil War society. The main actors were blacks, a vast majority ex-slaves; white allies, mainly northern missionaries and Republicans; and freedpeople's enemies, notably southern Democrats.

Blacks determined to "secure the blessings of liberty." As former Confederate states enacted laws to subjugate them, freedmen and women registered their marriages, reclaimed sold-away family members, formed protective associations, sent their children to old Sabbath and new Freedmen's Bureau Schools, and worked. Few freedpeople could rent or buy farmland; most contracted with planters to work for half the crop. Bureau agents oversaw labor relations while army patrols helped protect blacks from harassment and violence by diehards such as the Ku Klux Klan. Freedpeople, pursuing better livelihoods, engaged a growing black world of enterprises, churches, schools, fraternal orders, women's clubs, and civic organizations in the South and nation. Freedmen also rallied in branches of the Republican-backed Union League. About 660,000 white and 703,400 black men qualified to vote in 1867. Black votes also insured victory for many white and black Republican candidates in 1868 and after. Blacks comprised nearly 60% of the population in South Carolina; over 50% in Mississippi and Louisiana; 40% to 50% in Alabama, Florida, Georgia, and Virginia; 33% in North Carolina; and 25% to 33% in Arkansas, Tennessee, and Texas.

Until 1877, probably 2,000 black Republicans "had held federal, state, and local public offices, ranging from member of Congress to justice of the peace" (Foner, 1993, p. xi). Most were literate; one sample (714) showed more than half (387) to be slave-born. Many were Union veterans, militiamen, clergymen, educators, farmers, and artisans. Congress seated 16, including Hiram R. Revels and Blanche K. Bruce of Mississippi as Senators. South Carolina ranked first in the number of black congressmen (6) and officeholders (316). Pinckney B. S. Pinchback was governor of Louisiana from December 9, 1872 to January 13, 1873. Local and state officials, in spite of Democrats' attacks, pushed their communities' justice in schooling, work contracts, renting and buying land, physical protection, poor relief, and public jobs. Calling for equity in economics, education, law, and politics, they echoed the priorities of black leaders nationally not only among politicians but lawyers, ministers, teachers, trade unionists, women activists, and Negro nationalists too. State and national conventions of the ongoing convention movement, which had fought for freedom and citizenship since 1830, alongside the National Equal Rights League, "insisted upon the prime importance of education" and civil rights.

Black protest for equality lasted. In 1870 New York State Colored Voters protested "the continued existence of a feeling of caste which excludes colored people from hotels, workshops, and places of amusement" and "in persecuting and intimidating colored voters and their political friends at the South" (Foner and Walker, 1986, p. 420). They proclaimed bitter truths. Klansmen and other diehards harassed freedmen at the polls, in the fields, and in their homes, even as they murdered white and black Republican officeholders. Congress passed the Civil Rights Act of 1875, which opened public accommodations to all citizens, but neglected to enforce it. Democrats had "redeemed" every state by 1876, except Louisiana, South Carolina, and Florida. Indeed, they conceded those states' nineteen disputed electoral votes to the Republican candidate for president, who withdrew Union troops and terminated Reconstruction the next year. Abandoned by Republicans, black citizens persevered.

[*See also* Politics; Electoral.]

References

Foner, Eric. *Freedom's Lawmakers: A Directory of Black Officeholders During Reconstruction*. Baton Rouge: Louisiana State University Press, 1993, p. xi.

Foner, Philip S., and George E. Walker, eds. *Proceedings of the Black National and State Conventions, 1865–1900*, Vol. I. Philadelphia: Temple University Press, 1986, p. 420.

Further Reading

Fitzgerald, Michael W. *The Union League Movement in the Deep South: Politics and Agricultural Change During Reconstruction.* Baton Rouge: Louisiana State University Press, 2000.

Foner, Eric. *Freedom's Lawmakers: A Directory of Black Officeholders during Reconstruction.* Baton Rouge: Louisiana State University Press, 1996.

Franklin, John Hope. *Reconstruction: After the Civil War.* Chicago: University of Chicago Press, 2013.

REDISTRICTING

The process of drawing US electoral district boundaries due to population changes reflected by the census, known as redistricting, is regulated by federal law. Districts with a history of voting discrimination against racial-ethnic minorities, like many in the South, must meet requirements of the Voting Rights Act 1965). Section 5 requires that districts pre-clear any change in suffrage laws with the Department of Justice.

Early compliance was slow. Some southern states diluted black votes by instituting at-large elections and multimember districts, changing elective into appointive positions, and restricting minority candidates' ability to appear on the official ballot. But the Supreme Court rejected such measures in *Allen v. State Board of Elections* (1969) for Virginia and Mississippi, and in *White v. Register* (1973) for Texas. Black and Latino voters, it stated, must have "equal opportunity to participate in the legal processes and to elect legislators of their choice." This anticipated majority–minority Congressional Districts in the 1990s.

[*See also Baker v. Carr* (1962); *Shaw v. Reno* (1993); *Voting Rights Act of 1965*.]

Further Reading

Darling, Marsha J. Tyson, ed. *Race, Voting, Redistricting and the Constitution: Sources and Explorations on the Fifteenth Amendment.* New York: Routledge, 2001.

Yarbrough, Tinsley E. *Race and Redistricting: The Shaw-Cromartie Cases.* Lawrence: University of Kansas Press, 2002.

RELIGION

Contributing to religious pluralism, more and more slaves converted to Christianity over time, creating "what might be termed 'the invisible institution'–black religion under slavery" (Raboteau, 1978, p. ix). Forged in "hush harbors," slave Christianity spawned separate churches, mainly Baptist and Methodist, ca. 1760s. "The Negro Church is the only social institution of the Negroes which started in the African forest and survived slavery," W. E. B. Du Bois wrote in 1903, "under the leadership of priest or medicine man, afterward the Christian pastor, the Church preserved in itself the remnants of African tribal life and became after emancipation the center of Negro social life." He added "that today the Negro population of the United States is virtually divided into church congregations which are the real units of race life" (Du Bois, 2011, p. ii).

Congregations created major denominations. The African Methodist Episcopal Church (1816), African Methodist Episcopal Zion Church (1821), Christian Methodist Episcopal Church (1870), National Baptist Convention (1895), Church of God in Christ (1897), National Baptist Convention of America (1915), and Progressive National Baptist Convention (1961) aggregated 80 percent of black Christian memberships by the 1990s; 20 percent of black Christians were in historically white denominations.

Black churches led struggles for justice. From colonial times, they espoused freedom, literacy, and morality. The first interstate black institutions, beside Negro Masons, mutual aid, and temperance societies, churches resisted the colonizing of freed blacks in Africa; sponsored Canadian, Caribbean, and African missions; and sustained the Convention Movement (1830–93), the "most representative vehicle" of black uplift. State and national conventions advocated abolitionism, self-help, Union loyalty, emancipation, and citizenship. Churchmen and women were notable among post–Civil War delegates, who pursued federal and state enforcement of African American schooling; wage labor; and rights, notably suffrage and office holding; and security of black life, limb, and property. Denominational bodies enlarged regionally, nationally, and internationally post-Reconstruction, as churchmen and women fostered black progress. The ex-slave Union soldier William W. Browne preached economic unity at his Colored Methodist Episcopal Church in Richmond, Virginia. In 1881 he founded the Grand Fountain of the United Order of True Reformers, whose thrift and financial solidarity resulted in a three-story building, regalia factory, insurance company, and, by 1888, the first black-owned bank. They soon added a print shop, newspaper, department store, hotel, real estate firm, funeral and old folks' homes, and farm co-op. Reformers counted probably 100,000 members by 1900 and had opened firms in eighteen states. Equally resolute was slave-born Callie House, a washerwoman, widow, and mother of five from Nashville, Tennessee. She and a coworker formed the National Ex-Slave Mutual Relief, Bounty and Pension Association (1898) to seek federal reparations. From her Nashville headquarters, she traveled and enrolled a membership of more than 300,000 blacks, mostly Baptists, Disciples of Christ, and Methodists. She mobilized the association to petition, lobby, and ultimately sue Congress for ex-slave pensions. Prosecuted and imprisoned in 1917 for using "the mails to defraud," House was silenced but "praised by poor African Americans."

Churches provided spaces for blacks' spiritual, social, and civic striving preceding and following their first Great Migration north. Their "small, unpretentious wooden structures" in farm communities or "remodeled stores" or modern edifices in cities served as sanctuaries for affirmation. *The Negro's Church* (1933) surveyed 609 urban parishes in 12 cities (7 southern) and 169 rural parishes in 4 southern counties. "All of the Churches ... have cooperated with other churches, or with community institutions and agencies, through ministerial alliances and associations; in religious educational activities; in cooperative humanitarian movements; in social welfare, poor relief, and the like" (Mays and Nicholson, 1933, p. 157), it noted. They funded Boy and Girl Scouts; partnered with YMCAs and YWCAs, schools, and colleges; financed homes for delinquents, orphans, and elders; and sponsored nurseries; mission charities; health and Bible classes; and employment bureaus.

Building antiracist alliances, they helped preserve a moral conscience in America. For example, countless churches hosted local chapters and furnished foot soldiers in the NAACP's antilynching, equal education, and right to vote crusades. Formed in 1934, the Fraternal Council of Negro Churches "was the first self-consciously ecumenical body of national scope to be organized by black Americans" (Sawyer, 1990, p. 51). Fighting segregation, it later backed the 1955 Montgomery, Alabama bus boycott and Martin Luther King Jr.'s leadership. King's role in nonviolent protest hastened his departure from the National Baptist Convention, as its influential president, Joseph H. Jackson (1900–90), endorsed lawsuits rather than sit-ins to fight Jim Crow. In 1961 King joined other activist ministers such as Gardner C. Taylor (b. 1918) and Samuel D. Proctor (1921–97) to form the Progressive National Baptist Convention, which embraced liberation theology, rejected racism and poverty, and inspired opposition to the Vietnam War.

Memberships reflect the vitality of African American religion. By 1990 the National Baptist Convention was "by far the largest of all the black denominations, and is considered the largest organization of African Americans in existence." It had an annual budget of $4.5 million and 7.5 million members, 100,000 of them outside the United States. Its members were a fourth of black Americans and a third of black Christians. Some 29,000 pastors and 30,000 congregations were affiliated, together with 4,700 district and 59 state associations. Other black Baptists aggregated 3.6 million members, black Methodists 4.4 million, and the Church of God in Christ 3.7 million.

Churches continue to push black priorities in education, labor, healthcare, and housing; affirmative action; voting rights; criminal justice; and antipoverty and welfare. These are the major trends: black females join churches more than males, the middle-aged and elders more than youth, the lower and middle classes more than elites. Younger blacks abandon churchgoing at higher rates as their opportunities improve. Yet structural inequities persist, denying peoples of color and the poor equal life chances. C. Eric Lincoln called such disparities America's worst failure to secure "liberty and justice for all." Christians, Jews, Muslims, and all communions must help ensure equality, he warned, for America to avoid destructive racial and ethnic conflict.

[*See also* Civil Rights Movement; Conventions, National Negro; Education; Segregation; Slavery.]

References

Du Bois, W. E. B., ed. *The Negro Church*. 1903. Eugene, OR: Cascade Books, 2011, p. ii.

Mays, Benjamin E., and Joseph W. Nicholson. *The Negro's Church*. New York: Institute of Social and Religious Research, 1933, p. 157.

Raboteau, Albert J., *Slave Religion: The "Invisible Institution" in the Antebellum South*. New York: Oxford University Press, 1978. p. ix.

Sawyer, Mary R. "The Fraternal Council of Negro Churches, 1934–1964." *Church History*, Vol. 59 (March 1990), p. 51.

Further Reading

Collier-Thomas, Bettye. *Jesus, Jobs, and Justice: African American Women and Religion*. Philadelphia: Temple University Press, 2014.

Lincoln, C. Eric, and Lawrence C. Mamiya. *The Black Church in the African American Experience*. Durham, NC: Duke University Press, 1990.

Smith, R. Drew, ed. *Long March Ahead: African American Churches and Public Policy in Post-Civil Rights America*. Durham, NC: Duke University Press, 2004.

RESEGREGATION

School integration crested as 44 percent of southern black students attended majority-white schools (1988), reducing to 34.7 percent (1996) and 31 percent (2000). Most court-ordered plans to end school segregation, including busing, terminated by 2000. Forty percent of blacks and Latinos, compared to four percent of whites, were in majority–minority and high-poverty urban schools (2006). According to a 2012 report, "80% of Latino students and 74% of black students attended majority nonwhite schools (50–100% minority)" (Orfield and Sigel-Hawley, 2012, p. 9).

Resegregation bares the nation's retreat from *Brown*, exposing racial, ethnic, and class disparities; "white flight"; proliferating private and public charter schools and suburban school districts; and Supreme Court decisions like *Oklahoma City v. Dowell* (1991), terminating court oversight of that city's school desegregation. Moreover, in 2007 the Court disallowed Seattle, Washington and Louisville, Kentucky schools' voluntary steps to desegregate, enhance diversity, and terminate minority student isolation by means of a race-based assignment plan.

[*See also* Desegregation; Segregation.]

Reference

Orfield, Gary, John Kucsera & Genevieve Siegel-Hawley, *E PLURIBUS ... SEPARATION: Deepening Double Segregation for More Students.* Los Angeles: The Civil Rights Project, UCLA, 2012. p. 9.

Further Reading

Clotfelter, Charles T. *After Brown: The Rise and Retreat of School Desegregation.* Princeton, NJ: Princeton University Press, 2004.

Orfield, Gary, et al. "E Pluribus ... Separation: Deepening Double Segregation for More Students." The Civil Rights Project, UCLA, September 2012.

Parents Involved in Community Schools v. Seattle School District No. 1, 551 U.S. 701 (2007).

RICE, CONDOLEEZZA   NATIONAL SECURITY ADVISOR AND SECRETARY OF STATE

Born: November 14, 1954, Birmingham, AL
Education: University of Denver, B.A. cum laude, 1974, Ph.D., 1981; University of Notre Dame, M.A., 1975

When the president named her National Security Advisor (2001–05) and Secretary of State (2005–09), Rice became the first black woman and second black person appointed to both offices. A former Stanford University professor and provost, she was the youngest of President George Bush's advisors. She stayed close to him, as he had little experience in world affairs. Rice, pundits think, defined his foreign policy of democracy, development, and war on terror. A Soviet Union and Eastern Europe specialist, she evinced her toughness in US–Russian negotiations over missile defense. National interests and realities, not American military power alone, shaped her strategic thinking and advising.

Rice's education and faith in equality prepared her for such powerful roles. Growing up in the Jim Crow South, she instilled high ideals, in a *Newsweek* interview stating: "My parents had me absolutely convinced that, well, you may not be able to have a hamburger at Woolworth's but you can be president of the United States" (Brant, 2001). Racial, class, and gender equity must be pursued by embracing and practicing values of tolerance and social justice, she told a college commencement audience, because we live "in an age where too often difference is still seen as a license to kill."

Reference

Brant, Martha. "West Wing Story: America's Favorite Bushie." *Newsweek*, July 31, 2001.

Further Reading

Bumiller, Elisabeth. *Condoleezza Rice: An American Life*. New York: Random House, 2007.
Mabry, Marcus. *Twice As Good: Condoleezza Rice and Her Path to Power*. New York: Modern Times, 2007.

ROBESON, PAUL   SINGER, ACTOR, AND ACTIVIST

Born: April 9, 1898, Princeton, NJ
Education: Rutgers University, B.A. highest honors, 1919; Columbia Law School, LL.B., 1923
Died: January 23, 1976, Philadelphia, PA

Inspired by his father, an escaped slave and Baptist preacher, Robeson learned in boyhood to resist injustice.

He was a trailblazer. A scholar-athlete at Rutgers University, he finished Columbia Law School and worked in a New York law firm. But he soon quit because of race prejudice and, inspired by the Harlem Renaissance, joined a theatrical group. He acted in off-Broadway shows like *The Emperor Jones* (1923). A popular and recording singer of Negro folk songs and spirituals, he also starred on Broadway in *Othello* (1930). His film credits include *The Emperor Jones* (1933) and *The Song of the Rivers* (1954).

As he performed overseas, including in the Soviet Union, Robeson denounced racial, ethnic, and class injustices. From the 1930s he was an international activist. He rejected fascism and racism, "refusing to sing before segregated audiences," joining the leftist National Negro Congress, and performing fund-raisers for labor unions and civil rights organizations.

He faced a backlash. The House Committee on Un-American Activities interrogated him; the government revoked his passport (1950). When a Federal Court restored it (1958), he visited the Soviet Union and remained abroad. He returned in 1963 but was isolated by civil rights leaders; media blacklisted him. He received a posthumous Grammy Award for Lifetime Achievement (1998).

Further Reading

Duberman, Martin. *Paul Robeson*. New York: Alfred A.Knopf, 1989.
Le Blanc, Paul, ed. *Black Liberation and the American Dream: The Struggle for Racial and Economic Justice: Analysis, Strategy, Readings*. Amherst, NY: Humanity Press, 2003.

ROBINSON, JACK R. (JACKIE)
PRO BASEBALL PLAYER

Born: July 31, 1919, Cairo, GA
Education: Pasadena, California Junior College, 1938–40, UCLA, 1940–41
Died: October 24, 1972, Stamford, CT

Private Robinson resisted army segregation and was denied promotion, but boxer Joe Louis intervened successfully on his behalf.

Promoted and honorably discharged, Jackie played second base for the Negro Leagues' Kansas City Monarchs. Brooklyn Dodgers owner Branch Rickey soon began recruiting him and he signed in 1947, breaching "approximately eighty years of baseball segregation." He became a black hero and a few other Negro Leagues stars joined him in the majors.

Jackie was a leader. He endured racist treatment with dignity and fought by letting "his bat and glove do the talking." Thus he won the Rookie of the Year Award (1947) and many firsts, such as the first black player to win the National League Most Valuable Player Award (1949), in the Baseball Hall of Fame (1962), and on a commemorative US postal stamp (1982).

Retiring from the game in 1957, Jackie emerged as a strong advocate of civil rights and equal opportunity. He advocated broader and more expeditious desegregation of baseball. As blacks were excluded from coaching and managerial positions, he would not attend games or play on "old timers" days. But he did the opening pitch for the 1972 World Series and twenty-fifth anniversary of Major League integration. He died nine days later.

Further Reading

Carroll, Brian. *When to Stop the Cheering?: The Black Press, the Black Community, and the Integration of Baseball*. New York: Routledge, 2007.
Tygiel, Jules. *Baseball's Great Experiment: Jackie Robinson and His Legacy*. New York: Oxford University Press, 1997.

ROOTS

A respected writer, Alex Haley (1921–1992) won international acclaim for *Roots: The Saga of an American Family* (1976). It did "more than recapture the history of his own family." Rather, it reclaimed the African ancestry, slavery experience, and emancipation of African Americans.

The book was seminal. Some critics believe Haley blurred the line between fact and fiction in tracing Kunta Kinte and his descendants from Africa to freedom. Nevertheless, he earned the Pulitzer Prize Committee's Special Citation for literary achievement (1977). That year more than 90 million viewed a twelve-hour *Roots* television miniseries, depicting violent racial images, even as *Roots* vitalized African American genealogy. Scholars still question its historical accuracy.

[*See also* Film.]

Further Reading

Ryan, Tim A. *Calls and Responses: The American Novel of Slavery since Gone with the Wind*. Baton Rouge: Louisiana State University Press, 2008.
Taylor, Helen. "Everybody's Search for Roots: Alex Haley and the Black and White Atlantic." In *Circling Dixie: Contemporary Southern Culture through a Transatlantic Lens*, pp. 63–90. New Brunswick, NJ: Rutgers University Press, 2001.

ROSENWALD SCHOOLS

One to four-teacher wooden schoolhouses, financed partly by the Julius Rosenwald Fund, were symbols of self-help in black southerners' crusade for schools during the early twentieth century.

From 1914 to 1932 the Rosenwald school-building program assisted African Americans in 883 counties of fifteen southern states. That assistance facilitated the construction of 4,977 rural schools (capacity 615–63); teacher cottages; and vocational shops costing $28, 408,520. The Rosenwald brand and its building program's matching grants sustained the widespread notion that the Fund alone paid for those schools. Grants covered approximately 15 percent of the total costs, however, while blacks contributed 17 percent, whites donated 4 percent, and state taxes provided 64 percent. African American communities also observed an annual "Rosenwald School Day" to raise money and pledge in-kind contributions. They sacrificed to build and maintain schools for their children.

[*See also* Education.]

Further Reading

Hanchett, Thomas W. "The Rosenwald Schools and Black Education in North Carolina," *North Carolina Historical Review*, LXI (October 1988): 387–444.
Hoffschwelle, Mary S. *The Rosenwald Schools of the American South.* Gainesville: University Press of Florida, 2006.

RUSTIN, BAYARD T.
CIVIL AND HUMAN RIGHTS ACTIVIST

Born: March 17, 1912, West Chester, PA
Education: Attended Wilberforce University, Cheyney State Teachers College, City College of New York
Died: August 24, 1987, New York, NY

Rustin was the foremost organizer in the nonviolent freedom struggle between 1941 and 1965. As a Quaker, he embraced not only the War Resisters League (1936–41) but also racial and ethnic integration and equality.

He pursued civil and human rights and peace. Early on, his work in the Fellowship of Reconciliation (FOR) placed him at the forefront of anti-war activism. An assistant to A. Philip Randolph, he became chief advisor for the March on Washington Movement (1941). Cofounder of the Congress of Racial Equality (CORE, 1942), he went to California to protest the internment of Japanese Americans. Convicted of draft resistance, he served two and a half years in federal prison. He co-created CORE's Journey of Reconciliation (1947), joining an interracial team to challenge Jim Crow on interstate buses. Through FOR's affiliate, In Friendship, he organized both the Montgomery Bus Boycott and Southern Christian Leadership Conference. He was the major architect of the 1963 March on Washington and voting rights marches in Alabama. Rustin founded the Randolph Institute in 1965. Under his visionary leadership, the institute sponsored initiatives in nonviolence, union organizing, and building multiracial and ethnic voter coalitions. President Obama awarded Rustin the Presidential Medal of Freedom posthumously (2013).

Further Reading

D'Emilio, John. *Lost Prophet: The Life and Times of Bayard Rustin.* New York: Free Press, 2003.
Wink, Walter, ed. *Peace Is the Way: Writings on Nonviolence from the Fellowship of Reconciliation.* Maryknoll, NY: Orbis Books, 2000.

SCHOLARSHIP

Black scholarship creates and promotes knowledge of blacks, as well as racial, ethnic, gender, and class relations, in the United States and world. Its core creators and promoters before the 1960s were black secondary and higher education faculty in humanities, behavioral and social sciences, and their associations. It saw growing acceptance with desegregation of learned societies, colleges, and universities, which elected to membership and recruited to white faculties black scholars who helped establish Black Studies programs and promote research and teaching on race and the black experience. The programs indeed energized inquiry, instruction, and community service; minority group and women's studies; and demands to integrate academia.

African American history clearly provides a microcosm of black scholarly inquiries. Its development as a field, according to Earle E. Thorpe's *Black Historians: A Critique* (1971), is traceable via the lens of various schools, some historians contributing to more than one school. An increasing number of whites contributed. Schools researched and interpreted not only white racism and racial injustice but also the complexity and richness of black heritage and culture, institutions and organizations, and movements for justice.

The Beginning School (1800–96) affirmed African and African American humanity, dignity, and freedom. Chroniclers (slaves, free blacks, freedmen and women) renounced slavery and color caste. They championed abolitionism, Christianity, literacy, the Union, emancipation, black citizenship and uplift in their columns, essays, memoirs, sermons, and histories. William Wells Brown, former slave and abolitionist, defended *The Black Man: His Antecedents, His Genius, and His Achievements* (1863). Union veteran, Baptist minister, and legislator George Washington Williams did so in his *A History of the Negro Race in America from 1619 to 1880* (1882). Slave-born educator Anna J. Cooper's *A Voice from the South by a Black Woman of the South* (1892) urged educating girls and women to elevate "the whole Negro race." Episcopal rector Alexander Crummell preached black pride, self-help, and African repatriation. Former missionary in Liberia, he authored *Africa and America* (1891) and mentored W. E. B. Du Bois.

The Middle School (1896–1930) instituted black historiography. Members mostly had ties to Negro colleges, the American Negro Academy, and Association for the Study of Negro Life and History (ASNLH). Crummell created the Academy in 1897; it promoted art, literature, and science until 1928. Its first paper, "The Conservation of Races" by Du Bois, said we must "conserve our physical powers, our intellectual endowments, our spiritual ideals ... by race organization" (Blight and Gooding, 1997, 234). Using his tedious survey of 2,500 households, he wrote *The Philadelphia Negro: A Social Study* (1899). It unveiled the color line and black poverty in the North and arguably introduced empirical sociology in America. Joining the Atlanta University faculty, he organized its annual interdisciplinary Conference for the Study of Negro Problems. Between 1898 and 1912 alone, the conference produced seventeen monographs such as *The Negro Church* (1903) as well as defined methods for study. History and sociology departments in white and black institutions, accordingly, added scholars on race. In 1915 Carter G. Woodson formed ASNLH, sponsor of *The Journal of Negro History* (1916), Associated Publishers (1921), Negro History Week (1926), and *Negro History Bulletin* (1937). Author and editor of nineteen books, Woodson "was virtually single-handedly responsible for establishing Afro-American history as a specialty" (Collisson, 2008, p. 35). His *The Negro in Our History* (1922) was "the best textbook on the subject until the appearance in 1947 of John Hope Franklin's *From Slavery to Freedom*" (Thorpe, 1971, p. 118). Confirming Gunnar Myrdal's *An American Dilemma: The Negro Problem and Modern Democracy* (1944), Franklin said "that the treatment of the Negro is America's greatest scandal" (Provenzo, 2011, p. 195). That book is currently Franklin and Evelyn Brooks Higginbotham, *From Slavery to Freedom: A History of African Americans* 9th ed. (2011). Du Bois, Woodson, and Charles H. Wesley, author of *Negro Labor in the United States, 1850–1925* (1927), were "pioneers in Black Studies."

Franklin's generation established the New School (1930–60). Highly educated, often Ph.D.'s, members created a large body of work, including colonial, antebellum, and Civil War themes: Lorenzo J. Greene's *The Negro in Colonial New England, 1620–1776* (1943); Franklin's *The Free Negro in North Carolina, 1790–1860* (1943); Luther P. Jackson's *Free Negro Labor and Property Holding in Virginia, 1830–1860* (1942); Benjamin Quarles's *Frederick Douglass* (1948) and *The Negro in the Civil War* (1954); Kenneth M. Stampp's *The Peculiar Institution: Slavery in the Ante-Bellum South* (1956); Herbert Aptheker's *American Negro Slave Revolts* (1943); and Wesley's *The Collapse of the Confederacy* (1937). Postwar topics included *Black Reconstruction in America ... 1860–1880* (1935) by Du Bois; *The Negro in Tennessee, 1865–1880* (1941) by A. A. Taylor; *The Negro in American Life and Thought: The Nadir, 1877–1901* (1954) by Rayford W. Logan; *The Negro and Fusion*

Politics in North Carolina, 1894–1901 (1951) by Helen G. Edmonds; and *The Strange Career of Jim Crow* (1955) by C. Vann Woodward. Studies of black business, labor, politics, religion, and civil rights appeared. *The United States and Armaments* (1948), by Merze Tate, analyzed military weaponry. *The Militant South, 1800–1861* (1956), by Franklin, assessed the South's endemic militarism.

Desegregation in the United States, beside African and the Third World decolonization, inspired the Contemporary School (1960–present). In *The Mind of the Negro: An Intellectual History of Afro-Americans* (1961), Thorpe explores Afro-American letters, ideologies, and leadership from enslavement to "the growing integration movement." Franklin studied *Reconstruction: After the Civil War* (1961) and *The Emancipation Proclamation* (1963). Tracing developments in African Americans' intellectual and social life and continuing quest for equality, Thorpe and Franklin forecast many new works. *The Confederate Negro: Virginia's Craftsmen and Military Laborers, 1861–1865* (1969), by James H. Brewer, typified that work. So did "the arrival of David L. Lewis's *King: A Critical Biography* (1970), Mary Frances Berry's *Black Resistance/White Law* (1971), B. Joyce Ross's *J. E. Spingarn and the Rise of the NAACP* (1972), and John W. Blassingame's *The Slave Community* (1972)" (Meier, 1986, p. 179).

Published in subsequent years by racially diverse and numerous authors, such accounts engage key issues and varying sources aimed at "putting black people back at the center of their history" (Hine, 1986, p. 4). Evidencing this is Darlene Clark Hine, ed., *The State of Afro-American History: Past, Present, and Future* (1986), which explores historians' evolution; Slavery, Emancipation, and Urban Studies, the last stressing the Great Migration and post-1945 Civil Rights Movement; Black Women; and Black History education and communities. It views slavery, emancipation, and urbanization as the "three major periods of Afro-American history." Black agency is a central theme over time and place. How did "the African cultural inheritance" shape slaves, free blacks, freedpeople, sharecroppers, and migrants' struggles to build and sustain families, institutions, economic self-help, and resistance in spite of the "slave and postslavery labor systems"? For example, using plantation and legal records in *The Black Family in Slavery and Freedom, 1750–1925* (1976), Herbert G. Gutman foregrounds slaves and freedpeople's testimony, marriages, children, African naming practices, and religious traditions. They thus preserved "familial and social memory," a two-parent household, and an "extended family" tradition.

Leon F. Litwack, in *Trouble in Mind: Black Southerners in the Age of Jim Crow* (1998), draws on black voices from autobiography; memoir; literature; oral history; church; and folklife, especially blues lyrics, to depict sustaining values of hope and struggle. Historiography constitutes Manning Marable's main black source, but he culls bell-letters, journalism, interviews, speeches, and organizations as well to explain the evolution of black and multiethnic freedom struggles in *Race, Reform, and Rebellion: The Second Reconstruction and Beyond in Black America, 1945–2006*, 3rd ed. (2007).

[*See also* Afro-American studies; Education; Medicine; Science.]

References

Collisson, Craig. *The Fight to Legitimize Blackness: How Black Students Changed the University*. Ph.D. dissertation, University of Washington, 2008, p. 35.

"The Conservation of Races" (1897). In Blight, David W. and Robert Gooding-Williams, eds., The Souls of Black Folk by W. E. B. Du Bois. Boston: Bedford/St. Martin's, 1997, p. 234.

Hine, Darlene Clark, ed., *The State of Afro-American History: Past, Present, Future*. Baton Rouge: Louisiana State University Press, 1986, p. 4.

Meier, August, and Elliott Rudwick. *Black History and the Historical Profession, 1915–80*. Urbana: University of Illinois Press, 1986, p. 179.

Provenzo, Eugene F. *The Teacher in American Society: A Critical Anthology*. Thousand Oaks, CA: SAGE, 2011, p. 195.

Thorpe, Earl E. *Black Historians: A Critique*. New York: Morrow, 1971, p. 118.

Further Reading

Dagbovie, Pero Gaglo. *African American History Reconsidered*. Urbana: University of Illinois Press, 2010.

Meier, August, and Elliott M. Rudwick. *Black History and the Historical Profession, 1915–1980*. Urbana: University of Illinois Press, 1986.

White, Deborah Gray, ed. *Telling Histories: Black Women Historians in the Ivory Tower*. Chapel Hill: University of North Carolina Press, 2014.

SCIENCE

In spite of educational discrimination over time, blacks embraced careers in fields such as biology, chemistry, physics, engineering, and mathematics and helped advance scientific knowledge.

For example, Percy L. Julian (1899–1975) finished Depauw University (valedictorian, Phi Beta Kappa); an M.S. at Harvard, which would not continue him; and a Ph.D. (chemistry) at the University of Vienna. Then "potential employers snubbed him. 'We didn't know you were a Negro.'"

He became a Howard University professor, Depauw faculty visitor, an industry scientist, and created Julian Laboratories in Chicago (1953); he sold the labs "for more than $2 million in 1961" and established the nonprofit Julian Research Institute (1964). His research generated 130 chemical patents and financial aid for college students. In 1999 the American Chemical Society "recognized his synthesis of physostigmine, a glaucoma drug, as one of the top 25 achievements in the history of American chemistry. He was the first black chemist ever elected to the National Academy of Sciences" (Lee, 2007).

The record of African Americans in science mirrors Julian's career. Blacks earned 511 doctorates in graduate science programs of 34 institutions between 1876 and 1969. More than a third specialized in biological sciences. Ohio State and Iowa were first and second, with 45 and 36, and Howard, the only black institution included, was tenth with 18. Universities awarded 1,251 chemistry doctorates in 1999, including 46 or 4 percent to blacks.

Those statistics reflect inequality in schooling and graduate school admissions, as well as institutions' uneven adoption of affirmative action. A "controversial and politically sensitive" policy, it posits that denial of equal opportunity (past and present) adversely affects blacks' performance on standardized tests and measures. Blacks still contribute to science professions. Historically black North Carolina A. & T., Tennessee State, and Tuskegee universities award the Ph.D. in agronomy and engineering. Howard and Meharry medical schools, which enrolled and trained 85 percent of black M.D.'s in the twentieth century, made "strong showings in traditional measures of achievement." Similarly noted is the Morehouse School of Medicine (MSM), formed in 1975 by Louis W. Sullivan, Morehouse '54, hematologist, and Secretary of Health and Human Services (1989–92). MSM admitted its first class in 1981 and was accredited in 1985. By 2002 it had graduated 602 doctors, 68 percent in primary care; 84 percent of them practiced in underserved areas. Former civil rights activists Robert Moses and Charles Cobb started the Algebra Project (1982), teaching math and life skills to inner-city middle and high school students. Black colleges increasingly emphasized science, technology, engineering, and mathematics (STEM) fields. In 2012, of 31,338 black students in US graduate science and engineering programs, 4,162 or 13.3 percent were at Historically Black Colleges and Universities (HBCUs), including 35 percent in pharmacology.

[*See also* Medicine; Technology.]

Reference

Lee, Felicia R. "Reclaiming a Black Research Scientist's Forgotten Legacy." *The New York Times,* February 6, 2007.

Further Reading

Czujko, Roman, Rachel Ivie, and James H. Stith. "Untapped Talent: The African American Presence in Physics and the Geosciences." *AIP Report.* Pub. Number R-144, September 2008.

Mickens, Ronald E., ed. *The African American Presence in Physics: A Compilation of Materials Related to an Exhibit.* Atlanta: National Society of Black Physicists, 1999.

Warren, Wini. *Black Women Scientists in the United States.* Bloomington: Indiana University Press, 1999.

SEGREGATION

Also called *Jim Crow,* a moniker for slave, segregation was a system to enforce white–black, racial–ethnic separation and white supremacy.

Deep-rooted in customs and laws to control slaves and free blacks, it interfaced slavery, evolved after slavery's abolition, and was legal until 1964. In the North, where slave emancipation occurred ca. 1777–1846, blacks were separated by custom in churches, housing, jobs, schools, streetcars, and endured racist violence. Post–Civil War, only six northern states enacted black suffrage. In the South, domiciling more than 90 percent of African Americans, customary separation of the races morphed, legally and extralegally, into legalized apartheid. In face of Freedmen's Bureau efforts to educate and protect them, Black Codes and Ku Klux Klan terror restricted former slaves. Congress repealed the codes while approving states' constitutions and readmissions that vitiated blacks' citizenship, suffrage, and well-being. During Reconstruction and after, Democrats invented devices like the grandfather clause, poll tax, and registration reforms to suppress black and Republican voting; lynching; and convict leasing to abet separating blacks. Virginia declared a "white person" one who "has no trace whatever of any blood other than Caucasian." A "colored person" was one "in whom there is ascertainable any Negro blood" (Lewis, 1999, p. 5). Schools, churches, businesses, industries, civic and social organizations, cohabiting and marriage, public auditoriums, hospitals, parks, prisons, and transportation thus were segregated years before the proliferation of Jim Crow laws.

Jim Crow codified rapidly during the 1890s. Democrats defeated Populist–Republican–Negro voter coalitions and constitutionally eliminated black voters in Mississippi (1890) and South Carolina (1895) as the Supreme Court's *Plessy* decision (1896) instituted the "equal, but separate" doctrine. Southern states hardly equalized black institutions and opportunities. They also winked at mob murder. From 1880 to 1930 alone 3,220 blacks and 723 whites were lynched in the South. The "white primary" election and poll tax continued. The Court overturned the former in 1944; the latter persisted to 1964–65.

[*See also* Apartheid; Civil Rights Act of 1964; *Smith v. Allwright* (1944).]

Reference

Lewis, Ida. E. "Who Is An African American?" *The Crisis*, Vol. 106, (January/ February 1999), p. 5.

Further Reading

Litwack, Leon F. *Trouble in Mind: Black Southerners in the Age of Jim Crow.* New York: Alfred A. Knopf, 1998.

Valk, Anne M., and Leslie Brown. *Living with Jim Crow: African American Women and Memories of the Segregated South.* New York: Palgrave Macmillan, 2010.

SHARE CROPPERS' UNION (SCU)

With the assistance of American Communist Party organizers, Alabama black sharecroppers and tenant farmers created the SCU in 1931. Nate Shaw, a Tallapoosa County cropper, recalled that one organizer "was a colored fella … He wanted us to organize and he was with us a whole lot of the time holdin meetins with us" (Rosengarten, 2000, p. 297).

The members resisted economic and racial injustice. Meeting secretly, they discussed how to fight cheating, lien foreclosures, peonage (jail for debt), and lynching and how to get a nine-month school term and a county bus for their children. But news of the meetings leaked and the authorities retaliated. The sheriff and Ku Klux Klansmen killed more than a dozen members. They whipped many; arrested, convicted, and jailed others. Shaw served twelve years in the state prison. SCU went underground, recruited, and spread. It had a membership between 10,000 and 12,000 in Alabama, Georgia, Louisiana, and Mississippi by 1936.

[*See also Labor.*]

Reference

Rosengarten, Theodore. *All God's Dangers: The Life of Nate Shaw."* Chicago: University of Chicago Press, 2000, p. 297.

Further Reading

Kelley, Robin D. G. *Hammer and Hoe: Alabama Communists during the Great Depression.* Chapel Hill: University of North Carolina Press, 1990.

Rosengarten, Theodore. *All God's Dangers: The Life of Nate Shaw.* Chicago: University of Chicago Press, 2000.

SHARECROPPING

A post-bellum farming system that mirrored southern slavery, sharecropping entailed far more black than white tenant farmers. Blacks accommodated it to survive, to escape gang work and the whip. They hoped to support themselves while protecting their women and children.

Landlords and sharecroppers signed contracts for "halves." The landlord furnished the land, house, fuel, tools, work stock, feed for stock, seed, and half the fertilizer; he earned half the crop. The cropper supplied labor and half the fertilizer, earning half the crop. He also had to repay (at high interest) for food and supplies from the store, clearing little or nothing when he settled. Sharecropping fueled landlords' cheating as well as racial violence. It lasted until the twentieth century mechanization of cotton planting and harvesting saw croppers migrate by millions to seek better livelihoods in cities.

[*See also* Agriculture; Great Migration.]

Further Reading

Hurt, R. Douglas, ed. *African American Life in the Rural South, 1900–1950.* Columbia: University of Missouri Press, 2003.

Ransom, Roger L., and Richard Sutch. *One Kind of Freedom: The Economic Consequences of Emancipation.* New York: Cambridge University Press, 2001.

SHAW V. RENO (1993)

North Carolina's Suffrage Amendment (1900) disfranchised blacks and, while *Smith v. Allwright* (1944) overturned the white primary and revived black suffrage, southern African Americans did not vote widely until after the Voting Rights Act of 1965 (VRA). Civil rights groups also sued to broaden North Carolina black political participation, resulting in the state's 1991–92 Congressional redistricting. Whites comprised the majority in ten of its twelve districts, whose shapes and sizes varied considerably. Accordingly, the Democratic legislature created the black-majority First and Twelfth districts, whose voters elected the first blacks to Congress since 1898.

But the election of Melvin Watt and Eva M. Clayton (who broke a gender barrier too) was challenged successfully. Suing for Republicans, a Duke Law School professor claimed that the First and Twelfth Congressional Districts were "bizarre looking" and racially discriminatory. He never established any violation of the Fourteenth and Fifteenth Amendments. But in a 5–4 decision the Supreme Court upheld his claim. It ruled "that neither race-conscious efforts to comply with the VRA nor attempts to correct past discrimination were acceptable justifications for creating the particular minority opportunity districts at issue." The Court's ruling weakened a quarter century of electoral protections for underrepresented racial and ethnic minorities.

[*See also* Redistricting.]

Further Reading

Keyssar, Alexander. *The Right to Vote: The Contested History of Democracy in the United States.* New York: Basic Books, 2000.

Kousser, J. Morgan. *Colorblind Injustice: Minority Voting Rights and the Undoing of the Second Reconstruction.* Chapel Hill: University of North Carolina Press, 1999.

SIT-INS

Civil rights activists began using a sit-down at white-only restaurants and other facilities to fight segregation during the 1930s.

When four students from all-black North Carolina A & T College (Greensboro) sat at Woolworth's segregated lunch counter on February 1, 1960, they powerfully reclaimed that tactic of nonviolent protest. Sit-ins swept seventy-eight cities and towns in North and South Carolina, Florida, Georgia, Tennessee, and Virginia by April, when student leaders formed the Student Nonviolent Coordinating Committee (SNCC). By then more than 2,000 protesters had been arrested, many injured from violent attacks. SNCC used the sit-in and voter registration to promote desegregation, black enfranchisement, and "a coalition of conscience" for racial and social justice. Its campaigns won invaluable support from others, including Congress of Racial Equality (CORE), a sponsor of 1940s sit-downs; NAACP Youth Councils, sponsors of the Durham, North Carolina (1957) and Wichita, Kansas (1958) sit-ins; and Southern Christian Leadership Conference (SCLC), whose staff member organized the Nashville sit-ins (1959).

[*See also* Civil Rights Movement; Student activism.]

Further Reading

Morgan, Iwan, and Philip Davies, eds. *From Sit-ins to SNCC: The Student Civil Rights Movement in the 1960s*. Gainesville: University Press of Florida, 2012.
Lewis, Andrew B. *The Shadows of Youth: The Remarkable Journey of the Civil Rights Generation*. New York: Hill and Wang, 2009.

SLAVERY

For nearly two and a half centuries preceding the Civil War and general emancipation, slavery critically defined the economy and government; black life and culture; and race, ethnic, class, and gender relations in America.

Slavery on the North American mainland evolved with the Atlantic Slave Trade (1502–1870) and European slave systems in the Western Hemisphere. Enduring "physical and psychic hardships" on the 40–69-day crossing known as the Middle Passage, countless Africans died; 10–12 million lived. Europeans also enslaved native Indians and exploited white servants, usually indentured 5–7 years to repay costs of transport and rations. Indians escaped and rebelled; white-borne malaria, measles, and other diseases killed millions of them. Yet, as wages improved in Europe, importations of servants declined. Colonists thus imported more and more blacks from West Africa, where Portugal built its first slave fort in 1482.

Africans' enslavement braced western economies. Thought by whites to be heathen, plentiful, and strong, they were laborers on voyages of Spanish explorers. They supplied Spain's short-lived settlement near the Cape Fear River (1526) and permanent colony at St. Augustine, Florida (1565). Before 1600 about 75,000 Africans slaved in the fields and mines of Brazil, Hispaniola, Mexico, and Peru alone. British Caribbean colonies imported 2,339,000 Africans from 1630 to 1780, beside 650,000 in North America. Here, mostly as a result of rising births, slaves were 25% of inhabitants after 1740. Owner manumissions, escapes, and gradual emancipation in the North (1777–1846) increased the number of free blacks. Freedpeople were 8% of all blacks in 1790 and 11% by 1860. Slaves totaled 697,897 or 22% of the nation's population in 1790; 1,538,125 or 20% in 1820; 3,204,313 or 16% in 1850, when approximately 400,000 were urban dwellers; and 4,000,000 or 15% by 1860.

Slaving emerged along regional lines, creating color and class oppression by custom and law. Slaveholder and merchant elites accumulated wealth and controlled political power. A nonplantation economy developed in the North: New England, New York, New Jersey, and Pennsylvania, where farms and households had small slave holdings and close living conditions. Crews of bondmen tended iron forges, shipyards, and tanneries in cities (Philadelphia, New York, and Boston). Plantations spread in the South. Gang labor was the rule on the tobacco and wheat plantations of the Chesapeake (Maryland, Virginia, and North Carolina). But large indigo and rice estates in the Low Country (South Carolina, Georgia) used a "task system." Bondmen, for example, were assigned tasks of digging, sowing, or threshing every morning. They could finish those by mid-afternoon, receive permission to leave the fields, and use the rest of the day hunting, fishing, gardening, or networking.

Slaves forged a community. As in the Chesapeake by 1750, they created households, domestic groups, and families. The household was coresidential, including slaves in a "proximity of sleeping arrangements" or living under the same roof. By comparison, the domestic group comprised kin and nonkin in common or separate households, sharing activities such as cooking, eating, childcare, fieldwork, and religious services. Families included those related by blood or marriage; husband and wife or parents and children were immediate family. The family's close and distant kinfolk encompassed adult brothers and sisters, cousins, aunts, uncles, and "fictive" relatives. Family formation depended crucially on master–slave relationships, slaves' hope, and their resilience. Many masters encouraged bondmen and women to cohabit or marry, coaxing them to have children. Slaves' marriages and children often were victims of masters' sexual abuse, punishment, and separations at auction. Slaves devised extended-family and kin networks (derived from Africa) to survive. African naming practices, like a boy named for his sold-away father or grandfather, enabled them to preserve memories of loved ones.

Their shared sense of belonging, identity, and obligation mirrored "the life cycle of Afro-American slaves." First, infancy: a mother nursed and weaned her infant in the fields and quarters, where he or she learned to explore, relate, and play. Second, "leaving the matricentral cell": young children were cared for by older siblings and relatives, who trained them in work routines. Third, fieldwork: at age seven to ten children "were typically forced to leave home." Fourth, courtship and marriage: occurring in late teens for females and mid-twenties for males. Fifth, parenthood: mother and children bonded, ordinarily without the father; kinfolk helped with childcare. Sixth, old age: at sixty and older slaves faced increasing illness, poverty, and dependence on their kin.

Slaveholding markedly shaped America. Virginia slaves were half of its residents by 1700. South Carolina had a slave majority in 1765. While the American Revolution spawned hope for liberty and northern abolition, the Constitution preserved bondage. It allowed three-fifths of "persons held to service" to be counted for congressional representatives and direct taxes. Its ban of the foreign slave trade (1808) fueled smuggling, the Domestic Slave Trade, and emerging Cotton Kingdom. Companies, dealers, and kidnappers "who specialized in buying and selling human property" profited greatly. Border and Upper South owners, separating families, sold more than 1,800,000 so-called "surplus" slaves ca. 1790–1860, many to the Carolina–Georgia Piedmont. Most were transported to Deep South states. Slaveholding families, some of them black, were a third of all free families. North Carolina free blacks from 37 counties, for instance, owned 620 of the state's 245, 601 slaves in 1830. An owner of twenty or more slaves was a planter. By 1860 planters constituted 12 percent of slaveholders but possessed 50 percent of all slaves. An estimated three-fourths of white southerners were non-slaveholders. Antiblack, nevertheless, they provided the overseers, farmers, patrollers, and other vigilantes who assisted in preserving slavery.

The "'peculiar institution'" demanded brawn and entailed toil. Most slaves were field hands, toiling from sunup to sundown though ill-clothed, fed, and housed. Some were whip-toting drivers and foremen. Women, despite pregnancy and nursing, toiled in fieldwork with men. Slaves labored as domestics, artisans, mechanics, and washerwomen; others worked in the canal, railroad, naval stores, and turpentine industries. A great mass worked in factories (textile, tobacco), mines (coal, iron, salt), sawmills, and quarries. Often in the southwest, they were cattle herders and cowboys. They piloted river boats and frequently were crewmen or stevedores.

Slave codes and cruel discipline (whipping, maiming, torture, executions) hounded them. By 1800 it was illegal to manumit slaves at one's discretion; for them to read and write or obtain written material. Slaves could not host or visit free people; own property; or make contracts or sue, except through a freeholder. They could testify in court only against other blacks. Their marriages had no legal standing. Nor should they assemble in public, keep guns, strike white people, and travel without a pass. Some masters allowed them to worship separately; raise and barter produce from slave garden plots; and share earnings from being hired out. A family or its members could be sold to pay an owner's creditors. States levied severe fines for stealing slaves. When a slave was executed for arson, murder, rape, or rebellion, the state compensated her or his owner at fair market value. Between 1785 and 1865, Virginia alone tried, condemned, and put to death 628 slaves accused of capital offenses.

Slaves, nonetheless, survived, resisted, and struggled for freedom. Drawing upon an Afro-American culture formed and conveyed by African and Creole (American-born) forebears, who gradually adopted Christianity, they sustained families, communities, and social institutions while gaining allies among white and black abolitionists. Slaves' "invisible institution" of Afro-Christianity, nurtured in slave and free-black Baptist and Methodist churches before enlarging to northern Free African Societies (1787–1810), informed and inspired the fight for liberation, literacy, and justice. Probably 100,000 slaves evacuated with the British army, or fled to Canada and Florida, by the end of the Revolutionary War. Furthermore, slaves in the French Caribbean colony of St. Domingue launched a bloody rebellion (1791) that achieved emancipation and, by 1804, an independent Haiti, the second Republic in the hemisphere. Southern ports banned West Indian slavers, but news of the revolt traveled and catalyzed slave resistance across the Atlantic World. More and more American slaves escaped. In a random sample of twenty newspapers, one study found 1,407 runaway slave ads for 1790–1816 and 2,677 for 1838–1860.

At the same time, bond and free blacks were steadfast. Slave and ex-slave clerics led in forming the Negro Baptist, African Methodist Episcopal, and African Methodist Episcopal Zion denominations, plus major missionary associations, fraternal orders, and the Convention Movement. All partnered in the abolitionist movement and its Underground Railroad. Free-born David Walker, who moved to Boston from North Carolina, proclaimed the movement's central purpose in *Walker's Appeal* (1829, p. 79). "Remember Americans, that we must and shall be free ... in spite of you," he wrote. "You may do your best to keep us in wretchedness and misery ... but God will deliver us from under you." That faith infused the rebellions of Gabriel Prosser (1800) and Nat Turner (1831) in Virginia, of Denmark Vesey (1822) in South Carolina. Each hung with fellow rebels. The authorities terrorized blacks, closed their churches, and silenced black preachers. But thousands of bondmen, women, and children, aided in safe houses, made their way to freedom, forcing Congress' passing of a fugitive slave law (1850), North–South conflict on slavery expansion, and southern secession. Countless slaves ran to and found refuge in Union lines during the Civil War, making it a war to abolish slavery.

[*See also* Black Belt; Fugitive Slave Act (1850); Indentured servitude; Underground Railroad.]

Further Reading

Berlin, Ira. *Generations of Captivity: A History of African-American Slaves.* Cambridge, MA: Harvard University Press, 2003.

Kolchin, Peter. *American Slavery, 1619–1877.* New York: Hill and Wang, 2003.

White, Deborah Gray. *Ar'n't I a Woman?: Female Slaves in the Plantation South.* New York: W. W. Norton, 1999.

SMITH V. ALLWRIGHT (1944)

In the Jim Crow South whites disfranchised blacks by extralegal and legal practices. The latter included the "white primary," which allowed a political party to nominate its candidates for the general election. Blacks were excluded.

Pursuing "the Negro's right to vote," the NAACP battled suffrage restriction in Texas. Its initial case, *Nixon v. Herndon* (1927), convinced the Supreme Court to overturn Texas' law excluding blacks from primary elections. The legislature changed it by allowing the Democratic Party's executive committee to determine its eligible voters, but the Court disallowed the change in *Nixon v. Condon* (1932). The Texas Democratic Convention, a private body, thus restricted participation in primaries to whites-only. Enlisting black Houston dentist Dr. Lonnie Smith as plaintiff, NAACP counsel unsuccessfully contested the party's racial exclusion in state court. He appealed and the Court overturned the "white primary" in *Smith* 8–1. Black voter registration and voting increased in southern states.

[*See also* Segregation.]

Further Reading

Hine, Darlene Clark. *Black Victory: The Rise and Fall of the White Primary in Texas.* Columbia: University of Missouri Press, 2003.

Zelden, Charles L. *The Battle for the Black Ballot:* Smith v. Allwright *and the Defeat of the Texas All-White Primary.* Lawrence: University Press of Kansas, 2004.

SOCIETIES, MUTUAL AID

Beside churches, slaves and free blacks formed protective associations and fraternal orders whose memberships paid dues to help provide needed "mutual aid for members and their families."

Rising black freedom struggles in the South and gradual northern emancipation (1777–1846) paralleled the growth not only of separate Baptist, Methodist, and other congregations but also African schools and Free African Societies, the latter contributing sick and burial assistance even as they forged race literacy, economic cooperation, social progress, and liberty. Orders of Negro Masons (1787) and Oddfellows (1843) helped build national networks of support, as did women's United Order of Tents (1867). Societies buttressed African American business and commerce. Burial societies established funeral homes, cemeteries, banks, and real estate and insurance companies. North Carolina Mutual Life Insurance Company, blacks' largest black business before 1960, evolved from Richmond, Virginia's Grand Fountain of the United Order of True Reformers (1881).

[*See also* Fraternal orders and lodges.]

Further Reading

Fahey, David M. *The Black Lodge in White America: "True Reformer" Browne and His Economic Strategy.* Lanham, MD: University Press of America, 1994.
Trotter, Joe William. "African American Fraternal Associations in American History." *Social Science History,* 28 (Fall 2004): 355–66.

SORORITIES

Rooted in the nineteenth century, the "Black sorority idea" saw a revival when women created Alpha Kappa Alpha (1908), Delta Sigma Theta (1913), and Zeta Phi Beta (1920) at Howard University. Not long after, Sigma Gamma Rho (1922) formed at Butler University. Those forerunners evolved into transnational bodies. By 1985 the Zetas had more than 500 chapters in the United States, Africa, and the Bahamas, as opposed to Sigma Gamma Rho's 350 chapters in the United States, Bermuda, and the Bahamas. In 1988 the Deltas included more than 125,000 members in 730 US, African, and Caribbean chapters.

Sororities helped advance African American women and communities. They supported women's education, community service, and leadership. Patricia R. Harris became Delta's first executive director in 1953. She also was the first woman dean at Howard Law School, ambassador to Luxembourg, and Secretary of Housing & Urban Development. Accepting her ambassadorship, she said that "while there are many things in my life which have prepared me for what I am about to do, it is largely the experience in Delta Sigma Theta which gives me most security." Even as they competed, sororities shared ideals of sisterhood in the struggle for racial equality.

[*See also* Clubs; Fraternal orders and lodges; Fraternities.]

Further Reading

Brown, Tamara L. et al., eds. *African American Fraternities and Sororities: The Legacy and the Vision*. Lexington: University Press of Kentucky, 2005.

Hughey, Matthew W., and Gregory S. Parks, eds. *Black Greek-Letter Organizations 2.0: New Directions in the Study of African American Fraternities and Sororities*. Jackson: University Press of Mississippi, 2011.

SOUTHERN CHRISTIAN LEADERSHIP CONFERENCE (SCLC)

Founded in 1957 by Martin Luther King, Jr. with ministers such as Ralph D. Abernathy and Fred L. Shuttlesworth, Jr., SCLC strived "to redeem the soul of America." It advocated nonviolent direct action, racial integration, and justice for all. In the wake of the victorious Montgomery Bus Boycott and white "massive resistance" to desegregation, it powerfully influenced the freedom movement.

With headquarters in Atlanta, it recruited a national cross section of black and white churchmen and women, community organizers and activists. Early on, it sponsored "Citizenship Schools" to promote adult literacy, voter registration, and civic activism. Beginning at Albany, Georgia in 1961, SCLC pursued local campaigns against segregated public accommodations and employment. Nonviolence, including marches and sit-ins, marked its internationally publicized struggles to end Jim Crow. Its 1963 campaign in Birmingham, which saw much police repression and the murder of four black girls, not only helped compel Congress to pass the Civil Rights Act. Its massive march from Selma to Montgomery and rally catalyzed passage of the Voting Rights Act.

[*See also Civil Rights Movement; Desegregation;* Nonviolence.]

Further Reading

Cotton, Dporothy F. *If Your Back's Not Bent: The Role of the Citizenship Education Program in the Civil Rights Movement*. New York: Atria Books, 2012.

Fairclough, Adam. *To Redeem the Soul of America: The Southern Christian Leadership Conference and Martin Luther King, Jr*. Athens: University of Georgia Press, 1987.

SOUTHERN NEGRO YOUTH CONGRESS (SNYC)

Founded in Richmond, Virginia (1937), SNYC coalesced young black activists from the National Negro Congress, labor, and student movements. In 1939 it moved its headquarters to Birmingham, Alabama. Until the Red Scare, state prosecution, and white terror impeded SNYC's organizing, it advanced and bridged the civil rights and industrial union struggles. Women were critical among SNYC leaders and community organizers. Organizers reached out to many local partners: black churches, schools and colleges, NAACP chapters, civic associations, women's clubs, and fraternal orders. Youth legislatures, which met in various cities, engaged communities in equal education, anti-poll tax, and voter registration campaigns. W. E. B. Du Bois did the keynote address at the Columbia, South Carolina youth legislature (1946).

Further Reading

Gellman, Erik S. *Death Blow to Jim Crow: The National Negro Congress and the Rise of Militant Civil Rights*. Chapel Hill: University of North Carolina Press, 2012.

Jackson, Esther, ed. *Freedomways Reader: Prophets in Their Own Country*. Boulder, CO: Westview Press, 2000.

SPANISH-AMERICAN WAR

Driven by its pro-war press, hailing Cuba's fight for independence and alleging sabotage of the USS *Maine* (which killed 262, including blacks), America declared war on Spain in 1898 and wrested much of her empire.

African Americans, if wary of imperialists, were patriotic. War created a chance "to render service to our country that no other race can," Booker T. Washington asserted. Others believed that "economic opportunities would open up for blacks once the islands came under American influence." However, many worried "that a Jim Crow war would result in a Jim Crow empire" ("Black Participation in the Spanish-American War").

Blacks served. Beside the 9th and 10th Cavalry, 24th and 25th Infantry of Buffalo soldiers, more than 8,000 volunteered in the army. Three regiments (23rd Kansas, 3rd North Carolina, and 8th Illinois) had full rosters of black officers. The only unit to see action was the 6th Massachusetts in Puerto Rico. Black soldiers also fought in the Philippines (1899–1902).

[*See also* Military.]

Reference

"Black Participation in the Spanish-American War." Retrieved from www.spanamwar .com/AfroAmericans.htm.

Further Reading

Scott, Edward Van Zile. *The Unwept: Black American Soldiers and the Spanish-American War.* Montgomery, AL: Black Belt Press, 1998.

Steward, T. G. *Buffalo Soldiers: The Colored Regulars in the United States Army.* Amherst, NY: Humanity Books, 2003.

SPAULDING, CHARLES C.
BUSINESS AND CIVIC LEADER

Born: August 1, 1874, Columbus County, NC
Education: Whitted School, Durham, NC, graduated 1898
Died: August 1, 1952, Durham, NC

North Carolina Mutual Life Insurance Company, established in 1898, is one of the largest black businesses in America. Its first agent, Spaulding masterminded the company's success.

He personified self-help. "Success is carved out by the chisel of efficiency, integrity, and hard work," he said. Invoking race pride, "Greatest Negro Insurance Company in the World" appeared on Mutual's stationery in 1909. By 1916 it reported $3 million in policies along with offices in twelve states and Washington, DC. Local assets included Mechanics and Farmers Bank, a real estate firm, drugstore, and two newspapers. During the Great Depression, it reduced operations and recovered in the robust post–World War II economy.

Spaulding preached black unity, economically and politically; civil rights, especially use of the ballot; and interracial cooperation. A loyal New Deal Democrat, he urged equal relief and opportunity, "liberty and justice for all." Cofounder of Durham Committee's on Negro Affairs, he helped increase black voting, which leveraged concessions like better schools. He also signed the Durham Manifesto (1942) against Jim Crow. Fifty-seven signers, all influential southern blacks, were "fundamentally opposed to the principle and practice of compulsory segregation." Their statement forecast the President's Committee on Civil Rights (1947) and desegregation in the South and nation.

Further Reading

Brown, Leslie. *Upbuilding Black Durham: Gender, Class, and Black Community Development in the Jim Crow South*. Chapel Hill: University of North Carolina Press, 2008.

Weare, Walter B. *Black Business in the New South: A Social History of the North Carolina Mutual Life Insurance Company*. Durham, NC: Duke University Press, 1993.

SPORTS

From slavery to freedom, baseball, football and other games valorized blacks. Their institutions and organizations sponsored sandlot, amateur, and professional sports for recreation, race pride, solidarity, and uplift. Sponsors included schools and colleges, hubs of physical education and athletics; churches; fraternal orders; businesses; YMCAs and YWCAs; Boy and Girl Scouts.

As a rule, black athletes were segregated until the mid-twentieth century. Boxing was an early exception. Jack Johnson reigned as world heavyweight champion (1908–15), as did Joe Louis (1937–49). The National Football League (NFL) drafted a black player in 1946 and Jackie Robinson entered Major League Baseball (MLB) in 1947. Those, as well as other firsts, inspired African American athletes to pursue a level "playing field" for themselves and their community.

Black education and athletics related in their mission. For example, southern black high schools told "student athletes to excel at northern colleges and debunk negative stereotypes of the race" (Kuska, 2004, p. 215). Although the National Collegiate Athletic Association (NCAA) began in 1906, it neglected small and Negro colleges until 1937. Johnson C. Smith University and Livingstone College christened black college football in 1892. Virginia Union–Virginia State and Tuskegee–Talladega's games soon followed. In 1912 Hampton Institute, with Howard, Lincoln, and Shaw universities, created the first black association: the Colored Intercollegiate Athletic Association. The Southern Intercollegiate Athletic Conference and Southwestern Athletic Conference formed in 1913 and

1920, respectively. They pooled resources for programs, notably baseball, track and field, basketball, football, and tennis, besides fostering principles of dignity, hardwork, fairness, and teamwork. Teams enlisted huge followings and produced a number of All-Americans and Olympians, among them Tuskegee high jumper Alice Coachman, the first black female Olympic champion and only American woman gold medalist in the 1948 Olympics.

Pro conferences and players not only pursued profit but also displayed athleticism. In such venues, many "players from black colleges and universities were given an opportunity to display their talents" (Ross, 2001, p. 54). Teams competed on local, state, and national levels, and selected all-star players. This occurred in Negro basketball, the so-called "Black Fives" (1906–49), whose most dominant teams were the famed Harlem Renaissance Big Five (1923) and Chicago-born Harlem Globetrotters (1926). Created by businessmen, academics, and physicians, the American Tennis Association (1916–50s), in addition to regular competition, held an annual tournament to select men and women singles and doubles champions. Black baseball established its Negro National League (1920–31, 1933–48), which included twenty-four franchises. The Homestead Grays, of Pittsburgh and Washington, DC, won ten Negro World Series. Seeking "to gather all colored golfers and golf associations into one body" (www.aaregistry.org/historic_events/view/african-americans-and-golf-brief-history) was the United States Colored Golfers Association (1925–76). Also valuable were football leagues (1928–46) such as the Virginia Negro League, which had teams in Richmond, Norfolk, and Newport News.

The conditioning and drive that enabled sportsmen and women to perform at a high level enhanced blacks' recognition and respect. A writer for *Opportunity*, organ of the National Urban League, explained in 1933, "That the Negro is deficient in the qualities of which athletic champions are made was long one of the accepted shibboleths of the American people. That rare combination–stamina, skill, and courage–it was commonly believed were seldom found under a black skin," he wrote. "Like many other myths concerning the Negro, this myth is being exploded, not by theory, nor argument, but by performance."

His words were prophetic. Blacks (sixteen men and two women) performed remarkably in the Berlin Olympics (1936). They accounted for 83 of the US team's 167 points; they won 8 gold medals, 6 of them in individual events. Jesse Owens set an Olympic record, winning golds in the long jump, 100 and 200 meter sprints, and the 4 × 100 meter relay. Owens and Joe Louis, who became the heavyweight boxing champion

(1937), gained recognition as American heroes, inspiring desegregation of the NFL, MLB, National Basketball Association (1949), United States Professional Tennis Association (1957), and Professional Golf Association (1961).

MLB was emblematic. The Brooklyn Dodgers (National League) discarded its white-only label by recruiting Jackie Robinson from the Kansas City Monarchs of the Negro League. Within weeks the Cleveland Indians (American League) recruited Larry Doby of the Newark Eagles. In 1956 the Cincinnati Reds signed Frank Robinson, the first black Most Valuable Player and triple-crown winner (most home runs, runs batted in, and highest batting average) in both leagues. He rose to be MLB's first black manager in 1975 when Cleveland named him a player-manager. The Milwaukee Braves acquired Hank Aaron of the Indianapolis Clowns in 1952. A perennial all-star, he broke baseball's 714 home run record (1974). During his twenty-three-year career, which put him in the Hall of Fame, Aaron set records for runs batted in (2,297) and home runs (755).

Sports mirrored racial issues as well as efforts for inclusion. After Cassius Clay won the heavyweight boxing championship in 1964, he joined the Nation of Islam, a black nationalist religious body, and became Muhammad Ali. Also a conscientious objector, he denounced the Vietnam War. The World Boxing Association (WBA) voided his title in 1967. But the Supreme Court vacated WBA's action and Ali recaptured the title in 1974. In the meantime, calls for equal opportunity were echoing in the initiatives of LeRoy T. Walker. A revered track coach at historically black North Carolina College (1956–80), he coached several Olympians and the US Track & Field team in the 1976 Olympics. As the first black president of the United States Olympic Committee (USOC) in 1994, he appointed task forces to review sports, including the participation of "women and people of color." The reviews detailed advances and disparities in amateur and professional athletics.

How much had the field leveled in 2000? Northeastern University's Center for the Study of Sport in Society provided a snapshot with its Racial and Gender Report Card covering seven institutions. For instance, it assigned C+ to the USOC, NCAA (noting inequities in women's programs), and MLB (whose front office rarely hired women and minorities); B+ to the NBA (helped by its Women's NBA); and B to the NFL on race and D on gender, as women and minorities were underemployed in management. It awarded Major League Soccer and Hockey C on race and D on gender. "As in society itself," the Center added, "we have a long way to go to achieve equality in sport." African Americans are continuing the journey.

[*See also* Desegregation; Education; Television.]

References

Kuska, Bob. *How Washington and New York Gave Birth to Black Basketball and Changed America's Game Forever*. Charlottesville: University of Virginia Press, 2004, p. 215.

Ross, Charles K. *Outside the Lines: African Americans and the Integration of the National Football League*. New York: New York University Press, 2001, p. 54.

Further Reading

Dawkins, Marvin P., and Graham C. Kinloch. *African American Golfers during the Jim Crow Era*. Westport, CT: Praeger, 2000.

Demas, Lane. *Integrating the Gridiron: Black Civil Rights and American College Football*. New Brunswick, NJ: Rutgers University Press, 2010.

Wiggins, David K., and Patrick B. Miller, eds. *The Unlevel Playing Field: A Documentary History of the African American Experience in Sport*. Urbana: University of Illinois Press, 2003.

STATE CONVENTION OF COLORED MEN OF TEXAS (1883)

The Negro Convention Movement (1830–1893) not only advocated slavery abolition but also helped sustain struggles for citizenship. The post-Reconstruction era saw African Americans' freedom diminish amid segregation, suffrage restriction, and lynching. In 1883 the US Supreme Court struck down the Civil Rights Act of 1875, which granted all citizens the "full and equal enjoyment" of public accommodations.

African Americans called a national convention in Louisville, Kentucky to protest the Court's action. State delegates met in advance to draft statements, one of the most crucial being drafted in Texas. That statement, which has been preserved, testified powerfully against Jim Crow. It condemned the "bitter hatred and fixed prejudice" of caste laws and mob violence; sexual exploitation "of our most promising females"; state neglect of Negro education; and an inhumane convict-lease system. Finally, it demanded a restoration of blacks' civil rights, including the right to serve on juries.

[*See also* Conventions, National Negro.]

Further Reading

Barr, Alwyn. *Reconstruction to Reform: Texas Politics, 1876–1906*. Dallas: Southern Methodist University Press, 2000.

Foner, Philip S., and George E. Walker, eds. *Proceedings of the Black National and State Conventions, 1865–1900*. 2 vols. Philadelphia: Temple University Press, 1986.

STUDENT ACTIVISM

Black students' crusade for civil and human rights reached high tide circa 1954–82, then ebbed and flowed into the twenty-first century. Their post-1954 activities are far better studied, but they were crusading for rights long before.

From slavery to freedom and after, black communities linked the training of children and uplifting the race. Alongside literacy, schools and churches taught them "to be kind, honest, and trustworthy" and to seek justice. *The Negro Church* (1903), edited by W. E. B. Du Bois of Atlanta University, declared: "People who are thoroughly fitted for good citizenship and who show by their conduct that they have the disposition and purpose to be good citizens are not going to be permanently excluded in any part of this country from the responsibilities of citizenship" (Du Bois, 2011, p. 208). Many youths joined civic, educational, and religious groups fostering black pride and protest. National Urban League and NAACP Youth chapters picketed theaters showing *The Birth of a Nation* (1915), which glorified the Ku Klux Klan's bloody undoing of Reconstruction. Youths flocked to the NAACP's "Silent Protest Parade" on behalf of the blacks killed in the East St. Louis, Illinois race riot of 1917. About 10,000 people marched along Fifth Avenue in New York. Echoing the "New Negro" during World War I, many young people protested against the Jim Crow military and lynching; they rallied for black and women's suffrage. Students of Fisk, Howard, and Lincoln Universities, and other Negro colleges, resisted white presidents' antiblack policies in strikes ca. 1925–27.

During the 1930s–40s black collegians pushed not only to free "the Scottsboro Boys," nine Alabama blacks falsely convicted of raping two white women, but in "Don't Buy Where You Can't Work" boycotts; and pickets for equitable relief and work, labor's right of collective bargaining, and peace. They advocated different ideologies – liberalism, socialism, communism, antifascism, and pacifism, to name a few – in both black and interracial organizations. The latter included the Southern Negro Youth Congress (SNYC).

An offshoot of the National Negro Congress, which enlisted a spectrum of groups, the Communist Party (CP) among them, SNYC was cofounded in Richmond, Virginia by James E. Jackson in 1937. A graduate of local Virginia Union University, he joined the CP; served in the army 1943–46; and was CP southern regional director to his 1951 prosecution for subversion. SNYC organized tobacco workers before 1939, when it relocated to Birmingham, a center of the steel industry. In the World War II and postwar years, it pursued voter registration, union organizing, and peaceful protest, drawing help from churches, colleges, women's societies, fraternal orders, and civic associations. It convened annual youth legislatures on race and class issues and antiracist strategies. Du Bois delivered the keynote address to its 1946 legislature in Columbia, South Carolina.

Students increasingly used nonviolent direct action to battle racial and economic inequality. Many embraced the New York–based March on Washington Movement (MOWM), formed in 1941 to recruit 10,000 marchers against discrimination in defense industries. Thus the president created the Committee on Fair Employment Practice (FEPC) and MOWM aborted its march. Activists backed the Congress of Racial Equality (CORE), started in 1942 by Chicago seminarians. Their "sit-downs" at white-only restaurants and picketing to desegregate housing, hospitals, schools, and recreation energized nonviolence. Howard University students began sit down demonstrations at segregated accommodations in 1942–43. The next decade witnessed black elementary and high school strikes (some initiated by students) in eighteen northern and southern cities. Also, in 1944 and 1946, the Supreme Court outlawed the white primary election and Jim Crow on interstate buses; the president signed his 1948 order to integrate the military; and the Court in 1950 ordered the University of Texas law and University of Oklahoma graduate schools to enroll black applicants. In addition, a 1951 student walkout from a Farmville, Virginia high school generated *Davis v. County School Board of Prince Edward County* (1952), one of five cases in the Court's 1954 *Brown* decision.

Student dissent spread in the wake of *Brown*. More and more southern black parents filed petitions for their children to attend white schools, where they faced threats and attacks. Still, a boycott by South Carolina State and Claflin College students forced Orangeburg officials to begin school desegregation. Collegians were critical to bus boycotts in five cities (1953–57), including Montgomery, Alabama, where Martin Luther King, Jr. became spokesman and soon president of the Southern Christian Leadership Conference (SCLC). Heeding his call to peaceful resistance, black and white students and ordinary people conducted sit-ins in six cities (1956–59) prior to the Greensboro, North Carolina sit-ins of 1960, which transformed students' role in the freedom movement.

Their activism helped bring pivotal reforms between 1960 and 1975. Voter education, sit-in, and Freedom Ride strategies of the Southern Regional Council, Student Nonviolent Coordinating Committee (SNCC), SCLC, CORE, and NAACP, all protesting peacefully, encountered threats, beatings, and sometimes murders. SNCC gained supporters in the Free Speech Movement (FSM) based at the University of California, Berkeley and led by Mississippi Freedom Summer volunteer Mario Savio; Southern Student Organizing Committee (SSOC) and Students for a Democratic Society (SDS), both primarily white; and the Northern Student Movement (NSM). White partners worked for civil and voting rights and economic justice, too. But many pulled out when SNCC endorsed Black Power, the Black Panther Party for Self Defense (BPP), African Liberation Support Committee (ALSC), and Student Organization for Black Unity (SOBU). Many black students in majority-white colleges and universities demanded Black Studies, while supporting demands for women's and ethnic studies. Meantime, white students increasingly turned to the feminist, antipoverty, and antiwar movements. SSOC then organized among working-class whites. The NSM prioritized northern inner-cities hard hit by riots, crime, and poverty, as the FBI targeted two NSM groups: the BPP and Weather Underground Organization (WUO), a radical faction in SDS. Nevertheless, black poverty decreased from 55 to 30 percent between 1959 and 1974, thanks in no small way to student initiatives.

Circa 1980–2000, countering rollbacks on affirmative action, school resegregation by family income as well as color, and ongoing culture wars, African American student activists, as independents and in coalitions, championed "liberty and justice for all." They urged inclusion regardless of race, ethnicity, gender, class, and sexual orientation. They championed inclusive college and university admissions, courses, and faculties, not to mention equal employment opportunity. If accused of "political correctness" by opponents, a broad cross section of black and other students promoted pivotal causes: the "Free South Africa Movement," which catalyzed US and international sanctions to abolish apartheid; teach-ins to end racial profiling; campaigns for progressive black and nonblack candidates; advocacy of multicultural curricula; democratic reform in welfare policy; and reparations for slavery and Jim Crow. Joining in the Million Man March and Million Woman March, they backed projects to combat drug addiction, aids, gangs, domestic and street violence, teen pregnancy, and the effects of Hurricane Katrina (2005). They participated in the annual State of Black America forum, Hip-Hop Summit, and Martin Luther King, Jr. Holiday, propelling ideals of freedom and equality.

[*See also* Afro-American Studies; Civil Rights Movement; Desegregation; Politics.]

Reference

Du Bois, W. E. B., ed. *The Negro Church* 1903. Eugene, OR: Cascade Books, 2011, p. 208.

Further Reading

Biondi, Martha. *The Black Revolution on Campus*. Berkeley: University of California Press, 2012.
Bynum, Thomas L. *NAACP Youth and the Fight for Black Freedom, 1936–1965*. Knoxville: University of Tennessee Press, 2013.
Cohen, Robert, and David J. Snyder, eds. *Rebellion in Black and White: Southern Student Activism in the 1960s*. Baltimore: Johns Hopkins University Press, 2013.

STUDENT NONVIOLENT COORDINATING COMMITTEE (SNCC)

Established at Shaw University in April 1960, SNCC helped transform the role of students in the freedom movement. Ella J. Baker, former NAACP and Southern Christian Leadership Conference official inspired its formation. Her core ideas, especially "participatory democracy" and empowerment of ordinary people, grounded its organizing.

It pursued sit-ins and voter education campaigns; it called for Black Power in 1966. Women seldom served on its executive committee and never led the organization. But women were invaluable in civil rights activism, for instance as Freedom Riders and voter registration organizers. As teachers in Freedom Schools, they contributed to literacy, suffrage, and the hope for the "Beloved Community."

[*See also* Black Power movement; Freedom Rides; Sit-ins.]

Further Reading

Hogan, Wesley C. *Many Minds, One Heart: SNCC's Dream for a New America*. Chapel Hill: University of North Carolina Press, 2007.
Holsaert, Faith S. et al., eds. *Hands on the Freedom Plow: Personal Accounts by Women in SNCC*. Urbana: University of Illinois Press, 2010.

SWANN V. CHARLOTTE-MECKLENBURG BOARD OF EDUCATION (1971)

When the Supreme Court validated it on appeal, Swann had been in litigation since 1965, filed by Charlotte, North Carolina attorney Julius L. Chambers for parents Darius and Vera Swann. They petitioned that their son James be assigned to Seversville Elementary School, which was integrated and the closest school to his home.

But the city dragged in desegregation. It also missed the lessons of *Green v. County Board of New Kent County* (1968) and *Alexander v. Holmes County Board of Education* (1969), Virginia and Mississippi decisions, respectively, which invalidated "freedom of choice" student assignments and required "only unitary schools." Yet, when Chambers reargued *Swann* in 1969, two-thirds of the city's 21,000 black students attended schools that were predominantly or entirely black. Accordingly, the Federal District Court obtained an expert to propose an integration plan. His proposal would pair schools, integrate grades 1–3 and 4–6, redraw attendance zones, and bus students. Even so, the Supreme Court considered it "administratively awkward, inconvenient and even bizarre in some situations." In 1971, announcing the need to end school segregation urgent, the Court ordered student busing to create a unitary system. Busing thus became the Court's most effective, if legally contested, method for desegregating schools.

[*See also* Desegregation.]

Further Reading

Douglas, Davison M. *Reading, Writing, and Race: The Desegregation of the Charlotte Schools*. Chapel Hill: University of North Carolina Press, 1995.
Ogletree, Charles J., Jr. *All Deliberate Speed: Reflections on the First Half Century of Brown v. Board of Education*. New York: W. W. Norton, 2004.

SWEATT V. PAINTER (1950)

A pivotal case, *Sweatt* compelled the Supreme Court to overturn segregation in state-supported higher education, foreshadowing full repeal of its "equal, but separate" doctrine.

Denied admission at the University of Texas School of Law in 1946 due to his race, Heman Sweatt, a Wiley College graduate and postal worker, obtained NAACP counsel and sued. Heeding the trial court's ruling, the state soon opened a black law school in Houston. It was vastly unequal,

Thurgood Marshall argued. Both the Court of Civil Appeals and Texas Supreme Court rejected that argument. Marshall appealed to the US Supreme Court, where he emphasized the black school's inferior facilities and its students' professional isolation. Several institutions, including the Department of Justice, filed *ami curiae* briefs. Thus convinced of the inequality, the Court ordered the School of Law to enroll Sweatt. Its order, however, did not overturn *Plessy.*

[*See also* National Association for the Advancement of Colored People (NAACP).]

Further Reading

Pitre, Merline. *In Struggle against Jim Crow: Lula B. White and the NAACP, 1900–1957.* College Station: Texas A & M University Press, 1999.

Shabazz, Amilcar. *Advancing Democracy: African Americans and the Struggle for Access and Equity in Higher Education in Texas.* Chapel Hill: University of North Carolina Press, 2004.

TALENTED TENTH

Education and freedom were indivisible for W. E. B. Du Bois. "The Negro race, like all races, is going to be saved by its exceptional men" (Du Bois, 2003, p. 33), he asserted in 1903. We "must first of all deal with the Talented Tenth ... developing the Best of this race to guide the Mass." An educated elite would provide leadership. He renounced Booker T. Washington's program of industrial education and black accommodation. Yet the Talented Tenth embraced both leaders. Du Bois and his followers not only formed the Niagara Movement; they also agitated for political and civil rights, including access to higher learning in liberal arts.

[*See also* Education.]

Reference

Du Bois, W. E. B. "The Talented Tenth." In *The Negro Problem,* 1903. Amherst. NY: Humanity Books, 2003, p. 33.

Further Reading

Gates, Henry Louis, Jr., and Terri Hume Oliver, eds. *W.E. B. Du Bois The Souls of Black Folk: Authoritative Text, Contexts, Criticism.* New York: W. W. Norton, 1999.

Shaw, Stephanie J. *W. E. B. Du Bois and the Souls of Black Folk.* Chapel Hill: University of North Carolina Press, 2013.

TECHNOLOGY

African Americans influenced technological developments as consumers and creators during and following America's industrialization (1870s–1930s). As automation and the factory system powered the rise of cities, millions of rural black southerners migrated to the urban South, North, and West, where they interfaced whites and foreign immigrants in the nation's labor pool. An estimated 5.1 million or 43 percent of blacks were city residents by 1930.

Blacks contributed inventions along the way. Lewis H. Latimer devised the blueprint for Bell's telephone and remade Edison's electric light bulb with a longer-burning filament. Garrett A. Morgan invented the gas mask and traffic light. A number of others made women's hair straighteners and skin lighteners, creating a profitable beauty industry in a "race market" of banks, insurance firms, newspapers, funeral homes, groceries, eateries, and more. Black workers (especially those in coal, steel, automobile, meat packing, textile, tobacco, and timber industries) increasingly used new products. Those included cast-iron stoves, which domestics for white employers cooked on and cleaned, and factory-made clothes. More and more blacks bought tractors, cars, electricity, radios, and telephones, all mirroring intrablack educational, income, and cultural differences.

World War II and the postwar period brought shifts in race relations and influences of technology. Even as car, tractor, and television-buying increased among middle-class blacks, tractors and mechanical cotton pickers displaced black sharecropper and tenant farmer families. An estimated 1.5 million of them migrated to the North and West between 1939 and 1950. The percentage of all African American urban dwellers rose from 50 percent in 1940 to 80 percent in 1970. Desegregation and civil rights reforms leveraged blacks' progress in education, technical training, skilled occupations, and professions, including medicine, engineering, electronics, and computer science. But poor and unskilled blacks were left behind. Deindustrialization (severe in steel, auto, and other manufacturing plants by the late 1960s) brought massive layoffs and plant shutdowns. Plants also moved from industrial centers like Detroit, Michigan and reopened in Sun Belt states. Conspicuous among the jobless and unemployable were African Americans without skills as well as a growing black underclass, who, with their counterparts in Rural America, had become victims of America's service and information economy.

[*See also* Medicine; Science.]

Further Reading

Fouché, Rayvon. *Black Inventors in the Age of Segregation: Granville T. Woods, Lewis H. Latimer, and Shelby J. Davidson.* Baltimore: Johns Hopkins University Press, 2003.
Pursell, Carroll. *A Hammer in Their Hands: A Documentary History of Technology and the African American Experience.* Cambridge, MA: MIT Press, 2005.

TELEVISION

As this critical new medium emerged in America ca. 1950s, the NAACP and other civil rights organizations moved cautiously to monitor it. They demanded that television abandon negative and depict positive racial and ethnic images. Would the networks (ABC, CBS, and NBC Radio) agree? Abandon the racist imagery in journalism, radio, and film that mirrored the previous half-century of segregation? Employ people of color in nonmenial positions? Foster desegregation of American culture and society?

Yet the past was prologue. Radio, in spite of the Federal Radio Education Project's specials exploring cultural pluralism in the 1930s–40s, frequently degraded African Americans. To secure employment in radio and film, blacks had to play Coon, Uncle Tom, Aunt Jemima, shuffle, and dance roles. Television followed suit. Here blacks usually appeared as guests, not as regulars, and in musical roles. A typical role was the black butler or maid like Rochester on the *Jack Benny Show*, Louise on *The Danny Thomas Show*, and Willie on the *Trouble With Father*. Black caricatures abounded in *The Little Rascals*, featuring Sunshine Sammy and Buckwheat. The same was true of CBS's nationally popular comedy: *The Amos 'n Andy Show*, showcasing figures such as the Kingfish and his wife Sapphire.

African American protest leveraged reform. NAACP complaints against *Amos 'n Andy* began with its debut (1951) and persisted; the network agreed to cancel it in 1966, a year after *I Spy* premiered on NBC. Co-starring Robert Culp and Bill Cosby, *I Spy* showed until 1968. Winning two Emmy Awards for best actor, Cosby launched the career that made him so influential in reforming TV's portrayal of black characters. However, 1970s– 80s "black humor" shows, including *Good Times* and *Give Me a Break*, continued stereotyped black images. CBS did not cancel *The Little Rascals* but, despite protests of rights and education groups, spent "money to re-edit the series." Meanwhile, *The Cosby Show* (1984–92), portraying a middle-class black family, was highly rated and respected, proving that TV could abandon racial stereotypes and retain a cross-racial audience (30 million weekly). Founded in 1980, Black Entertainment Television (BET) provides multidimensional portrayals of blacks. Many media experts consider depictions of nonwhites crucial to achieving equality in America.

[*See also* Film; Journalism.]

Further Reading

Bodroghkozy, Aniko. *Equal Time: Television and the Civil Rights Movement.* Urbana: University of Illinois Press, 2012.

Dates, Jannette L., and William Barlow, eds. *Split Image: African Americans in the Mass Media.* Washington, DC: Howard University Press, 1993.

TEMPERANCE MOVEMENT

In 1788 the Free African Society of Philadelphia denied membership to liquor drinkers. Black sailmaker James Forten, Sr., backed by clerics Richard Allen and Absalom Jones, created a group to combat drunkenness in 1809. It joined the American Temperance Society and its campaigns in 1826.

Black women, ministers, and abolitionists formed temperance societies from Baltimore to Boston ca. 1829–33. They coalesced to instill values of sobriety, Christian morality, and racial respectability. Temperance became a priority of blacks' Convention Movement (1830–1893). In the twentieth century African American churches promoted alcohol abstinence for blacks' self-respect as well as to fight their high rate of diseases such as cirrhosis of the liver.

[*See also* Religion.]

Further Reading

Christmon, Kenneth. "Historical Overview of Alcohol in the African American Community." *Journal of Black Studies*, 25 (January 1995): 318–30.

Yacavone, Donald. "The Transformation of the Black Temperance Movement, 1827–1854: An Interpretation." *Journal of the Early Republic*, 8 (Fall 1988): 281–97.

TERRELL, MARY CHURCH
EDUCATOR AND ACTIVIST

Born: September 23, 1863, Memphis, TN
Education: Oberlin College, B.A. honors, 1884, M.A., 1888
Died: July 24, 1954, Washington, DC

Terrell fought for social justice. "A White Woman has only one handicap to overcome–a great one, true, her sex; a colored woman faces two–her sex and race," she said in *A Colored Woman in a White World* (Simian, 2006, p. 93). "A colored man has only one–that of race."

Espousing racial, class, and gender equality, she advanced black education and progress. Child of an ex-slave who amassed considerable wealth in Jim Crow Tennessee, well educated, and wife of a federal judge, Terrell served her community. She taught school; led women in charity service, and organized the National Association of Colored Women, whose motto was "Lifting as We Climb." With state and local affiliates, it supported schools, nurseries, and housing in underserved communities. It also espoused moral respectability. Cofounder of the NAACP, Terrell helped lead its antilynching and women's suffrage campaigns. A leader in the National Council of Negro Women, she became a forerunner in the use of sit-down protests at segregated restaurants ca. 1940s. During their 1950 "sit down," a Washington, DC café refused to serve Terrell and others. They sued. In 1953 the US Supreme Court approved their suit and ordered the desegregation of District of Columbia public accommodations.

Reference

Simian, Evelyn M. *Black Feminist Voices in Politics*. Albany: State University of New York Press, 2006, p. 93.

Further Reading

Jones, Beverly W. *Quest for Equality: The Life and Writings of Mary Eliza Church Terrell, 1863–1954*. Brooklyn, NY: Carlson, 1990.
McCluskey, Audrey Thomas. "Setting the Standard: Mary Church Terrell's Last Campaign for Social Justice." *Black Scholar*, 29 (1999): 47–53.

THEATRE

African Americans' theatrical performance has mirrored their quest for dignity and inclusion since slavery. Ordinarily stagehands for white performers, slaves and free blacks often performed plays in black churches or fraternal halls. In 1821 New York City freedpeople opened the African Grove Theatre, which presented classical dramas and even apprenticed Ira F. Aldridge, who became an acclaimed Shakespearean actor in England. By contrast, post–Civil War black performers such as the Georgia Minstrels played the vaudeville circuit, depicting a foolish "Stage Negro." Between 1893 and 1917 blacks also danced and occasionally acted in Harlem and Broadway productions.

During the Jim Crow era they enhanced their stage presence. They built viable and famous theatre companies, including Harlem's Anita Bush Players and Lafayette Players. Other troupes made the Pekin Theater in Chicago and the Karamu Theater in Cleveland, Ohio centers of African American dramatic arts. The Theater Owners Booking Association of New York booked black players at eighty theaters nationally by the 1920s. Meantime, the Harlem Renaissance created spaces for Apollo and Lafayette troupers in the Broadway musicals *Shuffle Along* (1922) and *Blackbirds* (1926). Blacks appeared off-Broadway in the likes of *The Chip Woman's Fortune* (1923), by black playwright Willis Richardson, and sponsored the Ethiopian Art Players. Paul Robeson starred in leading roles as *The Emperor Jones* (1923) and *Othello* (1930).

Such repertory contributions continued. As the Great Depression worsened, the Federal Theatre Project helped sustain black performers. The project's Negro Unit supported 22 affiliates, among them the Lafayette Theater. Its assistance was vital for Harlem Suitcase Theatre, founded by poet and writer Langston Hughes, whose play *Mulatto* (1935) enjoyed a long Broadway run. In 1940 other Harlem artists formed the American Negro Theater; its play *Anna Lucasta* (1944) had a record 957 Broadway performances. Comparably popular, *A Raisin in the Sun* (1959), by Lorraine Hansberry, explored conflicts in a working-class black family.

Raisin foreshadowed the 1960s Black Arts Movement. Its chief promoters included the Negro Ensemble Company of New York and Free Southern Theater of Jackson, Mississippi. Black consciousness writers and poets, notably Amiri Baraka and Nikki Giovanni, were the movement's major figures. They sang and spoke to issues in civil rights, Black Power, and radical politics. Later playwrights powerfully dramatized black identity in contexts of racial and ethnic coalescence and conflict. August Wilson and Anna Deavere Smith present black family and class striving for a common vision, respectively, in *The Piano Lesson* (1990) and *Twilight: Los Angeles, 1992.*

[*See also* Film; Harlem Renaissance; Music.]

Further Reading

Fraden, Rena. *Blueprints for a Black Federal Theatre, 1935–1939.* New York: Cambridge University Press, 1994.

Hill, Errol, and James V. Hatch. *A History of African American Theatre.* New York: Cambridge University Press, 2005.

Young, Harvey, ed. *The Cambridge Companion to African American Theatre.* New York: Cambridge University Press, 2013.

THOMAS, CLARENCE
US SUPREME COURT JUSTICE

Born: June 28, 1948, Pin Point, GA

Education: Immaculate Conception Seminary, 1967–68; Holy Cross College, B.A. cum laude, 1971; Yale Law School, J.D., 1974

Raised in rural Pin Point, Georgia by his grandparents, Thomas instilled strong values of dignity, education, faith, and hard work. He aspired to be a Catholic priest, but felt racially isolated at seminary and, instead, chose to study liberal arts. A racial activist in college, even joining the Black Panther Party, he became a social conservative and Republican at Yale. Attorney and legislative assistant, he was appointed to key positions, notably chairman of the Equal Employment Opportunity Commission (EEOC), federal judge, and later nominated to the Supreme Court.

His nomination met with fierce opposition. Civil rights, labor, and feminist groups, and liberal Democrats united in opposing him, frequently citing his anti-affirmative action views and judicial conservatism. Black attorney Anita F. Hill also accused Thomas of sexually harassing her when they were coworkers at EEOC. So, the Senate Judiciary Committee heard Hill's allegations in televised hearings. These fueled a national conversation on sexual harassment in the workplace, politics, and race, including black sexual stereotypes. Thomas rebutted that he had been the target of "a hi-tech lynching." The committee approved him 13–1 though without a recommendation, an unprecedented move. In spite of the charged political atmosphere, the full Senate voted 52–48 for confirmation.

Further Reading

Foskett, Ken. *Judging Thomas: The Life and Times of Clarence Thomas.* New York: W. Morrow, 2004.

Gerber, Scott Douglas. *First Principles: The Jurisprudence of Clarence Thomas.* New York: New York University Press, 2002.

THURMAN, HOWARD   RELIGIOUS LEADER

Born: November 18, 1900, Daytona Beach, FL
Education: Morehouse College, B.A. valedictorian, 1923; Rochester Theological Seminary, M. Div., 1926; Kent Fellow, Haverford College
Died: April 10, 1981, San Francisco, CA

Revered author, minister, mystic, and prophet, Thurman's teachings on nonviolence and peace inspired seminarian Martin L. King, Jr. In 1989 a panel of scholars ranked Thurman one of "the 50 most important figures in Black American history."

Nonviolence and human kinship were core precepts in his theological and social ethics. In college he joined the Fellowship of Reconciliation

(FOR), attracted by its focus on pacifism and racial equality. Leading a "pilgrimage of friendship" to India in 1935, he had "a three-hour visit with Mahatma Gandhi," whose uses of nonviolent civil disobedience to resist British colonialism and secure India's independence powerfully influenced him. He emphasized Gandhian principles in theology courses at Howard School of Religion, where dean Benjamin Mays and seminarian James Farmer integrated them in FOR's "sit-down" protests at segregated restaurants and a mission for the nascent Congress of Racial Equality (CORE).

Morehouse College honors Thurman's memory with a seventy-three-foot bell tower that contains his remains and a chapel. Located beside the Martin Luther King, Jr. Chapel, it is surrounded by a reflecting pool and eight eagle-inscribed flags. Recorded sermons and speeches are accessible in the chapel's listening room. Today, more than 100 Thurman Listening Rooms are available at colleges, churches, and prisons.

Further Reading

Dixie, Quinton Hosford. *Visions of a Better World: Howard Thurman's Pilgrimage to India and the Origins of African American Nonviolence*. Boston: Beacon Press, 2011.

Howard Thurman: Essential Writings. Selected, introduction by Luther E. Smith, Jr. Maryknoll, NY: Orbis Books, 2006.

TRANSAFRICA

Established in 1977 at the Congressional Black Caucus' behest and funded largely by corporations, TransAfrica is a critical institution. Using research and advocacy, it seeks to influence US foreign policy toward Africa and the Caribbean.

Directed by attorney and founding president Randall Robinson, who served until 2001, TransAfrica's role has been and is crucial. It lobbied successfully for more equity in African and Caribbean financial and humanitarian aid; immigration; and cultural exchange. It organized and headed protests against apartheid at the South African Embassy, which inspired demonstrations nationwide, the Anti-Apartheid Act (1986), and international sanctions that helped abolish South Africa's white-only government in 1994.

[*See also* Apartheid.]

Further Reading

Robinson, Randall. *Defending the Spirit: A Black Life in America*. New York: Dutton, 1998.

Waters, Robert Anthony, Jr. *Historical Dictionary of United States–Africa Relations*. Lanham, MD: Scarecrow Press, 2009.

TRUTH, SOJOURNER
ABOLITIONIST AND FEMINIST

Born: ca. 1797, Ulster County, NY
Education: Nonliterate
Died: November 26, 1883, Battle Creek, MI

Born Isabella Baumfree, enslaved by a Dutch family, Truth was sold several times, beginning at age eleven. One master claimed that she worked "better than a man … for she will do a good family's washing in the night, and be ready in the morning to go to into the field." Another owner flogged her repeatedly until she cohabited with his bondman.

Truth not only birthed five children but also became an activist of singular importance. In 1825 Quakers helped to rescue her son from Alabama, where slave traders took him. She also converted to Methodism and escaped carrying an infant. Freed by state law in 1827, she settled in New York City, did domestic work, and spoke at Methodist services. Between 1832 and 1846 she joined religious communes in New York, Connecticut, and Massachusetts. As an evangelist for the antislavery Northampton Association, she adopted the name Sojourner Truth, preaching and promoting slavery abolition, women's rights, and the Union. Her inspirational speeches on Christ, emancipation, and the equality of women drew large biracial audiences. She organized relief efforts on behalf of Washington, DC freedmen during the Civil War. Postwar, she fought for ex-slave homesteads on public lands in the West.

Further Reading

Painter, Nell Irvin. *Sojourner Truth: A Life, a Symbol*. New York: W. W. Norton, 1996.

Washington, Margaret. *Sojourner Truth's America*. Urbana: University of Illinois Press, 2009.

TUBMAN, HARRIET R.
ABOLITIONIST AND FEMINIST

Born: ca. 1820, Dorchester County, MD
Education: Nonliterate
Died: March 10, 1913, Auburn, NY

Resisting an overseer at a young age, Tubman incurred a head blow that left her a lifelong epileptic. She still toiled in the fields and continued to resist. Hearing that she and other slaves would be sold in 1849, she ran away, reached Pennsylvania, and worked as a domestic in Philadelphia.

Between 1830 and 1860 alone more than 9,000 fugitive slaves passed through that city and its abolitionist Vigilance Committee, directed by black author William Still, helped sustain their Underground Railroad. Tubman became a legendary figure in the underground, leading nineteen rescue trips into the South from 1850 to 1860. Armed and using creative methods, such as singing "Steal away" to begin an escape, she liberated 300 bondmen and women, including her parents.

Black and white abolitionists alike honored Tubman as "the Moses of her people." She befriended the radical John Brown and mourned his execution for insurrection (1859). In 1862 she served as a spy, scout, and nurse for the Union Army in South Carolina. During the postwar decades she cared for the disadvantaged, converting her own residence into a Home for Indigent and Aged Negroes. Also a women's rights advocate, she cofounded the National Association of Colored Women in 1896.

Further Reading

Clinton, Catherine. *Harriet Tubman: The Road to Freedom.* New York: Little, Brown, 2004.
Horton, Lois E. *Harriet Tubman and the Fight for Freedom: A Brief History with Documents.* Bedford/St. Martin's, 2013.

TUSKEGEE EXPERIMENT

Authorized by the US Public Health Service (PHS) and Tuskegee Institute, "Untreated Syphilis in the Negro Male" was one of the most inhumane medical experiments in the twentieth century. Centered in Macon County, Alabama and enrolling 600 poor black men, 399 infected and 201 noninfected, the experiment began in 1932 and lasted until 1972, when public censure forced its termination.

It enjoyed official sanction. Subjects received free meals, physical examinations, and burial costs. Syphilitic subjects were never informed of their disease, merely told that they had "bad blood." Penicillin became available for treatment of syphilis in the 1940s, but they did not get it. Instead, while infected men suffered, doctors studied their syphilitic symptoms. Many endured painful deaths; eight survived. Five of them attended a White House ceremony to hear the president's apology (1977). Since that time the federal government has paid more than $10 million in compensation to the men's survivors and heirs.

[*See also Medicine.*]

Further Reading

Jones, James H. *Bad Blood: The Tuskegee Syphilis Experiment.* New and expanded ed. New York: Free Press, 1993.

Reverby, Susan M. *Examining Tuskegee: The Infamous Syphilis Study and Its Legacy.* Chapel Hill: University of North Carolina Press, 2009.

TUSKEGEE MACHINE

Booker T. Washington bossed what W. E. B. Du Bois called the "Tuskegee Machine," a network of institutions and surrogates promoting racial accommodation and self-help. Surrogates "edited newspapers, owned businesses, and directed schools modeled on Tuskegee."

Washington thus wielded "quasi-dictatorial power." Years before the anti-Bookerites helped establish the NAACP, he controlled many black leaders, shaping Republican patronage for blacks and white philanthropy to African American education. He also proved benevolent. For example, his National Negro Business League assisted dozens of communities in starting banks, stores, and other enterprises. The "Rosenwald Fund School Building Program" was created at and coordinated by Tuskegee Institute.

[*See also* Rosenwald Schools; Talented Tenth.]

Further Reading

Harlan, Louis R. *Booker T. Washington: The Wizard of Tuskegee, 1901–1915.* New York: Oxford University Press, 1983.

Jackson, David H., Jr. *A Chief Lieutenant of the Tuskegee Machine: Charles Banks of Mississippi.* Gainesville: University Press of Florida, 2002.

UNDERGROUND RAILROAD

In 1844 a northern newspaper called the secret support network for run-away slaves "The Liberty Line," guiding them to freedom.

Many runaways followed the North Star. Slaves, free blacks, and sympathetic whites provided safe houses on the way. Frederick Douglass's home in Rochester, New York was a select stopover to Canada. His passengers increased greatly in the wake of the Fugitive Slave Act (1850). According to *The Underground Railroad* (1872) by William Still, black chair of the Philadelphia Vigilance Committee, 5,000 fugitives passed through the city ca. 1852–57. Today the Museum of the Underground Railroad (Cincinnati, Ohio) preserves that history.

[*See also* Antislavery movement.]

Further Reading

Bordewich, Fergus M. *Bound for Canaan: The Underground Railroad and the War for the Soul of America.* New York: Amistad, 2006.
Foner, Eric. *Gateway to Freedom: The Hidden History of the Underground Railroad.* New York: W. W. Norton, 2015.

UNITED NEGRO COLLEGE FUND (UNCF)

Private Negro colleges and universities struggled during Jim Crow. With few endowment dollars, they relied on black churches, communities, and philanthropies such as the American Missionary Association. As tuition income fell in the Depression, many institutions sought federal assistance.

In 1944, led by Tuskegee president Frederick D. Patterson, twenty-seven institutions formed UNCF to raise funds, advance black education, and promote interracial cooperation. "A mind is a terrible thing to waste" became its motto (1972). Its thirty-seven institutional members today are a vital source of support. Since 1944 the fund has raised more than $3.6 billion. If only partly supporting members' funding over time, it helped sustain financial aid, scholarships, internships, research, and teaching.

[*See also* Historically Black Colleges and Universities (HBCUs).]

Further Reading

Gasman, Marybeth. *Envisioning Black Colleges: A History of the United Negro College Fund.* Baltimore: Johns Hopkins University Press, 2007.

Samuels, Albert L. *Is Separate Unequal?: Black Colleges and the Challenge to Desegregation*. Lawrence: University Press of Kansas, 2004.

UNIVERSAL NEGRO IMPROVEMENT ASSOCIATION (UNIA)

Marcus Garvey founded UNIA in Kingston, Jamaica (1914). Immigrating to Harlem in 1916, he rebuilt it amid the Great Migration and World War I. UNIA preached black pride, self-help, Back-to-Africa, and African independence.

Its message attracted the African American masses, notably poor migrants from the rural South. Chapters formed across the country, in Central and South America, the West Indies, West Africa, England, and Canada. UNIA enlisted more than a million members by 1920. It sponsored uniformed corps, including the Black Cross nurses and Legions; it had parades and rallies to honor Africa and the race. The Negro Factories Corporation supported, among other enterprises, a black doll company, *Negro World* newspaper, and Black Star Steamship Line. The latter operated three ships but it collapsed in 1921 reportedly due to mismanagement, fueling much criticism from rival organizations like the NAACP. In 1922 the United States indicted Garvey for mail fraud involving Black Star stock sales. His conviction, incarceration, and eventual deportation in 1925 began UNIA's decline. But it inspired ongoing black nationalist movements in America and the African diaspora.

[*See also* Black nationalism; Garvey, Marcus M; New Negro movement; Pan-African movement.]

Further Reading

Harold, Claudrena N. *The Rise and Fall of the Garvey Movement in the Urban South, 1918–1942*. New York: Routledge, 2007.

Robinson, Mary G. *Grassroots Garveyism: The Universal Negro Improvement Association in the Rural South*. Chapel Hill: University of North Carolina Press, 2007.

VIETNAM WAR

An unsuccessful effort to defend South Vietnam from communist North Vietnam's invasion, the Vietnam War (1964–73) proved deadly. Probably 500,000 to a million North Vietnamese, 350,000 South Vietnamese, millions of civilians, and 58,000 Americans died.

Blacks, as did most citizens, were divided over American intervention. However, 30 percent of eligible blacks, compared to 18 percent of whites, were drafted in the 1960s. African Americans composed 12 percent of Vietnam combat soldiers and 20 percent of fatalities between 1966 and 1969. Such racial and class disparities steadily united the civil rights and antiwar movements. Black Muslim imam Malcolm X condemned the Kennedy administration's military policy in 1964. The next year, speaking before a Washington Monument rally, Student Nonviolent Coordinating Committee (SNCC) activist Bob Moses criticized the troop buildup. In 1967 Martin Luther King, Jr. opposed the war, renouncing US militarism, racism, and injustice. When the National Guard killed six college protesters in 1970, a majority of Americans had turned against the war.

[*See also* Cold War; Military; Student activism.]

Further Reading

Hampton, Isaac II. *The Black Officer Corps: A History of Black Military Advancement from Integration through Vietnam.* New York: Routledge, 2013.
Westheider, James E. *Fighting on Two Fronts: African Americans and the Vietnam War.* New York: New York University Press, 1997.

VIOLENCE, RACIAL

Reflecting ideologies and institutions of white supremacy, racial violence not only targets blacks and ethnic minorities such as Jews but also other peoples of color. Violent conflict between whites and blacks, deep-rooted in slavery and segregation, has been persistent, as seen in *Without Sanctuary: Lynching Photography in America* (2000) and *The Rise and Fall of Jim Crow* (2002), a documentary.

Slavery, the Civil War, and post-emancipation times were extremely violent. Slaves endured and resisted brutal treatment. Captured slave rebels were lynched on site or hanged after summary trials. Free blacks frequently suffered attacks, abduction, and enslavement. In New York City's draft riots (1863), white mobs, resentful of serving to free the slaves who could take their jobs, burned black neighborhoods, killing

105 blacks, before federal forces restored order. Black and white civilians often clashed in Union and Confederate states during the rest of the war; its end brought slavery's demise, northern Republican rule, and southern Conservatives' (Democrats) reign of terror. Ex-confederate vigilantes such as the Ku Klux Klan whipped, intimidated, and murdered former slaves, many of them sharecroppers; northern missionaries; white and black Republican voters and officeholders. Black and white Republicans fought back but, despite some army protection and anti-Klan laws, Democrats reestablished "home rule" in 1877.

Southern whites then codified the Jim Crow system of segregation, disfranchisement, and terror that lasted into the 1960s. The black sharecropper or domestic who demanded fairness could face whipping, arrest, jail, or worse. Whitecapping, arson, gunfire, and sometimes murder, usually by white dirt farmers, drove out many black landowners. Lynching or illegal killing, which targeted blacks too, peaked circa 1880–1910, as Democrats and the Klan finally crushed a biracial opposition of Populists and Republicans, known as fusionists, and legally disfranchised black men. Tuskegee Institute recorded 4,730 lynching victims, 72.6 percent of them black, for 1882–1951. The peak year of 1892 saw 230 victims, including 69 whites.

Riots caused a deluge of casualties. At least 43 happened in the urban South, North, and Midwest (1898–1921), taking more than 750 black and 103 white lives. Many were injured. Rioting also marked the Depression and World War II era, 180 outbreaks in 1943 alone. Well-armed and aggressive, white rioters sought "a terrorization of massacre, and ... a magnified, or mass, lynching" (Myrdal, 1996, p. 566), one scholar writes. Federal officials seldom arrested and prosecuted lynchers prior to the Civil Rights Act of 1957 or secure black suffrage until the Voting Rights Act of 1965. Meanwhile, the 1960s freedom movement and Urban Crisis, job discrimination, police brutality, murders of civil rights leaders and organizers, and Black Power advocates' insistence on armed self-defense fueled race riots in scores of cities across the nation. Such violence, concluded the National Advisory Commission on Civil Disorders in 1968, was perpetrated by *white racism*. The 1992 Los Angeles riot, leaving 58 dead, attested to its conclusion. So did the 1,360 "hate groups," 321 militias among them, which were active in 2012.

[*See also* Kerner Report; Ku Klux Klan (KKK); Segregation.]

Reference

Myrdal, Gunnar. *Black and African-American Studies: American Dilemma, the Negro Problem and Modern Democracy*. New Brunswick, NJ: Transaction, 1996, p. 566.

Further Reading

Collins, Ann V. *All Hell Broke Loose: American Race Riots from the Progressive Era through World War II.* Santa Barbara, CA: Praeger, 2012.
Pfeifer, Michael J., ed. *Lynching Beyond Dixie: American Mob Violence Outside the South.* Urbana: University of Illinois Press, 2013.
Potok, Mark. "The Year in Hate and Extremism." *Intelligence Report* (Spring 2013):1–5. Southern Poverty Law Center, Montgomery, Alabama.

VOTER EDUCATION PROJECT (VEP)

Funded by private foundations, NAACP, Congress of Racial Equality (CORE), Southern Christian Leadership Conference (SCLC), and Student Nonviolent Coordinating Committee (SNCC) formed VEP to enlarge the right to vote. It operated in the Southern Regional Council (Atlanta) from 1962 to 1965, when the Voting Rights Act (VRA) energized its work. It then worked autonomously through 1968.

The project stressed voter education, registration, and electoral representation of blacks and minorities in the South. Beside reporting on race and voting, it awarded grants to nonpartisan agencies or groups to register disfranchised citizens, $900,000 by the end of 1964 alone. At the same time, grantees, including civil rights activists and canvassers, registered more than 688,000 African Americans, mostly in the Upper South. By 1969 they had added 1,496, 200 more black voters in Deep South states. Their progress owed crucially to VRA, which authorized federal registrars, and to VEP's state projects, which used civics in schools and communities to promote black suffrage and political empowerment.

[*See also Smith v. Allwright* (1944).]

Further Reading

Frystak, Shannon L. *Our Minds on Freedom: Women and the Struggle for Black Equality in Louisiana, 1924–1967.* Baton Rouge: Louisiana State University Press, 2007.
Lawson, Steven F. *Black Ballots: Voting Rights in the South, 1944–1969.* Lanham, MD: Lexington Books, 1999.

VOTING RIGHTS ACT OF 1965

In wake of the Civil Rights Act (1964), activists pressed for equality of suffrage. Southern Christian Leadership Conference (SCLC), backed by Student Nonviolent Coordinating Committee (SNCC) and Congress of Racial Equality (CORE), launched its Selma right to vote campaign in

January 1965. Resulting demonstrations, arrests, murders of civil rights workers, brutal beatings of marchers (nationally televised in March), and massive march to Montgomery helped secure passage of the Voting Rights Act.

The act authorized the Justice Department to monitor voter registration and elections in states with discriminatory voting requirements and where registration or turnout had been less than 50 percent of the electorate in the 1964 presidential election. It banned the poll tax, literacy test, discrimination, and violence, methods used to restrict minority voting, in many jurisdictions of Alabama, Georgia, Louisiana, Mississippi, North Carolina, South Carolina, and Virginia. Federal registrars would register citizens where needed. In addition, no state or county could change its electoral laws without pre-clearance. A ten-year record of nondiscrimination also was required for clearance.

[*See also* Department of Justice, US]

Further Reading

Landsberg, Brian K. *Free at Last to Vote: The Alabama Origins of the 1965 Voting Rights Act*. Lawrence: University Press of Kansas, 2007.
May, Gary. *Bending Toward Justice: The Voting Rights Act and the Transformation of American Democracy*. New York: Basic Books, 2013.

WAGNER ACT (1935)

Proposing this measure, known as the National Labor Relations Act, Senator Robert F. Wagner (Dem–NY) argued that the government must ensure democracy in industry and workers the right to organize and bargain collectively through their representatives.

While eyeing such ends, the Wagner Act did not prohibit racial discrimination in hiring or cover farm and domestic labor. It formed a National Labor Relations Board with the authority to regulate interstate commercial work and employer–employee relations. It banned blacklisting or other reprisals against employees who joined unions, picketed, and participated in strikes. It required employers to recognize and negotiate with workers' spokesmen. In short, it aimed to elevate working conditions, increase wages, and secure a peaceful workplace. Employers widely rejected the law, as did many in the press and legal community. Even so, the Supreme Court upheld it in 1937. Workers continued to unionize, sometimes across the color line, in the steel, auto, tobacco, coal, meatpacking, railroad, and shipping industries, among others.

[*See also* Labor.]

Further Reading

McMahon, Kevin J. *Reconsidering Roosevelt on Race: How the Presidency Paved the Road to Brown*. Chicago: University of Chicago Press, 2004.

Morris, Charles J. *The Blue Eagle at Work: Reclaiming Democratic Rights in the American Workplace*. Ithaca: Cornell University Press, 2004.

WALKER, ALICE WRITER

Born: February 9, 1944, Eatonton, GA
Education: Spelman College, 1961–63; Sarah Lawrence College, B.A., 1965

Writing novels such as *The Color Purple* (1982), a Pulitzer Prize winner, Walker is a renowned literary feminist; she uses "womanist." A child of sharecroppers, she completed high school and received from her mother a sewing machine, suitcase, and typewriter, which helped her excel in college. She urges African American women to honor and sustain their mothers' gifts, including strong values of faith, love, and support.

Walker's writings engage racial, class, and gender identities; individual and collective freedom; familial conflict; the dignity of ordinary people;

personal survival and transformation. *The Color Purple* evinces those themes. Set in Jim Crow Georgia, it depicts a black family in which Celie, the main character, is subjected to her father's incest and husband's misogyny. Celie finds refuge in God, recalls her faraway sister, and relies on Shug, a family friend with whom she is infatuated. The novel sparked debates. Some reviewers believed it stereotyped black men, families, and religion; others criticized its romanticized images of Africa. Still, many praised its depiction of women's underappreciated strengths. In more recent works, for example *We Are the Ones We Have Been Waiting For: Light in a Time of Darkness* (2006), Walker encourages women to seek personal and spiritual renewal.

Further Reading

Warren, Nagueyalti, ed. *Alice Walker*. Ipswich, MA: Salem Press, 2013.
White, Evelyn C. *Alice Walker: A Life*. New York: W. W. Norton, 2004.

WALKER, DAVID　　　ABOLITIONIST

Born: September 1785, Wilmington, NC
Education: Methodist mission school
Died: August 3, 1830, Boston, MA

The child of an enslaved father and free mother, Walker had a short but significant life. A literate and fearless spokesman against racial slavery and oppression, he proved to be a forerunner, paving the way for influential black abolitionists like Frederick Douglass and Henry Highland Garnet.

After traveling at risk as a freeman in the Slave South, he moved to Boston by the mid-1820s to earn a living and join the abolitionist movement. A member of the May Street Methodist Church and Massachusetts General Colored Association, he emerged as a leader. He also became local agent for the New York *Freedom's Journal*.

Walker's Appeal, written on behalf of "my much afflicted and suffering brethren," was his singular contribution. He defied "the white Christians of America, who hold us in slavery" and finance "the colonizing plan," warning them that "America is as much our country, as it is yours." Vowing that "we must and shall be free," he called for slaves and free blacks to take up arms and "obtain our freedom by fighting" (*Walker's Appeal*, 1830, pp. 5, 22, 79). Slave state authorities quickly outlawed his

Appeal, jailed or executed its distributors, and silenced black preachers. Speaking to faith and force, Walker powerfully articulated blacks' freedom struggle.

Further Reading

Hinks, Peter P. *To Awaken My Afflicted Brethren: David Walker and the Problem of Antebellum Slave Resistance*. University Park: Pennsylvania State University Press, 1997.

Peters, James S., II. *The Spirit of David Walker, The Obscure Hero*. Lanham, MD: University Press of America, 2002.

WALKER, MADAM C. J. (SARAH BREEDLOVE)
BUSINESS AND CIVIC LEADER

Born: December 23, 1867, Delta, LA
Education: Self-taught
Died: May 25, 1919, New York, NY

Coming of age in post-Reconstruction Louisiana, Walker battled poverty, segregation, and sexism as a field hand and domestic. She became an entrepreneur, creative marketer, and America's first self-made woman millionaire.

She determined to succeed. Denied a request to address the National Negro Business League (1912), in spite of her membership in good standing, she addressed the largely male delegates on the final day without permission, declaring "I promoted myself into the business of manufacturing hair goods and preparations... I have built my own factory on my own ground."

Her products and marketing strategies were not original, however. Poro, her former employer, created the hot comb and "Wonderful Hair Grower" while other companies used mail order sales. But she was innovative via door-to-door sales, straightening and styling methods, opening a training school for her agents, and organizing a hair care workers' union. By 1919 more than 25,000 women were selling Walker-brand combs and conditioners made in factories with state of the art equipment. Assisted by her daughter A'Lelia Bundles, a benefactress of the Harlem Renaissance, Madam Walker financed beauty parlors across the United States and Caribbean. At the same time, she joined, donated money to, and helped provide leadership in organizations fighting for African American freedom, justice, and progress.

Further Reading

Bundles, A'Lelia. *On Her Own Ground: The Life and Times of Madam C. J. Walker*. New York: Scribner, 2001.

Lowry, Beverly. *Her Dream of Dreams: The Rise and Triumph of Madam C. J. Walker*. New York: Alfred A. Knopf, 2003.

WALKER, MAGGIE LENA
BUSINESS AND CIVIC LEADER

Born: July 15, 1867, Richmond, VA
Education: Armstrong Normal School, valedictorian, 1883
Died: December 15, 1934, Richmond

Child of a butler and former slave mother, Walker rose from humble circumstances to exemplary leadership in the Jim Crow era. A schoolteacher after Reconstruction, she became head of a growing fraternal order, the Independent Order of St. Luke. During her lifetime tenure, it enrolled more than 100,000 members in twenty-eight states and Washington, DC; established viable businesses; and empowered African American communities.

She advocated efforts for self-help and civil rights. Thrift was her core tenet, "a gospel of financial independence from the white world" (Hine and Thompson, 1999, p. 194). By saving pennies and nickels, blacks could accumulate dollars for homes, farms, and businesses. She founded the *St. Luke Herald* (1902) newspaper, which promoted industry, thrift, and moral character, as well as the St. Luke Penny Savings Bank (1903), becoming "the first woman bank president in America." One of six black banks nationally in 1941, it is now the Consolidated Bank and Trust Company. Walker helped finance black women and girls' literacy and welfare; lead blacks' boycott of Jim Crow streetcars (1904–06); and sustain the NAACP antilynching and women's suffrage campaigns. A candidate for Virginia State School Superintendent on the Lily–Black Republican ticket (1920), she received an honorary master's degree from Virginia Union University (1923). The Maggie Lena Walker National Historic Site honors her today.

Reference

Hine, Darlene Clark, and Kathleen Thompson. *A Shining Thread of Hope: the History of Black Women in America*. New York: Broadway Books, 1999, p. 194.

Further Reading

Brown, Elsa Barkley. "Womanist Consciousness: Maggie Lena Walker and the Independent Order of St. Luke." *Signs*, 14 (Spring 1989): 610–33.

Marlowe, Gertrude Woodruff. *A Right Worthy Grand Mission: Maggie Lena Walker and the Quest for Black Economic Empowerment.* Washington, DC: Howard University Press, 2003.

WASHINGTON, BOOKER T.
EDUCATOR AND LEADER

Born: April 5, 1856, Hale's Ford, VA
Education: Hampton Institute, B.A. honors, 1875; Wayland Seminary, 1878
Died: November 14, 1915, Tuskegee, AL

Washington founded Tuskegee Institute (1881) and industrial arts training was its model for racial uplift. "I believe that the negro problem can be worked out only in the south," he wrote, "and by education" (*Indianapolis Journal*, August 16, 1899).

He led pragmatically. In face of Jim Crow, lynching, and blacks' loss of civil rights, he solicited aid from northern industrialists to train black hands, promoting "self-help, industry, sobriety, and thrift." Also, he built a "Tuskegee Machine" of black businesses and organizations, which isolated his critics, controlled Republican patronage for blacks, and influenced white philanthropy to black education.

Washington's speech to the Atlanta Cotton States and International Exposition in 1895 elevated him "to the plateau of his power." Blacks must cultivate moral character and economic independence rather than agitate for suffrage and racial equality, he said. Deprecating migration, he told them to "cast down your buckets where you are." He addressed realities of segregation by telling the audience that "socially we can be as separate as the fingers, but one as the hand in all things essential to mutual progress." After his "Atlanta Compromise," Washington became African Americans' chief spokesman and, in the judgment of one editor, "the foremost educator among the coloured people of the world."

Further Reading

Brundage, W. Fitzhugh, ed. *Booker T. Washington and Black Progress: Up from Slavery 100 Years Later.* Gainesville: University Press of Florida, 2003.

Norrell, Robert J. *Up from History: The Life of Booker T. Washington.* Cambridge, MA: Harvard University Press, 2009.

WEAVER, ROBERT C.
ECONOMIST AND SECRETARY OF HUD

Born: December 29, 1907, Washington, DC
Education: Harvard University, B.S. cum laude, 1929, M.S., 1931, Ph.D., 1934
Died: July 17, 1997, New York, NY

Instilling familial values of education and service, Weaver rose to be Secretary of the Department of Housing and Urban Development (HUD, 1966–68), the first black cabinet secretary in American history.

He advocated racial equality. A member of the War Production Board and the Negro Manpower Commission in World War II, he opposed segregation. His studies of race and class discrimination in employment, housing, and the armed forces reinforced his call for civil rights laws. Weaver's *Negro Labor: A National Problem* (1946) and *The Negro Ghetto* (1948) detailed disparities that the nation could ill afford to ignore. During the postwar years, he worked in various agencies, including the American Council on Race Relations, pursuing remedies to inequality. As director of the Housing and Home Finance Agency, he pursued fairness in lending and anticipated the "affirmative action" policy later adopted at HUD. But HUD's other priorities (Demonstration Cities and the Metropolitan Development Act) were stillborn, due to rising costs of the Vietnam War as well as backlash to urban riots. He resigned in 1969, turning to college administration and teaching, as one of the nation's most respected advocates of social justice. Weaver also chaired the National Committee Against Discrimination in Housing (1973–87).

Further Reading

Pritchett, Wendell E. *Robert Clifton Weaver and the American City: The Life and Times of an Urban Reformer*. Chicago: University of Chicago Press, 2008.
Hill, Walter B., Jr. "Finding a Place for the Negro: Robert C. Weaver and the Groundwork for the Civil Rights Movement." *Prologue*, 37 (Spring 2005): 42–51.

WELFARE

While racial, ethnic, and class discrimination and disrespect stigmatized the poor over time, the public aid system has been more inclusive and situated to empower its recipients since the 1960s.

Public relief reflected the white–black color line early on. Colonies and states, the latter utilizing the Tenth Amendment of the Constitution, supported private households and charities for deserving indigent whites. When agriculture and industry spread, fueling the immigration of indentured servants, greater white destitution, and industrialism, state legislatures ordinarily funded orphanages, insane asylums, homes for the disabled, and poorfarms. Blacks were denied such assistance, with destitute slaves becoming wards of their masters and free blacks excluded. Accordingly, slave and free black families and churches formed secret societies and networks for subsistence and mutual support.

Federal welfare institutionalized in the wake of the Civil War and it encouraged the development of state programs. From 1865 to 1870 the Freedmen's Bureau aided ex-slaves and white refugees. Union military pensions, which were critical, also helped many black veterans and their survivors. Poverty had enlarged by the 1890s, however, particularly among southern black and white sharecroppers, farm tenants, and city migrants. Women and progressives gained indispensable reforms; forty-one states enacted Mothers' Aid and anti-child labor laws, and twenty-one passed workmen's compensation, between 1911 and 1920. States still discriminated against blacks and immigrants, as did the rural health initiative of the Children's Bureau (1912) and Women's Bureau (1919) in the Department of Labor.

Although the 1930s ushered in the Great Depression, causing massive unemployment and impoverishment, the New Deal Administration (1933) crucially expanded the national safety net. The Works Progress Administration, Civilian Conservation Corps, and Federal Emergency Relief Administration, while isolating minorities and women, provided employment and food. Social Security (1935) established universal old-age insurance and unemployment compensation, but tenant farmers, domestic workers, and other unskilled workers were overlooked for decades. Aid to Dependent Children, renamed Aid to Families with Dependent Children (AFDC) in 1950, assisted the disadvantaged.

Change proceeded. Civil and voting rights acts in 1964–65 inspired the formation of the Office of Economic Opportunity (OEO). OEO's indispensable "War on Poverty" program included AFDC; Food Stamps; Medicare, Medicaid, rent subsidies; preschool Head Start; Job Corps; Neighborhood Youth Corps; and the Community Action Program. Nationally, poverty decreased from 48 to 8 percent of whites, and from 87 to 31 percent of blacks, ca. 1965–1973 alone.

Welfare reform and retrenchment ensued, nevertheless, causing an expansion of race-based disparities. This trend mirrored not only rising costs of the Vietnam War but also growing conservative opposition to civil rights and antipoverty policies. To wit, in 1974 the Republican administration abolished OEO, thus shifting its funds and services to the states. The shift fueled conservative–liberal debates on welfare spending that, while ignoring policy options such as full employment, frequently described the poverty-stricken as immoral and irresponsible, justifying cuts in benefits. Activists on behalf of the "underclass," as well as the Welfare Rights Movement, Children's Defense Fund, and many grassroots groups, protested. Notwithstanding, the Personal Responsibility and Work Opportunity Reconciliation Act (1996) eliminated AFDC, the chief cash-aid program. It allocated block grants to states, giving them "increased flexibility" to provide assistance, job training, and regulations to "prevent and reduce the incidence of out-of-wedlock births." States also reduced their dependency rolls by adopting work requirements (twenty to thirty hours per week). Work-fare, which was instituted without supplements for childcare or transportation, caused "poor female-headed families with children to lose ground" (www.cnn.com/ALLPOLITICS/stories/1999/08/23/welfare.reform/). Surely this was true of the poorest groups, namely blacks, Latinos, and Native Americans, during the first decade of the twenty-first century.

[*See also* Cities; Great Depression; Poverty.]

Further Reading

DeParle, Jason. *American Dream: Three Women, Ten Kids, and a Nation's Drive to End Welfare.* New York: Viking, 2004.

Gordon, Linda. "Federal Welfare," 823–25. In Paul S. Boyer, ed. *The Oxford Companion to United States History.* New York: Oxford University Press, 2001.

Kornbluh, Felicia Ann. *The Battle for Welfare Rights: Politics and Poverty in Modern America.* Philadelphia: University of Pennsylvania Press, 2007.

WELLS-BARNETT, IDA B.
CIVIL RIGHTS AND POLITICAL ACTIVIST

Born: July 16, 1862, Holly Springs, MS
Education: Mississippi Freedmen's School, Rust College, Fisk University
Died: March 25, 1931, Chicago, IL

Wells-Barnett was an antilynching and civil rights activist in dangerous times, when the South disfranchised, segregated, and terrorized blacks, and the nation treated them as second-class citizens.

Teacher and journalist, she wrote for Memphis, Tennessee church weeklies before becoming editor of the *Free Speech*. Her editorials, using the pseudonym *Iola*, were factual and defiant. Two, which denounced the murder of three black storeowners, angered whites and a mob destroyed the newspaper in 1892.

She fled to New York and a crucial role in the black freedom struggle. Reporting for the *Age*, she bared southern lynching and became internationally respected. Moving to Chicago, Wells-Barnett's journalism and activism intersected familial obligations, for example, raising six children. But she reported for Chicago's *Conservator* and joined the militant wing of the Afro-American Council. The council held its first annual meeting there in 1899. An outspoken anti-Bookerite, she was a founder of the NAACP but did not join the Chicago branch because of political differences with Du Bois. A noted community leader all the same, Wells-Barnett collected church, clubwomen, and other group petitions for a federal law against lynching and presented them to Congress. She also expressed the concerns of the "colored woman" in the national women's suffrage movement.

Further Reading

Broussard, Jinx Coleman. *Giving a Voice to the Voiceless: Four Pioneering Black Women Journalists*. New York: Routledge, 2004.
Schechter, Patricia Ann. *Ida B. Wells-Barnett and American Reform, 1880–1930*. Chapel Hill: University of North Carolina Press, 2001.

WHEATLEY, PHILLIS   POET

Born: Circa 1753, Gambia, West Africa
Education: Taught by the Wheatley family
Died: December 5, 1784, Boston, MA

The first African woman and second American woman to publish a book, Wheatley rose to literary distinction. Born in the Gambia River region of West Africa and a member of the Fulani tribe, she was probably Muslim. Seized and shipped to America on the slaver *Phillis*, she was about eight when Boston merchant John Wheatley bought her (1761). Too frail for housework, she evinced aptitude to learn. So, using the Bible, English and Latin books, the family taught her to read and write. She accepted Christianity and baptism (1771), began writing letters and poems, and worshiped at the Old South Boston Meeting House, whose minister tutored her in the classics.

Freedom inspired Wheatley's works. *Poems on Various Subjects, Religious and Moral* (1773) sang that "new worlds amaze th' unbounded soul." Public praise for *Poems* and the author led John Wheatley to free her. "In every human Breast, God has implanted a principle, which we call Love of Freedom; it is impatient of Oppression, and pants for Deliverance," Wheatley testified. She married black freeman John Peters in 1778, but they were very poor and she eventually died in childbirth. Her poetry paved the way for "the founding of African American literature" (Gates and McKay, 1997, p. 167).

Reference

Gates, Henry Lewis Jr. and Nellie Y. McKay, eds. *The Norton Anthology of African American Literature.* New York: W. W. Norton, 1997, p. 167.

Further Reading

Carretta, Vincent. *Phillis Wheatley: Biography of a Genius in Bondage.* Athens: University of Georgia Press, 2011.

Gates, Henry Louis, Jr. *The Trials of Phillis Wheatley: America's First Black Poet and Her Encounters with the Founding Fathers.* New York: Basic Civitas Books, 2003.

WHITE, WALTER F.   CIVIL RIGHTS LEADER

Born: July 1, 1893, Atlanta, GA
Education: Atlanta University, B. A., 1916
Died: March 21, 1955, New York, NY

Light-skinned and blue-eyed, White fought for black equality. Armed beside his father during the Atlanta race riot (1906), he helped protect the family's home from a white mob. An Atlanta University alumnus, he joined the local NAACP staff and later moved to the National Office (1918). Able to "pass," once nearly caught passing in Arkansas (1919), he became the most fearless lynching investigator of the Jim Crow era. Using eyewitness and newspaper accounts, he wrote *Rope and Faggot: A Biography of Judge Lynch* (1929).

White defined the NAACP's agenda. He recruited Howard Law School dean Charles Houston as chief counsel. Houston shaped a legal strategy of "direct attack" on segregation that led to *Brown*. White forced *Crisis* editor W. E. B. Du Bois to resign (1934) for espousing black self-help within Jim Crow, instead of racial integration, as blacks' goal. He also backed A. Philip Randolph's threatened March on Washington, which gained an executive order for the Committee on Fair Employment Practice (1941) and more black employment in defense industries. White observed the United Nation's opening assembly (1945) in the US delegation, including Du Bois. The UN's human rights declaration and ongoing black protest foreshadowed the President's order to integrate the armed forces (1948).

Further Reading

Janken, Kenneth Robert. *White: The Biography of Walter White, Mr. NAACP.* New York: New Press, 2003.
Jonas, Gilbert. *Freedom's Sword: The NAACP and the Struggle Against Racism in America, 1909–1969.* New York: Routledge, 2005.

WILDER, L. DOUGLAS   GOVERNOR OF VIRGINIA

Born: January 17, 1931, Richmond, VA
Education: Virginia Union University, B.A., 1951; Howard University Law School, J.D., 1959

Core values of education, justice, and service were foundational to Wilder's political career. A Richmond native from a striving family, he finished Virginia Union University, went to the army, and earned a Bronze Star for valor in the Korean War. Finishing Howard Law School, he served a growing African American clientele, including veterans. Inspired by the civil rights movement, he organized a successful campaign (1969) for the Virginia State Senate, where he led Democrats' efforts to prohibit racial discrimination in employment and housing, earning statewide recognition and respect. He won election to lieutenant governor (1985).

Wilder became the first African American elected governor of any state in America (1990). His victory was particularly historic for the Old Dominion, once the center of "massive resistance" to *Brown v. Board of Education*. Indeed, several districts closed schools (1959–63) to thwart desegregation. Many black and white liberals and progressives criticized Wilder's policies, including budget cuts on social programs and support for capital punishment, which hurt Democratic turnout, causing losses, in midterm elections for the General Assembly. Even so, he entered the 1991 Democratic presidential primaries. Weakened politically, he withdrew but had enhanced his reputation. He delivered the vice presidential nominating speech at the Democratic National Convention (1992).

Further Reading

Edds, Margaret. *Claiming the Dream: The Victorious Campaign of Douglas Wilder of Virginia.* Chapel Hill: Algonquin Books, 1990.
Jeffries, J. L. *Virginia's Native Son: The Election and Administration of Governor L. Douglas Wilder.* West Lafayette, IN: Purdue University Press, 2000.

WILKINS, ROY O.   CIVIL RIGHTS LEADER

Born: August 30, 1901, St. Louis, MO
Education: University of Minnesota School of Journalism, graduated 1923
Died: September 8, 1981, New York, NY

Called "Mr. Civil Rights," Wilkins was recognized and respected for his steadfastness on legal strategy for equality. He rose from the Kansas City *Call* and NAACP to the NAACP National Office. Assistant secretary, editor of *Crisis*, chair of the Leadership Conference on Civil Rights, and executive secretary, he favored steps that would elicit and sustain Federal support. He prioritized integration of Central High School, Little Rock, Arkansas (1957) and the University of Mississippi (1962).

Wilkins guided the NAACP in the civil rights and public policy battles of the 1960s. Co-sponsor of the March on Washington for Jobs and Freedom, he led in lobbying Congress for the Civil Rights Act of 1964. His unwavering loyalty to the Kennedy–Johnson administration strained his relations with outspoken activists and black nationalists alike. He once called Black Power a backward step and criticized Martin Luther King, Jr.' s opposition to the Vietnam War, as it weakened government enforcement of racial equality. But rising antiwar sentiment turned President Johnson against seeking reelection. Wilkins was a member of the President's National Advisory Commission on Civil Disorders, which delivered its report in 1968. It concluded that white racism, resulting in black unemployment and poverty, was the root cause of America's many race riots.

Further Reading

Rosenburg, Gerald N. *The Hollow Hope: Can Courts Bring About Social Change?* Chicago: University of Chicago Press, 2008.

Wilson, Sondra Kathryn, ed. *In Search of Democracy: The NAACP Writings of James Weldon Johnson, Walter White, and Roy Wilkins (1920–1977)*. New York: Oxford University Press, 1999.

WILLIAMS, ROBERT F.   CIVIL RIGHTS ACTIVIST

Born: February 26, 1925, Monroe, NC
Education: High school graduate, Monroe, NC; attended Johnson C. Smith University
Died: October 15, 1996, Grand Rapids, MI

Malcolm X asserted that "Robert Williams was just a couple years ahead of his time." Rosa Parks, speaking at Williams's funeral, commended him "for his courage and his commitment to freedom. The work that he did should go down in history and never be forgotten."

He represented the tradition of black self-determination. His ex-slave grandfather was a Republican newspaper editor and equal rights advocate who owned a gun, which Williams inherited. Battling a white mob during the Detroit race riot (1943) and European fascism in the armed forces, he knew how to defend himself using guns. He did so on returning to Monroe, North Carolina, where he headed the local NAACP and the Ku Klux Klan terrorized blacks. Forming a rifle club, he espoused "meeting 'violence with violence' " in 1959. The NAACP then suspended him for violating its peaceful protest policy. Pursued by state police for inciting a Monroe race riot (1961), he fled alternately to Cuba, North Vietnam, and China. From exile, his *Radio Free Dixie* broadcasts and *The Crusader* journal denounced capitalism, racism, and imperialism. Returning in 1969, he helped organize "to eliminate prostitution, police brutality, and political corruption" (Stephens, 2003, p. 675) by nonviolent means but never renounced the human right of armed self-defense.

Reference

Stephens, Ronald J. "Narrating Acts of Resistance: Explorations of Untold Heroic and Horrific Battle Stories Surrounding Robert Franklin Williams's Residence in Lake County, Michigan." *Journal of Black Studies,* Vol. 33, May 2003, p. 675.

Further Reading

Cobb, Charles E. Jr. *This Nonviolent Stuff'll Get You Killed: How Guns Made the Civil Rights Movement Possible.* New York: Basic Books, 2014.

Tyson, Timothy B. *Radio Free Dixie: Robert F. Williams & the Roots of Black Power*. Chapel Hill: University of North Carolina Press, 1999.

WILMINGTON TEN

State v. Ben Chavis (1972) helped bring international attention to US racial injustice.

During 1971 black Wilmington, North Carolina high school students held nonviolent civil rights protests. But violence erupted when officials rejected their plan for a Martin Luther King, Jr. memorial service. After unidentified snipers burned a white grocery and fatally shot one man, a white female and nine black males, including United Church of Christ minister Benjamin Chavis, were arrested, unjustly convicted, and sentenced to prison an aggregate 282 years. In 1980 a Federal Court overturned their convictions. The state ceased its prosecution in 1981 and pardoned them in 2012.

[*See also* Law enforcement.]

Further Reading

Godwin, John L. *Black Wilmington and the North Carolina Way: Portrait of a Community in the Era of Civil Rights Protest*. Lanham, MD: University Press of America, 2000.
"Pardons for the Wilmington 10," *New York Times*, December 23, 2012, p. SR10.

WINFREY, OPRAH G.
MEDIA ICON AND PHILANTHROPIST

Born: January 29, 1954, Kosciusko, MS
Education: Tennessee State University, B.A., 1976

Born in Mississippi poverty and raised by her grandmother in Milwaukee, Winfrey had a difficult childhood (raped at a very young age). She came of age in Nashville, Tennessee with her father. Working at a radio station, she rose from high school and college newscaster to media icon.

Before fans embraced her as a talk-show host, she portrayed the tragic *Sofia* in *The Color Purple*, earning five Best Supporting Actress nominations. Critics also liked her in *Native Son*, based on the novel by Richard Wright.

She took television and America by storm. *The Oprah Winfrey Show* was peerless. Her keys for audience appeal turned on emotion, empathy, literature, self-improvement, and spirituality. Popular guests appeared and the show explored "uplifting, meaningful subjects." Race was rarely explicit but a subtext in guests' personal experiences of failure, faith, illness, and relating to others. Oprah's Book Club selections tended to entwine race in stories of class, gender, love, or religion. Oprah's Angel Network supported charities and antipoverty agencies around the world, helping the truly disadvantaged. Also, she created The World's Largest Piggy Bank to finance all college expenses for fifty students. Today a philanthropist of international significance, she donates generously to education, including black colleges, Chicago Public Schools, and Oprah Winfrey Leadership Academy for Girls in South Africa.

Further Reading

Garson, Helen S. *Oprah Winfrey: A Biography*. Westport, CT: Greenwood Press, 2004.

Illouz, Eva. *Oprah Winfrey and the Glamour of Misery: An Essay on Popular Culture*. New York: Columbia University Press, 2003.

WOODS, ELDRICK T. (TIGER)   PRO GOLFER

Born: December 30, 1975, Cypress, CA
Education: Stanford University, 1994–96

Hitting golf balls since his childhood, Woods succeeded as an amateur at Stanford before taking the men's professional tour by storm through the 1990s. He is a popular figure in media coverage of sports, race, and money.

Woods symbolizes the American Dream of success. After first-season wins in the Las Vegas International and Disney-Oldsmobile Classic, writers touted him as the "future of golf." They wowed over his commercial contracts, including Nike ($40 million), Titleist ($20 million), and millions more in prize money. They further commented on his mixed-race identity: African American father and Thai mother. In 1997, when he became the first black golfer to win The Masters Tournament, color was foremost in their reporting. In the victory statement, Woods thanked the early black golfers, such as Teddy Rhodes, Charlie Sifford, and Lee Elder, who paved the way for him.

He is committed to equal opportunity and a level playing field. Created in 1996, the Tiger Woods Foundation provides educational and recreational services for disadvantaged and minority children. For example, it awards scholarships to youths participating in its nationwide golf clinics.

It also partners with the Professional Golf Association, the National Minority Golf Association, and Target Stores to support wholesome after-school activities.

Further Reading

Londino, Lawrence J. *Tiger Woods: A Biography*. Westport, CT: Greenwood Press, 2005.

Sounes, Howard. *The Wicked Game: Arnold Palmer, Jack Nicklaus, Tiger Woods and the True Story of Modern Golf*. New York: Morrow, 2004.

WOODSON, CARTER G.
HISTORIAN AND ACTIVIST

Born: December 19, 1875, New Canton, VA
Education: Berea College, B.L., 1903; University of Chicago, B.A., M.A., 1908; Harvard University, Ph.D., 1912
Died: April 3, 1950, Washington, DC

Founder of the Association for the Study of Negro Life and History (1915), Woodson is revered as "the father of Negro history." Like W. E. B. Du Bois, he is iconic in black intellectual life. He sought white philanthropic support, usually unsuccessfully. So, he raised money for projects through black churches, civic, fraternal, and social organizations; book and journal sales of Associated Publishers (1921); and his schoolteacher or college salary. When communities began observing Negro History Week (1926), which he founded, Woodson also sold kits including photographs and stories of black heroes. The annual observance became Black History Month in the 1960s.

While he aimed primarily to produce and promote historical literature, Woodson used scholarship to influence black ideology and strategy. Research, publication, and teaching would ground activism and efforts for civil rights and racial equality. A member of the NAACP and National Urban League, he supported the militant Friends of Negro Freedom, the nationalist Universal Negro Improvement Association, and "Don't Buy Where You Can't Work" boycotts. As the National Negro Congress pushed workers' right of collective bargaining, he joined its call for black union organizing and economic solidarity. He especially promoted African American history and culture courses in schools and colleges.

[*See also* Scholarship.]

Further Reading

Conyers, James L. Conyers, Jr., ed. *Carter G. Woodson: A Historical Reader.* New York: Garland, 2000.

Goggin, Jacqueline. *Carter G. Woodson: A Life in Black History.* Baton Rouge: Louisiana State University Press, 1993.

WORLD WAR I

America entered the "Great War" (1914–18) in 1917 beside the Allies (Great Britain, France, and Russia) against Germany. The war witnessed 10 million fatalities, including 113,000 Americans, and a watershed in race relations.

Meantime, nativism, immigration restriction, anti-sedition laws, and labor shortages spread at home. In the first wave of their Great Migration, 500,000 to 1 million primarily rural southern blacks migrated north for better jobs and opportunities. The migration forecast the "new Negro" and Harlem Renaissance; notable growth of the NAACP, Urban League, and black press; and civil rights protests. *Crisis* editor W. E. B. Du Bois, commissioned an army captain, urged African Americans to "close ranks" and serve. A. Philip Randolph and Chandler Owen, editors of the socialist and pacifist *Messenger*, denounced and resisted the draft.

Segregation and racist violence strained the loyalty of blacks, 400,000 of whom served in the military. East St. Louis, Illinois, where factories hired large numbers of black migrants from the South, and Houston, Texas, near Camp Logan, saw riots in the summer of 1917. At least 2 whites and 150 blacks died in East St. Louis. Attacked by Houston civilians and police, black soldiers killed 16 whites; 4 soldiers died. The army hanged 14 of them and sentenced 43 to life in prison. Even so, the NAACP helped launch a Colored Officers' Training Camp at Fort Dodge in Des Moines, Iowa. It trained 639 officers, less than 1 percent of the army officer corps, while black men and women comprised 13 percent of all service personnel. Ninety percent of blacks mustered as support troops of the American Expeditionary Force and French Army, the latter being more racially tolerant. Black infantry regiments like the 369th and 371st fought bravely on the Western Front. Some 171 members of the 369th were awarded the *Croix de Guerre* and *Legion of Merit*, but no black soldier obtained the Congressional Medal of Honor; a member the 371st received it posthumously in 1991.

[*See also Military; Violence, racial.*]

Further Reading

Lentz-Smith, Adriane Danette. *Freedom Struggles: African Americans and World War I*. Cambridge, MA: Harvard University Press, 2009.
Williams, Chad Louis. *Torchbearers of Democracy: African American Soldiers in the World War I Era*. Chapel Hill: University of North Carolina Press, 2010.

WORLD WAR II

The Second World War (1939–45) caused 50,000,000 fatalities, including Jews in German death camps, Japanese deaths from atomic bombs, and 407,000 Americans of various racial and ethnic identities. After Japan's attack on Pearl Harbor (1941), America joined the Allied powers (Great Britain, France, and Russia) against the Axis powers (Japan, Germany, and Italy).

Blacks, like women and workers en masse, pursued equality on the home front. In the wake of the Selective Service Act (1940) some 2 million black men ages twenty to thirty-five registered for the draft, but service authorities rejected 33 percent of them (compared to 16 percent of white men). Blacks protested Jim Crow in defense industries and the Armed Forces. So, the War Department agreed to elevate a black officer to brigadier general, appoint black civilian aides to the War and Selective Service secretaries, and begin reserve officers' training at five black colleges. But the issue of fair employment dragged until blacks threatened a mass March on Washington, which forced an executive order that banned job discrimination and established the Committee on Fair Employment Practice (FEPC). Black newspapers campaigned for a "double victory," victory over racism at home and fascism abroad. Still, the army and War Relocation Authority relocated 120,000 Japanese Americans, 80 percent native-born, from the West Coast to the Southwest where they were held in detention camps to 1946. Xenophobia and job competition also fueled bloody race riots, more than 100 in 1943 alone. One of the worst broke out in Detroit, hub of the auto industry, taking the lives of twenty-five blacks and nine whites and destroying property worth millions. Nevertheless, black civilians continued pushing for equal citizenship.

Black servicemen and women's roles helped leverage that cause. Over 1,000,000 of them served, 701,000 in the army. Many saw duty in the navy, coast guard, marines, merchant marine, and army air corps. Half of them went overseas, there serving in infantry, coastal and field artillery, cavalry, tank, and transportation units; in signal, engineer, medical, nurses, and air corps. The army, navy, women's army and navy branches slowly began desegregating officers' training schools. Segregation was still the official policy, but one black platoon fought bravely with white troops in Germany. A number of blacks earned military honors, notably the Navy Cross and (after a 1997 staff review) seven Medals of Honor. In addition, fourteen US ships were christened in honor of black heroes such as abolitionist Harriet Tubman. Blacks' collective record in the military both grounded and inspired the postwar civil rights movement.

[*See also* G.I. Bill (1944); Port Chicago Mutiny (1944); Military.]

Further Reading

Jefferson, Robert F. *Fighting for Hope: African American Troops of the 93rd Infantry Division in World War II and Postwar America*. Baltimore: Johns Hopkins University Press, 2008.

McGuire, Phillip, ed. *Taps for a Jim Crow Army: Letters from Black Soldiers in World War II*. Santa Barbara, CA: ABC-Clio. Lexington: University Press of Kentucky, 1993.

Moye, J. Todd. *Freedom's Flyers: The Tuskegee Airmen of World War II*. New York: Oxford University Press, 2010.

WRIGHT, RICHARD   WRITER

Born: September 4, 1908, Roxie, MS
Education: Jackson, MS, 9th grade valedictorian
Died: November 28, 1960, Paris, France

Born on a Mississippi plantation, Wright came of age facing family poverty and Jim Crow. In 1927 he migrated to Chicago and did odd jobs prior to a post office job, where he began writing. He joined a communist literary group, the Communist Party, and steadily became an acclaimed writer.

Native Son (1940), his protest novel, places Wright among the best modern American writers. Its protagonist, Bigger Thomas, is a young black man from the ghetto and the chauffeur for the Daltons. He is attracted to Mary, their daughter. One night he takes a drunken Mary to her bedroom and kisses her but Mary's blind mother enters the room. To keep Mary quiet, he covers her face with a pillow and accidentally kills her. Frightened, he hides her in the furnace and writes a ransom note to feign kidnapping. But the body is found and he flees. Bigger also kills a girlfriend before his capture and prosecution. His counsel argues that the white-created ghetto caused Bigger's crimes, yet he is judged guilty and sentenced to death. "What I killed for I am," he confesses. Indeed, he had done something that white society could not ignore. Wright thus powerfully evoked the tragic consequences of racial inequality.

Further Reading

Rowley, Hazel. *Richard Wright: The Life and Times.* New York: Henry Holt, 2001.
Walker, Margaret. *Richard Wright: Daemonic Genius.* New York: Warner Books, 1988.

YOUNG, ANDREW J.   CIVIL RIGHTS LEADER

Born: October 23, 1932, New Orleans, LA
Education: Howard University, B.A., 1951; Hartford Theological Seminary, B.D., 1954

When the shot rang out, Young assumed it was a fire cracker or a car backfiring. Then he saw Martin Luther King, Jr. fall dead.

As Southern Christian Leadership Conference (SCLC) executive secretary, he remained steadfast. SCLC drew thousands to its 1968 Poor People's Campaign (PPC) in Washington, DC. From many racial and ethnic backgrounds, participants pitched tents on the Mall, marched, and rallied for racial and economic justice. Young also called for mass voter registration. After the campaign, Young and SCLC's staff turned to registering voters and organizing Charleston, South Carolina hospital workers.

Young's post-SCLC contributions are exemplary. Active in the Democratic Party, he won election to Congress (1972), the first black from the 5th Georgia Congressional District and the South since Reconstruction. He spoke out forcefully for implementing civil and voting rights and social programs. Appointed ambassador to the United Nations (1977–79), he was respected by Third World leaders. He criticized genocide and oppression, such as South African apartheid, enhancing America's moral stature. His unauthorized conversations with the Palestine Liberation Organization, however, resulted in his recall. As mayor of Atlanta (1982–90), he helped make it a hub of global commerce, interracial progress, and home of the King National Historic Site. He received the Presidential Medal of Freedom (1981).

Further Reading

DeRoche, Andrew J. *Andrew Young: Civil Rights Ambassador.* Wilmington, DE: Scholarly Resources Inc., 2003.
Hornsby, Alton, Jr. "Andrew Jackson Young: Mayor of Atlanta, 1982–1990." *Journal of Negro History,* 77 (Summer 1992): 159–82.

YOUNG, PLUMMER B.
NEWSPAPERMAN AND LEADER

Born: July 27, 1884, Littleton, NC
Education: St. Augustine's College, 1903–05
Died: October 9, 1962, Norfolk, VA

Young published and edited the Norfolk, Virginia *Journal and Guide*, a leading black newspaper in the segregated South. The "dean of Negro editors," respected "race man" and moderate, he advocated black self-help and interracial cooperation to fight segregation.

Young learned early on "to build from within." He apprenticed in printing under his parents, publishers of the Littleton, North Carolina *True Reformer*. As a student and instructor at St. Augustine's College, he honed his journalistic skills. Moving to Norfolk, he worked for *The Lodge Journal and Guide*, which he eventually bought and renamed in 1910. Its circulation rose from 500 to more than 30,000 by 1917, making it the largest black weekly in the South.

Young opposed Jim Crow. Yet, as did many African American moderates, he fought carefully, pursuing federal action as well as southern white liberals' support to abolish it. Black journalists chose him in 1918 to lead their conference on military and civilian injustices, including lynching, job discrimination, and unequal education. He chaired the 1942 Durham, North Carolina conference of southern black leaders. The conferees issued the historic Durham Manifesto, which condemned "the principle and practice of compulsory segregation in our American society" and inspired postwar civil rights struggles.

Further Reading

Lewis, Earl. *In Their Own Interests: Race, Class, and Power in Twentieth-Century Norfolk, Virginia.* Berkeley: University of California Press, 1991.

Suggs, Henry Lewis. *P. B. Young, Newspaperman: Race, Politics, and Journalism in the New South, 1910–1962.* Charlottesville: University Press of Virginia, 1988.

YOUNG, WHITNEY M.   CIVIL RIGHTS LEADER

Born: July 31, 1921, Lincoln Ridge, KY
Education: Kentucky State Industrial College, B.S., 1941; University of Minnesota, M.S.W., 1947
Died: March 11, 1971, Lagos, Nigeria

Young mastered the art of mediation as an army sergeant during World War II, settling disputes between black soldiers and white officers. As executive director of the National Urban League (NUL, 1961–71), he earned national recognition and respect. He lobbied employers to hire blacks, hereby increasing NUL's job placements from dozens to 40,000–50,000 annually.

Leaving as dean of Atlanta University's School of Social Work, he transformed NUL. He defined clear procedures of financial accounting, reorganized the national staff, and strengthened communication with local branches, which grew from sixty-three to ninety-eight. Skillfully involving NUL in the civil rights movement and federal social programs, he increased public and corporate funds for its educational and employment services.

Young thus became a crucial mediator. A co-sponsor of the March on Washington for Jobs and Freedom (1963), he proposed a "Domestic Marshall Plan" for Black America. Similarly, in 1968, he established a "New Thrust" program to dismantle riot-torn ghettos and build affordable housing. This would make education, job training, and health care accessible to the inner-city poor. Young also gained political influence as an informal adviser to presidents John Kennedy, Lyndon Johnson, and Richard Nixon. Official presidential advisers used his ideas in planning what became the War on Poverty.

Further Reading

Dickerson, Dennis C. *Militant Mediator: Whitney M. Young, Jr.* Lexington: University Press of Kentucky, 1998.
"History of the National Urban League," 153–57. In *The State of Black America 2005*. New York: National Urban League, 2005.

Index